— 最新修訂版 —

瑜伽秘要

瑜伽經、哈達瑜伽明燈、葛蘭達本集、希瓦本集

Patanjali's Yoga Sútras *Haṭha Yoga Pradípiká* *Gheraṇḍa Saṁhitá* *Śiva Saṁhitá*

— 合集 —

楊台基 —— 譯‧著

目 次

ॐ

謹將本書獻給
愛好瑜伽的朋友

〈總序〉
走在靈性的旅程中

時下瑜伽蓬勃流行，習之者眾！不過對瑜伽根本精神的認知，隨著流行似有逐漸隱微之勢。什麼是瑜伽？瑜伽的目的為何？瑜伽鍛煉的門徑有幾？等等問題的解答，並未因瑜伽的廣被而更清楚，反而由於答問雙方的經驗和認知所給予的解讀而益趨模糊，因此所獲得的了解仍有可能只是以偏概全的印象，不若追本溯源，從瑜伽原典來探究。原典中所載之瑜伽行法，是先哲系統性進化自我的集要；學人若無明師指引，則從瑜伽古籍來稍窺瑜伽原本之真意，亦可明其概要。《瑜伽秘要》即是為此需求呈現給繫心瑜伽者的禮物。

本書內容包含《瑜伽經》、《哈達瑜伽明燈》、《葛蘭達本集》和《希瓦本集》等四本最為瑜伽學人所知的瑜伽古籍，俱是一代瑜伽開士所留下的瑜伽哲學心要與行法結晶，是欲深窺瑜伽精義者必讀的經典。四書中，《瑜伽經》是勝王瑜伽的經典，其他三本被歸類為哈達瑜伽的經典。這四本瑜伽古笈在印度被發現的時間不一，然所述內容均有其關聯與互補，故亦可供相互參考；為方便研究，合此四典輯為一冊出版，或是世界先例，也是華人瑜伽界的里程碑。書名《瑜伽秘要》，是取內容為瑜伽奧旨精義的意思。修訂新版以文字錘鍊出經典內涵，內容將更有助於深入了解傳統瑜伽的心法與修法。

人類是生物學上靈長目中最特殊的物種，擁有高度發展的智力，能夠深入分析事理，判別善惡，善用時間，省思生死及探索靈魂的概念；亦能模擬創新，展現出不可思議的自我進化，推證出靈魂與神聖力量或神聖存在的關連。瑜伽即是建基於這種人類的特殊性所發展出來的實學，此歷史悠久的實學，實際上就是探索自我、活出自我、昇華自我的鍛煉。

瑜伽也是印度傳統哲學中的一支。大哲帕檀迦利所編寫的《瑜伽經》是瑜伽學派最被公認的經典，其中對於瑜伽的修習次第，亦即廣為瑜伽人所知的瑜伽八支功法理論部分多有著墨，唯缺少實際方法或細節上的陳述。《哈達瑜伽明燈》、《葛蘭達本集》乃至《希瓦本集》的出版，正好彌補了後人對這方面的需求，這三本著作遂成為哈達瑜伽主要的指引和張本。

印度詩哲泰戈爾在《吉檀迦利》詩集中有首詩，前半段是：「我要唱的歌迄今還沒有唱出，日子都消耗在調理樂器上的琴絃；拍子還沒調正，歌詞也尚未填好，只有渴望的苦惱在我心頭。」因為這個原因，筆者投入了瑜伽的行列。在長久浸身瑜伽的歷程裡，初欲由古典文本了解瑜伽，然由於文化之隔閡，這些書籍讀起來總有霧裡看花之感。耐心讀完這四本經典後決心揭開這些經典的面紗，將此極具探索價值的四本瑜伽經典譯出，讓華人世界的瑜伽愛好者也有機會窺得古典瑜伽原意，是為出版之緣起。

一般認為，勝王瑜伽著重如何安心，哈達瑜伽重點在呼吸與身心之調節。許多習者認為哈達瑜伽就是體位法，但體位法只是瑜伽八支功法之一。在修習瑜伽之初，習者可視哈達瑜伽和勝王瑜伽兩者為一種唇齒相依的關係；有了哈達瑜伽的修煉，更能加速勝王瑜伽的成就。然而不論瑜伽的外在形式如何變化，真正的瑜伽總會透過一些奇妙的事情不斷地傳承下去。

時人熱衷哈達瑜伽，但研究過四本瑜伽經典後，可知哈達瑜伽的鍛煉非僅止體式和調息。如《哈達瑜伽明燈》中「所知、已知和可知皆此一心，若已知和所知俱泯，即無二元之路。」（IV-60），「盡棄所知，心即不存；心若不存，所餘者唯不共之真常。」（IV-62）；如《葛蘭達本集》中「每當心馳外境，隨即收視返聽；必使之內攝而將心意收於控制之下」（IV-2），「行意醺持氣法，心意與真我融而為一，瑜伽行人緣此融合得入勝王瑜伽三摩地」（VII-16）；如《希瓦本集》中「透過瑜伽修習，明一切本來現成，如是悉心領會，何需任何其他教言」（I-18），「那些不欲受享此生或來世行為之果的行人，應捨棄對一切行為之果的關注；放下對日常行和特定行的執著，發心從事瑜伽的修習」（I-31），「猶如空性虛通五大卻不與之相混，宇宙神性於此無常世界亦如是恆保湛然」（I-51）隨文舉隅，常可見到典籍作者欲將哈達與勝王接軌的用心。

《瑜伽經》一書中，有關體位法之敘述僅寥寥數語，也沒談到靈能軍荼利，書中談的是瑜伽哲學，如「念想滅盡，心明淨若琉璃，由是能取、執取、所取泯歸清淨，謂之正受持定（三摩缽提）」（I-41），「因與果、所依與所緣彼此相互關聯，此若不生，彼亦不有」（IV-11），「不變不遷之淨識乃心之主，始終明了心相之變化」（IV-18）等等所言，對瑜伽哲理的認識極具參考價值，因此成為瑜伽學派的重要典籍。

研究心瑜伽者，必要重新檢視「梵」（*Brahma*）這個字；如果僅從佛教或西方宗教的角度論梵，將發現與「梵」的本義會有出入。印度哲學古典鉅作《瓦西斯塔瑜伽》第六章有篇對「梵」的釋義，其中第 16-20 節對梵的描述是：「一切於你眼下周遭所現的浩瀚世界，皆處於無邊無際之梵中。梵即此意識，即此世界與此世界中的一切有情、無情。梵是我，是你，亦是所有我們的朋友和敵人。梵是過去、現在和未來三際，猶如永恆汪洋中的波和浪，本質一如。是梵化現為無數我們所感受到的形形色色，成為行為者、行為和所為之事等不同面向；如同餵食之人、餵食的行為和所餵的食物；亦如接收器、接收作用和所接收的東西。梵透過自己之力於己身中擴展，透過自己之力展現自身……。」從這幾節描述有助於我們了解梵的內涵。

當今對「梵」剖析的最透徹的是阿南達瑪迦靈性組織的創始導師雪莉．雪莉．阿南達慕提先生（俗名普羅巴．阮將．沙卡），他指出「梵」是一體兩面無有終始的永恆組合，本身無限偉大亦可造就他人偉大如己。其作為形式因的一面名為造化力或運作勢能或宇宙力量，作為目的因或見證的一面名為清淨識或至上意識或宇宙意識，而宇宙力量從屬於宇宙意識。大千世界從無到有的演化即是部分宇宙意識接受宇宙力量影響的呈現。上述覺證的一面，也常名為靈魂、至上意識、真常自性、自性真我等等，此一真性隱於萬有之中，是人類乃至萬物真正的本性。在破除因心意識扭曲而覆於其上的一切習氣與遮障後，人自得體會到此無比喜悅的真性，進而融入其中，完成生命進化的終極目的。

緣此，印度不二哲學認為「梵」是絕對的存在，是一種具含覺性與見證作用的圓滿自在心體，是有為法、無為法或說形而上、形而下存在的合稱，別稱有本初、本體、至上本體、宇宙本體等。《瑜伽經》中所述及的至上主（*Iishvara*）是由意識居主導的本體之神格稱謂。如上所言，宇宙從本初的無所有到而今的森羅萬象皆是至上本體的創造遊戲，而所有受造的最終歸趨就是回歸其本，此一趨勢或有遲速，然無例外。

本書所呈現的是原典的完整內容，有些內容歷久彌新，有些或已不符時代，因此冀望讀者能持平常心閱讀，不宜以偏概全。本書有關體位法、坐式及身印部分維持原典樣貌，只有文字敘述。有興趣進一步研究的讀者，紅桌文化出版有《體位法、養氣法、身印、鎖印》一書，該書是印度比哈瑜伽學校的功法大全，書中有詳細的圖文可參考。讀者需注意的是書內所有的功法，有些是安全無虞的，有些則不宜在沒有指導之下練習。任何不熟悉的功法，若有心嘗試，建議先徵詢你所信任的瑜伽導師，以免產生不好的影響。

人生是一趟「無到有處有還無」的意境之旅，在這趟旅程中最大的困擾就是靈魂與心靈間的衝突。靈魂需要「返歸其本」，心靈需要「向外馳求維持生命存在之所需」。靈魂以返歸其本為喜，心靈藉攀緣馳求為樂，所求不遂即苦。人若想要在世俗層面成功，就必須努力執著於外；人若想在靈性層面成就，就必須努力離外向內。然而偏執任何一面，都可能造成障礙。一定要在向內深入的同時亦與外在的需求保持平衡，如此向內、向外的心行一致才能夠進入航向至上核心的軌道，才能夠品嚐三摩地的法味。對於想要了解或是準備啟程的人，對於已經走在靈性旅程中的行人，這本《瑜伽秘要》都提供了許多有用且值得參考的訊息，希望對讀者有所啟發。

本書琢磨十餘年方成冊付梓，感謝出版公司各方面的用心。初版校稿承同門陳新淦師兄惠賜寶貴意見，藉此文末一角，併致謝忱。

〈二版序〉
瑜伽之道在使妄心湛寂

科學日益證明，宇宙是一體的，萬化始於一復歸於一；這是萬化乃至人類的大命運，是本初意識設計的生命之旅，無可改變！而旅程的久暫，則可由人類的自由意志決定。瑜伽是加快此旅程的指引，其精髓不在名相，而在行持中的體悟。《瑜伽經》內容主要在闡明心作用與生命現象的哲學以及引領自心返本歸真的修持心法，餘《哈達瑜伽明燈》等三書則是或顯或密的修法集要。而以己心上合天心，以己空性合本初空性，以己之意識合至上意識，則為瑜伽鍛煉的終極目的。

回溯瑜伽之沿革，古典瑜伽能於近代拓展於世，誕生於十九世紀的幾位瑜伽士是先驅。一八九三年九月，為建立全球信仰對話的首屆世界宗教會議在美國芝加哥開幕。博聞強記，滿懷抱負的印度瑜伽僧辨喜尊者（*Swami Vivekananda*）在而立之年排除重重困難參加了這次會議，是第一位赴美的瑜伽僧；他的演講獲得熱烈的掌聲，會後受邀四處訪問，引起了西方人對印度玄學的注意。同年一月尤迦南達（*Paramahamsa Yogananda*）在印北出生，自幼慕道，十七歲遇依止上師，二十二歲出家。一九二零年以印度代表身份參加在波士頓舉辦的第七屆國際宗教自由大會，並創立「悟真會」，宗旨除了以科學方法教導瑜伽知識外，也致力消弭各種文化與宗教間的分歧。第三位是施化難陀（*Swami Shivananda*），行醫十年，自嘆所習醫術只能益人一時，遇業病則力有不逮，何不學永恆益人之道？於是虔心瑜伽，創立神聖生命協會，開辦瑜伽吠檀多學院，吸引了不少西方瑜伽愛好者。

在二十世紀瑜伽領域裡或非最知名，然為今後人類留下最重要思想資產的是雪莉．雪莉．阿南達慕提。他是國際阿南達瑪迦靈修組織的創立者及導師，以救度之心擇生應世，示現說法，彰顯一如之理。換句話說，宇宙實相和他之間了無遮障！故爾言論精闢，從圓明的視角，不憚勞煩，全面性地為紛紜的世情作出診斷，應病予藥；以理性和科學的思維闡明習者如何藉瑜伽及無私服務成就全人之道，道破古瑜伽形而上、形而下的迷思，揭露並讓人了解到個人、眾生與上主或至上意識的一體關係。他的生平著述抽絲剝繭地解析發明心性對人的必要和重要，教導適合現代人鍛煉的具體方法。他說：「就整體社會人類而言，信仰只有一種，宗教也只有一種。」「人類社會是一體不可分的，每個人不論或大、或小的問題，都是所有人的問題；當使他們明白全體人類的本源和終極目標都是相同的。」「這個宇宙是本初心靈的創造。透過靜坐的過程，當人類心靈與本初心靈合一時，他將立刻領悟到本初心靈所想或所做的一切事情，而此無所不知的種子本就深埋在人類心中。」「每一個人都擁有無限的潛能，沒有人是不重要的，每個人都是重要的；在整個宇宙中，只有一個不重要的存在，那就是『我』是不重要的。」「你永遠不會孤獨或無助，引導日月星辰的力量，也同樣引導著你。」誠然是和上古希瓦、中古克里斯那同一鼻孔呼吸的典型。

古之瑜伽因上述諸師得在今世開枝散葉，所宣揚的都是內見自心上主的瑜伽之道。早於《瑜伽經》千餘年的數論哲學並未有至上主的觀念；而帕檀迦利的瑜伽經中加入了這一觀念，經文第一章二十四節謂「至上主乃最勝妙之意識，不受任何煩惱、行為、果報、宿業等染著」。從語意學切入思考，所言至上主與真如自性、自性實相、大光明藏等，意思是一樣的；「內見自心上主」的修法亦可謂「內見自性實相」的修法，是正統瑜伽的禪定心法。儘管當今瑜伽練習流行的是身瑜伽亦即哈達瑜伽，然而身瑜伽的作用就是令人身心愈趨安穩，為心瑜伽亦即勝王瑜伽創造更有利的鍛煉條件。身瑜伽、心瑜伽雖有消長，但兩種瑜伽仍然微妙的相互影響著。

在鍛煉瑜伽的過程中，習者多能經驗到程度不一的恍惚之境。這種恍惚不是一般認為的失神狀態，而是老子《道德經》二十一章所言的「惚兮恍兮其中有象，恍兮惚兮其中有物」的恍惚，一種超越的喜悅體會。這種體驗，亦是讓人持續練習的動力。融入上主或與內心永恆的上主連結，向來是瑜伽的主旨，是人類完成生命之旅的最後行程。有些鍛煉即使不是以瑜伽為名，然究其目的則無有二致。而步上這條路是人類的宿命，也是人類走向真正文明的發端。而聖人之出，亦是為此一大事因緣。

唐玄奘法師自幼聰慧好學，少年出家，早發宿慧，聞經發悟；束髮加冠之年即窮盡諸家學說，以善解經論譽滿京師。公元六二七年為抉法疑，跋涉西域，求解《瑜伽師地論》，也因此名聞印度。《瑜伽師地論》是瑜伽行派的根本經論，探討瑜伽修行境界，定義瑜伽行者是聲聞、緣覺、菩薩三乘行者的通稱。其中卷一有兩句解釋瑜伽的名義，一是：謂一切乘境、行、果等所有諸法，皆名瑜伽，一切並有方便善巧相應義故。二是：究竟清淨真如名為瑜伽，理中最極，一切功德，共相應故。其中第二句「究竟清淨真如名為瑜伽」與《瑜伽經》第一章三摩地品第二節經句「瑜伽之道在使妄心湛寂」文義相通，透露同脈的淵源。他如三摩地品第二十五節經句「於其（至上主）中藏有無可等比之一切智種子。」若不論名相異同，究其義則與真如、如來藏等觀念呼應。惜二書文字若非專研者皆不易理解，否則必可尋出更多交集。不過起碼可以讓我們體會到瑜伽還有很深廣的領域有待現代廣大的瑜伽族去發掘。

瑜伽歷史發源古老，早在《梨俱吠陀》時代就有瑜伽行者的詩贊（卷十 136 節），贊誦一位長髮褐衣的飄逸行者，能御風而行，與天地為友，身心自在，通達生死，洞悉萬象同源奧秘。所描述的內容，顯示出當時對修行有成之人的崇仰。四吠陀是雅利安人知識的集總，卷帙浩繁，《奧義書》是吠陀梳理後的菁華。《奧義書》時期對瑜伽有了更多的著墨，《羯陀奧義書》第二章六輪十節中詮釋瑜伽是「五識不起，思惟亦靜，心定不動，是謂至境，此稱瑜伽，諸識寂寂。」在《白淨識奧義書》中對修行事理的指引更清楚，如「……頭胸中正，軀體安然，心一境性，以此梵筏，智渡湍流；氣息中和，舉止安適，息有若無；念如野馬，智者惕之，當馭以羈勒。修室簡樸，無塵無火，地處乾爽，環境無喧；意守安悅，視界無障，居所避風，是修行善地。」之後的章節內容，更有在真境顯現前可能經驗的幻象以及身內瑜伽能量生起時，可以克服老病死諸難，使身清體健、少濁寡欲；心生諸想，如塵染鏡，拂則光生；如是內見自性，體悟無生，諸縛盡解。其它冠名瑜伽的奧義書，尚有《瑜伽頂奧義書》、《瑜伽真性奧義書》等，更多面地展現出瑜伽的義涵。

兩千多年前，大哲帕檀迦利將所見修行之法歸納為外在控制、內在控制、坐式、調息法、內攝、專注、禪定及三摩地等八個次第，是為瑜伽八支功法。正宗修法是以禪定為本，然禪定不易，須下功夫始得，故禪定八支功法中的前六支乃是禪定支的前行，三摩地則是立基禪定上的結果。禪定舊譯禪那，取梵語「*Dhyana*」之音譯。禪定之義以禪宗六祖所言最為直捷，在《壇經》坐禪品中講到：「何名坐禪？心念不起，名為坐；內見自性不動，名為禪。」續說：「何名禪定？外離相為禪，內心不亂為定。」所說之「外離相及心念不起」豈不與「使妄心湛寂」意同？而「內見自性不動」和「內見自心上主」則幾無二致。再如《瑜伽經》四章二十五節「徹見真妄之別者，亦不生覓求真常自性之心」，與六祖惠能聞《金剛經》大悟之言「何期自性本自清淨，何期自性本不生滅，何期自性本無動搖！……」亦頗相契。可見西域瑜伽與東土禪門，實有異曲同工之效。了解了這一點，復閱讀經文，於經中文義必能會契於心。

印度史詩《摩訶婆羅多》，內容也有許多相關瑜伽修煉的故事貫穿其間。《摩訶婆羅多》是三千五百多年前發生在北印度的一場由上主克里希納編導的法性戰爭，當時視信守承諾為法性；上主克里希納帶進若為社會福祉毀諾亦為法性的觀念，這也是後人對他評價毀譽參半的原因。大哲毗耶娑將這場戰事筆之於書。從書中第六章毗史摩篇中摘錄出來的《薄伽梵歌》，是在開戰之際，代表法性一方的主將阿周納，思及與昔日親友即將互相屠戮，一時心亂喪志，意欲罷戰！上主克里希納是他的導師，戰陣中助其駕馭戰車，臨機開導。析理復加演示，全面且深入地揭開瑜伽和宇宙生命的奧義，教誨「莫為生命角色所惑，法身從來永恆；眾生皆是循業依其角色完成宇宙大戲，藉此大戲明了生命法性所在而回歸本源，回歸上主懷抱。」

讓阿周納明白了萬有中上主是最高展現之真理。從而一舉摎破了阿周納的迷思，無有懸念地重返戰事。而這番講話，歷久彌新，所以自成書以來，始終是瑜伽修行的指南。

生活的經驗告訴我們：人類智力愈趨發展，衍生的人際、社會和心理問題愈多，其中顯示出來的無常已是生命的常態，這是僧侶修士乃至社會各階層人士的共同感慨！這種感慨源自於集體意識對生命的誤解。人生的重點在學習，喜樂是自學習中來；學習生存，學習工作，學習親情、友情、愛情，學習割捨，學習憶起空諸所有的清寂大樂。而在此無常世界浮沉生死的人類，在輾轉來去之中究竟要學到什麼功課？此亦為世間古往今來心懷哲思之高士，無不思透窺的生命奧秘。間有洞悉者，緣走四方，於市廛山林，隨機接引、啟人心慧。如是拔俗之士，中有知名於世者，亦有少為人知之隱士。然哲人指示，必有契於心者錄傳於後世有緣之人；《瑜伽奧秘要》所輯錄之四書，即屬是類。翻譯初衷是為了明白經文確切的意旨，在中譯的過程中，領略到經典翻譯非易事，尤其是人謂晦澀甚至難以理解的《瑜伽經》。於是梳理辨析、靜心琢磨，終能理出完整經文；譯文詞句或簡，卻是一窺古瑜伽行派哲理不可缺的案頭書，其精神亦可為所有修行之參考。

本書所輯四典各有擅長，綜觀已勾勒出開啟瑜伽之秘的心要。其中所揭部分修法，還可看出一些與藏密、東密瑜伽之間的淵源，不過重點仍在文義。壓軸之《希瓦本集》披露本有現成之理與頓悟漸修之法，鎔瑜伽之空有心要於五章之中，對瑜伽事理有著最全面的解析，字裡行間蘊藏著可以讓生命發光的內涵，在四本經典中無疑是含金量最高的，讀之令人心曠神怡，靈智大開。誠心推薦讀者細品。

考量實際需求，《瑜伽秘要》二版拿掉了天城文體經句，保留梵文羅馬拼音並加入《瑜伽經》的英譯，選用的是一九一二年出版的《帕檀迦利瑜伽經（*Patanjali's Yoga Sutra*）》之英譯文；這是毗耶薩（*Viyása*）署名註解，由室利薩・旃德羅・婆藪作序，羅姆・帕拉薩文學碩士（*Rama Prasada*）翻譯的梵英對照本。羅姆・帕拉薩的譯筆精簡，最貼近梵文經句本義。而室利薩・旃德羅・婆藪是受勳的梵文學者，也是本書《葛蘭達本集》、《希瓦本集》梵文本的英文翻譯。唯就玄理而言，梵文在靈性上的表述深度非英文可及，有時很難找到貼切的英文譯詞，故不易從英譯了解經句意思，仍需酌參梵文字彙解釋，方能掌握經句本義。

加入英文譯文後，為了中譯更能信達雅地表現《瑜伽經》句義，《瑜伽秘要》二版修訂了初版《瑜伽經》中的一些譯文，其他疏漏部分也一併作了修訂。訂正部分的對照，初版讀者可參考下列任一網址或 QR 掃描碼：

https://drive.google.com/drive/folders/1E8P6yJxwmE7nf0Sqdb2BvhzXiwvKE-oB

https://bit.ly/ 瑜伽秘要初版修訂

梵文羅馬拼音說明

古印度哲學多以梵文的形式保存下來，考據印度最早的文字是婆羅米文，自十三世紀以後最接近婆羅米文的天城文成為梵語最普遍的書寫文字，也用來書寫印地語（印度第一官方語）、尼泊爾語。天城體梵文對非以其為母語之人不易親近，故西方國家改以羅馬拼音的方式流通，亦是本書所採用的方式。

梵語發音有清音與濁音、送氣音與不送氣音之分，凡字母 s 及 *h* 之後相連母音者多為送氣音；又字首字尾出現有 *c*、*k*、*p*、*t*、*s*、*ḥ* 等字相接母音者，多為清音。外於前述條件者，多為濁音與不送氣音。

梵文發音和英語習慣的發音有別，利用羅馬拼音可有輔助辨識作用。為方便讀者辨識及應用，根據字母上的輔助符號，舉例如下（單字下有劃橫線處即對照之近似發音）：

<table>
<tr><th colspan="2">元音（母音）部</th></tr>
<tr><td>單元音：
a- but
á- father
i- pin, england
í- beet
u- put
ú- wool
ṛ- cur, burl
ṛ́- 發音如 ṛ 但音更長些，亦可標為「rri」</td><td>雙元音：
e- fate、eight
ai- sigh、aisle，亦可標為「ae」
o- over、pole
au- cow 或 sour，亦可標為「ao」</td></tr>
<tr><th colspan="2">輔音（子音）部</th></tr>
</table>

喉音： *k-* s<u>k</u>ill、s<u>k</u>ip *kh-* <u>k</u>ill、<u>c</u>at *g-* <u>g</u>reat、<u>g</u>ame *gh-* 發音如 *g* 加上由喉發的送氣音「*h-*赫」 *ṅ-* su<u>ng</u>	顎音： *c-* <u>ch</u>urch *ch-* <u>Ch</u>urchill *j-* <u>j</u>ean *jh-* 發音如 *j* 加上前顎發的送氣音「*h-*赫」 *ñ-* ca<u>ny</u>on
捲舌音： *ṭ-* <u>t</u>ub *ṭh-* 發音如 *ṭ* 加送氣音「*h-* 赫」 *ḍ-* <u>d</u>og，<u>d</u> 發音時注意捲舌。 *ḍh-* 發音如 *ḍ* 加送氣音「*h-* 赫」 *ṇ-* re<u>n</u>own 或 a<u>nd</u>	齒音： *t-* <u>th</u>in *th-* <u>th</u>under *d-* <u>th</u>en，舌尖觸及上排牙齒內側
唇音： *p-* <u>p</u>ink *ph-* <u>p</u>ill、<u>p</u>it *b-* <u>b</u>omb、<u>b</u>one *bh-* 發音如 *b* 加送氣音「*h-* 赫」。 *m-* <u>m</u>ail	半元音： *y-* y 於字首音如 jump 的 *j*，於字尾音如 you 的 y *r-* <u>r</u>ub *l-* <u>l</u>oad、<u>l</u>ove *v-* v 於字首音如 victory 的 v，於字尾音如 awaken 的 w
摩擦音： *ś-* <u>sh</u>ave *ṣ-* di<u>sh</u>，<u>sh</u>all *s-* <u>s</u>ave	氣音： *h-* <u>h</u>um、<u>h</u>undred
鼻音： *ṃ-* <u>m</u>ine	止韻： *ḥ-* <u>h</u>er，如 *aḥ* 發音如 *a* 加送氣音「*h-*赫」

　　羅馬拼音可輔助梵文發音，但很難完全取代，因為發音時捲舌的應用及舌尖與出音的位置都需注意才能掌握。網路上有不少指導梵文發音的網站，可以試著模擬練習。推薦兩個網站如下：

https://www.sanskrit-trikashaivism.com/en/learning-sanskrit-pronunciation-1-1/456

https://sadvidyafoundation.org/online-lessons/yoga-sutra-chanting/sanskrit-pronunciation/

瑜伽經

Patanjali's Yoga Sútras

〈中譯本前言〉
《瑜伽經》是勝王瑜伽的代表經典

《瑜伽經》為古印度六派哲學瑜伽學派中的重要經典，作者是大哲帕檀迦利（*Maharsi Pantanjali*）。帕檀迦利因此經廣受瑜伽行人的敬重，然其生平不詳，但有傳說而無紀實；只知他誕生於加爾各答西北方的布德旺鎮帕通村，數論哲學的創始人迦毗羅亦生於這片古地。由於同名著作之故，推崇帕檀迦利的人認為他不但是哲學家而且還是醫生及文法學家。

本經原名《帕檀迦利瑜伽箴言集》，是其對瑜伽理法的梳理結集。十二世紀以後日益受到學人重視，後人遂將之更名為《瑜伽經》。經分四品一百九十六節 *，首篇三摩地品，敘述三摩地之性質、類別和目的；次篇修習品，敘述禪定之法；第三篇功德品，亦稱神通品，敘述得定後之功德妙用；第四篇獨存品，亦稱究竟品，敘述惑妄生滅及契入究竟之理。這四篇經文，有序地點出傳統瑜伽的修持哲學。

《瑜伽經》成書年代並不確定，比較多的學者認為是在公元前二世紀到公元四世紀間，當時大乘佛教已然興起。瑜伽鍛煉本身並不屬於任何宗教，但任何宗教的學子行人都可從瑜伽的鍛煉中獲益。而自《瑜伽經》內文的一些專有詞彙來看，奧義書、數論、佛學和瑜伽之間，彼此的哲理已有所交集。

---

* 譯按：本書選譯的《瑜伽經》是四品一九六節版本，其中第三品二十節及二十二節，似是權威註解者毗耶薩的釋文；故未錄入這兩節的就是四品一九四節版本；而將第三品二十二節、二十三節併成一節的，則是四品一九五節的《瑜伽經》版本。

當前瑜伽的兩大類是勝王瑜伽和哈達瑜伽，《瑜伽經》咸認是勝王瑜伽的代表經典。《瑜伽經》中未提及哈達瑜伽，只有提及體位法應保持安穩、舒適。而哈達瑜伽的主要經典皆有強調：哈達瑜伽是成就勝王瑜伽的階梯。所以欲要了解更深邃的身心成就，《瑜伽經》是很好的叩門磚。

帕檀迦利的瑜伽之道主要是建立在湛寂內心習氣的基礎，由此往上，才可能達瑜伽「合一」的宗旨。經中瑜伽八支的前五支都是去習氣的基本功；進階的修持則是透過後三支，亦即透過持續不斷地練習專一集中、禪定和三摩地，最後融入究竟不共的圓明空性。

整體觀之，《瑜伽經》偏重析理，較乏行門指引；哈達瑜伽的經典如《哈達瑜伽明燈》、《葛蘭達本集》等對練習方法著墨較多。另外一本頗受識者推崇的《希瓦本集》，內容在古本瑜伽經典中最為豐富，可說是密部瑜伽的隨身指導。瑜伽合一之道其實是虔誠、智慧、行業和持恆修習的結果，不宜偏廢。

《瑜伽經》被譯成各國文字，其中以英譯本最多。維基百科對於《瑜伽經》的現代註解和翻譯的評論是「現存有多種《瑜伽經》譯本，這些版本異文甚多，似未經過嚴謹的文本校勘，很多梵文詞彙的確切含義也未有定論。」

雖譯本繁多，然因文化語言的隔閡，對非以英文為母語之瑜伽學人，欲自英譯本來通解經中文義仍是不容易的事。為能有貼近經文的譯文，本書根據幾種古本之英譯，參考梵文字義，再根據譯者對瑜伽的了解筆之於文，期能以最貼近經文的意思呈現。並衷心希望所譯內容對有心深入瑜伽之道者有所助益。

〈中譯本導讀〉
瑜伽是修道、見道、合道、證道的過程

奎師那瑪阿闍梨被譽為是現代哈達瑜伽之父，因為他座下的四大弟子——艾揚格、帕達比・喬艾斯、茵卓・戴薇和他的兒子德西卡恰是今日世上大部分瑜伽名師的老師。若從印度瑜伽的發展史來看，瑜伽之父乃是七千多年前的上主希瓦，在《哈達瑜伽明燈》、《葛蘭達本集》和《希瓦本集》等經典中均敬稱他是瑜伽元尊（*adiyogi*），也就是瑜伽始祖的意思。不僅如此，在印度只要是涉及瑜伽、密學、舞蹈、音樂、醫藥以及精神文明的知識，祖師爺都是上主希瓦，其香火和傳承迄今不輟。希瓦在漢譯佛典裡名濕婆，從文字形義上看略含貶抑的味道；然而即使在今天，希瓦在印度人心目中的地位仍是無可比擬的，在佛教中則成了眾生的護法神。

《瑜伽經》的內文並未提到上主希瓦，或許帕檀迦利非為上主希瓦的傳承，但他對數論哲學很了解。數論哲學將一切有形無形的存在歸為二十五諦，其根本是原識（*purúsa*）與原質（*prakrti*），瑜伽哲學與數論哲學有相當多的交集。帕檀迦利在《瑜伽經》中另外提出了上主（*Íśvara*）的觀念，這是數論哲學中所欠缺的，惜未深述。

帕檀迦利的偉大在於他從卷帙浩繁的奧義經典中梳理出瑜伽的脈絡，雖然偏向知識面，但這是一項了不起的工作。帕檀迦利的這本原名《瑜伽箴言》的《瑜伽經》，沒有註解，沒有引言，就只有這精簡的一百九十六節經句。最早署名註解《瑜伽經》的是哲人毗耶薩（*Vyása*），和史詩《摩訶婆羅多》的作者同名，但兩者應不是同一人。毗耶薩的釋文是迄今仍被認為是最權威的註解，有說他生於公元六百年，不過亦無生平記載。由於《瑜伽經》從公元六世紀到十二世紀沉寂了近七百年，故益增考據困難。如前所言，世人對帕檀迦利的認識極少，僅知他出生在西孟加拉，生存年代約是兩千三、四百年前。至於和印度另兩位同名的古典梵文語法大學者和醫學家是否為同一人，學者多持保留態度。

《瑜伽經》的第一句經文是「現在闡述瑜伽旨要」。大多數人認為瑜伽是一種源自印度的曲伸扭轉身體的健身運動，但瑜伽在古印度的定義指的卻是一種人天合一的追求，有如中華道統中的修道，瑜伽鍛煉就是一門修道、見道、合道、證道的過程。帕檀迦利從哲學家的敏銳度或許觀察到時人對瑜伽的認識頗不一致，因此有藉這本小卷冊讓人深入認識瑜伽的用意。

帕檀迦利接著說：「瑜伽之道在使妄心湛寂。」也就是說若要達到瑜伽的目的，需要息止內心因念所起的波動；這種不時起伏的心念，這種因習氣而起的心念，這種心緒的傾向，這些癡心妄想，糾結著生命，演出一幕幕的人生戲碼！而瑜伽平息癡妄的鍛煉是讓這齣看似無盡的人生戲劇，或在今生或在來世有機會畫上完美的休止。後續經文圍繞在止心息妄為什麼重要，不如此會如何，其中道理在哪裡，這些道理涉及哪些生理和心理因素，須要怎樣才能克服，克服或對治的方法有哪些，有哪些選擇，練習時要注意什麼事情，關鍵緊要處為何，鍛煉過程中會有什麼光景出現，等等所有修行過程中行人會關心或會遇到的問題，會生起的疑點，可能有的困惑，帕檀迦利嘗試在《瑜伽經》中一一作出闡釋。

根據修行識見，瑜伽一詞有不同的詮釋，有說「心入三昧即是瑜伽」，有說「心住一境謂之瑜伽」等等。較為主要的定義則有三種，除前述帕檀迦利在《瑜伽經》中的解釋外，第二種定義是「內心全無思想、念頭的狀態」，第三種傳承自古老密乘的定義是「個體意識與至上意識融而為一」，此一定義最為大成就者所肯定。

《哈達瑜伽明燈》、《葛蘭達本集》的分章皆是以「三摩地」為終章，《希瓦本集》末章最後一節則提到「如是信受奉行吾之教導者，得永住於無上喜悅之境」。三本被歸類為哈達瑜伽的經典裡，都以「三摩地」作結尾，而《瑜伽經》第一章三摩地品，梵語「*Samádhi Páda*」，就是討論「三摩地」，圓滿了前述哈達瑜伽經典中談及三摩地時缺少的一些細述。

帕檀迦利將瑜伽的鍛煉分成八個次第，通名八支瑜伽，最後一個次第就是三摩地。三摩地一詞是梵語的音譯，意表「心與所緣或所觀等持不二」的一種空靈無我之定境，其中人心融入天心與個體意識融入至上意識是最終的兩種定境。哈達瑜伽的經典裡常提到可經由何種坐式、身印入三摩地，然而三摩地主要並非從坐式而來，它是一種靈修結果的呈現，也就是經由修持使得身體的感覺器官、運動器官和生命氣三者達到如如不動後，進一步融入空性或無上喜悅或至上意識的狀態。三摩地非一蹴可及，其中包含著許多細膩的工程，這些內在工程的道理和方法，在帕檀迦利的《瑜伽經》都有扼要的提點。

第二章修習品講解瑜伽修行之道在於利他、學習及以至上主為目標的靜坐。這一章的品名，梵語是「*Sádhaná Páda*」，詞義是「持續地努力朝心中的目標前去」。生活中最讓人不安、焦慮的就是各種煩惱，減少煩惱的繫縛是瑜伽修行首要之務，契入三摩地亦是為此。煩惱源於無明，帕檀迦利歸納出去無明之法，俾能持續地保持明辨覺智；而誠心地修習瑜伽各支功法，可斷諸雜染，發智慧光，通明辨智。藉此分析，引出完整的勝王瑜伽八支功法。其後便從內、外在規範開始介紹，依序講到坐式（體位法）、呼吸控制法和感官收攝。第二章探討了八支瑜伽中淨化身心的前五支功法，修行這五支瑜伽使知作根（五種感覺器官和五種運動器官）受到完全的控制，為修習勝王瑜伽的後三支，即專注、禪定、三摩地做好準備。

第三章功德品，梵語「*Vibhúti Páda*」，也稱神通品。功是付出的努力，德是得到的饒益；修行努力的收獲之一，就是突破身患，可能會通達一些神奇的能力，這些功德也會引起自他的驚詫，故又名神通品。神通有好幾種，依修而得的名修通。南懷瑾先生說：「神通是人修到了精神超越物質、超越肉體時，他的精神與天地宇宙法界的觀念相通了，自然就起各種變化。」而八支瑜伽後三支的「專注」是將心繫於一處，「禪定」是相續不斷的住心於一處，「三摩地」是於禪定中，唯存本初空性光明，此外無他；總合此三支同參一諦，謂之「合參法」或「總制行法」。依合參法成就之行人，其精神超越了物質的拘束，自然也會有某種駕馭物質的能力。從功德品第十六節到第五十六節，帕檀迦利講述了二十餘種觀法，從觀宿業、觀心、觀日、觀月、觀心、觀身、觀五大元素……等等，藉這些觀法，成就者皆能透析所觀奧秘，於身於心都能獲得饒益。不過在本章第三節帕檀迦利述及「然就無種三摩地而言，彼仍屬外支」，提醒了這些神奇能力都不是靈修目的。

瑜伽經第四章獨存品，梵語「*Kaivalya Páda*」；*Kaivalya* 字義為唯一、獨存、不共，意表解脫的絕對境界，故也稱解脫品。這一品主要是探討如何轉識成智，再利用此慧智達到瑜伽的目的。首先帕檀迦利提醒除前章所說的修通外，宿業、藥餌、咒術也可能生起神通。又說輪迴轉世其實是宇宙造化力量的作用，而這種作用無關獎懲，乃是為了平衡受造個體心靈的扭曲以及個體最終福祉的目的。個體心靈的變化來自於頻繁的起心動念，此心念之作用唯從「我見」產生；相續流轉之差別心念，亦是一心所化；如是因果相互關聯，輾轉相生，因其屬性、成相各異。而要超越此變化心的網罟，只有藉瑜伽行修證入寂，徹見身、命、意識間之差異，方能泯除無始以來之障垢，待得惑業盡消，識心融入本初淨識或至上意識中，是謂之「不共獨存境」，至此生命大戲圓滿謝幕，大事方畢。

瑜伽是智慧的哲學，也是一門反思人生、思考因果、尋求根源、尋求永恆的實學。如總序所言，人生是靈魂與心靈的拔河賽，靈魂的喜悅從「歸趨其本」而來，心靈的快樂自「向外攀緣」而得；前者須向內覓，後者要向外求，兩者的方向是衝突的。瑜伽修行的終極領悟，就是有一天於內在覓著的，也遍及在外；而一切所接觸到的外在，其根與內在所覓著的也無有二致。《瑜伽經》花了相當多篇幅分析心的作用以及必須從外求轉向內覓的道理，而內覓的捷徑——虔心皈依至上主，卻只有寥寥數語，算是美中不足之處。

本書中譯，在使讀者能夠理解的前題下，採最貼近梵文原義的文體輔以經句用詞註解，期望讀者體會一下類如梵文偈語的簡潔文句；然囿於筆力，信達雅未周延處尚祈寬容。

第一章

三摩地品

Samádhi Páda

•瑜伽旨要

Sutra I.1

atha yogánuśásanam//*1*//

Now a revised text of *Yoga*.

現在闡述瑜伽旨要。

atha - 現在、此刻

yoga- 瑜伽，相應、結合、融合；靈性上意指人天應合之學。

anuśásanam- 教、教導、講授、闡釋、闡揚論述，此字特別是指「透過紀律引領人獲得生命成功或福祉的教導」。

Sutra I.2

yogaś cittavṛtti nirodhaḥ//*2*//

Yoga is the restraint of mental modifications.

瑜伽之道在使妄心湛寂。

yogaḥ- 瑜伽之法、瑜伽之道；與本初相應，進而合一之道。

cittavṛtti—妄心、染妄之心，詞由 *citta* 及 *vṛtti* 組成。*citta* 音譯質多，字義為心、心靈質、集起心，能收集一切業力種子，待成熟後便藉事緣引生出各種覺受；*vṛtti* 本義「如旋渦般運動的」，含有轉、障、作用、職分、活動等意思。《瑜伽經》中指的是心緒、念想、妄想、心靈傾向等因內外緣而生的內心波動或變化，這種變化是苦樂感受的來源和維繫心靈存續的動力。由於心靈是相對的存在，故須臻至湛寂，方堪真實悟入瑜伽真境。

nirodhaḥ- 寂、滅；同四聖諦中滅諦之梵文，有時與涅槃同義。

譯按：經云「凡有所相，皆是虛妄」，禪言「動念即乖，心想成妄」；而瑜伽之重點即在使妄心回復湛寂。在實修上，若與本章第 23 節所述同時並進，則進境將無可限量，否則易陷頑空之病。

Sutra I.3

tadá draṣṭuḥ svarúpe avasthánam//*3*//

Then the Seer stands in his own nature.

如是，觀者住於本然自性。

tadá- 如是、是時、當彼之時
drașțuḥ- 觀者、見者、見證者
svarúpe- 自性、自相
avasthánam- 住、處於、安住於

Sutra I.4

vṛtti sárúpyam itaratra//4//

Identification with modifications elsewhere.

否則即易隨順心之所緣。

vṛtti- 心緒、心、相、念想、情緒傾向，因起心動念或所緣感受而生之波動。
sárúpyam- 認同、隨順、順應
itaratra- 不然、否則

• 心之緣相

Sutra I.5

vṛttayaḥ pañcatayyaḥ klișțá aklișțáḥ//5//

The modifications are five-fold, painful and not-painful.

心之所緣有五，或有染著或無染著。

vṛttayaḥ- 內心之染相，因起心攀緣外境而形成之心相，是心靈存在之資糧；若心中無人、我、眾生等等相，即見本心。
pañcatayyaḥ- 五種、五類
klișțá- 染、染著、雜染、煩惱；意指必然招至痛苦的。
aklișțáḥ- 不染、無染、無染污、無雜染、沒有痛苦的

Sutra I.6

pramáṇa viparyaya vikalpa nidrá smṛtayaḥ//6//

Real Cognition, Ureal Cognition, Imagination, Deep Sleep and Memory.

〔依次為〕為證量、顛倒、想像、睡眠和記憶。

pramáṇa- 量、理、證、驗證、辨證；依證據所有的度量或衡量。
viparyaya- 倒、顛倒、反、異；錯誤的概念、認知或想像。
vikalpa- 想像、空想、妄想、分別想；內心多變的想像或感覺。
nidrá- 眠、睡、睡眠
smṛtayaḥ- 憶念、憶持、記憶

Sutra I.7
pratyakṣa anumána ágamáḥ pramáṇáni//7//
Perception, Verbal Cognition and Inference are real cognitions.
「證量」有三，名為現量、比量和聖教量。
pratyakṣa- 現觀、現識、所證、現量；感知或直接而得的知識。
anumána- 比、比推、比量、推理、對照；由推理、推測或模擬而生的結論或知識。
ágamáḥ- 聖教、教法；從聖人或所信任之人的言教所得的知識。
pramáṇáni- 證量的、此處指證量的形態

Sutra I.8
viparyayaḥ mithyá-jñánam-atadrúpa pratiṣṭham//8//
Unreal Cognition is the knowing of the unreal, possessing a form not its own.
「顛倒」依立於不實的妄見。
viparyayaḥ- 反、倒、顛倒、顛倒識；對不實事物的錯誤知識，如水中月、鏡中花、造成貪、嗔、癡、慢、疑等五毒煩惱。
mithyá jñánam- 妄想、邪見、邪識
atadrúpa- 不實的形貌、非實相的
pratiṣṭham- 立於、基於、依止、建立

Sutra I.9
śabdajñána anupátí vastuśúnyaḥ vikalpaḥ//9//
Imagination is followed in sequence by verbal expression and knowledge, and is devoid of objective substratum.

「想像」依語文而非從事實所生之知見。

śabdajñána- 從語文得到的知識或知見

anupátí- 依隨、附隨、跟隨

vastuśúnyaḥ- 事境非實的、依止空泛的、根基不實的

vikalpaḥ- 想像、妄想、分別想

Sutra I.10

abháva pratyaya álambaná vṛttiḥ nidrá//10//

Sleep is the mental modification which has for its objective substratum, the cause of non-existence.

「睡眠」是心所對所緣境無所覺知的狀態。

abháva- 無、非有、空寂、無所覺知

pratyaya- 因、依、緣、緣起

álambaná- 憑、塵境、緣境、所緣境

vṛttiḥ- 念想、思想波的、心靈所緣的對象

nidrá- 睡、睡眠、深睡；一種心理上真空忘我的狀態。

Sutra I.11

anubhúta viṣaya asaṁpramoṣaḥ smṛtiḥ//11//

Memory is the not stealing away along with objective mental impressions (retained) (i.e., the reproducing of not more than what has been impressed upon the mind).

「記憶」是未忘失的塵緣經歷。

anubhúta- 受、領受、所識、經驗、覺知的

viṣaya- 所緣、外塵、外境、所知、諸境界

asaṁpramoṣaḥ- 未忘失的、無忘失的

smṛtiḥ- 憶念、憶持、記憶；於內心中重塑出過去已知事物。

• 論修行

Sutra I.12

abhyása vairágyábhyáṁ tannirodhaḥ//12//

They are restrained by practice and desirelessness.

透過修行與不執著可息而止之。

abhyása- 修行、修持、勤習

vairágyábhyáṁ- 透過或通過離欲、厭離、不執著或無染心

tannirodhaḥ- 控制、息止那些心念及變化

Sutra I.13

tatra sthitau yatnaḥ abhyásaḥ||13||

Of these, practice is the effort to secure steadiness.

故此，修行是使身心安住之努力。

tatra- 此處、於此、其中

sthitau- 在、坐、住、安住、安穩

yatnaḥ- 力使、勤於、努力、致力

abhyásaḥ- 修、修習、勤習、修行

Sutra I.14

sa tu dírghakála nairantarya satkára ásevitaḥ dṛḍhabhúmiḥ||14||

And this is firmly rooted, being well-attended to for a long time without interruption and with devotion.

此需持恆無間地虔心修習，根基方固。

sa- 彼、此、那個

tu- 然、但、唯

dírghakála- 持恆的、長久的

nairantarya- 綿延的、無間斷的、沒有中斷的

satkára- 虔敬、敬信、認真的

ásevitaḥ- 修、習、親近、多修習

dṛḍhabhúmiḥ- 穩固的、蒂固根深的、堅固的基礎

Sutra I.15

dṛṣta ánuśravika viṣaya vitṛṣṇasya vaśíkárasaṁjñá vairágyam||15||

Desirelessness is the consciousness of supremacy in him, who is free from thirst for perceptible and scriptural enjoyments.

對所見所聞之塵緣外境能心不動搖，謂之「不執著」。

dṛṣṭa- 見、所見、所看到的

ánuśravika- 聞、所聞、所聽到的

viṣaya- 塵、六塵、客塵、外境、所緣、外在的事物

vitṛṣṇasya- 離欲的、無欲的、不受欲望影響的

vaśíkára- 掌控、調伏、置於控制之下的

saṁjñá- 名、謂、概念、想蘊

vairágyam- 厭捨、離染、離欲行、不染著、不執著

譯按：緣心繫一切喜樂之源，故能不執著塵緣。

Sutra I.16

tatparaṁ puruṣakhyáteḥ guṇavaitṛṣṇyam//16//

The same is Higher, when there is indifference to the "qualities," due to the knowledge of the *Puruṣa*.

彼中最勝者，緣明了意識實相故，於一切造化功用無所執著。

tatparaṁ- 彼最高者、那個最高的、最卓越的；意指離欲行中成就最高者。

puruṣakhyáteḥ- 至上的顯現、最高的意識實相

guṇa- 宇宙運作勢能或造化力之功用或束縛作用，分悅性、變性與惰性三種。

vaitṛṣṇyam- 無所執著、不受造化功用或束縛的影響

•三昧定境

Sutra I.17

vitarka vicára ánanda asmitárúpa anugamát saṁprajñátaḥ//17//

The Cognitive Trance is accompanied by the appearances of philosophical curiosity, meditation, elation and egoism.

入正智定者仍伴隨有尋、伺、樂受及我相。

vitarka- 覺、尋、尋思、析理；指未臻至道心懷覺辨意尋之念。

vicára- 觀、伺、觀待；指未臻至道心懷觀待所專注的目標之念。
ánanda- 樂受、法悅、極樂、大樂、靈性的喜樂
asmitárúpa- 我相、自我感、自我意識
anugamát- 隨、相隨、伴隨、執持
saṁprajñátaḥ- 正知、正智、正了知、有想定；字面義為正確的般若定境，於此定境中逐漸能知過去、現在、未來，然仍有我相或我覺存留。有尋、有伺、樂受與我相是正智定的四個階段。

Sutra I.18
virámа-pratyayabhyása púrvaḥ saṁskáraśeṣaḥ anyaḥ||18||
Preceded by the constant repetition of the notion of cessation is the other; in which the residual potencies only remain.
修行至緣慮盡歇，唯存宿業，乃他種定境。
viráma- 歇息、停止、全然的放下
pratyaya- 依緣、所緣、心之所繫
abhyása- 修、修習、勤習
púrvaḥ- 先、前、前世、往昔、過去世
saṁskáraśeṣaḥ- 所餘伏業、業蘊、剩下的潛伏業力或反作用力
anyaḥ- 餘、餘類、別的、還有、其他的；或指無智定（*asaṁprajñátaḥ*），此處之無智非指沒有智慧，而是《心經》中「無智亦無得」之無智，亦即純粹本然，不假智用之圓鏡智相。無智定分有種無智定及無種無智定。

Sutra I.19
bhavapratyayaḥ videha prakṛtilayánám||19||
Is caused by Objective Existence for the *Videhas* and *Prakṛitilayas*.
如是定境亦因著「無身天」和「入造化力天」之宿緣而有。
bhava- 有、誕生、生而具有的、顯現出來的
pratyayaḥ- 緣、由、憑著、因著、緣著
videha- 無身的、無形的、無身天；生前厭離世間惱苦，持念

「空觀」有成之行者，離世後化為無有形體之天人。
prakṛtilayánám- 入造化力天；生前心懷敬信，一心解脫，因執著於有形神像，離世後融入造化力諸變化，成為入造化力天人。
譯按：大哲毗耶薩註解易有此定境之兩種宿緣，一是前世耽著空觀樂境之修行者，二是前世敬奉有相神像或聖物而未能超脫者。

Sutra I.20

śraddhá-vírya-smṛti samádhi-prajñá-púrvaka itareṣám//20//

For others it is preceded by faith, energy, memory, trance and discernment.

餘得此定者係依其信心、精進、憶持、定境及慧力等勤修而成。

śraddhá- 信心、信仰、虔信
vírya- 勤行、精勤、精進、精進力
smṛti- 憶念、憶持、記念、記憶
samádhi- 定境、三昧、等持、正定、正受、三摩地；泛指心識融入所觀，如：人心融入天心，小我融入真我，個體意識融入至上意識等。
prajñá- 明、慧、慧力、智慧、般若
púrvaka- 先、前；指前述之定境。
itareṣám- 其餘、餘者、而其他人

Sutra I.21

tívra-saṁvegánám-ásannaḥ//21//

Proximate for those whose consciousness of supremacy is keen.

發猛利厭離心者，定境亦日益近之。

tivra- 勇猛、猛利、熾誠
saṁvegá- 厭、厭離心；看破世情，志求解脫的心境。
ásannaḥ- 近、親近、接近

Sutra I.22

mṛdu-madhya-adhimátratvát-tato'pi viśeṣaḥ//22//

A further also differentiation by mild, middling, and intense.

是故下品、中品和上品修法之進境亦各有別。

mṛdu- 下、下品的、柔和的、溫和的

madhya- 中、中士、中品的、中等強度的

adhimátratvát- 上、上品的、勝、增上、熱切的

tatah- 因而、如是、從而

api- 也、且、又、此外

viśeṣaḥ- 別、殊異、各各差別

•至上主

Sutra I.23

Íśvara-praṇidhánát-vá//23//

Or, by feeling the omnipresence of God (*Íśvara*)

或，虔心皈依至上主。

Íśvara- 字義為控制者，能控制宇宙間一切萬有；以其不受世間苦惱及作用力之侵襲，故無須任何庇護，然能庇護萬物。依其特質，亦有譯為上主、至上主、宇宙的控制者等等。

praṇidháná- 安住於、融入於、庇護於、心住於所觀目標；英譯「亦或透過持念上主之無所不在」。

vá- 或、亦

譯按：凡事仰望主、以至上主為依歸，屬虔誠瑜伽之修法。西方著名代表人物是十二世紀的聖方濟各，印度是十五世紀的柴坦耶及十九世紀的羅摩克里希納。中世紀大哲商羯羅阿闍黎亦言「在各種達到解脫的方法裡，虔誠是最好的」。

Sutra I.24

kleśa karma vipáka-áśayaiḥ-aparámṛṣṭaḥ puruṣaviśeṣa íśvaraḥ//24//

Íśvara is a distinct *Puruṣa*, untouched by the vehicles of affliction, action and fruition.

至上主乃最勝妙之意識，不受任何煩惱、行為、果報、宿業等染著。

kleśa- 煩惱、痛苦、雜染、繫屬；亦即由無明，我慢，愛欲，怨憎和執著生命等引起的煩惱。
karma- 業、業行、因果、行為
vipáka- 果報、異熟果、取得成果的
áśayaiḥ- 宿業、業識、累業；未表發的業果、貯藏於潛意識中的心行印痕。
aparámṛṣṭaḥ- 無著的、不受染著的、不受影響的
puruṣaviśeṣa- 最殊勝、高妙的意識
íśvaraḥ- 控制者、宇宙的控制者、上主、自在主、自在天

Sutra I.25
tatra niratiśayaṁ sarvajña-bíjam//25//
In Him the seed of the omniscient is not exceeded.
於其中藏有無可等比之一切智種子。
tatra- 此中、於其中；即在至上主之中。
niratiśayaṁ- 不可超越的、無可等比的、無與倫比的
sarvajña- 一切智
bíjam- 種子

Sutra I.26
sa eṣah púrveṣám-api-guruḥ kálena-anavacchedát//26//
He is the Teacher of the Ancients too, not being limited by time.
至上主不受時輪所限，是亙古明師之師。
sa- 彼、那
eṣah- 此、這、彼之
púrveṣám- 最初的、最古老的
api- 也、且、又、此外
guruḥ- 上師；以靈性光輝驅逐弟子身心靈各層面黑暗的導師。
kálena- 時間、時輪
anavacchedát- 無盡無邊的、不受限制的、無間斷的

Sutra I.27

tasya vácakaḥ praṇavaḥ//27//

The Sacred word connotes Him.

聖音「唵（ॐ-*Oṁ*）」，即彼之象徵。

tasya- 彼、該；此處指祂（上主）。

vácakaḥ- 意含、意指、表詮

praṇavaḥ- 神聖的宇宙音聲（ॐ-*Oṁ*），*A*（表生）、*U*（表住）、*Ṁ*（表滅）的合成音。

Sutra I.28

taj-japaḥ tad-artha-bhávanam//28//

Its repetition and the understanding of its meaning.

反覆聆誦並思惟其音義。

tad- 其、那個

japaḥ- 念誦、持誦、覆誦

artha- 意義、目標、欲望的目標對象

bhávanam- 思惟、正行、熏習、觀想

譯按：*Oṁ* 聲是五大元素假合而成的有相宇宙的代表音聲，也是最常被唱頌的音聲，具沉澱及梳理身心之效。

• 心障

Sutra I.29

tataḥ pratyak-cetana-adhigamah-api-antaráya-abhavaś-ca//29//

Thence the understanding of the individual self and the absence of obstacles too.

如是修習可內證覺性，空諸心障。

tataḥ- 如此、如是、從彼

pratyak- 內向、內轉、從內證得

cetana- 意識、覺性

adhigamah- 了知、通達、證得、成就

api- 也、且、又、此外

antaráya- 障、阻礙、障礙
abhavah- 無、無有、滅除
ca- 和、與、及

Sutra I.30
vyádhi styána saṁśaya pramáda-álasya-avirati bhránti darśana-alabdha-bhúmikatva anavasthitatváni cittavikṣepáḥ te antaráyáḥ//30//
Disease, languor, indecision, carelessness, sloth, sensuality, mistaken notion, missing the point, instability, these causing distractions are the obstacles.
疾病、惛沈、猶疑、放逸、慵懶、縱情、散亂、誤解、未登地以及退墮等，皆屬亂心之障礙。
vyádhi- 疾病、病苦
styána- 頹廢、惛沈
saṁśaya- 猶疑、憂柔、徬徨
pramáda- 粗心、大意、放逸
álasya- 懶散、懈怠
avirati- 放縱、沒有節制的、偏重感官享受的
bhránti darśana- 誤解、錯誤的認知或看法
alabdha-bhúmikatva- 未登地，意指無有定境之經驗。
anavasthitatváni- 不安、不穩、退墮、退轉
cittavikṣepáḥ- 散亂心、分心、心障
te- 這些、這都是
antaráyáḥ- 障礙、阻礙

Sutra I.31
duḥkha-daurmanasya-aṅgamejayatva-śvásapraśvásáḥ vikṣepa sahabhuvaḥ//31//
Pain, despair, shakiness, inspiration and expiration are the companions of these distractions.

心障若起，苦惱、憂愁、搖顫、呼吸紊亂等隨之而至。
duḥkha- 苦、憂苦、痛苦、苦惱、苦受
daurmanasya- 憂惱、憂愁、愁苦
aṅgamejayatva- 顫抖、打顫
śvása- 息、入息、吸氣
praśvásáḥ- 出、出息、呼氣
vikṣepa- 心障，使人背離至上的力量。
sahabhuvaḥ- 隨著、伴隨著

Sutra I.32
tat-pratiṣedha-artham-eka-tattva-abhyásaḥ//32//
For their prevention, habituation to one Truth.
為破前述諸障，需勤習「一諦」之法。
tat- 該、那個、那些；即以上所舉諸障。
pratiṣedha- 破、滅、對治、防止、預防
artham- 令、為了、目的在於……
eka- 一、一相、單一的、專於一的
tattva- 真諦、真性、真理
abhyásaḥ- 勤習、反覆修習

• 對治之法

Sutra I.33
maitrí karuṇá mudito-pekṣáṇáṁ-sukha-duḥkha puṇya-apuṇya-viṣayáṇáṁ bhávanátaḥ citta-prasádanam//33//
By cultivating habits of friendliness, compassion, complacency and indifference towards happiness, misery, virtue and vice (respectively) the mind becomes pure.
以慈、悲、喜、捨之心對待樂、苦、善、惡之境；如是修行，心自悅淨。
maitrí- 慈心、友善、慈愛、大悲心
karuṇá- 悲心、慈悲、慈愍

mudita- 喜、喜心、歡喜
upekṣáṇáṁ- 捨、捨心、捨離、棄捨
sukha- 悅、快樂、安樂、樂受
duḥkha- 苦、憂苦、痛苦、苦惱、苦受
puṇya- 善行、美德
apuṇya- 惡行、非善行、非福行
viṣayáṇáṁ- 所緣、所行、目標、關注的事
bhávanátaḥ- 修、勤修、正念、態度、養成習慣
citta- 心、心靈、自心、念心
prasádanam- 淨、清淨、悅淨

Sutra I.34
pracchardana-vidh áraṇábhyáṁ vá práṇasya//34//
Optionally, by the expulsion and retention of breath.
或可擇調息法之呼氣與持氣。
pracchardana- 呼氣、經由呼氣
vidháraṇábhyáṁ- 住氣、持氣、經由持氣
vá- 或、或是、可選擇的
práṇasya- 呼吸的、調息法的、生命能控制法的

Sutra I.35
viṣayavatí vá pravṛttih-utpanná manasaḥ sthiti nibandhiní//35//
Or, Higher sense-activity appearing, causes mental steadiness.
或凝心專注外在所觀，令心安住。
viṣayavatí- 所感覺的、所知覺的對象
vá- 或、或是
pravṛtti- 高度專注於可感知的外在客體，如集中點、山色、星空、聖像、聖器或海潮音等；反之專注於內心平靜者稱為 *nivṛtti*。
utpanná- 出現、引發、生起
manasaḥ- 意、心意的

sthiti- 安住、安穩、堅穩
nibandhiní- 令、執持、導致、使得

Sutra I.36
viśoká vá jyotiṣmatí//36//
Or, the state of painless lucidity.
或心繫於無憂之內在慧光。
viśoká- 無憂的、沒有悲哀的
vá- 或、或是、亦可選擇
jyotiṣmatí- 慧光、慧明之境

Sutra I.37
vítarága viṣayam vá cittam//37//
Or, the mind having the desirelessness, for its object.
或觀想對所緣塵境已清淨無欲之成就者。
vítarága- 離欲之人、清淨無欲之人
viṣayam- 所緣境、塵境界、所感知到的事物
vá- 或、或是、亦可選擇
cittam- 心靈、心識

Sutra I.38
svapna nidrá jñána álambanam vá//38//
Or, having the knowledge of dream and sleep as its object of study.
或靜慮夢境與深眠中之慧見。
svapna- 夢、夢境
nidrá- 睡眠、深眠、無有夢擾的睡眠
jñána- 智、慧、覺境、正智、深慧
álambanam- 觀、所依緣、所緣境界、依緣靜慮之意
vá- 或、或是、亦可選擇

Sutra I.39

yathá-abhimata dhyánád vá//39//

Or, by meditating according to one's predilection.

或循所欲願之禪法修持。

yathá- 依、如、隨、循

abhimata- 求、選擇、依所偏好的

dhyánát- 經由思惟、靜慮、禪定、禪那

vá- 或、或是、亦可選擇

Sutra I.40

paramáṇu parama-mahattva-antah asya vaśíkáraḥ//40//

His power reaches down to the minutest, and up to the largest.

如是習者之控制力能從極微擴至無窮。

paramáṇu- 極微、最微細的粒子

paramamahattva- 最高、最大、最極、最無窮處

antah- 邊際、終點、終止處

asya- 於此、如是、修習者之……

vaśíkáraḥ- 調伏、降伏、掌控、主控力

•三摩缽提與無種子三摩地

Sutra I.41

kṣíṇa-vṛtter abhijátasyeva maṇer grahítṛ-grahaṇa-gráhyeṣu tatstha tadañjanatá samápattiḥ//41//

Becoming like a transparent crystal on the modifications disappearing (the mind acquires) the power of though-transformation (*Samápatti*), the power of appearing in the shape of whatever object is presented to it, be it the knower, knowable or the act of knowing.

念想滅盡，心明淨若琉璃，由是能取、執取、所取泯歸清淨，謂之正受持定（三摩缽提）。

kṣíṇa- 已滅、已盡、滅盡

vṛtti- 心念、心緒、內心擬向、情緒傾向、妄心所念的
abhijátasya- 清明、剔透、純淨的
iva- 似、如、等同
maṇeh- 水晶、琉璃；喻斷惑證真後的心相。
grahítṛi- 能取、能知、知者、能取者、認識主體、能識別事物者
grahaṇa- 執取、取境、攝受、執持；認識或認知的作用。
gráhyeṣu- 所知、所取、所證；認識的對象、被執取的事物
tatstha- 由是、由於
tadañjanatá- 取所見之形色
samápattiḥ- 三摩缽提、正受持定（心離邪亂、止於一念、而後內見自性不動之謂）

Sutra I.42
tatra śabdártha-jñána-vikalpaiḥ saṁkírṇá savitarká samápattiḥ//42//
There, the thought-transformation in which the options of word, meaning and idea are mixed up, is called Indistinct (verbal).
於其中若仍雜有覓求音義、慧智之想，謂之「有尋等至三摩缽提」。
tatra- 彼處、於其中、於此中、於……之中
śabdá ártha- 音義、名相、內心的欲望或目標對象
jñána- 正智、慧智、靈性的知識
vikalpaiḥ- 思、念、想；向內在追求的念想
saṁkírṇá- 混合、混雜、交織
savitarká- 有覺、有尋、正念不斷之謂
samápattiḥ- 三摩缽提、正受、正定、正受持定

Sutra I.43
smṛti-pariśuddhau svarúpa-śúnya iva arthamátra-nirbhásá nirvitarká//43//
Distinctive (wordless) thought-transformation is that in which the mind shines out as the object alone on the cessation of memory,

and it were devoid of its own nature.

若諸憶念清淨，唯存自性無相妙光明，謂之「無尋等至三摩缽提」。

smṛti- 念、憶念、憶持、記憶

pariśuddhau- 清淨的、純淨的

svarúpa- 本相、自相、自性

śúnya- 空、空性、妙空；無有相狀的。

iva- 似、如、等同

artha- 義理、欲望的目標對象

mátra- 唯、唯有

nirbhásá- 光、光明、光輝

nirvitarká- 無覺、無尋、受想心、覺知心，分別心盡滅之謂。

Sutra I.44

etayaiva savicárá nirvicárá ca súkṣma-viṣaya vyákhyátá//44//

By this the meditative and the ultra-meditative, having the subtle for their objects, are also described.

由此亦說明了「有伺等至」和「無伺等至」定境之精微。

etaya- 由此、藉此

iva- 也、如、亦、等同

savicárá- 念、有觀、有伺；仍存有某種精細念頭之定境。

nirvicárá- 無觀、無伺；任何覺觀尋伺俱無之定境。

ca- 和、及、與

súkṣma-viṣaya- 微細境界、精細的所緣境

vyákhyátá- 顯、說、釋、解釋

Sutra I.45

súkṣma-viṣayatvam-ca-aliṇga paryavasánam//45//

And the province of the subtle reaches up to the noumenal.

又此精微所緣，盡歸無相之究竟本源。

súkṣma- 精細的、精微的、微妙的

viṣayatvam- 境界、所知境界、所緣境界
ca- 和、及、與、又
aliṇga- 無形相、無有相狀的；尤指無狀無相的萬化源頭。
paryavasánam- 盡歸、終究、究竟

Sutra I.46
tá eva sabíjah-samádhiḥ//46//
They are the seeded trance only.
唯前述諸境界，仍屬具含種子之三摩地。
táh- 彼等、那些
eva- 唯、僅、遍
sabíjah- 有種、具種、具有種子的、仍有業識種子伏存的
samádhiḥ- 三昧、定境、三摩地

Sutra I.47
nirvicára vaiśáradye adhyátma-prasádaḥ//47//
The undisturbed flow of the ultra -meditative causes Subjective Luminosity.
證入無伺定境，內生妙明淨信，行人無怖無畏。
nirvicára- 無觀、無伺、任何觀伺俱無之境地
vaiśáradye- 無疑、無怖畏；證得本初不受擾動之清淨空性後的無畏心態。
adhyátma- 內在的、靈性的；對內在真我的靈性直覺經驗。
prasádaḥ- 明、清淨、淨信、吉祥、妙喜、妙明、獻供
譯按：本節敘述無種子三昧之心境。梵文 *Prasada* 又有獻供的意思，隱含有將個體小我交付給宇宙大我的究竟供養。

Sutra I.48
ṛtaṁbhará tatra prajñá//48//
Therein the faculty of Essential Cognition.
此中所證般若妙慧即圓明真理。

ṛtaṁbhará- 圓證、經驗到的圓明至理、證得真如實諦
tatra- 此中、此處、於此中、於其中
prajñá- 慧、妙慧、正慧、般若

Sutra I.49
śruta-anumána-prajñá-abhyám anya-viṣayá viśeṣa-arthatvát//49//
It has different objects from those of verbal and inferential cognition, as it refers to particulars.
如是妙慧義旨殊妙，與塵境耳聞、推比之智，自是不同。
śruta- 聞、聽聞、耳聞；從外聆聽到的知識
anumána- 推測、推論、推比、比量；推論比較得出的知識。
prajñábhyám- 從如是慧智、源自彼妙智的
anya- 餘、除、其他、不同的、別異、區別、辨別
viṣayá- 境、塵境、所緣境
viśeṣa- 特殊的、殊妙的、別異的
arthatvát- 目的、宗旨、義意、勝義

Sutra I.50
tajjas-saṁskárah anya-saṁskára pratibandhí//50//
Residual potencies born therefrom impede other residual potencies.
由彼妙慧所生慧力能遮斷所餘諸業。
tajjas- 由此所生、從彼所出的
saṁskárah- 宿業、伏業；此處意指由般若妙慧生起的作用力。
anya-saṁskára- 餘由過往作為形成的業力、其他未表發的行蘊、所餘未顯現的反作用力
pratibandhí- 能斷、能遮、能覆

Sutra I.51
tasyápi nirodhe sarva-nirodhán-nirbíjaḥ samádhiḥ//51//
All being suppressed, by the suppression of that too comes the

seedless trance.

當此妙慧亦復寂滅之時，由於悉皆滅盡，即契入無種子三摩地。

tasya- 彼、該、從彼、從其中

api- 也、且、又、此外

nirodhe- 斷、滅、已滅、止寂、息止、寂靜

sarva- 一切、從一切、悉皆、盡所有

nirodhat- 由於滅盡

nirbíjaḥ- 無種、不具種子的；二元泯除、唯存圓明之一相三昧。

samádhiḥ- 寂定、等持、三昧定、三摩地

第二章

修習品

Sádhana Páda

•瑜伽行法

Sutra 2.1

tapaḥ svádhyáy-eśvarapraṇidhánáni kriyá-yogaḥ ||1||

Purificatory action, study and making God the motive of action, is the *Yoga*, of action.

瑜伽之修行在於利他、誦習經典與皈依至上主。

tapaḥ- 苦修、苦行、淨心行、精進行、利他行；有二義、一為自苦、一為利他，此處作利他解，即不思己利而盡己能力為他人服務的行為。

svádhyáya- 誦讀、學習、誦經、研讀屬靈的經典

Iśvarapraṇidhána- 意譯為融入至上主，*Iśvara* 謂理事無礙、心能作主之境；*praṇidhána* 意為安住於、融入於。

kriyá-yoga- 瑜伽鍛煉、瑜伽修業；利他屬行瑜伽，誦習經典屬智瑜伽，皈依至上主屬虔誠瑜伽。

Sutra 2.2

samádhi-bhávana-arthaḥ kleśa tanú-karaṇa-arthaś ca ||2||

For the purpose of bringing about trance and for the purpose of attenuating afflictions.

旨在減少煩惱繫縛及契入三摩地。

samádhi- 定、三昧、等持、三摩地；個體心融入觀想目標之謂。

bhávana-arthaḥ- 為成就某種目的

kleśa- 煩惱、雜染、痛苦、不淨

tanu- 少、細、減少、削弱

karaṇa-artha- 使達到或促成某種目的

ca- 和、及、與

•論煩惱

Sutra 2.3

avidyá-asmitá-rága-dveṣa-abhiniveśaḥ kleśáḥ ||3||

The afflictions are Nescience, Egoism, Attachment, Aversion and Love of Life.

煩惱起自無明、我見、貪戀、怨憎和迷執。

avidyá- 愚昧、無知、無明；一種帶往離心的作用。

asmitá- 我見、我慢、自我感；將心靈認作是自性本體。

rága- 貪、貪欲、愛戀、貪戀

dveṣa- 瞋、瞋恨、憎惡、厭惡

abhiniveśaḥ- 迷執、執取、心靈的執著；尤指對生命之迷執。

kleśáḥ- 煩惱、染著、痛苦、本惑

Sutra 2.4

avidyá kṣetram-uttareṣám prasupta-tanu-vicchinn-udáráṇám //4//

Nescience is the field for the others, whether dormant, tenuous, alternated or fully operative.

無明是其後四煩惱之溫床，無論它們是處於蟄伏、衰減、中斷或是現行。

avidyá- 愚昧、無知、無明；一種導向離心的作用、是我見等後四煩惱的溫床。

kṣetram- 地、領域、田野、塵剎、國土

uttareṣám- 其後、其餘的；指前句經文所說的後四種煩惱。

prasupta- 蟄伏的、睡眠中的

tanu- 少、細、減少、削弱

vicchinna- 隔、間斷、中斷

udáráṇám- 擴張的、持續著的、現行中的

Sutra 2.5

anityá-aśuci-duḥkha-anátmasu nitya-śuci-sukha-átmakhyátir-avidyá //5//

Nescience is the taking of the non-eternal, the impure, the painful and the not-self to be the eternal, the pure, the pleasurable and the self.

無明是將無常、不淨、苦受和假我當作是恆常、清淨、樂受和

真我。
anitya- 斷、無常、非永恆的
aśuci- 穢、不淨
duḥkha- 苦、憂苦、痛苦、苦惱、苦受
anátmasu- 無我、假我、非真正的我、非自性靈魂的；意指俗世的我。
nitya- 常、恆常、永恆、不滅、不變異
śuci- 淨、清淨、潔淨
sukha- 樂、輕安、安樂、樂受
átma- 我、真我、大我、自性、靈魂、真如自性
khyáti- 概念、想法、認知、觀點
avidyá- 愚昧、無知、無明；一種導向離心的作用。

Sutra 2.6
dṛg-darśana-śaktyor ekátmata-iva-asmitá ||6||
Egoism is the appearance of identity in the natures of the subjective power of consciousness and the instrumental power of seeing.
我見來自認為能見之性與能見之力相同。
d g-**同** d k**，見性、見元、見證者**、能見之性、意識的見證本質
darśana śaktyoh- 能見之力；識蘊功能相互合作，生起能見知相分或所知的作用力。
ekátmata- 認同、同化、一致化；亦即認為兩者是相同的。
iva- 似、如、等、猶如、認為、認作
asmitá- 我見、我慢、自我感、自我意識；認為自心所感知者為真，以自我感知為主來論斷事情的作用。

Sutra 2.7
sukha-anuśayí rágaḥ ||7||
Attachment is the sequential attraction to pleasure.
貪戀緣隨樂受而生。

sukha- 快樂、輕安、安樂、樂受
anuśayí- 隨、隨附、緊密的連接著
rágaḥ- 貪、貪欲、貪愛、愛戀、貪戀

Sutra 2.8
Aversion is the sequential repulsion from pain.
duḥkha-anuśayí dveṣaḥ ||8||
怨憎緣隨苦受而起。
duḥkha- 苦、憂苦、痛苦、苦惱、苦受
anuśayí- 隨、隨附、緊密的連接著
dveṣaḥ- 瞋、瞋恨、怨憎、憎惡、厭惡

Sutra 2.9
svarasváhi viduṣo-'pi tathárúḍho-'bhiniveśaḥ ||9||
Flowing on by its own potency, established all the same even in the wise, is Love of Life.
迷執是俱生的內在傾向，在智者身上也同樣具有。
svarasváhi- 自然的本能之流、俱生的本能傾向
viduṣah- 智者、賢達、聰慧之人
api- 也、且、又、此外
tathárúḍhah- 一樣的成立、同樣的具有；同樣有這種傾向。
abhiniveśaḥ- 迷執、固執，尤指對生命的執著。

Sutra 2.10
te pratiprasava-heyáḥ súkṣmáḥ ||10||
These when but potential, are destroyed along with the passing out of activity.
這些深細煩惱，可藉反觀其生起處而斷之。
te- 此、這些
pratiprasava- 反轉還原、反觀其根本
heyáḥ- 斷、滅、棄、避免

súkṣmáḥ- 細、深細、微細；微細根深、錯綜糾結的。

Sutra 2.11

dhyána heyáḥ tad-vṛttayaḥ //11//

Their modifications are destroyed by meditation.

禪定可斷內心諸相變化。

dhyána- 禪、禪那、禪定；「外離諸相、內見自性不動」之境。

heyáḥ- 斷、滅、棄、避免

tad- 彼、那些、那個

vṛttayaḥ- 心妄、心之染相、心之變相

•因果業力

Sutra 2.12

kleśa-múlaḥ karma-aśayo dṛṣṭa-adṛṣṭa-janma-vedaníyaḥ //12//

The vehicle of actions has its origin in afflictions, and is experienced in visible and invisible births.

宿業根植於煩惱，形成今生和來世的經歷感受。

kleśa- 煩惱、雜染、痛苦、不淨

múlaḥ- 根、本、根本

karma- 業、業行、行為、行動

aśayah- 依、積、累、宿處

dṛṣṭa- 睹見、已見、所見、現世的

adṛṣṭa- 未見、不可見、未來的、來世的

janma- 生、世、出生、受生

vedaníyaḥ- 感受、應報、領受、經歷

Sutra 2.13

sati múle tad-vipáko játy-áyur-bhogáḥ //13//

It ripens into life-state, life- experience and life- time, if the root exists.

只要煩惱根尚存，異熟果報就會以身家、壽限、運數等方式呈

現。

sati- 現有的、存在的

múle- 為其根的

tat- 其、彼、那個

vipákah- 成熟、異熟、異熟果報；因過去善惡而有的果報總名。

játy- 種、類、種姓、出身、身家、身世、生相、種種的

áyur- 人生、生命、性命、壽命、命數、生命期

bhogáḥ- 受、受用、所受用的、利養資糧；泛指生命在器世間所經驗到的苦樂。

Sutra 2.14

te hláda paritápa-phaláḥ puṇya-apuṇya-hetutvát //14//

They have pleasure or pain as the fruit, by reason of virtue or vice.

果報的樂與苦，肇因於行為的善與惡。

te- 此、這些

hláda- 樂、快樂、歡喜、愉悦

paritápa- 苦、惱苦、悲苦、惱熱

phaláḥ- 果、業果、果報

puṇya- 善、善行、功德、福德、美德

apuṇya- 惡、罪行、惡行、非福行

hetutvát- 肇因、因緣於

•論苦

Sutra 2.15

pariṇáma tápa saṁskára duḥkhaiḥ guṇa-vṛtti-virodhácca duḥkham-eva sarvaṁ vivekinaḥ //15//

By reason of the pains of change, anxiety and habituation and by reason of the contrariety of the functionings of the 'qualities,' all indeed is pain to the discriminating.

無常、熱惱之苦因，緣自業識之牽引以及造化屬性形成的念想衝突，由是善分別者深明一切皆苦。

pariṇáma- 變化、轉變、無常
tápa- 熱、熾熱、熱惱、劇苦
saṁskára- 伏業、業蘊、潛伏的業力
duḥkhaiḥ- 苦因、苦惱的原因
guṇa- 造化力的屬性、特質；宇宙造化力的三種作用性質（悅性、變性、惰性、舊譯喜、憂、闇三德）。
vṛtti- 心念、心緒、念想、情緒傾向、內心擬向
virodhát- 對立、抵觸、衝突、相矛盾、乖違的
ca- 和、及、與
duḥkham- 由於此苦受
eva- 確實、只有
sarvaṁ- 一切、所有、普悉
vivekinaḥ- 善分別者、善明辨之人、具有辨識力者

Sutra 2.16
heyaṁ duḥkham-anágatam ||16||
Pain not-yet-come is the avoidable.
未來之苦可斷而除之。
heyaṁ- 可斷、可滅、可以避免的、可以防止的
duḥkham- 苦、憂苦、痛苦、苦惱、苦受
anágatam- 未來的、尚未到來的

Sutra 2.17
draṣṭṛi-dṛśyayoḥ saṁyogo heyahetuḥ ||17||
The Conjunction of the knower and the knowable is the cause of the avoidable pain.
須斷之因在於能見與所見塵境之和合。
draṣṭṛi- 見者、能見者；即根識之作用，識托於眼所生之作用。
dṛśyayoḥ- 見、現、所見、可見、塵境、所見的對象
saṁyogo- 結、合、融合、繫結、和合
heyahetuḥ- 應斷之因、須避免之因、應滅的致苦之因。

•造化三德

Sutra 2.18

prakáśa-kriyá-sthiti-śílaṁ bhútendriya-átmakaṁ bhoga-apavarga-arthaṁ dṛśyam ||18||

The knowable is of the nature of illumination, activity and inertia; it consists of the elements and the powers of sensation, action and thought; its objects are emancipation and expedience.

世間所見皆由五大暨諸根假合而成，並具悅性、變性及惰性等屬性；其目的在於經驗苦樂及通達解脫。

prakáśa- 光、光明、喻悅性

kriyá- 行、活動、喻變性

sthiti- 住、慣性、喻惰性

śílaṁ- 性質、具有的某種天性

bhúthạ- 世間、地大等元素群

indriya- 知作根等身根及意根之總稱，亦即身體運動器官、感覺器官與意根的作用。

átmakaṁ- 組構而成、事物的本質

bhoga- 受、受用、利養、資糧；物質層面的苦樂

apavarga- 解脫、自在；意指覺行圓滿而證涅槃之謂。

arthaṁ- 目的、法義、為求；為了某種目的的。

dṛśyam- 境、見、現、所見、所見或所經驗到的對象

Sutra 2.19

viśeṣa-aviśeṣa-liṅga-mátra-aliṅgáni guṇaparváṇi ||19||

The Specialized, the Unspecialized, the Undifferentiated phenomenal and the noumenal are the stages of the qualities.

無相、有相以及無別、有別，皆是造化屬性的階段相狀。

viśeṣa- 有別、差異、殊異；緣惰性屬性影響，我執有心之用，五大、五唯因之次第而出，漸成殊異萬象，是為有別階段。

aviśeṣa- 平等、無二、無別、無異；緣變性屬性之作用，大覺執

有我，但仍處無實質顯現可資分別之無別階段。

liṅga- 有相、有形相的；指造化力三屬性悅性屬性開始勝出，元明生所、大覺相出、萬象生焉。

mátra- 唯、只、只是、但是

aliṅgáni- 無相、無形相的；指造化力三屬性處於平衡無有勝出的無相狀態。

guṇa- 造化力的屬性、特質；宇宙造化力的三種作用性質（悅性、變性、惰性、舊譯喜、憂、闇三德）。

parváṇi- 型態、相狀、狀態、階段、層次

•本初淨識

Sutra 2.20

draṣṭá dṛśimátraḥ śuddho-'pi pratyaya-anupaśyaḥ ||20||

The seer is consciousness only; even though pure, he cognizes ideas by imitation.

能見者實此能見之性，雖湛寂虛靈，然依虔心修觀可得覺證。

draṣṭá- 見者、能見者

dṛśimátraḥ- 見分：字義唯一能見者，指的是清淨識或意識本身，亦即能見之性，亦可謂本心或本性。

śuddhah- 淨、清淨、純淨

api- 也、且、又、雖、即使、此外

pratyaya- 緣、信、虔信、依緣、類似的、虔心繫念、心理上的努力；本字若作為後綴詞，意思依文會有多種變化；而虔信或虔心繫念也是一種心理上的模仿（imitation）。

anupaśyaḥ- 觀、觀見、證知、察見，覺知

Sutra 2.21

tadartha eva dṛśyasya-átmá ||21||

For his purpose only is the being of the 'knowable.'

如是所見，唯是為明此自性實相。

tadartha- 為彼目的、為了那個目標

eva- 唯、只、皆
dṛśyasya- 所見的、可見的、被映現之事物
átmá- 自我、自性、真我、淨識、靈魂、個體意識、真如自性
譯按：一切變現皆是本初之心的幻化，其目的亦是為復歸本初而有；亦可謂吾人之一切因緣、一切所見，皆是為返本歸源之目的。

•成就者所見

Sutra 2.22
kṛtárthaṁ pratinaṣṭaṁ-apy-anaṣṭaṁ tadanya sádháraṇatvát //22//
Although destroyed in relation to him whose objects have been achieved, it is not destroyed, being common to others.
故此，大成就者雖與他人共見壞滅，然知實無壞滅。
kṛtárthaṁ- 完成、成就者、受供者；指成就之人
prati- 依、向、對、就
naṣṭaṁ- 毀、壞、滅、泯滅。
api- 也、且、然、雖
anaṣṭaṁ- 無壞、無滅、無失
tadanya- 除此之外，意指除了成就者之外的人。
asádháraṇatvát- 共通、共有、共性、普遍性
譯按：如前節所言意旨，所謂壞滅亦是回歸本初，故實無壞滅。

Sutra 2.23
svasvámi-śaktyoḥ svarúp-oplabdhi-hetuḥ saṁyogaḥ //23/
Conjunction is that which brings about the recognition of the natures of the power of owning and the capacity of being owned.
人我與其所有事物間之和合作用，旨在了別自性本相。
sva- 人的、我的、自有的、我所擁有的塵緣事物
svámi- 擁有者、能夠擁有事物的人或我
śaktyoḥ- 力能，此處指結合擁有者與其所擁有事物的作用力。
svarúpa- 自相、本相、原本的樣貌

uplabdhi- 了別、了知、察覺、識知
hetuḥ- 因、理由、要旨、目的
saṁyogaḥ- 結、合、和合、聯結
譯按：老子「夫物芸芸，各歸其根」之語，可佐參本節意旨。

Sutra 2.24
tasya hetur-avidyá //24//
Nescience is its effective cause.
彼和合之因，緣起於無明。
tasya- 此、彼（指和合、聯結的作用）
hetuh- 因、理由、要旨、目的
avidyá- 愚昧、無知、無明；一種帶往離心的作用。
譯按：無明 (離心力) 是相對覺明 (向心力) 而說，然就本然清淨之自性而言，無有相對之存在 : 故凡有無明或覺明之想，亦皆無明生起之因。之所以結果有別，在於前者是因假亂真，後者是藉假修真。

Sutra 2.25
tad-abhábát-saṁyoga-abhávo hánaṁ taddṛśeḥ kaivalyam //25//
Removal is the disappearance of conjunction on account of its disappearance that is the absolute freedom of the knower.
去彼無明，和合即不有；和合既除，獨存不共之境即現。
tad- 彼之、那個
abhábát- 除去、消去、使消失
saṁyoga- 結、合、認同、聯結
abhávah- 不存、無有
hánaṁ- 滅、拔除、中止
tad- dṛśeḥ- 即見、即證見
kaivalyam- 不共、獨存、絕對、究竟解脫

•去無明之法

Sutra 2.26

viveka-khyátir-aviplavá hánopáyaḥ //26//

The means of the removal is discriminative knowledge undisturbed.

去彼無明之法，在持續地保持明辨覺知。

viveka- 辨、明辨、辨別、區別

khyátih- 了別、覺知、洞察力

aviplavá- 無有斷續的、不受影響的、沒有動搖的

hánopáyaḥ- 去除的方法、斷除之道

Sutra 2.27

tasya saptadhá pránta-bhúmiḥ prajña //27//

His discrimination becoming final at each stage, sevenfold.

循是法可通透瑜伽七種大慧。

tasya- 彼之、依循這個方法

saptadhá- 七、此處指七種大慧；瑜伽經權威毗耶薩註解這七種智是：1. 遍知智（應知已知）、2. 斷盡智（應斷已斷）、3. 證得智（寂定已證）、4. 所作清淨智（作行清淨）、5. 所修已成智（所修已證）、6. 超越三德智（束縛已解）、7. 自相光明智（知獨存境）等七種慧智。

pránta-bhúmiḥ- 極、遠、清智、終極境地

prajña- 真智、覺慧、完全的知識

•瑜伽八支功法

Sutra 2.28

yoga-aṅga-anuṣṭhánád-aśuddhi-kṣaye jñána-díptir-áviveka-khyáteḥ //28//

On the destruction of impurity by the sustained practice of the accessories of *Yoga,* the light of wisdom reaches up to discriminative knowledge.

虔修瑜伽各支功法可斷諸雜染，發智慧光，通明辨智。

yoga- 瑜伽、相應、融合、合一、結合

aṅga- 肢、支、支分、部分

anuṣṭhánád- 透過持續的修持、通過虔修、實修

aśuddhi- 不淨、雜染

kṣaye- 滅、壞、盡、斷、失

jñána- 智、智識、正智、智慧、深慧

díptih- 光明、光輝、光耀

á- 直到、通達

viveka-khyáteḥ- 明辨智、知識的本質

Sutra 2.29

yama niyama-ásana práṇáyáma pratyáhára dháraṇá dhyána samádhayo-'ṣṭávaṅgáni //29//

Restraint, Observance, Posture, Regulation of breath (Pranayama), Abstraction, Concentration, Meditation and Trance are the eight accessories of *Yoga*.

瑜伽八支功法是——外在規範、內在規範、坐式、調息法、內攝、專注、禪定及三摩地。

yama- 禁制、制戒、禁戒、持戒、約束、外在規範、外在行為控制，屬物質與心理層面的修持。*yama* 意思是控制或禁行之事，是如何於社會中生活應持守的大律，故有譯為持戒，然與佛門菩薩六度中防非止惡之持戒（*síla-* 音譯尸羅）不盡等同。

niyama- 勸制、遵行、律儀、精進、內在規範、內在行為控制，屬在世、出世和靈性層面同須著重的修持。故 *niyama* 意指是決定或必然要做之事，早期譯為精進，然與佛門菩薩六度中，練心於法而不懈怠之精進（*vírya*）亦不盡等同。

ásana- 坐式、體式、體位法、調身法、安坐法

práṇáyáma- 調息法、呼吸控制、生命能控制法

pratyáhára- 制感、攝心、收攝、內攝、感官收攝、感官回收

dháraṇá- 執持、總持、集中、專注、凝神
dhyána- 禪那、禪定、入定、靜慮、思惟、禪定、冥想
samádhi- 三昧、正受、正定、定境、等持、三摩地
áṣṭáu- 八
aṅgáni- 肢、支、支分、部分

•外在規範與內在規範

Sutra 2.30
ahiṁsá-satya-asteya brahmacarya-aparigraháḥ yamáḥ ||30||
Of these the restraints are: Abstinence from injury (*Ahimsá*); Veracity; Abstinence from theft; Continence; Abstinence from avariciousness.
「外在規範」包括—不傷害、真實語、不偷盜、心不離道、不役於物。
ahiṁsá- 不害、不傷害、不殺生、非暴力；不以言語、行為、思想造成他人的痛苦。
satya- 真理、真實語、真諦理、不虧於心、心懷真誠；言語、行為、思想以對方最終的福祉為出發點。
asteya- 不偷盜、不偷竊；不偷盜亦不起偷盜之想。
brahmacarya- 淨行、梵行、清淨行、心不離道；視一切際遇盡歸於梵或本體所現，而得心清淨。
aparigrahá- 不貪、不役於物、不為物所役
yamáḥ- 外在規範、外在行為規範

Sutra 2.31
játi-deśa-kála-samaya-anavacchinnáḥ sárvabhaumá-mahávratam ||31||
They are the Great Vow, universal, and not- limited by life-state, space, time, and circumstance.
此為普世性大願，不受身家、時間、方所等情況限制。
játi- 種姓、出身、身家、階級；出生時的地位。

deśa- 地方、方所、境地、國土、國家
kála- 時間、時輪
samaya- 境況、情況、狀況
anavacchinnáḥ- 不受限的
sárvabhaumá- 普遍、普世、世界、宇宙、一切層面
mahávratam- 大戒、大律、誓約、弘願、大行願

Sutra 2.32
śauca saṁtoṣa tapaḥ svádhyáy-eśvarapraṇidhánáni niyamáḥ ||32||
The observances are Cleanliness, Contentment, Purificatory action, study and the making of the Lord the motive of all action.
「內在規範」包括——潔淨、知足、利他行、研讀經典、皈依至上主。
śauca- 淨化、清淨、潔淨；包括內在清淨與外在整潔。
saṁtoṣa- 安足、知足、適足；保持內心處於適足狀態。
tapaḥ- 苦修、苦行、利他行、帶有犧牲性的服務
svádhyáya- 讀誦、研讀聖典或屬靈的經典
Iśvarapraṇidháná- 心住至上、皈依至上主、以至上主為庇護
niyamáḥ- 內在規範、內在行為規範

Sutra 2.33
vitarka-bádhane pratiprakṣa-bhávanam ||33||
Upon, thoughts of sin troubling, habituation to the contrary.
有因思惑而煩惱不安時，即以反向思維對治。
vitarka- 尋伺、疑惑、思惑
bádhane- 不安、憂惱、煩惱
pratiprakṣa- 反思、逆向的、對治之道
bhávanam- 想法、意念、思維

Sutra 2.34

vitarká himsádayaḥ kṛta-kárita-anumoditá lobha-krodha-moha-púrvaká mṛdu-madhya adhimátrá duḥkha-ajñána-ananta-phalá iti pratiprakṣa-bhávanam //34//

The sins are the causing of injury to others and the rest. They are done, caused to be done and permitted to be done; they are slight, middling and intense; their result is an infinity of pain and unwisdom; thus comes the habit-of-thinking to the contrary.

種種傷害由思惑而來，其作因多起於貪、瞋、癡；所作無論是輕微、中等或強烈，結果均導致無盡之苦惱與蒙昧，故當反思對治。

vitarká- 尋伺、疑惑、思惑
himsádayaḥ- 傷害等等……
kṛta- 已作、已做、已辦、已發生的
kárita- 所作因、誘因
anumoditá- 意欲、想要、屬意
lobha- 貪、貪著、貪婪、貪愛
krodha- 瞋、生氣、忿怒、瞋恚
moha- 癡、愚癡、癡迷、迷戀
púrvaká- 先前的、前述、以上
mṛdu- 輕微、微細、柔和、柔軟
madhya- 溫和、中間、處中
adhimátrá- 過激的、強烈的、極端的
duḥkha- 苦、憂苦、痛苦、苦惱、苦受
ajñána- 無知、愚昧、蒙昧、沒有智慧
ananta- 無盡、無邊、無窮、無限
phalá- 結果、所得果
iti- 因而、從而、由是、於是
pratiprakṣa- 反思、逆向的、對治之道
bhávanam- 想法、意念、思維

•外在規範之功

Sutra 2.35

ahiṁsá-pratiṣṭháyaṁ tat-sannidhau vairatyághaḥ //35//

(The habit of) not-causing-injury being confirmed, hostilities are given-up in his presence.

落實「不傷害」之人，近其身者不生敵意。

ahiṁsá- 不害、非暴力、不傷害、不殺生

pratiṣṭháyaṁ- 依住、落實、貫徹、確立

tat- 在彼之、在他的、在其之

sannidhau- 面前、左近、附近

vaira-tyághaḥ- 放棄敵意、不生敵意

Sutra 2.36

satya-pratiṣṭháyaṁ kriyá-phala-áśrayatvam //36//

Veracity being confirmed, action and fruition become dependents.

信守「真實語」，其所作事與所得果必信實可依。

satya- 真理、真實語、真諦理、不虧於心、心懷真誠

pratiṣṭháyaṁ- 依住、落實、貫徹、確立

kriyá- 行、行為、作為、所作事

phala- 果、報、所得果、行為的結果

áśrayatvam- 可依止的、可相信的

Sutra 2.37

asteya-pratiṣṭháyáṁ sarvaratn-opasthánam //37//

(The habit of) not-stealing being confirmed, all, jewels, approach him.

恪遵「不偷盜」，種種妙財利養自然現前。

asteya- 不偷盜、不偷竊

pratiṣṭháyáṁ- 依住、落實、貫徹、確立

sarva- 一切、悉皆、種種、諸所有
ratna- 珍寶、珠寶、珍貴的事物
upasthánam- 供侍、供養、現前、親近

Sutra 2.38
brahma-carya pratiṣṭháyáṁ vírya-lábhaḥ //38//
Continence being confirmed, vigour is obtained.
秉持「心不離道」，滋長勇健精進之力。
brahmacarya- 淨行、梵行、清淨行、心不離道
pratiṣṭháyáṁ- 依住、落實、貫徹、確立
vírya- 力、勇健、精勤、精進力
lábhaḥ- 得、獲得、證得、成就

Sutra 2.39
aparigraha-sthairye janma-kathaṁtá saṁbodhaḥ //39//
Non-covetousness being confirmed, the knowledge of-the-how of births.
堅持「不役於物」，即可了知當世云何受生。
aparigraha- 不貪、不役於物
sthairye- 穩固、堅定、堅持
janma-kathaṁtá- 因何誕生、云何受生、何故出生
saṁbodhaḥ- 覺知、了知、明知

•內在規範之功

Sutra 2.40
śaucát sváṅga-jugupsá parairasaṁsargaḥ //40//
By cleanliness, disinclination to-one's-body, and cessation-of-contact with-others.
「潔淨」者，厭離色身，少與他人接觸。
śaucát- 淨化者、清淨者、潔淨者
sváṅga- 自身、色身

jugupsá- 嫌、厭、厭嫌、不喜歡
paraiḥ- 與他人、和其他人
asaṁsargaḥ- 遠離、不接觸、不往來

Sutra 2.41
sattva-śuddhiḥ saumanasya-ikágry-endriyajaya-átmadarśana yogyatváni ca //41//
And upon-the-essence becoming-pure, come high mindedness, one-pointedness, control of the senses and fitness for the knowledge of the self.
身心嚴淨者，內心常喜，諸根調伏一處，足堪內觀自性真我。
sattva- 人、我、有情、眾生、悅性、精細悅性的存在
śuddhiḥ- 淨、嚴淨、清淨、聖潔
saumanasya- 喜、喜受、喜悅之心、歡喜的心
ekágry- 一點、一處、一境、專一
indriyajaya- 降伏了知作根，調伏了感覺器官和運動器官。
átmajaya- 真我、大我、自性、靈魂
darśana- 見、覲、覲見、照見
yogyatváni- 堪、宜、適合的、正好可以
ca- 和、及、與

Sutra 2.42
saṁtoṣát-anuttamas-sukhalábhaḥ //42//
By contentment the acquisition of extreme happiness.
能「知足」故，可得上勝喜樂。
saṁtoṣát- 從知足中、從安足中
anuttamah- 上勝的、極高的
sukha- 快樂、喜樂、安樂、樂受
lábhaḥ- 得、獲得、證得、成就

Sutra 2.43

káyendriya-siddhir-aśuddhi-kṣayát tapasaḥ //43//

By-purificatory-actions, the removal of impurity and the attainments of the physical-body and the senses.

修「利他行」者，雜染盡除，得色身成就。

káya- 身、色身、生身、身體

indriya- 身根、色身諸根

siddhih- 成、成就、悉地；指身心的潛力被喚醒的成就。

aśuddhi- 不淨、雜染

kṣayát- 壞、斷、滅、除

tapasaḥ- 苦修、苦行、利他行、帶有犧牲性的服務

Sutra 2.44

svádhyáyád-iṣṭa-devatá saṁprayogaḥ //44//

By-study comes communion with the desired deity.

常「誦習經典」，可與本尊相應交流。

svádhyáyát- 讀誦、誦習聖典或屬靈的經典

iṣṭaa-devatá- 本尊、所愛的、所信服的、所觀想的神明

saṁprayogaḥ- 交流、相應、共相應

Sutra 2.45

samádhi siddhiḥ-íśvarapraṇidhánát //45//

The attainment of trance by making *Íśvara* the-motive- of-all-actions.

凡事皈依至上主，三摩地自然成就。

samádhi- 三昧、正受、正定、定境、等持、三摩地

siddhiḥ- 成、成就、悉地

íśvarapraṇidhánát- 皈依至上主，此字為由 *íśvara+praṇidhánát* 組成的複合字。*íśavra* 概念上為上主、上帝的稱號之一，漢音譯伊希筏羅、意譯自在、如心經之「觀自在 - *avalokitesvara*」即是

avalokita+íśavra 組成。*íśavra* 字義有三：一是「控制者」，意指心靈的控制者或控制宇宙間一切萬有之作用者。其次是指「具有八大妙神通者，見第三章 46 節註」。第三義是指「不受世俗苦惱染著者、不受因果業力侵襲者」，綜此三義故，唐玄奘法師漢譯此字為「自在」。*praṇidhánát* 意思是「了悟洞明」及「以之為庇護」。此處 *Íśvarapraṇidhánát* 中譯為「皈依至上主」、即是「以至上主為依皈、以之為終極庇護、融入其中」之意。

•坐式（體位法）

Sutra 2.46
sthira-sukham-ásanam ||46||
Posture is steadily easy.
「坐式」是安穩、舒適的體位。
sthira- 不動、堅穩、安住
sukham- 安穩的、舒適的
ásanam- 坐式、體式、體位法、調身法；強化身體的鍛鍊。
譯按：練習體位法過程中，欲掌握安穩、舒適之要領，除需仔細體會一下一節的心法外，練習時切忌用強，儘量以意氣導引之法帶動體式之進行。

Sutra 2.47
prayatna-śaithilya-ananta-samápatti-bhyám ||47||
By-slackening of effort and by thought- trans formation as infinite.
此需放鬆身心，持觀無限，勤習方得。
prayatna- 努力、用功、精勤修習
śaithilya- 放鬆、放寬、鬆透
ananta- 無盡、無邊、無窮、無限
samápatti-bhyám- 修得、等至、入觀、入於所觀
譯按：本節須著眼注意。

Sutra 2.48

tato dvaṅdva-an-abhighátaḥ //48//

Thence cessation-of- disturbance from the-pairs-of-opposites.

如是可不受二元對立之影響。

tatah- 由此、由彼、從此、此外、上述

dvaṅdva- 相對的、對立的、二元性的

an-abhighátaḥ- 不受……干擾、不受……所逼

•調息法

Sutra 2.49

tasmin sati śvása-praśvásyor-gati-vicchedaḥ práṇáyámaḥ //49//

Regulation-of -breath (*Práṅáyáma*) is the stoppage of the inspiratory and expiratory movements (of breath) which follows, when that has-been-secured.

通達「坐式」後，復以懸止出、入息之法來調控生命能，是為「調息法」。

tasmin- 彼之、於彼、於此

sati- 做到後、通達後、完成後

śvása- 入息、吸氣

praśvásyah- 出息、呼氣、吐氣

gati- 行、動、往來、運動、方法、辦法

vicchedaḥ- 斷、中斷、中止、懸止

práṇáyámaḥ- 調息法、呼吸控制、生命能控制法

Sutra 2.50

báhya-ábhyantara-sthambha vṛttiḥ deśa-kála-sankhyábhiḥ paridṛṣto dírgha-súkṣmaḥ //50//

Manifestation as external, internal and total restraint is regulated by place, time and number; and thus it becomes long-induration and subtle.

無論是外懸息、內懸息或完全止息，宜隨其方所、時間和次數

作調節，以使息相逐漸細長。

báhya- 外息、外部的；外懸息、意指呼氣後的停息。

ábhyantara- 內在的、內部的；內懸息意指吸氣後的停息。

sthambha- 克制、懸止、暫止、止息、停息

vṛttiḥ- 活動、表現出來的、內心所緣的對象

deśa- 境、界、處所、方所；字義或意指身處位置，或指守意位置，或指肺活量。

kála- 時間，即意指懸息或持氣時間之長短。

sankhyábhiḥ- 數的、計數、次數

paridṛṣṭah- 監測、量度、感測、調整

dírgha- 長、拉長、延長的

súkṣmaḥ- 細、微細、深細、極細

Sutra 2.51

báhya-ábhyantara viṣaya-akṣepí caturthaḥ ||51||

The fourth is that which follows when the spheres of the external and internal have-been-passed.

第四種息相超越了外懸息和內懸息的範疇。

báhya- 外懸息

ábhyantara- 內懸息

viṣaya- 境界、範圍、領域、所緣對象

akṣepí- 越過、超越

caturthaḥ- 第四、第四種；指不同於懸息、內外懸息的第四種息相；一種若有若無、息相精細的呼吸狀態。

Sutra 2.52

tataḥ kṣíyate prakáśa-ávaraṇam ||52||

Thence the cover of light is destroyed.

由是光明之遮障遂漸消散。

tataḥ- 由此、因此、由是、從而

kṣíyate- 衰滅、消散、消失、消除
prakáśa- 明、光明、光輝
ávaraṇam- 遮、障、遮蓋、遮障、障礙

Sutra 2.53
dháraṇásu ca yogyatá manasaḥ //53//
And the fitness of the mind for concentration.
心意更能專注執持。
dháraṇásu- 為了集中、專注、執持
ca- 和、與、以及
yogyatá- 能、宜、適合、便於
manasaḥ- 意、心、心靈、心意

•內攝

Sutra 2.54
svaviṣaya-asaṁprayoge cittasya svarúpánukára-iv-endriyáṇáṁ pratyáháraḥ //54//
Abstraction (*Pratyáhára*) is that by which the senses do not-come-into-contact with their objects and follow as-it-were the nature of the mind.
「內攝」是不令自身諸根與所緣外境相應，以使心靈歸復其本相。
sva- 我的、自身的，指自身所有的感官或知作根。
viṣaya- 境界、範圍、領域、所緣對象
asaṁprayoge- 不與之連結、不與之相應
cittasya- 內心的、心靈的
svarúpá- 自相、自性、本相、原貌
ánukára- 仿傚、貼近、隨順、歸復
iva- 相似、似乎、就好像
indriyáṇáṁ- 感官、諸根、知作根（眼耳鼻舌身及喉舌手足大小

遺加意根共十一根）
pratyáháraḥ- 制感、攝心、收攝、感官內攝，客體融入主體。

Sutra 2.55
tataḥ paramá-vaśyatá indriyáṇám //55//
Thence the senses are under the highest control.
如是知作諸根完全受控。
tataḥ- 由此、由彼、從此、如是
paramá- 最勝的、究竟的、最完全的
vaśyatá- 主控、控制、調伏、受控
indriyáṇám- 感官、諸根、知作根

第三章

功德品

Vibhúti Páda

•專注、禪定與三摩地

Sutra 3.1

deśa-bandhaḥ cittasya dháraṇá ||1||

Concentration is the steadfastness of the mind.

「專注」是心繫一境而不動。

deśa- 處、地、境地、國土

bandhaḥ- 結、縛、繫縛

cittasya- 心的、心靈的

dháraṇá- 執持、總持、集中、專注、凝神

Sutra 3.2

tatra pratyaya-ikatánatá dhyánam ||2||

The continuation there of the mental-effort (to understand) is meditation (*dhyána*).

「禪定」乃是相續不斷地心住一境。

tatra- 於其中、在其中

pratyaya- 緣、緣事、在於，住於某一所緣境上。

ekatánatá- 持續的、相續不斷的、無有斷續地

dhyánam- 禪、禪那、禪定

Sutra 3.3

tadeva-artha-mátra-nirbhásaṁ svarúpa-śúnyam-iva-samádhiḥ ||3||

The same when shining with the light of the object alone, and devoid, as-it-were, of itself, is trance (or contemplation, Samádhi).

於此定中所觀，唯存本初空性光明，謂之「三摩地」。

tadeva- 如同、由此、如是、同樣的

artha- 對象、目標、塵境、目的物

mátra- 唯、唯有、只有、僅有

nirbhásaṁ- 光明的、閃耀的、閃亮的

svarúpa- 自相、本相、本初的樣貌
śúnyam- 空、空性、空相
iva- 似、如、如同、等同
samádhiḥ- 定、三昧、等持、正定、正受、三摩地

•合參法

Sutra 3.4
trayam-ekatra saṁyamaḥ ||4||
The three together are *Saṁyamá*.
總此三支同參一諦，謂之「合參法」。
trayam- 三者、此三者，意指專注、禪定、三摩地三支。
ekatra- 一處、一同、於一、共同
saṁyamaḥ- 音譯「三雅瑪」字義是克制、克己、調控；此處意指「合專注、禪定與三摩地三支同參一個目標」；意譯為「合參法」或同參法、總制行法、總持行法；「參」字唸ㄘㄢ、即禪宗參話頭的參，有探究、領悟之意。此同參法與釋教禪法之奢摩他、三摩鉢提、禪那等，有異曲同功之效。

Sutra 3.5
tajjayát prajñálokaḥ ||5||
By the achievement thereof comes the visibility of the Cognition.
修「合參法」成就者，散發出般若慧光。
tad- 那個、這個；意指「能如法行持者」。
jayát- 掌握、掌控了、成就了、實現了
prajñá- 慧、智慧、般若智、直覺的知識
alokaḥ- 光、光明、光輝；可見、看到

Sutra 3.6
tasya bhúmiṣu viniyogaḥ ||6||
Its application is to the planes(*bhúmiṣu*).
習者應如法循序鍛煉。

tasya- 彼法
bhúmiṣu- 等地、次第、階段 . 順序地、依進度計劃的；即應依同參法循專注、禪定、三摩地之順序鍛煉。
viniyogaḥ- 應用、使用、鍛煉、從事

Sutra 3.7
trayam-antarangaṁ púrvebhyaḥ //7//
The three are more-intimate than-the-preceding.
此三支修法較前五支更為深細。
trayam- 此三者（指專注、禪定、三摩地後三支）
antar- 內、更精細的、更為內在的
angaṁ- 各支、各部分
púrvebhyaḥ- 先前的、較之前面的；此處係指瑜伽八支功法中的前五支。

Sutra 3.8
tadapi bahiraṅgaṁ nirbíjasya //8//
Even that is non-intimate to the seedless.
然就「無種三摩地」而言，彼仍屬外支。
tad- 那個、這個；意指前述專注、禪定、三摩地等三支。
api- 也、且、雖、即使、乃至
bahiraṅgaṁ- 屬外在的部分
nirbíjasya- 無因的、無種子的、無種三摩地；無有業力餘習潛伏於心的三摩地。

Sutra 3.9
vyutthána-nirodha-saṁskárayoḥ abhibhava-prádurbhávau nirodhakṣaṇa cittánvayo nirodha-pariṇámaḥ //9//
The suppressive modification is the conjunction of the mind with the moment of suppression (*nirodha*), when the outgoing and

suppressive potencies disappear and appear respectively.

宿業或顯或隱隨緣生滅，繫心滅處即能剎那轉寂。

vyutthána- 出、離、轉、生、起

nirodha- 捨、滅、斷、抑止、寂滅

saṁskárayoḥ- 宿業、業緣之力、肇因於行為的反作用力。

abhibhava- 伏、隱、沒、隱蔽、消失的，指業緣消隱。

prádurbhávau- 現、出、生起、出現，指業緣顯現。

nirodha- 捨、滅、斷、寂滅、滅盡

kṣaṇa- 剎那、瞬間、當下

cittá- 心、念心、自心、心靈質、集起心

ánvayo- 合、隨、關聯、繫合

nirodha-pariṇámaḥ- 轉寂、托空、使斷、令滅；即以慧觀使心念湛寂之法。

Sutra 3.10

tasya praśánta-váhitá saṁskárat ||10||

By potency comes its undisturbed flow.

依此修行之功，入彼澄寂之流。

tasya- 彼、彼之、那個

praśánta- 澄淨、平靜、寂然、最寂靜、深邃的寧靜

váhitá- 流、轉、流轉、任運轉

saṁskárat- 依此修行之功、由此業行之功用

Sutra 3.11

sarvárthatá ekágrátayoḥ kṣayodayau cittasya samádhi-pariṇámaḥ ||11||

The trance modification of the mind is the destruction and rise of all-pointedness and one-pointedness, respectively.

如是諸緣頓斷，心一境性生起，遂入三摩地。

sarvárthatá- 一切、諸事、一切事、一切義、所有的

ekágrátayoḥ- 在一境、一心、一處或一點上

kṣaya- 退失、衰滅、滅除、頓斷
udayau- 生、升、出現、生起、浮現
cittasya- 心的、心靈的
samádhi- 定境、三昧、等持、正定、正受、三摩地；個體心融入觀想目標之謂。
pariṇámaḥ- 變、異、改變、轉變、進入

Sutra 3.12
tataḥ punaḥ śántoditau tulya-pratyayau cittasya-ikágratá-pariṇámaḥ ||12||
Thence again comes the mental modification of one-pointedness, when the subsiding and rising cognitive acts are similar.
復由此定，得生滅一如淨相，心即融於一境。
tataḥ- 因此、從而、由此、那麼
punaḥ- 復、還、再、次第
śánta- 滅、寂、息、平息、已滅狀態
uditau- 生、出、現、升起、已生狀態
tulya- 如、同、一致、等同、相同的
pratyayau- 因、緣、憑著、緣其、由是……
cittasya- 心的、心靈的
ekágratá- 一緣、一境、正定、心一境性；止心於一境之謂。
pariṇámaḥ- 變、異、改變、轉變、進化、導致

•性、相、位的變化

Sutra 3.13
etena bhútendriyeṣu dharma-lakṣaṇa-avasthá pariṇámá vyákhyátáḥ ||13||
By this are described the changes of characteristic (*dharma*), secondary quality (*lakṣaṇa*), and condition (*avasthá*) in the objective and instrumental phenomena.
前述說明了諸根所感受之現象在「性」、「相」和「位」上的變

化。

etena- 藉此、若此、如此；指從第九到第十二節的經句。

bhúta- 被創造出來的現象、五大元素所形成的客體世界

indriyeṣu- 官感、感官或知作根所感受到的

dharma- 法性、本性、屬性、天性、法性，天賦的秉性。

lakṣaṇa- 相、狀、特徵、性狀、體相、身相，形成的特質相狀。

avasthá- 位、位置、情況、境界、狀態，呈現的境界狀態。

pariṇámá- 變、異、改變、轉變、進化

vyákhyátáḥ- 說、釋、敘述、講說、解說

Sutra 3.14

śántodita avyapadeśya-dharmánupátí dharmí ||14||

"The object characterized" is that which is common to the latent, the rising and un-predicable characteristic.

「法性」是眾生已顯、方顯或是未來將顯之俱生秉性。。

śánta- 息、冷、寂、平息、已滅狀態，往昔曾出現過的。

udita- 生、出、現、升起、已生狀態，現在正持有的。

avyapadeśya- 未知的、未表現的；尚處於潛伏狀態、將會在未來顯現的。

dharmá- 性、法性、本性、天性、秉性

ánupátí- 共有的、緊隨的，與生俱來的；英譯作「共有秉性」。

dharmí- 具法性之人、具有法性之眾生、含藏法性的個體

Sutra 3.15

kramányatvaṁ pariṇámányateve hetuḥ ||15||

The distinctness of succession is the reason for the distinctness of modifications.

因緣有別，其〔性、相、位〕亦漸生別異。

kramá- 漸、漸次、順序、沿襲

ányatvaṁ- 別相、差異性、特異性，意指第 3.13 節所述性相、位

之差異。
pariṇámá- 變、異、改變、轉變、進化，此處指秉性之轉變。
ányateve- 有別、不同
hetuḥ- 因、緣、原因、因地；眾生因緣有別、隨其差異結果亦自不同。

•修合參法之功

Sutra 3.16
pariṇámatraya-saṁyamát-atítánágata jñánam ||16||
By *Saṁyamá* over the three-fold change, comes the knowledge of the past and the future.
依「合參法」深觀前述三種變化圓成者，可通曉過去與未來的知識。
pariṇáma- 變、異、熟、能轉、轉變、圓融
traya- 三、三重，意指經文 3.13 節所述之三種變化。
saṁyamát- 通過「合參法」
atítánágata- 過去與未來的
jñánam- 知識、知曉

Sutra 3.17
śabdártha-pratyayámám-itaretarádhyását-saṅkaraḥ tat-pravibhága-saṁyamát sarvabhúta-ruta-jñánam ||17||
The word, the object and the idea appear as one, because each coincides with the other; by *Saṁyamá* over their distinctions comes the knowledge of the sounds of all-living- beings.
音義、信念常交相混淆，然以「合參法」思惟辨別，可明一切眾生言語。
Śabda- 聲、語、言、字詞、聲量，亦指吠陀(耳聞經）之教導。
ártha- 事義、法義、義理、道理
pratyayámám- 信、信念、概念、觀念、因緣而生之信解。
itaretara- 各自、彼此、相互

adhyását- 重疊、疊合、交疊
saṅkaraḥ- 混雜、混淆、迷亂
tat- 彼、彼之、那個
pravibhága- 分別、差別、區別
saṁyamát- 通過「合參法」、透過「總制行法」
sarva- 悉、遍、一切、諸所有、全部的
bhúta- 五大元素、所被創造出來的萬有、五大元素所形成的客體世界
ṛuta- 言說、話語、音聲
jñánam- 知識、知曉

Sutra 3.18
saṁskára-sákṣátkaraṇát púrva-játi-jñánam ||18||
By bringing residual-potencies into consciousness, the knowledge of previous life-state (*Játi*).
依「合參法」現證宿業因果，可了知往昔生世。
saṁskára- 伏業、潛藏的業力、未表發的業力
sákṣátkaraṇát- 現證、親證、頓悟
púrva- 昔、往昔、宿世、過去世
játi- 生、出生、身世、生世
jñánam- 知識、知曉

Sutra 3.19
pratyayasya para-citta-jñánam ||19||
Of the notions, the knowledge of other minds.
依「合參法」觀緣生法，可知他人心想。
Pratyayasya- 緣起、眾緣、諸緣、緣生法；輾轉相因，環環相扣之生起、運作發相續的作用。
para- 別人的、他人的、其他的
citta- 心、心念、心思、心想、心靈
jñánam- 知識、知曉

Sutra 3.20

na ca tat sálambanaṁ tasya-aviṣayí bhútatvát ||20||

But not of its object, that not being the direct object of the *Yogi*'s mind.

然非是知彼所緣塵境，蓋此並非修法意旨。

註：本節與 3.22 節經句或是維耶索的釋文，故有些文本未收錄。

na- 無、不、非、不是、非是

ca- 及、與、和

tat- 彼、彼之、那個

sálambanaṁ- 彼之所緣、彼所依緣；意指非合參法的用功旨趣。

tasya- 彼之、他的、它的

aviṣayí- 非所趣的、非所緣的、非所趣向的

bhútatvát- 所緣之對象或境物

譯按：上節主述觀緣生法可知他人心想，本節進一步說明所謂知他人心想是了知他人的心理狀態，但他人所想的人事或塵境，則非是行人所觀的對象。毗耶索就本節經句舉了一個例子：譬如觀者知道對方愛的心理情感，但不會知道對方所愛的對象。

Sutra 3.21

káya-rúpa-saṁyamát tat-gráhyaśakti-stambhe cakṣuḥ prakáśásaṁprayoge-'ntardhánam ||21||

By *Saṁyamá* over the form of the body, on perceptibility being checked, and thus there being no contact with the light of the eye, comes disappearance.

依「合參法」觀照色身，得暫止身光外散，使之不與他人眼根相應，身形即隱。

káya- 身、色身、生身

rúpa- 形、色、色相、形相

saṁyamát- 由「合參法」、通過「總制行法」

tat- 彼、彼之、那個

gráhya- 取、受、感受、可覺察到的

śakti- 力、能、能力、能量波頻
stambhe- 僵住、凍結、停止、禁止
cakṣuḥ- 眼、眼根、眼睛
prakáśá- 光、明、顯示
asaṁprayoge- 不相應、無有映射，即隱匿吸收或反射的光。
antardhánam- 隱形、消失、不見、入於無形

Sutra 3.22
etena śhabdádi antardhánam uktam ||22||
By this the cessation of the perception of sound and other similar things, must be understood as explained.
理同前說，依此法修其餘諸根，聲音等亦得隱匿。
etena- 依此法、透過這個方法
śhabdádi- 聲音等、聲音及其他（如香、味、觸等）
antardhánam- 隱形、消失、不見、入於無形
uktam- 前說、前云、如前所云

Sutra 3.23
sopa-kramaṁ nirupa-kramaṁ ca karma tatsaṁyamát-aparántajñánam ariṣṭebhyo vá ||23||
Karma is either fast-in-fruition or slow; by *Saṁyamá* over these comes knowledge of death; or, by portents.
業報或有遲速，依合參法觀照修持，即能明了或預知死亡。
sopa-kramaṁ- 快速的、顯現的、正活動著的
nirupa-kramaṁ- 緩慢的、不顯的、尚蟄伏中的
ca- 及、與、和、或
karma- 業、作為、行為、業報，會招致因果業力的行為。
tat- 彼、彼之、那個
saṁyamát- 通過合參法、透過總制行法
aparánta- 死亡、未來、未來世
jñánam- 知識、屬靈的知識

ariṣṭebhyah- 預知、預示
vá- 或

Sutra 3.24
maitry-adiṣu baláni //24/
Over friendliness and so on the powers.
依是法修慈悲心等，能得所修之力。
maitry- 慈、慈悲、慈愍、慈愛
adiṣu- 等等（如慈、悲、喜、捨等等）
baláni- 力、力量

Sutra 3.25
baleṣu hastibaládíní//25//
Over the powers, the powers of elephant and so forth, the powers.
依是法觀修諸力，能得如象等所具之種種力。
baleṣu- 於力之上、在力量上
hasti- 象、大象
baládíní- 等等諸力、種種的力量；意指隨所觀之諸力，而得所觀對象之種種力。

Sutra 3.26
pravṛtty-áloka-nyását súkṣmá-vyávahita-viprakṛṣṭa-jñánam //26//
The knowledge of the subtle, the veiled, the remote, by directing the light of higher sense-activity towards them.
依是法深觀內心光明，能知精微、隱蔽以及極遠的知識。
pravṛttah- 內心深處的、更深細的感官知覺、更高的直覺活動
áloka- 光、光明、明相、出世的光明
nyását- 投射、引導、擴展
súkṣmá- 深、細、最細、微細、極細
vyávahita- 隱藏、隱晦、被遮掩的、遭隱蔽的
viprakṛṣṭa- 去、行、遠方的、遙遠的

jñánam- 知識、知曉

Sutra 3.27

bhuvana-jñánaṁ súrye-saṁyamát //27//

By *Saṁyamá* on the sun; knowledge of the regions.

依合參法觀日輪，能知曉此世界。

bhuvana- 界、世界、地球、居住地、有形宇宙

jñánaṁ- 知識、知曉

súrye- 日輪、太陽

saṁyamát- 通過「合參法」、透過「總制行法」

Sutra 3.28

candre táravyúha-jñánam //28//

On the moon, the knowledge of the starry systems.

依是法觀月輪，能明星宿系統。

candre- 月輪、月亮

táravyúha- 星象的系統、星宿的系統

jñánam- 知識、知曉

Sutra 3.29

dhruve tadgati-jñánam//29//

On the pole-star the knowledge of their movements.

依是法觀北極星，能知彼之運行。

dhruve- 不動的、恆在的、極星、北極星、北斗星

tat- 彼、彼之、那個

gati- 進、行、運行、運轉

jñánam- 知識、知曉

Sutra 3.30

nábhicakre káyavyúha-jñánam//30//

On the plexus of the navel, the knowledge of the system of the body.

依是法觀臍輪，能曉色身結構。

nábhi- 臍、肚臍

cakre- 輪、脈輪、圈形物、神經叢

káya- 身、形、名色、色身、生身、身體

vyúha- 結構、系統、整體的排序

jñánam- 知識、靈性的知識

Sutra 3.31

kanṭha-kúpe kṣutpipásá nivṛttiḥ ||31||

In the pit of the throat, subdual of hunger and thirst.

依是法觀喉穴，能不生饑渴。

kanṭha- 喉、喉嚨

kúpe- 坑、凹洞、空穴

kṣut- 饑、饑餓的

pipásá- 渴、渴愛、口渴的

nivṛttiḥ- 止、離、滅、息除、不生

Sutra 3.32

kúrma-náḍyáṁ sthairyam ||32||

On the tortoise tube (*kúrma nádi*), steadiness.

依是法觀龜脈，能令身心堅穩。

kúrma- 龜、烏龜；此處係指龜脈（毗耶薩註文說此是位於喉嚨下方近胸處的龜形脈管，凝心觀之，能有靜若蛇、鱷不動之效）。

náḍyáṁ- 經脈的、神經的

sthairyam- 嚴整的、堅固的、不動的

Sutra 3.33

múrdha-jyotiṣi siddha-darśanam ||33||

In the coronal light, vision of the Perfected-Ones.

依是法觀頂首之光，得見成就者之所見。

múrdha- 冠、頂、頂首、頭頂；泛指頂輪位置。
jyotiṣi-……的光上
siddha- 具成就者、完美的存在、天人中之最上者
darśanam- 洞見、深見、所見

Sutra 3.34
prátibhád-vá sarvam //34//
Or, all knowledge by prescience (*prátibhád*).
或由此慧光，洞悉一切。
prátibhát- 慧光、明慧、生自慧光的智慧
vá- 或
sarvam- 總、遍、悉皆、諸所有、一切的、一切所有的

Sutra 3.35
hrḍaye citta-saṁvit//35//
In the heart, the knowledge of the mind.
依是法觀心，能明心作用。
hrḍaye- 心（心臟）、心輪位置
citta- 心、心靈、心靈質、集起心
saṁvit- 領會、明了、明白

Sutra 3.36
sattva-puruṣáyoḥ atyatá-saṁkírṇayoḥ pratyayáviśeṣo bhogaḥ para-arthat-vát-sva-arthasaṁyamát puruṣa-jñánam //36//
Experience consists in the absence of the notion of distinction between the *Puruśa* and Objective-Essence, which we really quite distinct-from-each-other, because it exists for another. By *Saṁyamá* on his own object, comes the knowledge of the *Puruśa*.
世間的苦受、樂受在於不明我覺與淨識畢竟不同，我覺依淨識而有，淨識則自有永有。依「合參法」修證，能明淨識真知。
sattva- 人、我、我覺、心靈悅性的部分、精細的客體本質，淨

識受悅性力量影響轉成的我覺。
puruṣáyoḥ- 以及淨識、真我、靈魂、純意識
atyatá- 頗為、畢竟、絕對
asaṁkírṇayoḥ- 不同的、有所區別的
pratyay- 在於、由於、意識到
áviśeṣah- 不明的、缺少的、不能區別的
bhogaḥ- 物質世界或器世間的苦、樂經驗
para-arthat-vát- 依彼存在的、意指我覺自淨識而出。
sva-arth- 自有的、自行存在的、不依他而存在的，意指淨識本自存在、無有倚賴。
saṁyamát- 透過合參法，亦即透過集中、禪定與三摩地。
puruṣa-jñánam- 真我的知識、淨識的知識

Sutra 3.37
tataḥ prátibha-sráváṇa-vedana-ádarśa-ásváda-vártá jáyante //37//
Thence proceed prescience, higher hearing, touch, vision, taste, and smell.
如是，可生起靈明之耳聞、觸受、視見、舌嚐和鼻嗅能力。
tataḥ- 由此、由彼、從此、因此、如是；由於明了淨識真知
prátibha- 靈光、明光、靈明；超然的直覺感應力。
sráváṇa- 聲聞、聽覺
vedana- 受、觸覺
ádarśa- 見、視覺
ásváda- 嚐、味覺
vártá- 香聞、嗅覺
jáyante- 可生起、形成、產生

Sutra 3.38
te samádhau-upasargáh-vyuttháne siddhayaḥ //38//
They are obstacles to trance, but perfections to the outgoing mind.
然此成就令心外馳，乃修三摩地之障礙。

te- 彼、此、這些
samádhau- 寂定的、三昧定的、三摩地的
upasargáh- 阻礙、干擾、障礙
vyuttháne- 外馳心、內心向外投射、心靈趨向世俗
siddhayaḥ- 成就、神通、法力、超能力、神秘力量

Sutra 3.39
bandha-káraṇa-śaithilyát pracára-saṁvedanácca cittasya paraśaríráveśaḥ //39//
The mind may enter another body, on relaxation of the cause of bondage, and by knowledge of the passages of the mind.
心靈束縛之因開解後，得循其所知進入他身。
bandha- 繫縛、束縛的
káraṇa- 因、原因、肇因
śaithilyát- 鬆解、解開、放下
pracára- 通路、通過、透過、作用途徑
saṁvedanát- 透過知識、依循所知道的
ca- 和、與、及
cittasya- 內心的、心靈的
para- 他、別、別的、其他的
śarírá- 身、身體、色身、形身
aveśaḥ- 進入、進占

Sutra 3.40
udána-jayát jala-paṇkha-kaṇṭakádiṣu-asaṅga-utkrántiśca //40//
By mastery over *Udána*, ascension and non-contact with water, mud, thorns and so on.
掌控住「上行氣」，能於水面、沼澤和荊棘叢等處浮行，無有滯礙。
udána- 上息、通首氣、上升氣、上行氣，為五種內在生命能量之一，位於喉嚨、控制聲帶及發聲。

jayát- 通達、主宰、掌控、征服
jala- 水、液體
paṇkha- 泥沼、沼澤
kaṇṭaká- 荊棘、障礙
ádiṣu- 等等、其餘的、其他的
asańgah- 無著、無滯、不相接觸於……
utkrántih- 升起、浮起、於其上
ca- 和、與、以及

Sutra 3.41
samána-jayáj-jvalanam ||41||
By mastery over *Samána* comes effulgence.
掌控住「平行氣」，周身煥發光彩。
samána- 平行氣，為五種內在生命能量之一，位於臍腹，負責持命氣和下行氣間的平衡。
jayát- 通達、主宰、掌控、征服
jvalanam- 火、光明、光輝、光彩

Sutra 3.42
śrotra-ákáśayoḥ saḿbandha-saḿyamát divyaḿ śrotram ||42||
By *Saḿyamá* over the relation between *Ákása* and the power-of-hearing, comes the higher power-of-hearing.
依合參法觀耳根與虛空之關聯，可得殊妙之耳力。
śrotra- 耳、耳根
ákáśayoḥ- 乙太、虛空、空元素
saḿbandha- 依止關係、相應關聯
saḿyamát- 依「合參法」
divyaḿ- 天、微妙、深妙、天上的、神性的、能得聞天籟的
śrotram- 耳力、聽力

Sutra 3.43

káyákáśayoḥ saṁbandha-saṁyamát laghu-túla-samápatteh ca-ákáśa gamanam ||43||

By *Saṁyamá* on the relation between the body and the *Ákása*, or by attaining to (the state of thought transforming as) the lightness of cotton, &c., passage through space (*Ákása*).

依合參法觀色身與虛空之關聯，可使身輕若絮乃至飄行空中。

káyá- 身體、軀體

ákáśayoḥ- 乙太、虛空、空元素

saṁbandha- 依止關係、相應關聯

saṁyamát- 以「合參法」、透過「總制行法」

samápatteh- 三摩鉢提、善定、等至、正定、成就、合一

laghu- 少、輕、輕安、輕便

túla- 棉、棉花、棉絮

ca- 和、與、以及

ákáśa- 空中、虛空中

gamanam- 飄行、飛行、騰行、浮遊漫行

Sutra 3.44

bahir-akalpitá vṛttiḥ mahá-videhá tataḥ prakáśa-ávaraṇa-kṣayaḥ ||44||

Actual-passing-out and acting outside the body is the Great corporeal; by that is destroyed the veil of light.

出神身外無有計執之心識名「大無身」，依法修之，可袪除光明之遮障。

bahih- 外在的、外界的、身外的

akalpitá- 無著的、無分別的，無計執的；不為計度執著心所攀緣，一切即一，無所分別。

vṛttiḥ- 念想、心念、思想波的、內心所緣的對象

mahá- 大、廣大、摩訶

videhá- 無身的、無身的神識、無身的靈體，近義詞為「元神」。
tatah- 如是、如此、藉此，指依合参法成就者。
prakáśa- 字面義思是明、光明；光明是悦性的特質，此處光明的遮障指的是變性與惰性的影響。
ávaraṇa- 面紗、遮障、覆蓋
kṣayaḥ- 滅、盡、斷、失、壞、崩解、毀滅

Sutra 3.45
sthúla-svarúpa-súkṣma-anvaya-arthavattva-saṁyamát bhútajayaḥ ||45||
By *Saṁyamá* on the gross (*sthúla*), the substantive (*svarúpa*), the astral (*súkśma*), conjunction (*anvaya*) and purposefulness (*arthavattva*), is obtained mastery over the elements (*bhútas*).
依合參法觀照諸大元素之粗相、實相、細相及其關聯性和目的性，得掌控諸元素。
sthúla- 重、麤、粗相、粗鈍面
svarúpa- 本相、本質、實相；意指諸元素本貌。
súkṣma- 輕、精、細相、精細面
anvaya- 族、類、比、種類、關聯性、相互性；如諸大元素與六根六塵之關係、諸大之法性及與悦性變性惰性之關聯等等。
arthavattva- 目的性，從其相之變化與關聯察其為何如此之原由。
saṁyamát- 通過「合参法」
bhútajayaḥ- 主宰或掌控了諸元素(地、水、火、風、空等諸元素)

Sutra 3.46
tato-aṇimádi-prádurbhávaḥ káyasaṁpat tad-dharma abhighátśca ||46||
Thence the manifestation of attenuation (*aṇimá*) and the other (powers); as also the perfection of the body and non-resistance by their characteristics.
如此可顯示「能小」等諸神通力，身形相好莊嚴，且不受諸元

素屬性之拘束。

tatah- 如是、如此、藉此、那麼

aṇimá-「能小」，八種妙自在成就之一，其餘七種為：能大、能輕、能得、能主、能支配、能隨所欲、能透視，詳見《哈達瑜伽明燈》第三章第 8 節譯註。

prádurbhávaḥ- 顯示、示現

káya- 身體、軀體

saṁpat- 圓滿、具足、莊嚴

tad- 彼之、他們、他（它）們的

dharma- 秉性、屬性、賦性、法性

anabhighátaḥ- 無礙、無壞、不受拘束的

ca- 和且、與、以及

Sutra 3.47

rúpa-lávaṇya-bala-vajra-saṁhananatváni káyasaṁpat ||47||

The perfection of the body consists in beauty, grace, strength and adamantine hardness.

其身莊嚴優雅健實，堅若金剛。

rúpa- 身、形、形相、形色、色貌、色身

lávaṇya- 優雅、美麗、迷人、有魅力、有吸引力的

bala- 力、力量、有大力的、強健的

vajra- 鑽石、金剛、金剛石

saṁhananatváni- 堅固、堅實、緊實

káya- 身體

saṁpat- 圓滿、具足、莊嚴

Sutra 3.48

grahaṇa-svarúpa-asmitá-anvaya-arthavattva-saṁyamát-indriya jayaḥ ||48||

By *Saṁyamá* over the act, the substantive appearance, the egoism, the conjunction and purposefulness (of sensation) comes mastery over them.

依合參法內觀「取受因緣」、「自相本質」、「內在我見」及其相互間之關聯性和目的性，可降伏諸根。

grahaṇa- 取、受、攝、攝受、取受因緣、知覺和行動的過程
svarúpa- 自身、自相、自性、本質、自身的形貌
asmitá- 我見、我慢、我執、自我感、自我意識
anvaya- 類、比、種類、關聯性、相互性
arthavattva- 目的性
saṁyamát- 以「合參法」、透過「總制行法」
indriya- 根（五知根與五作根）、身根、感官
jayaḥ- 戰勝、克服、征服、控制

Sutra 3.49

tato mano-javitvaṁ vikaraṇa-bhávaḥ pradhána-jayaś-ca ||49||

Thence come quickness as of mind, un-instrumental-perception and mastery over the *Pradhána* (First Cause).

如是，心意機敏靈動，覺知不假諸根，且具功參造化之能。

tatah- 如是、如此、藉此、那麼
mano- 意、心意
javitvaṁ- 馳、速、快速的
vikaraṇa-bhávaḥ- 意指心思 可與感官分離而作用
pradhána- 勝因、起意、造化因、物化的最初因
jayaḥ- 降、伏、克服、戰勝、掌控
ca- 和、且、與、以及

Sutra 3.50

sattva-puruṣa-anyatá-khyátimátrasya sarva-bhává-adhiṣṭhátṛtvaṁ sarva-jñátṛtvaṁ ca ||49||

To him who recognizes the distinction between consciousness and pure-objective-existence comes supremacy over all states of being and omniscience.

唯有徹見「我覺」與「淨識」之不同，方得感通一切萬有及至高之一切種智。

sattva- 人、我、我覺、有情、心靈悅性的部分、精細的客體本質；淨識受悅性力量影響轉成的我覺。
puruṣáyoḥ- 以及淨識、靈魂、真我、純意識
anyatá- 異、別、異處、不同處
khyáti- 了別、辨悉、洞悉、能見
mátrasya- 唯、只、僅僅
sarva- 一切、所有、全部
bhává- 有、萬有、萬象、顯現的宇宙
adhiṣṭhátṛtvaṁ- 至高的、至上的、無上的
sarva-jñátṛtvaṁ- 全知、遍知、一切種智、直覺洞見的知識
ca- 和、且、與、以及

Sutra 3.51

tad-vairágyád-api doṣa-bíja-kṣaye kaivalyam ||51||

The seed of bondage having been destroyed by desirelessness, even for that, comes absolute-independence (*Kaivalya*)

乃至對此感通與一切種智亦不執著，即能斷除過患種子，入獨存不共之境。

tad- 彼、彼之、那個
vairágyát- 透過捨離、不執著、離染、離欲
api- 復、乃至、甚至、兼之
doṣa- 咎、病、罪、障、過失、過患
bíja- 因、種、種子、根源
kṣaye- 滅、盡、斷、失、壞、滅除、毀滅、頓斷
kaivalyam- 究竟境、不共境、絕對境、解脫境

Sutra 3.52

sthány-upa-nimantraṇe saṅga-smaya-akaraṇaṁ punar-aniṣṭa-prasaṅgát //52//

When the presiding-deities invite, there should be no attachment and no smile of satisfaction; contact with the undesirable being again possible.

若受上位者之奉請，但莫起貪著與自得，蓋亦有不受青睞之時。

stháni- 居高位者，或指權貴、師長、神明、高靈、神靈等等。

upa-nimantraṇe- 延請、受邀、奉請；被邀請的人。

saṅga- 貪著、愛著、執著、親近

smaya- 自得、自滿、自豪

akaraṇaṁ- 不起、不興、不作、莫作

punah- 又、復、還、還復

aniṣṭa- 不喜、不愛、不欲、怨憎

prasaṅgát- 墮、失、墜、際遇

Sutra 3.53

kṣaṇa-tat-kramayoḥ saṁyamát vivekajaṁ-jñánam //53//

By *Saṁyamá* over the moments and their succession, comes knowledge born-of-discrimination.

依合參法念念相續觀照，慧見即從明辨而生。

kṣaṇa- 剎那、瞬間、念念

tat- 彼之、他們、他（它）們的

kramayoḥ- 依序、相續、漸次、次第

saṁyamát- 以「合參法」、透過「總制行法」

vivekajaṁ- 由離而生、緣明辨力而生、由空寂生出

jñánam- 知識、慧見、直覺智、靈性的知識

譯按：思緒擾人、難得清淨！針對此、當代瑜伽行者斯瓦米韋達曾言：「你為什麼要去聽滴水聲，而不去傾聽每一滴水聲之間

的寧靜？」這句話是本節經句很好的註解。

Sutra 3.54

játi-lakṣaṇa-deśaiḥ anyatá-anavacchedát tulyayoḥ tataḥ pratipattiḥ ||54||

Two- similars are thereby distinguished when not separately distinguishable by genus, differentia and position-in-space.

藉此慧見可了知在類別、性相、方所上都兩相類似而難以辨識之事物。

játi- 生、出生、類、種類

lakṣaṇa- 相、性相、身相、特徵

deśaiḥ- 方、方所、處所、地點、位置

anyatá- 異、相異、不同的

anavacchedát- 未分的、未定義的、難以辨識的

tulyayoḥ- 類同的、同樣的、無異的、兩相類似的

tataḥ- 如是、如此、藉此、那麼

pratipattiḥ- 了知、明了、明白、領會

Sutra 3.55

tárakaṁ sarva-viṣayaṁ sarvathá-viṣayam-akramaṁ-ceti vivekajaṁ jñánam ||55||

And it is the intuitional; has everything for its sphere-of-operation; has all-condition for its sphere-of- operation; has no succession. This is the entire discriminative knowledge

如是自明辨所生慧見，能直接感通一切塵境事物，亦可趣入一切塵境事物。

tárakaṁ- 直觀的、直覺的、直接感通的

sarva- 一切、所有、全部

viṣayaṁ- 塵、境、事物、外塵、外境、緣境、所緣之境；塵泛指色身香味觸法等六塵，對應眼耳鼻舌身意等六根。

sarvathá- 全、皆、一切種、一切諸相、一切境況的

viṣayaṁ- 塵、境、事物、外塵、外境、緣境、所緣之境
akramaṁ- 深入、趣入、證入
ca- 和、且、與、以及
iti- 此、此是、如是
vivekajaṁ- 生出明辨力、生出覺察力
jñánam- 知識、慧見、直覺智、靈性的知識

Sutra 3.56
sattva-puruṣayoḥ śuddhisámye kaivalyam iti||56||
When the purity of the Objective-Essence and that of the *Puruśa* become equal, it is absolute independence.
「我覺」嚴淨至與「淨識」等同，是即「獨存不共」之究竟解脫。
sattva- 人、我、我覺、有情、心靈悅性的部分、精細的客體本質；淨識受悅性力量影響轉成的我覺。
puruṣayoḥ- 以及淨識、靈魂、真我、純意識
śuddhi- 淨、清淨、嚴淨、能淨、淨化
sámye- 等同、平等、相等、相同
kaivalyam- 究竟境、不共境、絕對境、獨存境、解脫境；與所觀融而為一。
iti- 此、此是、如是

第四章

獨存品

Kaivalya Páda

•一切唯心造

Sutra 4.1

janma-aṣadhi-mantra-tapas-samádhi-jáḥ siddhayaḥ //1//

The attainments are by birth, drugs, incantations, purificatory action (*tapas*) or trance.

超然能力或是俱生帶來，或是由藥餌、持咒、利他行、三摩地產生。

janma- 天生、俱生、出生就有的

auṣadhi- 藥餌、藥物、藥材

mantra- 梵咒、明咒、神咒、密語、真言；經過揀選的音聲，用於靜坐以助解脫。

tapas- 苦行、極簡樸的生活，犧牲己利、服務眾生的行為

samádhi- 寂定、等持、三昧定、三摩地

jáḥ- 生出、產生、誕生

siddhayaḥ- 成就、法力、神通力、特異能力、超自然能力

Sutra 4.2

játy-antara-pariṇámaḥ prakṛty-ápúrát //2//

Change to another life-state by the filling up of the creative causes *(prakrityápúra)*.

異世轉生之變易乃造化力功用參和使然。

játy-antara- 異生、隔世，於不同時空及不同的生命樣貌輪迴出生之意。

pariṇámaḥ- 轉、變、熟、變易、轉變

prakṛty- 冥諦、自性、造化力、造化勢能、原初物質或勢能

ápúrát- 注入、參與、流布

Sutra 4.3

nimittam-aprayojakaṁ prakṛtínáṁ-varaṇa-bhedastu tataḥ kṣetrikavat //3//

The creative-causes are not-moved-into-action by any incidental-cause; but that pierces-the-obstacle from it like the husbandman.

造化成相無偶因，但為祛除覆障而作，如田農之所為。

nimittam- 相、因相、動機；因故而有之相。

aprayojakaṁ- 非是、無故、無用的、無因的

prakṛtínáṁ- 造化力、最精微的物質因、自然進化的促力

varaṇam- 覆、障、遮障

bhedastu- 但為祛除……、然為移開……

tataḥ- 如此、由彼、好似、猶如

kṣetrikavat- 像田農般的……；意指田農除蕪。

譯按：「上帝不擲骰子。」——愛因斯坦名言

Sutra 4.4

nirmáṇa-cittány-asmitá-mátrát ||4||

Created minds proceed from egoism alone.

「變化心」唯出自「我見」。

nirmáṇa- 化、化生、幻化、變化、順應變化而生的

cittáni- 發心、動念、心思作用

asmitá- 我見、我慢、我執、自我感；認為一切都是我所做之感。

mátrát- 唯、由、只、單獨的

Sutra 4.5

pravṛtti-bhede prayojakaṁ cittam-ekam-anekeṣám ||5||

There being difference of activity, one mind the director of the many.

相續流轉之差別心念，俱是由一心化為無量數。

pravṛtti- 生起、相續、流轉相、生生不息的心念活動

bhede- 不同、別異、差別

prayojakaṁ- 所為、導致、引起、主導；由因緣之所需而引起。

cittam- 心、心質、心靈、集起心

ekam- 獨、一、一相

anekeṣám- 眾多、無數的、非一的；意指心念活動數量無邊。

Sutra 4.6
tatra dhyánajam-anáśayam ||6||
Of these the meditation-born is free-from-the vehicles.
然於禪定中生起者，不受業染。
tatra- 此、於此、此中、彼處、於其中
dhyánajam- 由定境生起，指由禪定中生起之淨念。
anáśayam- 不受業染、不受業力影響的

Sutra 4.7
karma-aśukla-akṛṣṇaṁ yoginaḥ trividham-itareṣám ||7||
Yogi's karma is neither-white nor-black; of-the-others it is three-fold.
瑜伽師之業行非白非黑，其他人之業行三種兼具。
karma- 業行、行動、行為、作為；從業力所生之行為。
aśukla- 非白；喻非求善果
akṛṣṇaṁ- 非黑；喻不招新殃
yoginaḥ- 瑜伽師的、瑜伽行者的
trividham- 三、三重、三種；意指或白、或黑、或黑白混雜。
itareṣám- 他人、別人、對其他的人

Sutra 4.8
tataḥ tad-vipáka-anugṇánám-eva-abhivyaktiḥ vásanánám ||8||
Thence proceed the residual-potencies competent-bring-about their fruition alone.
如是業行餘習，皆在彼之果報異熟後展現。
tataḥ- 如是、是故、因之、猶如、好似
tad- 彼、其、從彼、從而、因此；指前述「或白、或黑、或黑白混雜的行為種子」。
vipáka- 果、熟、成熟、果報、異熟果報

anugṇánám- 順、隨順、因而、對應於
eva- 唯、皆、必定
abhivyaktiḥ- 顯、顯現、展現、現前
vásanánám- 餘習、習氣、熏習、結習、潛伏的欲望

Sutra 4.9
játi deśa kála vyavahitánám-apy-ánantaryáṁ smṛti-saṁskárayoḥ ekarúpatvát ||9||
Memory and potential-residua being the same in appearance, there is sequential non-interruption, even when there is distinction of life-state, locality and time.
記憶與宿業之顯現具一致性，即使在出身、方所和時間上有所障隔，仍然持續不斷。
játi- 類、別、種類、種姓、階級、家世、出身
deśa- 境、域、處、處所、土地、地點、方所、國土
kála- 時、時間的
vyavahitánám- 障、隔、被障、間斷、隔開
api- 又、雖、乃至、即使
ántaryáṁ- 無間、不中斷的、相續的
smṛti- 記憶、憶持、憶念
saṁskárayoḥ- 業、業力、伏業、潛伏狀態下的心理反作用力
ekarúpatvát- 相同的形式、顯現時的一致性或類同性

Sutra 4.10
tásám-anáditvaṁ cáśiṣo nityatvát ||10||
And there is no-beginning for them, the desire-to-live being eternal.
如是作用並無起始，緣生存欲望恆有故。
tásám- 那些〔業習作用〕
anáditvaṁ- 無始的；意指業緣作用類如迴圈現象。
ca- 亦、及、和、與

áśiṣah- 生存的意志或欲望
nityatvát- 恆、常、常住的、恆有的

Sutra 4.11
hetu-phala-áśraya-álambanaiḥ-saṁgṛhítatvát-eṣám-abháve-tad-abhávaḥ ||11||
Being held together by Cause, motive, Substratum and Object, they disappear on-the-disappearance of-these.
因與果、所依與所緣彼此相互關聯，此若不生，彼亦不有。
hetu- 因、緣、因緣、原因；如十二因緣之無明緣行，無明即是行之因，無明不生，行即不有。
phala- 果、報、果報、結果；如十二因緣之行緣識，識即行之果，行不生，識即不有。
áśraya- 依、心、身、所依、依處、相依、身命、身心；如前例，無明緣行，無明是行之所依；無明不生，行即不有。
álambanaiḥ- 依止、依靠、攀緣、所緣之外境；如前例，行緣識，識是行之所緣，行不生，識即不有。
saṁgṛhítatvát- 攝受、關聯在一起；此節言業習的因果關係。
eṣám- 此、這、這些
abháve- 滅、不生、不有、非有、不住
tad- 彼、其、從彼、從而、因此
abhávaḥ- 無、消失、沒有、無所有

Sutra 4.12
atíta-anágataṁ svarúpato-'sti-adhvabhedád dharmáṇám ||12||
The past and the future exist in-reality, there being difference of the paths of being of the characteristics.
過去、未來皆存於自相中，依其法性而展現各異。
atíta- 過、過去、過去世、過去時
anágataṁ- 來、未來、未來時、未來世
svarúpataḥ- 自相、形相、實相、自己的形貌

asti- 有、在
adhvabhedát- 不同的途徑或不同的展現
dharmáṇám- 法性、天性、秉性、本質的、天生本性的

Sutra 4.13
te vyakta-súkṣmáḥ guṇa-atmánaḥ ||13||
They are manifested and subtle, and of the nature of the qualities.
法性之明顯或隱微，取決於自身三德屬性。
te- 此等、彼之，此處係指上述之天賦秉性。
vyakta- 顯、顯示、明了、分明；變性、惰性屬性居主導時，秉性較明顯。
súkṣmáḥ- 微細、精細、精微、極微細、深妙；悅性屬性居主導時，秉性較精細。
guṇa- 德、屬性、束縛、功德；舊譯喜、憂、闇三德，通指造化力之悅性、變性、惰性三種屬性。
atmánaḥ- 自性的、生命體的。

•變易與永恆

Sutra 4.14
pariṇáma-ikatvát vastu-tattvam ||14||
The reality of the object on account of the unity of modification.
變易是世間相之通性。
pariṇáma- 變、轉變、變化、變易
ekatvát- 一、通性、一性、一致性、共同性、統一性
vastu- 物、世事、塵境、事境、現象界、世間相、物質世界
tattvam- 實相、本質、性質、特性、本質屬性、基本真理

Sutra 4.15
vastusámye citta-bhedát-tayorvibhaktaḥ pantháḥ ||15||
There being difference of mentality in the case of the external-object being the same, their ways-of-being are different.

緣心思有別，雖所遇事境相同，感知各異。

vastu- 物、世事、塵境、事境、現象界、世間相、物質世界

sámye- 同、等、平等、相同

citta- 心、心思、心識、心靈質

bhedát- 差異、有別、不同的、不一樣的

tayoḥ- 彼、此、彼之

vibhaktaḥ- 別異、分別、別釋

pantháḥ- 路、途徑、方式；內心對事境的反應或處理方式。

Sutra 4.16

na caika-citta-tantraṁ cedvastu tad-apramáṇakaṁ tadá kiṁ syát ||16||

And if an object dependent upon one mind were not cognized by that, would it then exist?

又若依緣一心之事境未被意識到，則彼是否存在？

na- 不、非、未

ca- 亦、又、及、和、與

eka-citta- 一心、一念、一想；此處指個體心靈。

tantraṁ- 緣、緣於、依於、依他起

ced- 若、若是、假如、如果

vastu- 物、世事、事境現象界、世間相、物質世界

tat-apramáṇakaṁ- 那未認知的、那未意識到的、那未觀察到的

tadá- 就、則、彼時、爾時

kiṁ- 不、何、誰、何者、何義、什麼（反問句）

syát- 則、即為、成為；是否存在、是否發生

Sutra 4.17

tad-uparága-apekṣitvát cittasya vastu-jñátájñátaṁ ||17||

The mind needing to be coloured thereby an object may be known or unknown.

心因所需而擇染著，由是對境或能知或不知。

tad- 彼、其、從彼、從而、因此
uparága- 色、色染、觸染、染著、受影響
apekṣitvát- 視需要、因為需要
cittasya- 心之、心靈的、內心的、頭腦的、精神的
vastu- 物、世事、事境現象、世間相、物質世界
jñátájñátaṁ- 知或不知、明了或不明了、被知道或不被知道
譯按：對事境現象明了之多寡，端視心靈所受染著之深淺。

Sutra 4.18
sadájñátáḥ citta-vrttayaḥ tat-prabhoḥ puruṣasya-apariṇámitvát //18//
To its lord, the *Puruśa,* the modifications of the mind are always known on-account-of-unchangeability.
而不變不遷之淨識乃心之主，始終明了心相之變化。
sadá- 始終、總是、一直
jñátáḥ- 已知、被知道的
citta- 心、心思、心相、心靈的、心識的
vrttayaḥ- 念想的、變化的、心念所向的
tat- 彼之、他們、他（它）們的
prabhoḥ- 主人、主宰、控制者、主導者
puruṣasya- 淨識、真我、本我、神我的、淨識的、純意識的
apariṇámitvát- 緣其不變、不遷不變的、由於不會變化的

Sutra 4.19
na tat-svábhásaṁ dṛśyatvát //19//
It is not self-illuminating, being the knowable.
彼不能自明，因其可被知覺。
na- 不、非、未
tat- 彼之、他（它）們的；此處意指受染之個體心。
svábhásaṁ- 自見、自明、自發光的
dṛśyatvát- 可知的、可見的、可覺察的
譯按：反之能自明、自了，即成圓明真心。

Sutra 4.20

eka samaye cobhaya-an-avadháraṇam //20//

Nor can both, be cognized at the same time.

亦不能同時明了自他二者。

eka samaye- 同時、一時

ca- 亦、及、和、與

ubhaya- 彼此、自他；此處意指能知與所知（即主體和客體）。

an-avadháraṇam- 不能理解、不能認知、不能察知

譯按：個體心靈一次也只能專注於一件事。

Sutra 4.21

cittántara dṛśye buddhi-buddheḥ atiprasaṅgaḥ smṛti-saṁkaraś-ca //21//

In case of being knowable by another mind, there will be too many wills-to-know the Wills-to-know; and there will be confusion of memories.

若心為可為他心所見，則智見交相糾葛，記憶因之惑亂。

cittántara dṛśye-cittántara 字面義為內心、*dṛśye* 字面義為可見、得見；兩字合義為「內心若為可見」。

buddhi-buddheḥ- 覺知與從覺知而生的，指覺知或智用交相作用。

atiprasaṅgaḥ- 過度的、過多的、錯雜的思量；意指心若為可見，有如覺智能自相交互作用，則一時主客難分，訊息錯亂且反覆擴增而生謬失。

smṛti- 念、記念、記憶、憶念

saṁkaraś- 雜亂、雜煣、混亂、混淆、困惑

ca- 亦、及、然、若、則

Sutra 4.22

citer-aprati-saṁkramáyáḥ tad-ákára-ápattau svabuddhi saṁvedanam //22//

Consciousness knows its own Will-to-be by transforming its

appearance, though not-itself moving-from place-to-place.
本心無有遷流變易，但藉點化所幻妙有，自覺自證。
citeh- 本心、心之本相、純意識
aprati-saṁkramáyáḥ- 不遷流的、不流轉的、不變易的、不改變的
tad- 彼、其、從彼、從而、因此
ákára- 相、萬相、萬有、妙有、幻有；萬化的外顯相狀。
ápattau- 取、生、設想、轉化、投射
svabuddhi- 自覺、自證、我覺悟
saṁ-vedanam- 親、覺、覺知、見識到、經驗到

Sutra 4.23
draṣṭṛ-dṛśy-opa-raktaṁ cittaṁ sarva-artham ||23||
The mind being coloured by the knower and the know-able is omni-objective (*sarvárth*).
心受見分與相分之染著而遍知諸事義。
draṣṭṛ- 見分、感知者、能見之人（主體）；主觀的認知功能。
dṛśya- 相分、所見、所緣、被感知者、所見之物（客體）
upa-raktaṁ- 色染、受染著、受影響；擷取或接受所知見對象之熏染，理同成語「近朱者赤，近墨者黑」。
cittaṁ- 心、心思、心相、心靈、心質；此處係指個體心。
sarva-artham- 一切、全體、一切事、一切義

Sutra 4.24
tad-asaṅkhyeya vásanábhiḥ citram-api parártham saṁhatya-káritvát ||24||
And the mind exists-for-another, also because it is variegated by innumerable residua, inasmuch as it acts by combination.
故知心是依他起用，復因此攀緣聚合之作用，受無數熏染而現種種色。
tat- 彼之、他們
asaṅkhyeya- 無數的、無盡的、不可勝數的

vásanábhiḥ- 習氣、熏習、餘習
citram- 斑斕、嚴麗、種種色
api- 又、雖、乃至、即使
parártham- 依他故、為他故、由於……之故
saṁhatya- 聚、聚合、結合、和合
káritvát- 作、作用、作為
譯按：心性本淨，因受色染而遭覆蔽。唐禪師馬祖道一語錄有言——凡所見色，皆是見心；心不自心，因色故有。

Sutra 4.25
viśeṣa-darśinaḥ átmabháva-bhávaná-nivṛttiḥ //25//
For the seer of the distinction, ceases the curiosity as to the nature and relations of the Self.
徹見真妄之別者，亦不生覓求真常自性之心。
viśeṣa- 殊妙、殊異、特殊性、特別之處。
darśinaḥ- 見、能見者；意指能見此真心與妄心之殊異者。
átmabháva- *bháva* 字義是顯化出的萬有，*átmá* 即淨識、本識、靈魂，兩字組合之義為萬有內在之真常或個體意識。
bhávaná- 修、修行、修習、修觀；外向心思轉往內覓的狀態。
nivṛttiḥ- 止、滅、息、滅、不生
譯按：徹見真妄之別者，知心性本淨，緣依他起性故，能淨亦能染；染濁則迷，染淨則悟，迷時是妄，悟時即真，真妄皆性空無相。故明此者，但守本真，而不起覓求雜想。

Sutra 4.26
tadá viveka-nimnaṁ kaivalya-prág-bháraṁ cittam //26//
Then the mind inclines towards discrimination and gravitates towards absolute-independence(*kaivalya*).
由是識心隨順明辨，直趨獨存不共之究竟解脫。
tad- 彼、其、從彼、從而、因此
viveka- 能辨、明辨、明辨智

nimnaṁ- 下、隨、隨順、沒入、趣向
kaivalya- 究竟、不共、絕對、究竟解脫
prág-bháraṁ- 向、朝向、導往、被吸引向
cittam- 心、心思、心靈、識心

Sutra 4.27
tac-chidreṣu pratyaya-antaráṇi saṁskárebhyaḥ ||27||
In the breaks arise other thoughts from residua.
或於隨順明辨之間隙，復生起由業習而來之種種雜想。
tac-chidreṣu- 自彼隙間、從…間隙裡
pratyaya- 緣、緣想、雜染、雜想、煩惱想
antaráṇi- 其他、諸般、種種、不同的
saṁskárebhyaḥ- 從宿業、從業識習氣。

Sutra 4.28
hánam-eṣáṁ kleśavad-uktam ||28||
Their removal has been described like that of the afflictions.
如是塵緣煩惱，須依前述修法泯除。
hánam- 泯、捨、消除、移除
eṣáṁ- 此、這些、對這些
kleśavad- 惑、雜染、煩惱、塵勞、結使
uktam- 前已說、前已述及，如前所述的（如第 2 章 1、2、10、11、26 等節所述方法）。

•自我的圓成

Sutra 4.29
prasaṁkhyáne e-'py-akusídasya sarvathá vivekakhyáteḥ dharma-meghas-samádhiḥ ||29||
Having no-interest left even in the Highest Intellection there comes from constant discrimination, the trance known as the Cloud-of-Virtue.

緣明辨了別一切故，乃至於上勝智境亦無有執念，是謂法雲三摩地。

prasaṁkhyáne- 上勝智，洞明一切幻妄，悟得吾非此身的智境。
api- 又、雖、乃至、即使
akusídasya- 定義不忮求；喻內無妄念，心定而不受事境誘惑。
sarvathá- 皆、一切、始終、全部的、持續的
vivekakhyáteḥ- 透過明辨而了別、透過明辨而能見
dharma-meghas- 法雲、法雲定；意謂行人所獲清淨成就如雲，能滋潤法種，長養眾生善根。
samádhiḥ- 定、入定、三昧、三摩地

Sutra 4.30

tataḥ kleśa-karma-nivṛttiḥ ||30||

Thence the removal of actions and afflictions.

由是惑業煩惱不生。

tataḥ- 如是、是故、因之
kleśa-karma- 惑業、煩惱業；由行業引生的迷惑與煩惱。
nivṛttiḥ- 止、滅、息、除、不生、不轉、無有心之擬向

Sutra 4.31

tadá sarva-ávaraṇa-malápetasya jñánasya-ánantyát jñeyamalpam ||31||

The knowable is but little then, because of knowledge having-become infinite, on account of the removal of all obscuring impurities.

彼時一切塵垢業障泯除，無量真知現前，原所知境已不足道。

tadá- 就、則、彼時、爾時
ṣarva- 盡、皆、全、一切、所有
ávarana- 遮、蓋、障、業障、覆障
malá- 垢、塵垢、塵勞、不淨
ápetasya- 泯除、去除、斷除
jñánasya- 知識的

ánantyát- 無量、無邊、無際
jñeyam- 可知、應知、所緣、所知境、知境界
alpam- 極少、貧瘠、微乎其微、微不足道

Sutra 4.32
tataḥ kṛtárthánaṁ pariṇáma-krama-samáptir-guṇánám ||32||
By that, the qualities having fulfilled their object, the succession of their changes ends.
緣此定境，造化三德功成圓滿，其遷流變化亦隨之而止。
tataḥ- 如上、此後、由彼…
kṛtárthánaṁ- 功成圓滿、達成了作用的目的
pariṇáma- 轉、變、熟、結果、變易、轉變
krama- 漸、漸次、次第、相繼、遷流、演替
samáptih- 終、畢、竟、結束、告終
guṇánám- 屬性、特性，造化的悅性、變性、惰性三德或屬性。

Sutra 4.33
kṣaṇa-pratiyogí pariṇáma-aparánta nirgráhyaḥ kramaḥ ||33||
Succession is the uninterrupted-sequence of moments, cognized as distinct on the cessation of evolutionary change.
遷流變化剎那不止，然於變易後際可辨而明之。
kṣaṇa- 瞬間、剎那
pratiyogí- 連續、相續、連綿、綿延、不間斷
pariṇáma- 轉、變、熟、所變、變易、轉變
aparánta- 終、終止、結束、後際、未來際
nirgráhyaḥ- 被辨明的、被辨別的、被理解的
kramaḥ- 漸、漸次、次第、相繼、遷流、演替
譯按：本節「變易後際」的「後際」，梵文是 *aparánta*，一般英譯作結束、停止；此字意味的是一個波段的盡頭，有如波谷與波峰，一個結束是另一段新的開始，而在波谷之處回顧容易辨明變易的因緣始末。自瑜伽哲理來看，最終的辨明須待修證入寂，回

歸本初意識，屆時世緣盡了，遷流頓斷，一切變易消融於本初空性中，從而洞明一切幻有真空之究極真理。

Sutra 4.34

puruṣartha-śúnyánáṁ guṇánáṁ-pratiprasavaḥ kaivalyaṁ svarúpa-pratiṣṭhá vá citiśaktiriti ||34||

Absolute freedom comes when the qualities, becoming devoid of the object of the *Puruśa,* become latent; or the power of consciousness becomes established in its own nature.

如是造化屬性歸伏本處，行人識性融入本初淨識，安住獨存不共之境。

puruṣartha- 個體識性、瑜伽行人之識性

śúnyánáṁ- 空、空性、空寂、真空

guṇánáṁ- 屬性、特性、造化的悅性、變性、惰性三德或屬性

pratiprasavaḥ- 歸元、返本、回歸本處

kaivalyaṁ- 獨存、不共、絕對、究竟解脫

svarúpa- 本相、自相、自性、本來的形相

pratiṣṭhá- 住、安住、依止、建立

vá- 或、若、如

citiśaktiḥ- 淨識、至上意識、至上認知力，英譯作意識之力。

iti- 是、如是、即此、由是

Om Tat Sat

哈達瑜伽明燈

Haṭha Yoga Pradípiká

〈中譯本前言〉
瑜伽行者的重要踏腳石

《哈達瑜伽明燈》是哈達瑜伽的開山經典，作者是大瑜伽師史瓦特瑪拉（*Swatmarama*），名字的意思是從至上真我（atman）得到喜悅的人。他的出生年代不詳，學者們推估約莫是在十五世紀前後，本書是現存最古老的哈達瑜伽文本，譯名尚有《哈達瑜伽燈論》、《哈達瑜伽經》、《哈達瑜伽之光》等。

《哈達瑜伽明燈》的論述重心在體式、調息、身印和三摩地，瑜伽的身清淨法包含在調息章中。本書原典是以梵文書寫，一直到一九一四年才有學者潘強辛（*Pancham Sinh*）譯成英文；次年他又為本書寫了一篇導讀，語重心長地指出當時有關瑜伽的一些錯誤觀念，並提出若干懇切的建議。由這篇文章，可見潘強辛本人即是一位務實的瑜伽行人，這也是筆者對他的翻譯版本產生興趣的原因。

現代流行的瑜伽，幾都是哈達瑜伽推廣到西方世界後的變體；而在古典瑜伽的分類裡，勝王瑜伽才是主流，另外還有一支古老且較少為人所知的王中之王瑜伽（*Rajadhiraja Yoga*）也有不少瑜伽人修習。《哈達瑜伽明燈》的作者大瑜伽師史瓦特瑪拉肯定勝王瑜伽才是修行的依歸，在第一章第一節就明確地說道：「這門知識是志道者成就最高勝王瑜伽的階梯。」然而勝王瑜伽不易立即上手；因此為了想學瑜伽，又不能進入勝王瑜伽堂奧的準瑜伽學子們歸納出一套完整的哈達瑜伽練習方法，包括修習場地的選擇條件、學習時應具備的心態和戒律、建議練習的體位動作及其利益、靜坐的姿勢、修習的次序，飲食的取捨、修學的態度、各種呼吸調息和身印的知識及內外淨化的方法等等。待習者身心都有進展了，還有一章專介紹集中入定之法，教導如何靜心冥想。有趣的是在介紹身印法的篇章中，將近有二十節的篇幅，教導的是在家人應如何固本培元。然後在第四章第七十九節再次強調「僅練習哈達瑜伽而未明勝王瑜伽之人，我認為這些修習者是白費力氣，得不到努力的成果」，似乎是不希望習者被部分內容所誤導。由於內容豐富，後世有人將本書譽為是哈達瑜伽的聖經。

現代讀者若看本書經句，會覺得大部分的內容陳述過簡，事實也確是如此。筆者認為或許這只是一本綱要性的指導。緣古代印度，瑜伽是種師徒式的傳承，有相當的學習規矩；在學習過程中，自然會學習到個中細節。所以不能以現代商業社會的觀點審度，也因為如此，不少人認為當今是歷來瑜伽最興盛的時代，但真正的瑜伽精神卻模糊了。

《哈達瑜伽明燈》內容分四章三百八十九節經句，第一章體位法，第二章調息及淨化法，第三章身印法，第四章三摩地。就第一義諦而言，《哈達瑜伽明燈》揭櫫之法雖非究竟，卻是有心瑜伽者一塊很重要的踏腳石；使學人能藉之準備好自已，也開了一扇指引進階瑜伽學人未來方向的窗。

本書中譯版是以一九一四年潘強辛所翻譯的梵英文本為藍本，再參考布拉瑪難陀（*Brahmananda*）的英註本以及印度比哈瑜伽學院斯瓦米．慕克提博達難陀（*Swami Muktibodhananda*）的英譯本，試還原出梵文原旨。由於時空背景不同，部分經文已不符當今之社會體制與風氣，故不宜以今日之視角論斷。本書文字力求信達，部分亦採意譯，俾易於了解。然百密或不免一疏，尚祈賢達砌磋指教。

〈英譯本導讀〉
透過明師，一定能找到「祂」

目前存在著許多哈達瑜伽練習上的誤解。人們很容易相信那些自己聽來的二手訊息，卻不思直接從一些專著找出事實真相。比如，一般認為哈達瑜伽中的六種淨化法是學員必須的練習，否則便會招致不淨，而使練習中充滿了危險。這並非事實，這些淨化法只有在經脈不淨時才需要練習，非為其他。

在呼吸法方面也有著相同的誤解。人們把他們所相信的隱於故事中，然後訴說進行練習的危險性，卻沒有自己費心去查證其中的事實。我們從一出生就開始呼吸，也會繼續呼吸直到百年，這種行為不用任何老師的幫忙。呼吸法只是將緊促、不規律的氣息適當的規律化，並不需要使用多少力氣或過分的克制；如果練習時能耐心地保持氣息徐緩而穩定地出入，是不會有什麼危險的。所謂的危險，是因為有些沒有耐心的練習者在練習時過度地施壓器官，從而導致眼、耳和胸腔等部位的不適或疼痛。若能在練習呼吸法時小心地進行三鎖印（*bandhas*），是不致於會有任何危險的。

瑜伽學人有兩類：一是以研究學理為主，二是結合學理與修持。如果只是研究瑜伽學理而少應用，瑜伽從來不是這樣學的。甚且，在瑜伽的實際形式裡，學人修學之路充滿著艱辛。瑜伽書籍上的指示，截至目前，都屬於可以用語言來表達的方法；問題在於有的讀者，並未真正地用心遵循書中所言及的指示，因而達不到他們所期望的目的。這樣的人需要一位熟諳瑜伽鍛煉的老師。要找到一位能夠詮釋書中言語的老師不難，但若說要令人滿意就不容易了。例如，一位沒有任何藥材學知識的智者，可能把「*Kantakari* －黃果龍葵」解釋作「*Kantakasyaarih Kantakaari* －荊棘的敵人」，亦即鞋子；而事實上它是一種藥用植物的名稱。

就瑜伽學人而言，不能低估真正瑜伽行者在指導上的重要性；缺少這樣的老師，想要有所成就幾乎是難有可能。這種明智且經過熟慮的密行方式係源於此一體系的創始人和長久以來沿襲祖師們此一作法的追隨者，是具有其深意的。細看此一與人體重要器官有密切關係的主題及其鍛煉的重要性，其中最重要的是——為了避免練習過程中任何可能的差錯，唯有通過身具實學的老師，才可使一般能力的學生也可領會這些指示。概括說來，並非人人都適合接受相同詞句的指示。人類出生時的身體和心智能力是據前生的因果業力，因此不論智愚，要增加能力就必須透過歷練。是故，吾人不是一世間就能夠成為瑜伽行者的。上主克里希納曾言：「歷經多生累劫，有識者終必以我為依歸。」(《薄伽梵歌》7.19)，又言「於解脫道上因精進而得成就者，千人中唯只一人。」(《薄伽梵歌》7.3)

緣宿業之力，有人不顧一切地試圖完成內心解脫之願，也有人累世輪迴必須為資糧忙碌。如果學人是屬於這樣的靈魂且衷心渴望擺脫生死苦海，他總會找到辦法。眾所周知，真正的瑜伽行者不為利誘所惑，因此認為他保守知識的奧秘是為了待價而沽，是很荒謬的。瑜伽對眾生皆有裨益，一位真瑜伽士總是希望有越多的人受益越好。但是他也不會不加揀擇地胡亂拋灑這項珍寶，他細心地挑選傳人，在找到一個實在、認真，不會輕忽這門知識的弟子之前，繼承者是絕對不會任意地處置自己這份珍寶的。他要找的是真正渴求這門知識的人，那種渴求會令他輾轉反轍直到如願滿足，那種渴求會令他無視於身處的世界以及這個世界所有的享受。簡言之，他應該是全心想要求解脫的人。對於這樣的人，沒有什麼會比達悟自性更形重要。若真心愛其所愛，會像篤悉達＊般冒著生命之險，求與自己心愛的對象結合。真心愛其所愛的人會在任何方所、任何樹木及其樹葉裡、或任何一株小草中見著自己的最愛。這一整個世界的美，若少了自己的最愛，那麼在他眼裡便都一文不值。甚至為了自己的最愛，即便會喪失生命，他也會毫不猶豫地投身巨壙之口。

內心燃燒著強烈渴望想與至上靈魂合一的學人，必須要找到一位明師，透過明師，學人一定能找「祂」。這是一種嘗試，去體會這種隨著內心渴望強度而有的啄啐同時的經驗。若有幸，甚至祂會親自成為你的嚮導，在成功之路上指引你；或是讓你找到一位明師，或是把明師帶到你的面前。

有句俗話說的貼切：三心二意導致失敗！如果人們心中對世俗財富的執著勝過他們的上主，那麼就上主而言他們並不值得祂的特別青睞。奧義書有言：「自性或靈魂（*átmá*）會在汝心彰顯，唯只因為你值得這樣的恩典，而非其他。」所以瑜伽學人首先必須值得讓祂接受，準備好自己成為適合祂駐足的殿堂；掃除一切陳腐以及令殿堂不適合至上駐留的不淨，把心殿佈置好準備迎接造物主的到來。若是你已經努力為祂證明了自己是虔心的，即不需要為祂花太長的時間裝飾殿堂；如是機

＊ 篤悉達（*Tulasidas*）：十五世紀印度虔誠瑜伽最偉大的聖人之一，本身是位梵文學者及作家。在成婚生子盡到社會責任後，很早就離開家庭過著出家人的生活。一生中創作了十二部具有靈性義意的文學作品。

緣成熟，祂會在你內心展現出祂的一切榮耀。在你最艱困的時刻，在你最窘迫的時候，如是靜心思惟，謙恭地親近你的根本上師，向祂訴說你的困難，你一定會從祂那兒獲得適當的忠告。祂是恆古的明師，不受時間所限；祂指導古今之行人，如同明師一般。如果你一直無緣找到一位在世明師，那麼深入你內心的殿堂，請求這位從來與你同在的根本明師，指引你一條道路。祂知道什麼對你是最好的。不同於一般人，祂是超越過去和未來的；祂可以分派一位祂的代理指導你，或是親自引領你步上正確的道路。他一向樂於指引認真懇切的志道者，等待著你提供給祂一個機會引領你。但是如果你還沒有完成你的職責以及備足進入上主之門的條件，或是去到祂的面前卻仍然馱負著不潔的負擔，散發著慾樂及貪、瞋、癡等臭味，那麼可以肯定，這會使你與祂相隔離的。

體位法是一種取得坐姿安穩，令心不外馳以幫助冥想成功的輔助方法。如果坐式不安舒，即便些微的不適也會使人從修觀中分心，如是心不得靜，直到從規律的練習中消除導致坐姿不適的癥結為止。

在所有為專注心靈所設的各種方法中，持誦或半持誦「ॐ-*Oṁ*」音，並思惟其意涵是最好的。想要讓心思靜若雕像般一秒鐘都很難！因此，為了讓心處於清靜，讓對治的念頭進入，宜練習持誦「ॐ-*Oṁ*」音；並持續反覆練習，直到引發瑜伽定境現前，周身肌肉鬆透，內心會感應到極大的激勵。如是莊嚴與神聖之思溢滿心靈，輕而易舉地就沒入合一之境。

透過練習呼吸控制法，無比的秘音被喚醒。在晨晚各做幾週八十次的呼吸控制練習將有助於聆聽到明晰的音聲，隨著練習次數的增加，習者還能聽到不同的音聲。藉由細聽這些音聲，習者的內心獲得集中，從而體驗到本然三摩地。在經驗過瑜伽定境時，學人應任其生滅，以平常心觀照；逐漸地，這些聲音愈趨微細，漸至不聞。內在心靈的不安由是消失，變得平和而溫順，亦即內心藉由此法而得完善圓融，遂自發地進入三摩地。不過，此是修習的最高階段，需要許多上主的恩典並且只屬於少數幸運者。

在靜坐之時，習者所見非由雙眼而得，然猶如世間所見諸物般色彩繽紛，有的瑜伽書作者稱此為五大元素之色。有時候，星星看起來閃閃發光，閃電劃過天際，但這些都是世間相的無常本性。

起初這些顏色看起來是非常不規律的振波，呈現出內心的不穩定狀態。而隨著日增的修煉，心靈漸趨平靜，這些顏色波動也轉趨穩定、沉寂，而顯現為一片深深的光海。習者應忘卻世界，潛入這片光海，與此最高極樂之境的上主融而為一。

在瑜伽修煉裡，行人以一己之力完成前人也曾經歷過的考驗，其間信心是確保能早日成就的重要條件。如同俗話所說的「精誠所至，金石為開！」不論事情有多麼困難，皆可藉信心完成，沒有什麼是不能透過修煉來完成的。上主希瓦在《希瓦本集》第四章 9-10 節中提到：

> 透過精勤的修行取得成就，透過精勤的修行獲得解脫。
> 圓滿悟境是從修行獲得，瑜伽果位亦是從修行獲得；
> 身印成就來自修行，經由修行得御氣成就；
> 經由修行，死神可能受其獵物欺瞞。

所以讓我們繫緊身上的纏腰布，以堅強的決心從事修習，抱持著對祂的信心（你有權履行應盡的職責，但不應冀求行為的成果。——《薄伽梵歌》2.47），成功必定是我們的。願全能的父，歡喜地將祝福遍灑給那些忠誠地履行其職責的修行者們。

Oṁ，一切吉祥平安。

潘強辛（*Pancham Sinh*），1915 年 1 月 31 日

第一章

瑜伽體位法

Ásanas

1. Salutation to *Ádinátha* (*Śiva*) who expounded the knowledge of *Haṭha Yoga*, which like a staircase leads the aspirant to the high pinnacled *Rája Yoga*.

   頂禮元始至尊主，彼開示哈達瑜伽之學；此學是志道者登上勝王瑜伽之階梯。

   元始至尊主：意為最初始的那位受尊敬的人格神，此處是上主希瓦的代稱。

   哈達瑜伽：勝王瑜伽的加行法，平衡身內陰陽的修行法，用心理力量來控制身體能量的鍛煉；也可說，哈達瑜伽是以控制腺體荷爾蒙分泌並強化各脈輪的鍛鍊。

   勝王瑜伽：瑜伽學中藉收攝、禪定來開展身、心、靈的修行法門。更確切的說，是藉控制內在能量，使之從身體導向心理，從心理導向俱屬性靈性本體的修行。

2. *Yogin Swátmaráma*, after saluting first his *Guru Srinátha* explains *Haṭha Yoga* for the attainment of *Rája Yoga*.

   禮畢本師，大瑜伽師史瓦特瑪拉為欲成就勝王瑜伽者講述哈達瑜伽之學。

   史瓦特瑪拉：本書作者，大瑜伽師，師承葛拉克夏尊者。

3. Owing to the darkness arising from the multiplicity of opinions people are unable to know the *Rája Yoga*. Compassionate *Swátmaráma* composes the *Haṭha Yoga Pradipiká* like a torch to dispel it.

   由於紛紜眾說而生迷惘的人無法知曉勝王瑜伽，慈悲的史瓦特瑪拉為之撰述《哈達瑜伽明燈》以昭迷暗。

   紛紜眾說：作者觀察到，對於如何成就瑜伽道果，當時真假莫辨、令人生惑的說法很多。

4. *Matsyendra, Gorakṣa*, etc., knew *Haṭha Vidyá*, and by their favour *Yogí Swátmaráma* also learnt it from them. The following *Siddhas* (masters) are said to have existed in former times.

瑪茲央卓尊者、葛拉克夏尊者等瑜伽師們深明哈達瑜伽之道，承眾師青睞，瑜伽師史瓦特瑪拉也從彼處習得了這門知識。以下是過去知名的成就者：

瑪茲央卓尊者：約生於十世紀左右，印度八十四位大成就者之一，扭轉式以其名傳世。

葛拉克夏尊者：瑪茲央卓尊者弟子，法門傳承至今仍有人從習，著有《葛拉克夏本集》等書。

5. *Sri Ádinátha (Śiva), Matsyendra, Nátha, Sábar, Anand Bhairava, Chaurangi, Mína nátha, Gorakṣanátha, Virupákṣa, Bileśaya*.

   元始至尊主希瓦，瑪茲央卓尊者，夏巴拉尊者，阿難陀拜拉瓦尊者，喬蘭吉尊者，密納拿塔尊者，聖葛拉克夏尊者，毘盧帕夏尊者，毘雷夏雅尊者；

6. *Mantháná, Bhairava, Siddhi Buddha, Kanthadi, Karantaka, Suránanda, Siddhipáda, Charapati*.

   蒙達納尊者，拜拉瓦尊者，悉諦覺尊者，空塔地尊者，寇蘭塔卡尊者，蘇爾南達尊者，悉達帕達尊者，恰帕諦尊者；

7. *Kánerí, Pújyapáda, Nityanátha, Nirañjana, Kapáli, Vindunátha, Káka Chandíśwara*.

   勘列里尊者，普傑帕達尊者，尼帖拿塔尊者，無相尊者，卡帕林尊者，聖賓杜尊者，寇卡羌第自在王尊者；

8. *Alláma, Prabhudeva, Ghodá, Cholí, Tintiṇi, Bhánukí Nárdeva, Khanda Kápálika, etc*.

   奧拉瑪尊者，自化天尊者，果達尊者，秋林尊者，定提尼尊者，巴努金那羅提瓦尊者，坎達卡帕力卡尊者等。

9. These *Mahásiddhas* (great masters), breaking the sceptre of death, are roaming in the universe.

   這些大成就者藉哈達瑜伽之功已不再為死亡節杖所拘，遨遊於世。

譯按：修行悟達不生滅之常住真心，即不為世間生死所拘。

10. Like a house protecting one from the heat of the sun, *Haṭha Yoga* protects its practiser from the burning heat of the three *Tápas*; and, similarly, it is the supporting tortoise, as it were, for those who are constantly devoted to the practice of *Yoga*.

哈達瑜伽猶如遮陽屋舍，為受三苦煎熬之人提供依止；虔修瑜伽者，哈達瑜伽如同載世神龜般給予支持。

苦：受何種苦，諸譯本說法有異。然根本苦有三，是為 (1) 內因苦，(2) 外因苦，(3) 自然因苦。

載世神龜：和多數民族一樣，古印度亦認為地球是平的，由站在神龜背面四隅的四隻神象承載著。

11. A *Yogí* desirous of success should keep the knowledge of *Haṭha Yoga* secret; for it becomes potent by concealing, and impotent by exposing.

渴望成就之瑜伽行者應謹守哈達瑜伽密意；如是方能受益良多，一旦泄漏便成徒然。

哈達瑜伽密意：修行是身心的淬煉，不宜張揚，故本節意在提醒習者莫嘩眾取寵，當以實修為本。

修舍

12. The *Yogí* should practise *Haṭha Yoga* in a small room, situated in a solitary place, being 4 cubits square, and free from stones, fire, water, disturbances of all kinds, and in a country where justice is properly administered, where good people live, and food can be obtained easily and plentifully.

哈達瑜伽行者應住於僻靜處小修舍內修習，舍外四腕尺距離內無水患、火災及落石之虞；居地宜選由明君轄理，四鄰良善，飲食無虞，不受干擾之地。

四腕尺：又名肘尺，一腕尺約 50 公分，四腕尺約兩公尺。

13. The room should have a small door, be free from holes, hollows, neither too high nor too low, well plastered with cow-dung and free from dirt, filth and insects. On its outside there should be bowers, raised platform (*chabootrá*), a well, and a compound. These characteristics of a room for *Haṭha Yogís* have been described by adepts in the practice of *Haṭha*.

修舍應有一扇小門，不設窗戶；地面平坦無有坑洞，室內不宜太高或太低。保持修舍整潔，牆面塗牛糞杜絕蚊蟲。舍外要有廁所，廁所地面墊高，並用牆遮圍。此為哈達瑜伽成就者所描繪的哈達瑜伽士修舍特點。

14. Having seated in such a room and free from all anxieties, he should practise *Yoga*, as instructed by his *Guru*.

棲身如是修舍，行人應心無旁騖，遵循上師之教誨修習瑜伽。

內、外在規範

15. *Yoga* is destroyed by the following six causes:—Over-eating, exertion, talkativeness, adhering to rules, *i.e.*, cold bath in the morning, eating at night, or eating fruits only, company of men, and unsteadiness.

瑜伽行者退轉的六種原因是：飲食過量、操勞過度、言語太多、拘泥規矩（例如晨浴冷水、晚上進食、只進食水果等）、結交損友以及心意不定。

退轉的六種原因：對應的梵文是 *atyáhára*、*prayása*、*prajalpa*、*niyamagraha*、*janasaṅga*、*laulya*。

16. The following six bring speedy success:—courage, daring, perseverance, discriminative knowledge, faith, aloofness. from company.

瑜伽行者成功的六個要素：決心、勇氣、毅力、正知見、正思維、不交損友。

成功的六個要素：對應的梵文是 *utsáhát*、*sáhasát*、*dhairyát*、*ttattvajñáná*、*niścayát* 和 *Janasaṅgaparityágát*。

16a. The ten rules of conduct are: *ahiṃsá* (non-injuring), truth, non-stealing, continence, forgiveness, endurance, compassion, meekness, sparing diet and cleanliness.

不傷害、真誠為懷、不偷盜、淨行、自制、堅忍、慈憫、正直、飲食有度、淨化身心等是十條外在規範。

十條外在規範：對應的梵文依次是 *ahiṁsá*、*Satyam*、*asteya*、*brahmacarya*、*kṣamá*、*dhṛtiḥ*、*dayá*、*árjavam*、*mitáháraḥ* 以及 *śauca*。

16b. The ten *niyamas* mentioned by those proficient in the knowledge of *Yoga* are: *Tapa*, patience, belief in God, charity, adoration of God, hearing discourses on the principles of religion, modesty, intellect, *Japa* and *Yajña*.

苦行、知足、自律、佈施、敬信神、聆聽經典、謙遜、慧智、持咒、奉獻等是十條內在規範。

十條內在規範（*niyama*）：對應的梵文依次是 *tapas*、*santoṣa*、*ástikya*、*dána*、*íśvarapújana*、*Siddhántavákyaśravaṇa*、*hrí*、*matí*、*japa* 以及 *hutam*。

體位法

17. Being the first accessory of *Haṭha Yoga*, ásana is described first. It should be practised for gaining steady posture, health and lightness of body.

首先解說體位法，它是哈達瑜伽的初階；習後可使人姿勢安穩、身輕體健。

18. I am going to describe certain *ásanas* which have been adopted by

Munís like *Vasiṣṭha*, etc., and *Yogís* like *Matsyendra*, etc.

我要講述一些得到聖哲瓦西士塔和大瑜伽士瑪茲央卓尊者等推舉的體位法。

聖哲瓦西士塔：古印度神話級聖者、詩人和先知，中古世紀有人托蟻垤之名將他的教導編纂整理成《瑜伽 瓦西斯塔》一書。

● 吉祥坐

19. Having kept both the feet under both the thighs, with the body straight, when one sits calmly in this posture, it is called *Swastika*.

保持身軀中正，兩腳置於對側膝、腿之間，以此式靜坐即名吉祥坐。

吉祥坐：坐法簡易，予人吉祥舒適之感，為習見靜心姿勢之一，適合較長時間的靜坐。雙手可分置於膝上，掌心朝上或朝下。

● 牛面式

20. Placing the right ankle on the left side and the left ankle on the right side, makes *Gomukha-ásana*, having the appearance of a cow.

右腳踝置於左股側，左腳踝同樣的置於右股側，形若牛首，故名牛面式。

牛面式：又名牛頭式；此式需兩臀穩置地面，雙膝上下交疊，兩腳方能置於左右股側。雙手可置於膝上，或雙手持握兩腳，亦可雙臂一上一下於背後以手指搭扣住。

● 勇士式

21. One foot is to be placed on the thigh of the opposite side; and so also the other foot under the same thigh. This is called *Vírásana*.

一腳穩置於對側腿內側，再將另一腳置於同側腿下；是名勇士式。

勇士式：依本節所述，「再將另一腳置於同側腿下」，意指將腳置同一條腿之下或外側。雙手可置於膝上。此式現今做法多採屈膝跪坐於兩腿間。此式為禪坐式，故雙手可置於膝上。依特定功用，另有採併膝跪姿，腳掌豎立腳趾後曲，坐於兩腳跟上，手背置於胯上，亦名勇士式。

● 龜式坐

22. Placing the right ankle on the left side of anus, and the left ankle on the right side of it, makes what the *Yogís* call *Kúrma-ásana*.

    右踝置於後陰左側，左踝置於其右側，此式瑜伽師謂之龜式坐。

    龜式坐：此式需採跪坐姿，雙手分置於膝上。《葛蘭達本集2-32》敘述此式做法為足跟反向置於會陰下，直身端坐。此式現今常見做法是：坐正後兩腿前伸，左右分開；上身前俯，兩手分別自左右腿下同側穿出，貼近股外側。

● 公雞式

23. Taking the posture of *Padma-ásana* and carrying the hands under the thighs, when the *Yogí* raises himself above the ground, with his palms resting on the ground, it becomes *Kukkuṭa-ásana*.

    採取蓮花坐式，雙手伸入同側膝、腿之間，以雙掌穩撐於地，將身體懸空離地，是為公雞式。

    公雞坐：此式困難處在於雙手穿過大腿股二肌及小腿腓腸肌之間。功效可強化腸胃系統及腰腹、手臂肌群。

● 困難龜式

24. Having assumed *Kukkuṭa-ásana*, when one grasps his neck by crossing his hands behind his head, and lies in this posture with his back touching the ground, it becomes *Uttána Kúrma-ásana*, from its appearance like that of a tortoise..

採取公雞式，彎曲雙臂，雙手交置於後頸，背躺地板如仰龜，是為困難龜式。

困難龜式：此式屬於高難度的體位法，需熟練公雞式後，方宜練習。雙手亦可搭於後頸大椎與肩峰中點之肩井。《葛蘭達本集 2-33》敘述此式做法之動作如上，豎立如龜，名龜立式。

● 弓式

25. Having caught the toes of the feet with both the hands and carried them to the ears by drawing the body like a bow, it becomes *Dhanura ásana*.

雙手分別持握雙腳拇趾，如彎弓般將之拉向耳朵；是為弓式。

弓式：符合此描述者有二式，本節經句較貼近第二種：第一種是兩腿前伸坐正，兩手分握對側腳大趾，然後一腳伸直，一腳拉向對側耳朵，左右交替施作，又名拉弓式。二為身體俯臥，以雙手於肩後上方分握左右腳大趾，身軀反彎，將腳拉向耳朵（頭部）。第二種做法對一般習者頗有難度，現今做法多是俯臥後，雙手後伸握住腳踝附近，向上彎身。進行此式時，需注意腰背客觀條件的配合。

● 瑪茲央卓式

26. Having placed the right foot at the root of the left thigh, and place the left foot at the side of the right knee, then twist the bodythe body and catch hold of the feet with opposite hands, remain steady in theis position. This is the *ásana*, as explained by *Śri Matsyanátha*.

將右腳平置於左大腿根部，左腳曲立置於右膝外側；然後，以右手握住左腳，向左扭轉腰身，保持姿勢安穩；此式為由瑪茲央卓尊者所授。

瑪茲央卓式：此式因其形簡稱扭轉式。本式藉扭轉背脊活化神經，可以激活大腦和身體的精細能量。腳背無法置於腿根者，可先置於腿股外側。此式右手握住左腳，左手反繞於右腰，然後扭身轉頭向左，左右側交替施作。

27. It increases appetite and is an instrument for destroying the group of the most deadly diseases. Its practice awakens the *Kundaliní,* stops the nectar shedding from the moon in people.

瑪茲央卓式能增進食慾，為弭除諸難纏疾病之利器。常習此式有助喚醒靈能，阻止身內月甘露蒸耗。

增進食欲：本節經句原義是指能助燃胃火，亦即刺激脾胃的消化能力。

靈能：根本靈性勢能，蜷眠在脊椎底部的海底輪，梵名*Kundalini*。常見的譯名有軍荼利、昆達里尼、靈性能量、靈能、拙火、靈熱、靈力、靈蛇等等。靈能軍荼利一詞常見於哈達瑜伽經典中，認為她屬於陰性的靈性能量；密乘瑜伽定義其為受到造化力禁錮的悅性意識，當其脫離造化力的束縛後，即能沿著中脈上行至頂輪融入神性，證得修行之果。不同的傳承對此靈能的詮釋並不一致。

月甘露：月甘露係指由松果體分泌，能滋生靈性喜悅的內分泌，因部分作用受到月亮的控制而有此名。

● 背伸展式

28. Having stretched the feet on the ground, like a stick, and having grasped the toes of both the feet with both the hands, when one sits with his forehead resting on the thighs, it is called *Paśchima Tána*.

坐地兩腿向前直伸如杖，雙手抓握腳趾，彎身以額近膝腿；名之為背伸展式。

背伸展式：本式主要的伸展部位是下背及腿後側，前傾時背部保持不拱起，胸腹儘量貼近膝腿。進行本式時，注意練習強度，以免腿、背受傷。

29. This *Paśchimat tána* carries the air from the front to the back part of the body (*i.e.*, to the *suṣumna*). It kindles gastric fire, reduces obesity and cures all diseases of men.

背伸展式是諸體位法中之上品，此背伸展式可引導生命能通達脊背中脈，揚升胃火，緊實腰腹，令身無病。

背伸展是諸體位法中之上品：本節首句梵文 *Iti paśchimatánamásanághryam* 之中譯，英譯未錄，中譯補入。

脊背中脈：原句式名 *paścima*，意思是身體後部的脊背，故亦有助督脈之活絡。本書各版本多譯為中脈。

● 孔雀式

30. Place the palms of both the hands on the ground, and place the navel on both the elbows and balancing thus, the body should be stretched backward like a stick. This is called *Mayúra-ásana*.

跪地開膝，雙掌撐地，以雙肘頂於臍側支撐並掌握平衡，身應向後伸展平懸如杖；此為孔雀式。

孔雀式：本式除完成式形若孔雀外，其對腹腔的壓力可以給腸胃強力的按摩，是加強胃功能的補藥。本式準備式先採跪姿兩膝打開，上臂緊抵上腹，然後再雙掌撐地；撐身離地時重點在於找到平衡點，方能穩定展身懸空。

31. This *Ásana* soon destroys all diseases, and removes abdominal disorders, and also those arising from irregularities of phlegm, bile and wind, digests unwholesome food taken in excess, increases appetite and destroys the most deadly poison.

孔雀式可速解一切疾疫，消除脾腹腫脹以及所有因體風、膽汁或黏液三要能過剩導致的疾病；並能輕易地消化過雜、過量的食物，甚至能緩解劇毒。

要能：意指體內的三種要能（*dośa*）。印度生命醫學認為人之所以生病是因為體內的三種要能失衡之故，這三種要能是風能（*Vata*）、火能（*Pitta*）和水能（*Kapha*）。風能主理身體之行動，火能主理新陳代謝及消化，水能主理生理結構及體液之平衡。人體內的三種要能對應體風素、膽汁素和黏液素三種病素，這三種病素影響三種要能的平衡，三種要能的平衡則影響著身心的健康。

● 攤屍式

32. Lying down on the ground, like a corpse, is called *Śava-ásana*. It removes fatigue and gives rest to the mind.

仰面平躺於地，有如屍體一般，故名攤屍式；此式消除周身疲勞，回復心靈平靜。

攤屍式：又名大休息式；此式放空身、心，能迅速消除疲憊，恢復元氣。

33. *Śiva* taught eighty-four *ásanas*. Of these the first four being essential ones, I am going to explain them here.

希瓦講過八十四種體位法，我現在講述其中主要的四種。

希瓦：常被尊稱為上主希瓦或永恆的希瓦 *Sadáśiva*。約七千年生於印度的密宗聖師，永處於至上合一之境的大瑜伽士，後世尊為瑜伽及密宗之父，全方位的將屬靈的觀念帶給世人。訂定婚姻制度和印度音律法則，亦是密宗瑜伽和吠陀醫學的發明人，被認為是人類文明之父。*Śiva* 一詞在哲學上亦是清淨識、至上意識的代名詞。

34. These four are: The *Siddha*, *Padma*, *Sinha* and *Bhadra*. Even of these, the *Siddha-ásana*, being very comfortable, one should always practise it.

這四種最主要的體位法是成就坐、蓮花坐、獅子坐和普賢坐，其中最殊勝、最安穩舒適的是成就坐，當常習之。

● 成就坐

35. Press firmly the heel of the left foot against the perineum, and the

right heel above the male organ. With the chin pressing on the chest, one should sit calmly, having restrained the senses, and gaze steadily the space between the eyebrows. This is called the *Siddha Ásana*, the opener of the door of salvation.

一足腳跟緊抵會陰，另一足腳跟置於前陰之上；下巴觸胸，靜心端坐，雙眼凝注於眉心；此名成就坐，能打開究竟解脫之門。

成就坐：獲得修法成就的主要坐式，故譯為成就坐，又名完美坐。手結智慧手印（拇指、食指相觸，餘三指自然伸展，手心向上）或秦手印（手心向下，餘同智慧手印）。

究竟解脫：入無分別定成就；另一種解脫名 ***Mukti***，入有別定成就。

36. This *Siddhásana* is performed also by placing the left heel on *Meḍhra* (above the male organ), and then placing the right one on it.

將左足腳跟置於前陰上方，另一足腳踝交疊其上，此亦為成就坐。

腳跟：泛指腳、足、踝。本節另一重點在下巴可不必觸胸，頂懸中正。

37. Some call this *Siddhásana*, some *Vajrásana*. Others call it *Mukta Ásana* or *Gupta Ásana*.

此名成就坐，亦有說此為金剛坐式，還有人稱之為自在坐或笈多坐。

譯按：此式於《葛蘭達本集》中名為自在坐。

38. Just as sparing food is among *Yamas,* and *Ahiṃsá* among the *Niyamas*, so is *Siddhásana* called by adepts the chief of all the *ásanas*.

猶如外在規範中飲食有度最為重要，內在規範中不傷害最為重要；而所有體式之首，諸成就者則認為是成就坐。

譯按：本章第 16 節 a 及 b 述及外在規範和內在規範，不過此處有個小小的矛盾，因為節制飲食和不傷害俱在第 16 節 a 中。為何如此，不得而知。因此有學者懷疑第 16 節的 a 和 b 有可能是後人添補的。而且第 16 節的內外在規範與瑜伽經中的內外在規範儘管梵文相同，但內容多出十條，表示勝王瑜伽的內外在規範準則是經過帕檀迦利進一步的梳理。內外在規範中何者最重要？可能會視時代的需求而改變。當代密宗瑜伽導師雪莉．雪莉．阿南達慕提在專講內外在規範的《人類行為準則》一書中有言，外在規範中「心不離道」(*Brahmacarya*) 最為重要，內在規範中「安住至上」(*Iishvara pranidana*) 最為重要，其它八條都是依附在這兩條之上的。

39. Out of the eighty four *Ásanas*, the *Siddhásana* should always be practised, because it cleanses the impurities of 72,000 *náḍís*.

八十四種體位法中，當常習成就坐，可以淨化七萬二千經脈。

七萬二千經脈：分佈於身內的能量管道。其中較重要的有十四條；最重要的則是左脈、右脈與中脈，又稱月脈、日脈與中脈。右脈由臍輪以下的三個脈輪支配，左脈由心輪以上的脈輪支配

40. By contemplating on oneself, by eating sparingly, and by practising *Siddhásana* for 12 years, the *Yogí* obtains success.

思惟自性真我，調節飲食，持續以此成就坐式修行十二年，瑜伽行者可獲成就。

自性真我：梵文 *Átman*（*Átmá* 的呼格），意指最終的實相、宇宙靈魂、真如自性、至上意識；於個體身名個體靈魂 。

41. Other postures are of no use, when success has been achieved in *Siddhásana*, and *Práṇa Váyú* becomes calm and restrained by *Kevala Kumbhaka*.

當修習成就坐有成，何用修習其他體位法？當體內生命能藉本然持氣法調伏歸寂，則空境大樂自現。

本然持氣法：形容出入息呈不需意識作用的自發引動狀態，接近的名詞是胎息。

空境大樂：字義指心寂、無對待，此處指內心空明安樂之瑜伽定境。

譯按：「空境大樂自現」為本節梵文末句 *utpadyate niráy-ásátsvayamevonmaní kalá*. 之中譯，英譯未錄，中譯依從梵文原經句。

42. Success in one *Siddhásana* alone becoming firmly established, one gets *Unmaní* at once, and the three bonds (*Bandhas*) are accomplished of themselves.

是故只要成就坐式如實成就，一旦證此心寂定境，三鎖印亦自通達。

三鎖印：意指根鎖印、揚升鎖印和收頷鎖印等三鎖印，詳《瑜伽明燈》第三章身印篇第 55、61、70 節經文。

43. There is no *Ásana* like the *Siddhásana* and no *Kumbhaka* like the *Kevala*. There is no *mudrá* like the *Khechari* and no *laya* like the *Náda* (*Anáhata Náda*).

沒有一種體位法堪比成就坐，沒有一種持氣法堪比本然持氣，沒有一種身印法堪比明空身印，也沒一種深定法堪比秘音圓通。

明空身印：詳第三章 32 節。

深定法：意為消融、甚深禪定，心靈消融的狀態。

秘音圓通：是意識在提升到極高境界時聆聽到的神聖音聲。

● 蓮花坐

44. Place the right foot on the left thigh and the left foot on the right thigh, and grasp the toes with the hands crossed over the back.

Press the chin against the chest and gaze on the tip of the nose. This is called the *Padmásana*, the destroyer of the diseases of the *Yogís*.

將右足置於左腿根處，左足同樣置於右腿根處，雙手背後交叉握緊雙腳拇指；下巴抵向胸口，繫意鼻端，此名蓮花坐式，能除習者各種疾病。

蓮花坐：式名取蓮花出淤泥而不染之意。依本節所述，實為體式中的「鎖蓮式」，現今流行之蓮花坐式如下一節所述。

下巴抵向胸口：一般不會觸及胸骨上窩，下巴與鎖骨間約莫會有三指的距離。

45. Place the feet on the thighs, with the soles upwards, and place the hands on the thighs, with the palms upwards.

將雙腳分置於對側腿根處，腳心朝上，雙手掌心朝上交疊於兩腿中間。

46. Gaze on the tip of the nose, keeping the tongue pressed against the root of the teeth of the upper jaw, and the chin against the chest, and raise the air up slowly,*i.e.*, pull the *pavana* gently upwards.

繫意鼻端，舌抵上顎，下巴微扣胸，徐徐地提引生命氣向上。

47. This is called the *Padmásana*, the destroyer of all diseases. It is difficult of attainment by everybody, but can be learnt by intelligent people in this world.

此式名蓮花坐，能破一切疾恙；然非人人可由此式成就，唯世間慧智者能得其要。

48. Having kept both the hands together in the lap, performing the *Padmásana* firmly, keeping the chin Fixed to the chest and contemplating on Him in the mind, by drawing the *apána-váyú* up (performing *Múla Bandha*) and pushing down the air after inhaling it, joining thus the *práṇa* and *apána* in the navel, one gets the highest intelligence by awakening the *śakti* (*kundaliní*) thus.

以蓮花坐姿坐定，雙手掌心向上交疊，下巴觸胸，心入禪觀；藉根鎖印反覆提引下行氣向上，復令命根氣下行，使兩氣結合於臍；如是藉甦醒靈能之助，習者得獲本覺。

心入禪觀：令心關注坐禪時的集中標的，即自性真我（*Átman*）。

提引下行氣向上，後令命根氣下行：天地間激活萬有的生命能，在人身中分為五種形式，分別是命根氣（亦名持命氣）、下行氣、平行氣、上行氣（亦名通首氣）和遍行氣。在印度阿育吠陀醫學中，分析上述五氣的作用位置是：命根氣——頭、面（包括耳鼻舌）、胸（含心臟）；下行氣——大腸與骨盆內的臟器；平行氣——胃、腸、臍，整個腸道及活動；上行氣，亦稱通首氣——咽、肺、臍，向上至頸與鼻，向下至臍；遍行氣——心臟，行佈全身。瑜伽八支功法中的生命能控制法即呼吸調息法，包含了吸氣、呼氣和停息三方面。印度聖典《薄伽梵歌》第四章 29 節也提到「有行人鍛煉生命能調息，控制精微的出入息；以命根氣獻予下行氣，復將下行氣獻予命根氣。」

本覺：本覺意指本自俱有之覺照作用。

NḄ.—When *Apána Váyú* is drawn gently up and after filling in the lungs with the air from outside, the *práṇa* is forced down by and by so as to join both of them in the navel, they both enter then the *Kundaliní* and, reaching the *Brahmarandhra* (the great hole), they make the mind calm. Then the mind can contemplate on the nature of the *átmana* and can enjoy the highest bliss.

英註：當下行氣徐徐上提，待外氣填入肺腑後，命根氣如是被推向下而與下行氣會合於臍，然後兩氣與靈能循中脈上達梵穴（*Brahmarandhra*），內心由是歸於平靜。而能專心思惟自性真我，得享無上之大樂。

49. The *Yogí* who, sitting with *Padmásana*, can control breathing, there

is no doubt, is free from bondage.

依此蓮花坐姿修習之瑜伽行人，如是控制出入息，毫無疑問，可從束縛中解脫。

出入息：即透過鼻孔所進行的吸氣與呼氣。

● 獅子坐

50. Press the heels on both sides of the seam of Perineum, in such a way that the left heel touches the right side and the right heel touches the left side of it.

跪坐，兩腳足踵交叉抵於會陰兩側前陰之下；左踵近右側坐骨，右踵近左側坐骨。

51. Place the hands on the thighs, with stretched fingers, and keeping the mouth open and the mind collected, gaze on the tip of the nose.

雙手覆於膝上，掌指撐開；開頷張口，集中心神，目視鼻端。

52. This is *Siṃhásana*, held sacred by the best of *Yogís*. This excellent *Ásana* effects the completion of the three *Bandhas* (The *Múlabandha, Kanṭha* or *Jálandhar Bandha* and *Uḍḍiyána Bandha*).

此獅子坐式頗受上品瑜伽士們推崇，是對練習三鎖印極有助益的上品體式。

獅子坐：本式模擬獅子吼，開頷張口時吸氣，吐氣時意注眉心，像獅子般發出長「啊」聲。獅子式生理上刺激頭頸舌喉，具恢復面部、頸部肌肉彈性及防治喉嚨不適；心理上藉吐氣開聲，亦可增加自信心。

● 普賢坐

53. Place the heels on either side of the seam of the Perineum, keeping the left heel on the left side and the right one on the right side,

兩腳互抵於會陰兩側前陰之下，左踝置左側，右踝置右側。

54. hold the feet firmly joined to one another with both the hands. This *Bhadrásana* is the destroyer of all the diseases. The expert *Yogís* call this *Gorakśa ásana*.

以雙手緊握雙腳前側使腳掌相互貼牢，此普賢坐能除一切疾恙，已成就之瑜伽師稱此式為葛拉克夏式。

普賢坐：梵語 *Bhadrá*，意思仁、賢、善、普賢，故譯為普賢坐。

葛拉克夏式：以其姿像牧牛人遠觀牛群的坐姿，故亦名牧牛式；亦有說葛拉克夏尊者常習此式，故以之為名。

譯註：本節末句英譯原置於第 55 節，因原梵文經句是在第 54 節，故循原梵文經句置回本節。

55. Thus an advanced *Yogí* who gets rid of fatigue by the practice of various *ásanas* and *bandhas*, should practise *nádisuddhi, múdrás* etc. such *kriyás* which are related with *prána*.

已藉各種體式擺脫疲勞之進階行人，應續進行身印法、脈淨化法等練習，這些鍛煉都和生命能相關。

身印法：具有內在理念的特定姿勢，作用兼及於神經和肌肉，也翻成手印。

脈淨化法：清除身內經脈之法，這是訓練習生命能控制法前的必要先修，詳述於第二章。

56. The *Nádis* should be cleansed of their impurities by performing the *mudrás*, etc., *Ásanas, Kumbhakas,* various curious *mudrá*, and concentration on the *nádá*(inner sound).

依次通過體位法、持氣法、各種身印法以及諦聽秘音法等練習，經脈得淨除其雜染。

諦聽秘音：摒除外緣，靜心息慮，凝心細聞內在音聲的修煉。

譯按：根據《哈達瑜伽明燈》之權威註解《慧光》（*Jyotsna*）譯文，本節旨在述明哈達瑜伽之修習依次應是：體位法、各種持氣法與身印法（包括鎖印法），然後是諦聽秘音。

進階的修持

57. By regular and close attention to *Náda* (*anáhata náda*) in *Haṭha Yoga*, a *Brahmachari*, sparing in diet, unattached to objects of enjoyment, and devoted to *Yoga*, gains success, no doubt, within a year.

飲食有度，捨離欲樂，一心趣向瑜伽之梵行闍黎，無疑地於一年之內必有所成就。

趣向瑜伽：內心歸依或趣向瑜伽者。

梵行闍黎：志向梵行之瑜伽出家師。

譯按：本節經句英譯首句原為 By regular and close attention to *Náda* (*anáhata náda*) in *Haṭha Yoga*（常密切關注哈達瑜伽內在秘音之梵行闍黎），應是為承接上節「諦聽秘音」而寫；然原經句梵文是 *Brahmachárí mitáhárí tyághí yogaparáyanah*（飲食有度，捨離欲樂，一心趣向瑜伽之梵行闍黎），故中譯仍以梵文經句為本。

58. Abstemious feeding is that in which ¾ of hunger is satisfied with food, well cooked with ghee and sweets, and eaten with the offering of it to *Śiva*.

「飲食有度」是指保留胃部四分之一的空間，取用甘味與佐以醍醐之熟食，食時當先獻禱希瓦而後食。

飲食有度：屬外在規範之一，請見本章第 16b。

飲食的選擇

59. Bitter, sour, saltish, hot, green vegetables, fermented, oily, mixed with til seed, rape seed, intoxicating liquors, fish, meat, curds, *chhaasa* pulses, plums, oil-cake, asafœtida (*hínga*), garlic, onion, etc., should not be eaten.

苦、酸、辛、鹹及燥熱的食物，生菜、發酸的食物、油膩的食物、混雜的胡麻與芥子、含酒精飲料、魚鮮；各種肉品、凝乳、馬豆、槳果、油粕、阿魏、蔥蒜等食物不宜取食。

譯按：酒精傷肝，折損人的腦力與活力！洋蔥切開能吸附病氣，熟食可將體內病灶引發至表，宜藥用但不宜選做食物；大蒜阻礙淋巴作用，常食易罹患皮膚疾病。

60. Food heated again, dry, having too much salt, sour, minor grains, and vegetables that cause burning sensation, should not be eaten.
亦當避免一再加熱的食物，過鹹、過酸、過粗以及燒焦的食物。

61. As said by *Gorakṣa*, one should keep aloof from the society of the evil-minded, fire, women, travelling, early morning bath, fasting, and all kinds of bodily exertion.
葛拉克夏尊者曾說：「當遠損友、火、女人和長途旅行，凌晨沐浴、強制性禁食以及苦力勞動等亦不宜。」
女人：飲食男女，非關性別，只是在十九世紀以前，習瑜伽者畢竟以男性為主，故用詞難免本位。

62. Wheat, rice, barley, *shástik* (a kind of rice), good corns, milk, ghee, sugar, butter, sugar candy, honey, dried ginger, *Parwal* (a vegetable) the five vegetables, moong, pure water, these are very beneficial to those who practise *Yoga*.
小麥、稻米、大麥、薩提米、良質玉米，牛奶、醍醐、粗糖、奶油、製糖、蜂蜜，乾薑、胡瓜、五種時蔬、綠豆和淨水等，是對瑜伽行人甚有裨益的食物。
薩提米：印度一種表皮帶紅斑，容易消化、微甜有點黏性的區域性米。
醍醐：印度一種從牛奶提製，能健脾胃的純淨無鹽奶油。
五種時蔬：《葛蘭達本集》第五章20節敘述這五種蔬菜是：新鮮的綠色和黑色蔬菜、節瓜葉、菠菜、水田芥等五種時蔬；因為各地風土不同，選擇當令之悅性蔬菜即可。

63. A *Yogí* should eat tonics (things giving strength), well sweetened, greasy (made with ghee), milk, butter, etc., which may increase

humors of the body, according to his desire.

瑜伽行人可從其意願，取食營養、可口、易嚥食及醍醐、奶品、奶油等能滋養身體之食物。

譯按：飲食與身心健康有著緊密的關連，故宜選擇意識發展較低、刺激性較小以及容易消化的食物。

64. Whether young, old or too old, sick or lean, one who discards laziness, gets success if he practises *Yoga*.

不論青壯、老年、耄年、瘦弱甚至罹病之人，只要能勤習瑜伽不輟，便成就可期。

65. Success comes to him who is engaged in the practice. How can one get success without practice; for by merely reading books on *Yoga*, one can never get success.

成就來自於不懈的修持，不事修習者豈能有所成；僅是記誦瑜伽文本，永難獲致瑜伽成就。

66. Success cannot be attained by adopting a particular dress (*Veṣa*). It cannot be gained by telling tales. Practice alone is the means to success. This is true, there is no doubt.

成就非從身穿之法衣或是清談玄理而來，成就唯從實修而來；此乃真理，真實不虛。

67. *Ásanas* (postures), various *Kumbhakas*, and other divine means, all should be practised in the practice of *Haṭha Yoga*, till the fruit—*Rája Yoga*—is obtained.

各種體位法、持氣法以及其他殊妙哈達瑜伽功法，在未親證勝王瑜伽之果前，皆須持續為之。

第二章

淨化六法與生命能控制法

Shatkarma and Práṇáyáma

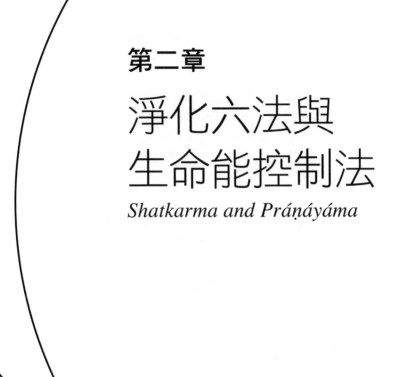

1. Posture becoming established, a *Yogí*, master of himself, eating salutary and moderate food, should practise *Práṇáyáma*, as instructed by his *Guru*.

   瑜伽行者得益於體位法之後，身得控制，飲食有度；即應從師指導，修習生命能控制法。

   生命能控制法：藉由控制呼吸來調控生命能的練習，此練習有助專注與靜坐，而在生命能調息中宜加入生命理念的觀想。

2. Respiration being disturbed, the mind becomes disturbed. By restraining respiration, the *Yogí* gets steadiness of mind. (By this the *Yogí* attains steadiness, hence should thus restrain the inner air.)

   息亂心亦亂，故藉調氣止息，瑜伽行人內心可得平靜（藉此瑜伽行人身心得穩，故應控制內息）。

   息：即生命氣之息，《內經》言「出氣曰呼，入氣曰吸；一呼一吸，謂之一息。」

   調氣止息：藉控制呼吸由粗至細，漸入身心俱寂之境。

   譯按：參考其他版本，本節經句後半英譯缺括弧內之譯文，中譯補入。

3. So long as the (breathing) air stays in the body, it is called life. Death consists in the passing out of the (breathing) air. It is, therefore, necessary to restrain the breath.

   只要一息存身，生命即在，息盡即命亡，故應調控出入息。

4. The breath does not pass through the middle channel (*suṣumná*), owing to the impurities of the *nádís*. How can then success be attained, and how can there be the *unmaní avasthá*.

   經脈不淨，生命氣便無法行入中脈；如是豈能獲得成就？又如何臻入心寂定境？

   中脈：位於脊椎中最重要的經脈，靈能循此融入頭頂千瓣蓮花輪之時，即證大圓滿。

心寂定境：一種內心空明寂靜的瑜伽定境。

5. When the whole system of *nádís* which is full of impurities, is cleaned, then the *Yogí* becomes able to control the *Práṇa*.

唯有不淨之經脈及脈輪全得淨化，行者才能控制生命能。

脈輪：瑜伽生理學認為人身擁有七個主要的能量中心或脈叢結，這七個中心幾都座落在位於脊髓內的三脈交點上；這七個從尾椎向上依序是海底輪（又稱根持輪）、生殖輪、臍輪、心輪、喉輪、眉心輪和頂輪。

生命能：維繫著生命及造化的生命能，遍存於小宇宙、大宇宙以及萬有之中。

6. Therefore, *Práṇáyáma* should be performed daily with *sáttvika buddhi* (intellect free from raja and tama or activity and sloth), in order to drive out the impurities of the *suṣumná*.

故當以悅性覺知每日習練生命能控制功法，中脈即得由濁轉趨清淨。

悅性覺知：不受變性和惰性或說不受心念起伏或耽著的靈明狀態。

譯按：本節末句英文直譯應是「為逐除中脈之不淨」，中譯依原句梵文「*yathá suṣhumṇá-náḍísthá maláḥ śuddhiṃ prayánti cha*」之義譯為「中脈即得由濁轉趨清淨」。

左右脈淨化呼吸法

7. Sitting in the *Padmásana* posture the *Yogí* should fill in the air through the left nostril (closing the right one); and, keeping it confined according to one's ability, it should be expelled slowly through the *súrya* (right nostril).

行人以蓮花坐姿安坐，由月脈口（閉右鼻孔）吸入生命能後，隨己身能力盡可能的持氣，然後由日脈口緩緩地呼出氣息。

月脈：原經句梵文 *chandra nádí*，又名 *Idá*，色淡藍，交纏於中脈的兩條經脈之一，當心靈涉及心理導向靈性活動時，即趨活躍。因月脈終於左鼻孔，故也稱左脈。由月脈口吸氣，意即由左鼻孔吸氣。

日脈：原經句梵文 *súrya nádí*，又名 *Pingalá*，色泥黃，交纏於中脈的兩條經脈之一，當心靈涉入物質或身體活動時，即轉活躍。因日脈終於右鼻孔，故也稱右脈。由日脈口吸氣，意即由右鼻孔吸氣。

譯按：練習淨化呼吸法時，以右手拇指控制右鼻孔出入息，以無名指、小指控制左鼻孔出入息，原則上不用左手。

8. Then, drawing in the air through the *súrya* (right nostril) slowly, the belly should be filled, and after performing *Kumbhaka* as before, it should be expelled slowly through the *chandra* (left nostril).

續由日脈口（右鼻孔）徐徐吸入生命能，滿息後如前述盡量持氣，再由月脈口（左鼻孔）緩緩地呼出。

持氣：瑜伽鍛煉將呼吸分成吸氣、持氣與呼氣，也就是入息、停息與出息。持氣意指將氣息持於身內，亦即吸氣與呼氣之間的狀態。

9. Inhaling thus through the one, through which it was expelled, and having restrained it there, till possible, it should be exhaled through the other, slowly and not forcibly.

復由呼氣之鼻孔徐徐吸氣，盡力持氣於內，再由另一鼻孔自然平緩地呼出。

10. If the air be inhaled through the left nostril, it should be expelled again through the other, and filling it through the right nostril, confining it there, it should be expelled through the left nostril. By practising in this way, through the right and the left nostrils alternately, the whole of the collection of the *nádís* of the *yamís* (practisers) becomes clean, *i.e.*, free from impurities, after 3 months

and over.

若是由左鼻孔吸入氣息，持氣後便由右鼻孔呼出氣息；續由右鼻孔吸氣後，盡力持氣，再由左鼻孔呼氣。規律地行此左、右脈交替呼吸法之行人，所有經脈能於三個月後淨化。

11. *Kumbhakas* should be performed gradually 4 times during day and night, *i.e.*, (morning, noon, evening and midnight), till the number of *Kumbhakas* for one time is 80 and for day and night together it is 320.

持氣功法宜在清晨、中午及黃昏、午夜四時練習，從四息開始直到漸增至八十息，如是一日夜總計三百二十息。

12. In the beginning there is perspiration, in the middle stage there is quivering, and in the last or the 3rd stage one obtains steadiness; and then the breath should be made steady or motionless.

在修習初期身體會發汗，修習中期會感到全身震顫，修習末期身止不動，氣息得到控制。

13. The perspiration exuding from exertion of practice should be rubbed into the body (and not wiped), as by so doing the body becomes strong.

將修習時所出的汗水抹回身上（非擦拭），可使身體堅實穩健。

譯按：南宋和尚濟癲搓垢可為藥丸，是故汗水益身也不無可能，需注意的是並非任何汗水都能益身。

14. During the first stage of practice the food consisting of milk and ghee is wholesome. When the practice becomes established, no such restriction is necessary.

修習初期須攝取含有牛奶和醍醐的飲食，當練習趨穩，便不需受此限制。

15. Just as lions, elephants and tigers are controlled by and by, so the breath is controlled by slow degrees, otherwise (*i.e.*, by being hasty or using too much force) it kills the practiser himself.

如同獅、象、虎等需逐步地馴服，生命氣亦應依法漸次調伏，否則（如草率練習或用力太過）行人可能自傷其身。

16. When *Práṇáyáma*, etc., are performed properly, they eradicate all diseases; but an improper practice generates diseases.

適當地修習生命能控制等法，行人可漸除一切疾恙；然若修習不當，則將產生諸多疾病。

17. Hiccough, asthma, cough, pain in the head, the ears, and the eyes; these and other various kinds of diseases are generated by the disturbance of the breath.

不當的修習，造成氣息紊亂，導致打嗝、氣喘、咳嗽、頭疼、眼耳不適以及其它諸疾。

18. The air should be expelled with proper tact and should be filled in skillfully; and when it has been kept confined properly it brings success.

如法地呼吸，如法地吸氣，如法地持氣，即能有所成就。

NḄ.—The above caution is necessary to warn the aspirants against omitting any instruction; and, in their zeal to gain success or *siddhis* early, to begin the practice, either by using too much force in filling in, confining and expelling the air, or by omitting any instructions, it may cause unnecessary pressure on their ears, eyes,etc,, and cause pain. Every word in the instructions is full of meaning and is necessarily used in the *slokas*, and should be followed very carefully and with due attention. Thus there will be nothing to fear whatsoever. We are inhaling and exhaling the air throughout our lives without any sort of danger, and *Práṇáyáma* being only a regular form of it, there should be no cause to fear.

英譯註：上述警告有其必要，以提醒瑜伽行人不要忽視任何指示；尤其是初期那種想要有所成就的熱心，使得習者在開始練習時，無論是過度的吸氣、持氣或是呼氣，還是任何指示被忽略了，都可能對習者的耳膜、眼睛等造成不必要的壓力，甚至引起疼痛。經句中的每一字詞都充滿了意義，應該非常謹慎小心地遵循。若是如此，就沒有什麼可擔心的。我們無時不在呼吸而無任何危險，而生命能控制只是將之規律化，應該沒有理由擔心。

19. When the *nádís* become free from impurities, and there appear the outward signs of success, such as lean body and glowing colour, then one should feel certain of success.

經脈淨化以後，或有徵兆顯現於習者之身；如身體輕捷，面有光采等，顯示修習有成。

20. By removing the impurities, the air can be restrained, according to one's wish and the appetite is increased, the divine sound is awakened, and the body becomes healthy.

濁脈清淨後，行人能隨意地控制氣息，身內胃火強旺；內在秘音聲現，身體更趨健康。

淨化六法

21. If there be excess of fat or phlegm in the body, the six kinds of *kriyás* (duties) should be performed first. But others, not suffering from the excess of these, should not perform them.

體內脂肪或黏液過多者，應於調息前先修習淨化六法；然若身內三種要能已處於平衡狀態，則不用練習。

黏液過多：黏液過多，造成痰濕體質，身易肥胖。

三種要能：印度傳統醫學認為人身的實質係由地、水、火、風四大組成；此四大依其在人體內比例的多寡，可分為水能、火能和風能三種要能。水能對應黏液素，位於身體上部，類如身體的基本成分、養分和水液；火能對應膽汁素，位於身體中部，將「黏液素」化為熱能；風能對應體風素，位於身體下部，將「膽汁素」所化熱能轉為身體功能。健康的關鍵即在保持體內三種要能之平衡。

22. The six kinds of duties are: *Dhauti*, *Basti*, *Neti*, *Trátaka*, *Nauti* and *Kapála Bháti*. These are called the six actions.

六種淨化法分別是：淨胃法、淨腸法、淨鼻法、淨目法、滾腹法與淨腦法。

23. These six kinds of actions which cleanse the body should be kept secret. They produce extraordinary attributes and are performed with earnestness by the best of *Yogís*.

是法具有調整體質之宏效，深受上品瑜伽行者推崇，當善護此淨化六法之密意。

● 淨胃法

24. A strip of cloth, about four fingers wide and 15 cubits long, is pushed in (swallowed), when moist with warm water, through the passage shown by the *Guru*, and is taken out again. This is called *Dhauti Karma*.

取一寬四指，十五腕尺長的細淨紗布，以溫水潤濕後，從師示範緩緩地嚥下；稍後再慢慢地拉出，此為淨胃法。

四指寬，十五腕尺長：四指寬五腕尺長約是 7.5 分 x 6.5 公尺，印度比哈瑜伽學校的建議是從 2.5 公分 x 3 公尺的尺寸開始，隨熟悉度漸增至 7.5 分 x 6.5 公尺。

NḄ.—The strip should be moistened with a little warm water, and the end should be held with the teeth. It is swallowed slowly, little by little; thus, first day 1 cubit, 2nd day 2 cubits, 3rd day 3 cubits, and so on. After swallowing it the stomach should be given a good, round motion from left to right, and then it should be taken out slowly and gently.

英譯註：紗布使用時應以溫水沾濕，尾端需以牙齒咬住。吞嚥速度宜緩，一點一點地嚥下；第一天吞嚥一掌長，次日增加為兩掌長，第三天三掌長，如是逐日增加。紗布吞入腹內之後，小心的從左至右做腹部滾圓運動，然後緩慢小心地將紗布拉出來。

25. There is no doubt, that cough, asthma, enlargement of the spleen, leprosy, and 20 kinds of diseases born of phlegm, disappear by the practice of *Dhauti Karma*.

咳嗽、氣喘、脾病、痲瘋，以及其它二十種由水能失調所引起的疾病，都可通過練習胃道清潔法而消除，毋庸懷疑。

水能失調：印度生命科學將人的體質分成水、火、風三型。水能型是五大元素中水和土的組合，梵文 *kapha*，水能對應體內黏液素，水能失調常見的疾病有——肥胖、水腫、消化不良、缺乏食欲、體內痰多、氣喘、糖尿病、膽固醇過高等等，呼吸道和脾胃方面的疾病。

● 淨腸法

26. Squatting in navel-deep water, and introducing a six inches long, smooth piece of ½ an inch diameter pipe, open at both ends, half inside the anus; it (anus) should he drawn up (contracted) and then expelled. This washing is called the *Basti Karma*.

蹲於水深及臍的水中，取一表面潤滑之小竹管插入穀道，再收放張弛穀道；此為淨腸法。

穀道：體內五穀殘渣泄出之通道，泛指直腸至肛門區域。

收放張弛穀道：蹲坐時重心置於腳掌前緣，臀輕抵足踵。小竹管長約 15 公分直徑 1.25 公分，一半插入穀道；收放張弛穀道（括約肌）是為將水吸入及排出，以達清洗之效。若能使水在腸內攪動，然後排出，效果更好。

譯按：原梵文經句無竹管之尺寸，故中譯從原經句；英譯增入之尺寸於中譯註中說明。現代多改用草藥或油灌腸或咖啡灌腸來淨腸。

27. By practising this *Basti Karma*, colic, enlarged spleen, and dropsy, arising from the disorders of *váta* (air), *pitta* (bile) and *kapha* (phlegm), are all cured.

練習淨腸法可防治腹、脾腫大以及其他因風能、火能、水能等三要能失調所引發的種種疾病。

28. By practising *Basti* with water, the *Dhátás*, the *Indriyas* and the mind become calm. It gives glow and tone to the body and increases the appetite. All the disorders disappear.

適當地練習此水灌腸法，可淨化七種體組織、知作根與內在器官；能滋補身體、煥發容光並增進消化力。由是消除所有體液的失調。

七種體組織：印度醫學認為五大構成的身體包含七種組織：血漿、血液、筋肉、脂肪、骨骼、骨髓和神經、腎精。

知作根：知作根即身體之五知根和五作根的合稱，五知根（感覺器官）——眼、耳、鼻、舌、身；五作根（運動器官）——舌、手、足、大小便道。

● 淨鼻法

29. A cord made of threads and about six inches long, should be passed through the passage of the nose and the end taken out in the mouth. This is called by adepts the *Neti Karma*.

準備一條一掌尺長的細繩，從一鼻孔穿入，由口中拉出來，此為成就者所謂之淨鼻法。

細繩：這是指清潔鼻腔專用的鼻繩，原梵文經句 *vitasti* 字義是一掌尺，合十二指長（約是 20 到 25 公分），實際可更長些。細繩不可有結，使用時需先潤濕。工業不發達時代是使用上蠟的棉繩，今則多使用專用之橡皮繩，粗 3 公厘長 42 公分，更好用。穿入時，先將一端伸入鼻孔，至細繩進入喉嚨時，再用手從口拉出細繩，穿入後可輕柔的前後拉動幾下，增加清潔效果。

譯按：現在採行較多的方式是用鼻壺或以手捧水灌鼻（頭微仰，引水入鼻腔再由口吐出）的方式淨鼻。

30. The *Neti* is the cleaner of the brain and giver of divine sight. It soon destroys all the diseases of the cervical and scapular regions.

淨鼻法可淨化顱腔，有助開啟靈視能力，還能消除肩頸一帶的所有疾患。

● 淨目法

31. Being calm, one should gaze steadily at a small mark, till eyes are filled with tears. This is called *Trataka* by *ácháryas*.

靜心凝神，目不稍瞬地將視線凝注於一小點，直到淚水泛出。此即諸阿闍黎所說的淨目法。

阿闍黎：靈性教師，又名軌範師；以身為楷模教導他人的導師。

32. *Trátaka* destroys the eye diseases and removes sloth, etc. It should be kept secret very carefully, like a box of jewellery.

淨目法可防治眼疾和消除懶散，應慎如藏寶篋般善護其秘。

● 滾腹法

33. Sitting on the toes with heels raised above the ground, and the palms resting on the ground, and in this bent posture the belly is moved forcibly from left to right just, as in vomiting. This is called by adepts the *Nauli Karma*.

（踵趾高於地面盤坐，兩掌鬆擺地上）上身前傾，鼓出肚腹將之由左至右滾動，如作嘔般，成就者名此為滾腹法。

踵趾高於地面盤坐：括號內文字為英譯者所加之輔助說明，未出現於梵文經句；依此說明，應是取蓮花坐式，無法蓮花坐者，方便坐亦可。另一通行的姿勢是立姿曲膝半蹲，微傾上身，雙手撐置膝上大腿，放鬆肚腹後進行滾腹法。

雙肩前傾：雙肩前傾，是為放鬆肚腹以方便滾腹法之進行。

如作嘔般：查本節梵文經句亦無此句，是為英譯所加；用意在為使讀者在進行滾腹法時所感覺到的肚腹狀況，有如作嘔時肚腹急速向內收縮一般。另有版本形容進行滾腹時有如漩渦般左右旋轉。

34. It removes dyspepsia, increases appetite and digestion, and is like the goddess of creation, and causes happiness. It dries up all the disorders. This *Nauli* is an excellent exercise in *Haṭha Yoga*.

此法改善消化不良，能增強食欲和消化力，是幸福的泉源，調理一切要能失衡，是哈達瑜伽中重要的一項練習。

幸福的泉源：英譯於此句之前有加一形容詞，英譯全句是-如同創造女神，是幸福的泉源。

調理一切要能失衡：印度阿育吠陀醫學認為疾病來自於身內水能、風能、火能等三要能失去平衡所致。

● 淨腦法

35. When inhalation and exhalation are performed very quickly, like a pair of bellows of a blacksmith, it dries up all the disorders from the excess of phlegm, and is known as *Kapála Bháti*.

有如鐵匠抽送風箱般地快速呼氣和吸氣，是為淨腦法，功能消解所有因水能（黏液）引起的失衡。

淨腦法：梵文直譯是閃亮頭顱淨化法，由於此法能增加頭顱清明之光，故亦有「頭顱清明法」之譯。習之可控制食慾、欲望以及強化意志力。

36. When *Práṇáyáma* is performed after getting rid of obesity born of the defects phlegm, by the performance of the six duties, it easily

brings success.

藉由上述六淨化法的鍛煉，可擺脫因黏液過多引起的擁腫，如此再練習生命能控制法，即易帶來成功。

37. Some *ácháryás* (teachers) do not advocate any other practice, being of opinion that all the impurities are dried up by the practice of *Práṇáyáma*.

有些瑜伽闍黎認為單練生命能控制法，即可祛除所有的不淨，故未推崇此六法。

● 清胃法

38. By carrying the *Apána Váyú* up to the throat, the food, etc., in the stomach are vomited. By degrees, the system of *Nádís* (*Śankhiní*) becomes known. This is called in *Haṭha* as *Gaja Karaṇi*.

提引下行氣至喉，令吐胃中物；如是可逐漸明了控制諸脈叢之法，哈達瑜伽名之為清胃法。

脈叢：能量管道的叢集部分，脈輪是其控制點。

譯按：本法非屬淨化六法，而是阿育吠陀中的催吐洗胃法。

生命能控制法

39. *Brahmá*, and other *devas* were always engaged in the exercise of *Práṇáyáma*, and, by means of it, got rid of the fear of death. Therefore, one should practise *práṇáyáma* regularly.

以梵天為首的半人神乃至其他諸神明，為克服對死亡的懼意，亦常修煉生命能控制法，故當勤習此法。

以梵天為首的半人神乃至其他諸神明：具有部分神力的人及三界諸神。

40. So long as the breath is restrained in the body, so long as the mind is undisturbed, and so long as the gaze is fixed between the eyebrows,

there is no fear from Death.

只要一息尚存於身，只要心神不受外擾，只要內視定於眉心，何有懼於死亡。

41. When the system of Nádis becomes clear of the impurities by properly controlling the práṇa, then the air, piercing the entrance of the Suśumṇá, enters it easily.

如法調伏生命能後，諸脈叢由濁轉淨，內息透入中脈之口，順達其中。

意摩尼定

42. Steadiness of mind comes when the air moves freely in the middle. That is the manonmaní condition, which is attained when the mind becomes calm.

當內息順達中脈之後心意寂然安止，這種心靈定境，謂之意摩尼定。

意摩尼定：息入中脈，心作用轉趨安寂的瑜伽定境。

43. To accomplish it, various *Kumbhakas* are performed by those who are expert in the methods; for, by the practice of different *Kumbhakas*, wonderful success is attained.

為達此成就，明其理者修習各種持氣功法；通過如是修習，行人達此勝妙定境。

不同的持氣法

44. *Kumbhakas* are of eight kinds, viz., *Súrya bhedan*, *Ujjáyí*, *Sítkarí*, *Sítalí*, *Bhastriká*, *Bhrámarí*, *Múrchhá*, and *Pláviní*.

持氣法有八種，是為日脈穿透法、勝利持氣法、嘶聲持氣法、清涼持氣法、風箱持氣法、蜂鳴持氣法、微醺持氣法與漂浮持氣法。

譯註：持氣法又稱瓶氣或寶瓶氣修法。

45. At the end of *Púraka*, *Jálandhara bandha* should be performed, and at the end of *Kumbhaka*, and at the beginning of *Rechaka*, *Uddiyána bandha* should be performed.

在吸氣終了時，完成收頷鎖印；在持氣結束開始呼氣之前，完成揚升鎖印。

收頷鎖印：詳見第三章第 70 節。

揚升鎖印：詳見第三章第 55 節。

NḄ.—Púraka is filling in of the air from outside. *Kumbhaka* is the keeping the air confined inside. *Rechaka* is expelling the confined air. The instructions for *Puraka*, *Kumbhaka* and *Rechaka* will be found at their proper place and should he carefully followed.

英譯註：吸入外氣名吸氣（即入息 -*Púraka*），吸氣後保留氣息於內名持氣（即停息 - *Kumbhaka*），吐出體內保留的氣息名呼氣（即出息 - *Rechaka*）。練習吸氣、持氣和呼氣需尋一合宜之場所，小心如法進行。

46. By drawing up from below (*Múla Bandha*) and contracting the throat (*Jálandha Bandha*) and by pulling back the middle of the front portion of the body (*i.e.*, belly), the *Práṇa* goes to the *Brahma Nádí* (*Suṣumná*).

藉迅速提肛（行根鎖印）、下巴抵喉（收頷鎖印）以及吊腹貼背（揚升鎖印）等三鎖印，促使生命能流往梵脈。

三鎖印：此處需三印齊施，意即以根鎖印要領提肛，以收頷鎖印要領收頷，以揚升鎖印要領吊胃之謂。

梵脈：中脈最內裡的中空層。

NḄ.—The middle hole, through the vertebral column, through which the spinal cord passes, is called the *Suṣumná Nádí* of the *Yogís*. The two other sympathetic cords, one on each side of the spinal cord, are called the *Idá* and the *Pingalá Nádís*. These will be described later on.

英譯註：穿過脊柱、穿過脊髓的中空脈管，瑜伽人稱之為中脈；另外兩條交纏於脊髓兩側的經脈，分別是左脈和右脈，這些會在後文說明。

47. By pulling up the *Apána Váyu* and by forcing the *Práṇa Váyu* down the throat, the *Yogí*, liberated from old age, becomes young, as it were 16 years old.

提引下行氣上行，接著力催命根氣自喉下行，如是瑜伽行者不見老態，猶若十六歲之青年。

下行氣：作用在穀道、臍腹之間，主管大小二遺。

命根氣：又名持命氣，作用在臍、喉之間，主管呼與吸。

NḄ.—The seat of the *Práṇa* is the heart; of the *Apána* anus; of the *Samána* the region about the navel; of the *Udána* the throat; while the *Vyána* moves throughout the body.

英譯註：命根氣坐於心，下行氣連結後陰，平行氣在臍輪一帶，上行氣通喉嚨，遍行氣周行全身。

● 日脈穿透法

48. Taking any comfortable posture and performing the *ásana*, the *Yogí* should draw in the air slowly, through the right nostril.

瑜伽行人採取任何安適坐式坐妥，然後通過右鼻徐徐地吸氣。

49. Then it should be confined within, so that it fills from the nails to the tips of the hair, and then let out through the left nostril slowly.

續持氣於身內，直到感覺氣息透達髮根和指尖；然後再由左鼻孔極緩慢的呼氣。

Note.—This is to be done alternately with both the nostrils, drawing in through the one, expelling through the other, and vice versa.

英譯註：此練習藉由左右鼻孔交替呼吸來完成，若由一鼻孔吸氣，即由另一鼻孔呼氣，反之亦然。

50. This excellent *Súrya bhedana* cleanses the forehead (frontal sinuses), destroys the disorders of *Váta*, and removes the worms, and, therefore, it should be performed again and again.

此勝妙日脈穿透法具淨化顱腔（前額竇）、平衡風能失調及祛除身內寄生蟲等效，故宜持續地反覆練習。

● 勝利持氣法

51. Having closed the opening of the Nádí (Larynx), the air should be drawn in such a way that it goes touching from the throat to the chest, and making noise while passing.

微閉唇喉，徐徐吸氣，感覺氣息拂觸過喉咽而入胸，同時發出擦喉的氣音。

擦喉的氣音：意其音類如閉口的嘆息聲或海水的潮聲。

52. It should be restrained, as before, and then let out through *Idá* (the left nostril). This removes *śleṣmá* (phlegm) in the throat and increases the appetite.

繼之如前文所述持氣，然後由左鼻孔呼氣。依此習練，可消除咽喉痰液，並激活體內胃火。

53. It destroys the defects of the *nádís*, dropsy and disorders of Dhátu (humours). Ujjáyí should be performed in all conditions of life, even while walking or sitting.

此持氣法名勝利持氣法，能除脈疾以及體組織的浮腫與失調；此法於日常行住坐臥任何時候均可練習。

勝利持氣法：藉輕壓喉部聲門發出氣摩擦聲，以克服老病取得勝利的呼吸法，又名喉呼吸法。

體組織：古印度生命科學認為人體主要由七種基本組織構成，分別是——血漿、血液、肌肉、脂肪、骨骼、骨髓和神經、腎精。

譯按：「此持氣法名勝利調息法」，原經文有此句 *kárya-mujjáyyákhyaṃ tu kumbhakam*，故等中譯補入。

●嘶聲持氣法

54. *Sítkárí* is performed by drawing in the air through the mouth, keeping the tongue between the lips. The air thus drawn in should not be expelled through the mouth. By practising in this way, one becomes next to the God of Love in beauty.

嘶聲持氣法進行的方式是置舌於兩唇之間，由口吸入外氣，滿息後由鼻呼氣。依此法練習，習者有若愛神。

嘶聲持氣法：因吸氣時發出類似「嘶」的聲而得名；文述置舌於兩唇之間，今較常行的方式是闔齒張唇，舌輕置於口腔內進行吸氣。做完後通常接著進行收頷鎖印，然後結束。

有若愛神：梵文原意是愛神第二，意思是印度神話故事中的愛神雖無由取代，但可以有如愛神一樣。

55. He is regarded adorable by the *Yoginís* and becomes the destroyer of the cycle of creation, He is not afflicted with hunger, thirst, sleep or lassitude.

習之有成者，不生饑、渴、睡意或懈怠，能行造作與毀壞，於明妃圈中備受欽敬。

習之有成者：此句英譯無，為中譯所加，以聯結上節經句。

能行造作與毀壞：表示成就者亦可引用意識的創造力與造化勢能的毀滅力來工作。

明妃：意指女性瑜伽行者，亦是宇宙造化力的化身。印度密宗有六十四位明妃代表著密宗六十四法以及六十四種瑜伽成就。

56. The *Sattva* of his body becomes free from all the disturbances. In truth, he becomes the lord of the *Yogís* in this world.

緣其身之悅性特質，得不受一切憂惱所苦；事實上，彼將成為世間瑜伽士之最勝者。

● 清涼持氣法

57. As in the above (*Sítkári*), the tongue to be protruded a little out of the lips, when the air is drawn in. It is kept confined, as before, and then expelled slowly through the nostrils.

如上述持氣，之法，當吸入外氣時，使經過略伸出唇外的舌頭；如前述持氣，然後徐緩地自鼻孔呼出氣息。

略伸出唇外的舌頭：伸出唇外的舌頭自兩側內捲成管狀，由管口吸入氣息；不能捲舌者，由舌面吸入氣息。

譯按：本節經文主要在說明—由舌頭吸氣，再依前述說明持氣，然後由鼻呼出氣息。清涼持氣法吸氣時不刻意發聲。

58. This *Śítalí Ḳumbhiká* cures colic, (enlarged) spleen, fever, disorders of bile, hunger, thirst, and counteracts poisons.

此清涼持氣法有助療治腹、脾腫脹以及身熱、饑、渴與膽汁失調等疾，並可中和體內毒素。

清涼持氣法：現今習法為將舌伸於唇外，捲舌如吸管，令氣息自捲孔吸入；此調息能使身覺清新。做完後亦可接著進行收頷鎖印，然後結束。

● 風箱調息法

59. The *Padma Ásana* consists in crossing the feet and placing them on both the thighs; it is the destroyer of all sins.

兩足交叉置於對側大腿之上，是為蓮花坐，此坐式能除一切罪愆。

60. Binding the *Padma-Ásana* and keeping the body straight, closing the mouth carefully, let the air be expelled through the nose.

依蓮花坐式要領坐好，保持頸腹中正，口唇輕闔，由鼻子呼出氣息。

譯按：由鼻子呼出氣息時需深有力，以達排毒及增強免疫力之效。

61. It should be filled up to the lotus of the heart, by drawing it in with force, making noise and touching the throat, the chest and the head.

然後強力吸氣透入心中蓮輪，發出吸氣聲並使之透達喉嚨、胸腑以及顱骨。

心中蓮輪：意即胸腑、心肺、心輪一帶。

62. It should be expelled again and filled again and again as before, just as a pair of bellows of the blacksmith is worked.

如是依前述方法反覆吐納，猶如鐵匠抽送風箱一般。

63. In the same way, the air of the body should be moved intelligently, filling it through *Súrya* when fatigue is experienced.

依此法，有意識地覺知體內生命氣息的流動；若身感疲累，可改以右鼻孔吸氣。

64. When that the abdomen is completely filled with air quickly, then it should be kept confined without using the middle and index fingers.

〔用無名指按住左鼻孔，以右鼻孔〕快速吸氣充滿胸腹；然後以中指和食指以外的手指按住鼻孔閉氣。

食指和中指以外的指頭：意思是只使用右手拇指和無名指及小指按住鼻子兩側，不過現代對中指的限制沒那麼嚴。

譯按：原梵文經句詞簡，〔〕內文字為中譯加入。英譯詞係按梵文原意修訂。

65. Having confined it properly, it should be expelled through the *Idá* (left nostril). This destroys *Váta*, *pitta* (bile) and phlegm and increases the digestive power (the gastric fire).

在適當地持氣之後，續由左脈鼻孔呼氣；如是可消除因風能、火能、水能失衡所引起的諸病，並增加脾胃的消化之火。

66. It quickly awakens the *Kuṇḍaliní*, purifies the system, gives pleasure, and is beneficial. It destroys phlegm and the impurities

accumulated at the entrance of the Brahma *Nádí*.

風箱調息法能快速地喚醒靈能，具淨脈、開心及利益身體之效；且能清除痰濕及梵脈入口處之不淨。

67. This *Bhastriká* should be performed plentifully, for it breaks the three knots.

此法可以打開中脈上的三個結縛，故行者當善加習練此風箱調息法。

三個結縛：中脈上阻礙靈能軍荼利上升的三大結縛是——位於下腹的梵結，位於喉胸的維世努結和位於眉心輪的魯德羅結。此三結的目的是將心靈綑綁在物質、心理與靈性三個領域，以阻礙生命能上行。打開這些結無法一蹴可即。當命根氣與下行氣結合，喚起靈能，可打開梵結；第二個結縛需藉生命能行入心輪之力，甚至需要好幾世的時間；直到打開第三個結縛，生命能才能從中脈通達頂輪，得大圓滿。又結縛位置，亦有梵結在眉心輪，魯德羅結在下腹尾之主張。

● 蜂鳴調息法

68. By filling the air with force, making noise like *Bhringi* (wasp), and expelling it slowly, making noise in the same way; this practice causes a sort of ecstacy in the minds of *Yogíndras*.

快速地吸氣，並發出類似雄黑蜂的聲音；繼之緩緩呼氣，發出類似雌黑蜂的聲音。如是練習，得其法要之行者心中將浮起深邃的喜悅。

譯按：現在常行的蜂鳴持氣法是用拇指封耳，食指輕貼眉眼間封眼，中指抵於鼻翼處，無名指貼於唇上方，小指置於唇下方；吸氣時不發聲，於呼氣時輕輕發出如蜂鳴般的聲音。也有僅用食指塞耳發蜂鳴聲之簡易行法。

● 微醺持氣法

69. Closing the passages with *Jálandhar Bandha* firmly at the end of *Púraka*, and expelling the air slowly, is called *Múrchhá*, from its causing the mind to swoon and giving comfort.

吸氣終了以及確實完成收頷鎖印後，徐徐地吐出肺腔之氣；此法名微醺持氣法，蓋能使心生醺茫，帶來愉悅感之故。

醺然持氣法：譯名取其練習後的內在感受有如微醺，故有此名。

● 漂浮調息法

70. When the belly is filled with air and the inside of the body is filled to its utmost with air, the body floats on the deepest water, like the leaf of a lotus.

服飲外氣直至胸腹飽滿達極限，行人於深水中亦能如蓮葉般輕鬆漂浮。

漂浮持氣法：此是不常見的瑜伽食氣法，實際上食氣的時辰、方式和禁忌都應有所講究，故應從師授，不宜自行冒然練習。

71. Considering *Púraka* (Filling), *Rechaka* (expelling) and *Kumbhaka* (confining), *Práṇáyáma* is of three kinds, but considering it accompanied by *Púraka* and *Rechaka*, and without these, it is of two kinds only, *i.e.*, *Sahita* (with) and *Kevala* (alone).

有說生命能控制法分三種息相：吸氣、呼氣和持氣；(然因呼與吸不可分，若不計呼吸之不同)，持氣法只有兩種分別，即意隨持氣和本然持氣。

意隨持氣：以心意控制來進行的持氣修習。

本然持氣：氣息循環自發，勿需意使；出入息若有似無，綿綿相續。

譯按：本節經句中間括弧內的文字係英譯所加，為原梵文經句所無。

72. Exercise in *Sahita* should be continued till success in *Kevala* is gained. This latter is simply confining the air with ease, without *Rechaka* and *Púraka*.

直至成就本然持氣，都應繼續修習意隨持氣；當行人練至出入息似有若無之時，即能持氣無礙。

73. In the practice of Kevala Prá áyáma when it can be performed successfully without Rechaka and Púraka, then it is called Kevala Kumbhaka.

待行人習此本然調息法臻至無有出入息之相，即稱之為本然持氣成就。

74. There is nothing in the three worlds which may be difficult to obtain for him who is able to keep the air confined according to pleasure, by means of *Kevala Kumbhaka*.

成就此法者透過本然持氣，能隨意地持氣懸息，在三界中無有不可企及之事。

三界：意指醒、夢、眠或現在、過去、未來或意識、潛意識、無意識（致因心靈層）等三界。

75. He obtains the position of *Rája Yoga* undoubtedly. *Kuṇḍaliní* awakens by *Kumbhaka*, and by its awakening, *Suṣumná* becomes free from impurities.

藉持氣之法當能趣入勝王瑜伽無疑，亦可藉之喚醒身內靈能，透過甦醒的靈能，中脈轉淨，哈達瑜伽功成。

哈達瑜伽功成：此句英譯漏譯。瑜伽認定思想波動受呼吸的影響很深，所以對呼吸的控制很重要。1990 年密乘瑜伽上師雪莉．雪莉．阿南達慕提在一場主題為〈達到極至的修持法門〉的演講中提及「……最後當呼吸和思想波流合一時，此一階段稱為哈達瑜伽三摩地。」是故呼吸控制是瑜伽修法裡的重點鍛煉。

76. No success in *Rája Yoga* without *Haṭha Yoga*, and no success in *Haṭha Yoga* without *Rája Yoga*. One should, therefore, practise both of these well, till complete success is gained.

沒有哈達瑜伽，勝王瑜伽無法有成；沒有勝王瑜伽，哈達瑜伽亦無法有成；是故兩者宜當雙修，直至成就圓滿。

77. On the completion of *Kumbhaka*, the mind should be given rest. By practising in this way one is raised to the position of (succeeds in getting) *Rája Yoga*.

持氣法圓成後，心行轉寂；循此法要修習，行人可通達勝王瑜伽之境。

78. When the body becomes lean, the face glows with delight, *Anáhatanáda* manifests, and eyes are clear, body is healthy, *bindu* under control, and appetite increases, then one should know that the *Nádís* are purified and success in *Haṭha Yoga* is approaching.

體形清癯、容顏光悅、密音明了、目光清澈、身體健康、明點調伏、胃火強盛、脈道純淨；以上皆是成就哈達瑜伽的表徵。

明點：明點在瑜伽中，被認為是生命能的凝聚，是一種生命力的精華。密續認為明點類分為四，物質明點即精液、氣明點、咒明點與智慧明點。其中物質明點屬世俗明點，是維持生命、健康、思維等等的基礎；餘為勝義明點，需於脈淨、心淨後方生，而精細的明點皆都是自性光明的反映。

第三章

身印與鎖印

Mudrás and Bandhás

1. As the chief of the snakes is the support of the earth with all the mountains and forests on it, so all the *Tantras* (*Yoga* practices) rest on the *Kuṇḍaliní*. (The Vertebral column.)

   如同龍王是大地與山林的支持者，靈能軍荼利亦如是支持著一切瑜伽行法。

   瑜伽行法：梵文 *yogatantránám*，藉瑜伽以達脫黏解縛之法。

2. When the sleeping *Kuṇḍaliní* awakens by favour of a *Guru*, then all the lotuses (in the six *chakras* or centres) and all the knots are pierced through.

   承上師恩典，當沉睡的軍荼利被喚醒，彼時所有的蓮輪和縛結都將被貫穿。

   上師：即本師、靈性導師或傳法上師；祛除弟子心中暗霾、無知，關照並引領弟子解脫者。

   蓮輪：脈輪的別名。

   縛結：人身內的三大結縛，分別是位於下三輪區的梵結、胸喉一帶的維世努結和眉心輪的魯德羅結。

3. *Suṣumná* (*Súnya Padaví*) becomes a main road for the passage of *Práṇa*, and the mind then becomes free from all connections (with its objects of enjoyments) and Death is then evaded.

   如是空脈成為生命能的康莊大道，彼時內心無所掛礙，乃至死亡亦受欺瞞。

   空脈：中脈的名稱之一。

   死亡亦受欺瞞：原句梵文是 *tadá kálasya vañcanam*，*kála* 時間之義，時間催人老，故亦指死亡。此句意為到此階段，時間止步，打破了命有定數之理，死亡亦受欺誑。

4. *Suṣumná*, *Sunya Padaví*, *Brahmarandhra*, *Mahá Patha*, *Śmaśána*, *Śambhaví*, *Madhya* Márga, are names of one and the same thing.

   中脈、空脈、梵竅、最勝脈、焚葬地、神變脈、中道等，都是中脈的不同名稱。

5. In order, therefore, to awaken this goddess, who is sleeping at the entrance of *Brahma Dvára* (the great door), *mudrás* should be practised well.
是故當勤習各種身印，盡力喚醒沉睡於梵竅口的靈能女神。
身印：又譯手印，結合了內氣與理念的一種鍛煉，作用兼及於神經和肌肉。

6. *Mahá mudrá*, *Mahá Bandha*, *Mahá Vedha*, *Khecharí*, *Uḍḍiyána Bandha*, *Múla Bandha*, *Jálandhara Bandha*.
大身印、大鎖印、大穿透印、明空身印、揚升鎖印、根鎖印、收頷鎖印，

7. *Viparíta Karaṇí*, *Vajroli*, and *Śakti Chálana*. These are the ten *Mudrás* which annihilate old age and death.
倒轉身印、金剛力身印和力動身印等，是克服老邁和死亡的十種身印。

8. They have been explained by *Ádi Nátha* (*Śiva*) and give eight kinds of divine wealth. They are loved by all the *Siddhas* and are hard to attain even by the *Marutas*.
Note.—The eight *Aiśwaryas* are:
Animá (becoming small, like an atom),
Mahimá (becoming great, like ákás),
Laghimá (l becoming very ight things, like cotton.)
Garimá (becoming very heavy, like mountains.)
Prápti (coming within easy reach of everything; as touching the moon with the little finger, while standing on the earth.)
Ísatá (mastery over matter and objects made of it.)
Vaśitva (controlling the animate and inanimate objects.)
Prákámya (non-resistance to the desires, as entering the earth like water.)
前述身印係至尊主希瓦所傳，習之能得八種妙自在成就；每種成就皆為諸大成就者所看重，然即便是眾神亦難通透。

八種妙自在成就：（第四至第七項括弧內及透視力之註釋引自 Gurukul Publication 之 *Ananda Márga Dictionary*）

能小（*Aṇimá*）：能成極小的能力，如原子

能大（*Mahimá*）：能成極大的能力，如虛空

能輕（*Laghimá*）：能成極輕甚至空行的能力，如柳絮

能重（*Garimá*）：能成極重之能力，如大山

能得（*Prápti*）：能得到或創造自他真正所需之能力（隨處可及一切事物，如立地以指觸月）

能主（*Íśitvá*）：能控制引導生靈心智之能力（具掌握一般物質及其由物質所造之物的能力）

能支配（*Vaśitva*）：能支配任何有情和無情之心理能力（主宰他物之心理能力）

能隨所欲（*Prákámya*）：能從心所欲，入地猶如入水（能取得一切事物形象及助人成就所願的能力）

譯按：哈達瑜伽和勝王瑜伽對八神通的說法不一，差異在第四項「能重」；勝王瑜伽無此項，但加入了第八項「能透視」（*Antaryámitva*），意思是「透視萬物內在所思及所需的能力」。

9. These *Mudrás* should be kept secret by every means, as one keeps one's box of jewellery, and should, on no account be told to any one, just as husband and wife keep their dealings secret.

如是身印應如寶篋藏珍般地嚴守其秘，猶如夫婦保守閨房之秘般，不得隨意語人。

● 大身印

10. Pressing the *Yoni* (perineum) with the heel of the left foot, and stretching forth the right foot, its toe should be grasped by the thumb and first finger.

左踵抵住會陰，右腿伸直；兩手握牢前伸之右足大趾。

11. By stopping the throat (by *Jálandhara Bandha*) the air is drawn in from the outside and carried down. Just as a snake struck with a stick becomes straight like a stick,

隨後下巴抵喉，使吸入之氣下行，〔令蜷伏之靈能〕有如眼鏡蛇受到杖擊般伸直。

下巴抵喉：此時收頷持氣，配合收頷鎖印。

使吸入之氣下行：配合根鎖印將吸入的氣息引入根輪後循中脈上行。

12. In the same way, *śakti* becomes straight at once. Then the *Kuṇḍaliní*, becoming as it were dead, and, leaving both the *Idá* and the *Pingalá*, enters the *suṣumná* (the middle passage).

如是甦醒的軍荼利倏然伸直進入中脈，左右兩脈因之萎頓若亡。

13. It should be expelled then, slowly only and not violently. For this very reason, the best of the wise men call it the *Mahá mudrá*. This *Mahá mudrá* has been propounded by great masters.

然後逐漸緩慢呼氣，切不可急躁；上智行人名此為大身印，此為大成就者所授之大身印訣。

大身印：大身印是最重要的身印之一，屬於哈達瑜伽鍛煉的技術，也是淨化瑜伽的練習之一；此法涉及體位法、持氣法、身印和鎖印，能在冥想時自發地調伏強大的生命力。

14. Great evils and pains, like death, are destroyed by it, and for this reason wise men call it the *Mahá mudrá*.

此法破除根本煩惱和致死之因；緣是之故，智者稱之為大身印。

根本煩惱：原經句梵文名 *Mahá Klesha*，是為無明、欲貪、嗔恚、我慢、迷執等五大煩惱之總名。

15. Having practised with the left side, it should be practised with the right side; and, when the number on both sides becomes equal, then the *mudrá* should be discontinued.

此身印於左側練習完之後，繼續練習右側；兩側交替至相同次數後結束身印。

譯按：練習次數一般可以三次為度。

16. There is nothing wholesome or injurious; for the practice of this *mudrá* destroys the injurious effects of all the *rasas* (chemicals). Even the deadliest of poisons, if taken, acts like nectar.

習此身印者，食無有宜與不宜之分，任何飲食之不利影響都可以運化，甚至惡毒亦能如甘露般消化。

譯按：粗淡的食物也能甘之如飴。

17. Consumption, leprosy, prolapsus ani, colic, and the diseases due to indigestion, all these irregularities are removed by the practice of this *Mahá Mudrá*.

勤習此大身印，可克服肺癆、痲瘋、便秘、腹絞痛及消化不良症候群等諸疾。

便秘：原經句梵文 *ghudávarta* 或 *gudávarta*，英譯為脫肛，然此梵文字義為便秘，中譯從梵文原義。

18. This *Mahá Mudrá* has been described as the giver of great success (*Siddhi*) to men. It should be kept secret by every effort, and not revealed to any and everyone.

此大身印咸認能賦予習者大成就，當嚴守其密意，莫輕易示人。

● 大鎖印

19. Press the left heel to the perineum and place the right foot on the left thigh.

左踵抵住會陰，右足置於左腿之上。

20. Fill in the air, keeping the chin firm against the chest, and, having pressed the air, the mind should he fixed on the middle of the eyebrows or in the *suṣumná* (the spine).

吸氣，下巴牢牢抵胸，提縮會陰，心意安住眉心。

心意安住眉心：此處梵語原句 *manomadhye niyojayet*，其中 *madhye* 使是中、中間、處中之意；有版本認為是指中脈，有的認為是指眉心，譯者採與葛蘭達本集第三章 6、7 節相同的觀點。

21. Having kept it confined so long as possible, it should be expelled slowly. Having practised on the left side, it should be practised on the right side.

盡可能地持氣於內，然後徐緩地呼氣，左側練習完後應再練習右側。

22. Some are of opinion that the closing of throat is not necessary here, for keeping the tongue pressed against the roots of the upper teeth makes a good *bandha* (stop).

亦有認為此處不必帶入收頷鎖印，將舌尖緊抵上顎即可。

23. This stops the upward motion of all the *Nádís*. Verily this *Mahá Bandha* is the giver of great *Siddhis*.

如此可阻擋生命能自諸氣脈上行。勤習此大鎖印必能予人大成就。

大鎖印：鎖印法是以特定的姿勢收縮並控制身體器官與肌肉，促使內氣或生命能進入特定的部位。大鎖印意指「非常的鎖」。根據葛蘭達本集和哈達瑜伽串珠（*Haṭharatnávali*）記載，大鎖印涉及內在持氣、收頷鎖印、根鎖印和希瓦身印。

譯按：意使生命氣只往中脈而行。

24. This *Mahá Bandha* is the most skilful means for cutting away the snares of death. It brings about the conjunction of the *Trivení* (*Idá*,

Pingalá and *Suṣumná*) and carries the mind to *Kedár* (the space between the eyebrows, which is the seat of *Śiva*).

此大鎖印是擺脫死神桎梏最善巧的方法，使三脈會聚於眉心輪，引領心靈登抵希瓦的寶座。

三脈：左、右、中三脈，亦名月脈、日脈、空脈。

希瓦的寶座：傳說中希瓦的聖座，在人身則位於眉心輪。

25. As beauty and loveliness, do not avail a woman without husband, so the *Mahá mudrá* and the *Mahá-Bandha* are useless without the *Mahá Vedha*.

如同娉婷女子若無丈夫即無有後，大身印、大鎖印若缺少了大穿透印亦無功果。

大穿透印：又名大貫穿印。練習此身印時以臀輕擊地板，強使靈能穿透中脈升至眉心輪。

● 大穿透印

26. Sitting with *Mahá Bandha*, the *Yogí* should fill in the air and keep his mind collected. The movements of the *Váyus* (*Práṇa* and *Apána*) should be stopped by closing the throat.)

瑜伽行人以大鎖印姿勢坐定，凝神吸氣，以收頷鎖印來阻止生命氣竄行。

生命氣：泛指呼吸或生命能，此處指的是命根氣與下行氣。

27. Resting both the hands equally on the ground, he should raise himself a little and strike his buttocks against the ground gently. The air, leaving both the passages (*Idá* and *Pingalá*), starts into the middle one.

雙手撐地使身體些微上升，繼之以臀部輕輕觸擊地面；藉此使生命氣逸離左右脈而行入中脈。

譯按：此式雙臂撐穩，以臀部輕擊地面時，由兩鼻孔呼氣。

28. The union of the *Idá* and the *Pingalá* is affected, in order to bring

about immortality. When the air becomes as it were dead (by leaving its course through the *Idá* and the *Pingalá*) (*i.e.*, when it has been kept confined), then it should be expelled.

月亮、太陽和聖火三者融合，即達不朽；當氣息呈現若亡之象時，徐徐呼出氣息。

月亮、太陽和聖火：原梵文經句用詞是 *soma-súryá-agni*，喻左、右、中三脈。

若亡之象：意指當左右兩脈之生命氣漸弱時產生的類死亡現象。

29. The practice of this *Mahá Vedha*, the giver of great *Siddhis*, destroys old age, grey hair, and shaking of the body, and therefore it is practised by the best masters.

習此大穿透印能予人大成就，功能消除老態、灰髮和耄年顫抖，是故上勝行者亦力行之。

30. These three are the great secrets. They are the destroyers of old age and death, increase the appetite, confer the accomplishments of *Anima*, etc.

此三大秘印，能破老邁和死亡，強化胃火，賦予「能小」等神通。

譯按：生死是生命常態，瑜伽深知生死無常，然亦認為在無常生死之中，存在著無有生死之永恆，與之相契合即是瑜伽之目的。

31. They should, be practised in eight ways, daily and hourly. They increase collection of good actions and lessen the evil ones. People, instructed well, should begin their practice, little by little, first.

前述鎖印每日應習八回，功能消罪立德；有心依此練習者，應從少分漸次開始。

每日應習八回：一日 24 小時，亦即包含練習時間，從少分開始，漸增至每間隔三小時練習一回。

●明空身印

32. The *Khechari mudrá* is accomplished by thrusting the tongue into the gullet, by turning it over itself, and keeping the eyesight in the middle of the eyebrows.

將舌回捲伸入顎咽，雙眼內視眉心，是為明空身印。

顎咽：生理位置上即顎咽與鼻咽腔一帶。

明空身印：亦稱虛空身印，斯瓦米施化難陀又名之為軟顎瑜伽。

33. To accomplish this, the tongue is lengthened by cutting the fraenum lingua, moving, and pulling it. When it can touch the space between the eyebrows, then *Khechari* can be accomplished.

可透過輕割舌筋與握擠、拉伸舌頭來漸增舌頭長度，直到舌尖能觸及眉心，方得成就明空身印。

34. Taking a sharp, smooth, and clean instrument, of the shape of a cactus leaf, the fraenum of the tongue should be cut a little (as much as a hair's thickness), at a time.

取一把鋒利、潔淨、薄如葉片之小刀，每次將舌下繫帶切一道細如髮絲的口子。

35. Then rock salt and yellow myrobalan (both powdered) should be rubbed in. On the 7th day, it should again be cut a hair's breadth.

然後取岩鹽末與薑黃粉調勻，以此粉揉搓舌繫帶切口。待七天後，於原切口再往內切一細如髮絲之深度。

譯按：早晚皆需用岩鹽末和薑黃粉揉搓，如習者禁食鹽，可以肉桂枝燒灰代替。

36. One should go on doing thus, regularly for six months. At the end of six months, the fraenum of the tongue will be completely cut.

如是反覆行之，連續六個月，直到舌下繫帶都被切開為止。

37. Turning the tongue upwards, it is fixed on the three ways

(esophagus, windpipe and palate.) Thus it makes the *Khechari mudrá*, and is called the *Vyoma Chakra*.

此時，習者舌頭上捲，可逆向伸入顎咽腔三脈會合處；是即明空身印，又稱空輪身印。

38. *The Yogí who sits for a minute turning his tongue upwards, is saved from poisons, diseases, death, old age, etc.*

瑜伽行者若能保持舌頭上捲，即便只半剎那，亦得免於毒害、疾病、死苦和老衰等事。

譯按：意指明空身印即便只進行了極短的時間，也有短的時間的功效。常人可以虛空身印取代（葛蘭達本集 III-9）

39. He who knows the *Khechari mudrá* is not afflicted with disease, death, sloth, sleep, hunger, thirst, and swooning.

成就明空身印之人，即不為疾病、死亡、疲倦、睡眠、飢渴和昏沉所困擾。

40. He who knows the *Khechari mudrá*, is not troubled by diseases, is not stained with karmas, and is not snared by time.

了知明空身印之人，不受疾病折磨，不遭業行染污，亦不為時輪所拘。

不為時輪所拘：不受時光、死亡或輪迴的束縛。

41. The *Siddhas* have devised this *Khechari mudrá* from the fact that the mind and the tongue reach *ákáśa* by its practice.

因行功時舌頭捲向顎咽空穴之引導，心靈得專注於空境，故諸成就者稱之為明空身印。

42. If the hole behind the palate be stopped with *Khechari* by turning the tongue upwards, then *bindu* cannot leave its place even if a woman were embraced.

能以明空身印捲舌封住軟顎後方咽腔穴孔之行人，縱使少艾在懷，精亦不漏。

軟顎：軟顎即上咽前之懸擁垂，一名小舌，梵文名 *Lambika*，其後即為上咽腔。

精：又名精氣或明點，氣之淨分，可昇華為智慧明點。

43. Even though the fluid flows and comes down to the genital organ, still arrested by *Yoni mudrá* it is taken by force upwards.

即便精液已入根門，仍能藉根門身印力使其向上。

根門身印：梵文 *Yoni mudrá* 的意譯，又名胎藏身印。*Yoni* 意為根門、女根、產門，雖然多指女根或女陰，但本節經句適用男、女根，故譯為根門身印。根門身印亦是金剛力身印（見本篇第 86 節）的別名。

44. If the *Yogí* drinks *Somarasa* (juice) by sitting with the tongue turned backwards and mind concentrated, there is no doubt he conquers death within 15 days.

若有瑜伽行人宴坐之時，以舌上抵顎咽，飲下月甘露，無疑可在十五天之內戰勝死亡。

宴坐：安坐、打坐、靜坐之同義詞。龍樹菩薩著《大智度論》言「不依身，不依心，不依於三界，於三界中，不得身心，是為宴坐」，

月甘露：因心神集中而得定時，從松果體自然泌出的精華液。

45. If the *Yogí*, whose body is full of *Somarasa* (juice), were bitten by *Takshaka* (snake), its poison cannot permeate his body.

身常注滿月甘露之瑜伽士，即便為毒龍咬傷，亦不受毒染。

毒龍：的神話中蛇王之名，音譯陀剎迦。

46. As fire is inseparably connected with the wood and light is connected with the wick and oil, so does the soul not leave the body full of nectar exuding from the *Soma*.

猶如火因薪材而燃，燈因油芯而明；只要身內月甘露具

足，生命主便不會逸離此身。

Note.—Soma (*Chandra*) is described later on located in the thousand-petalled lotus in the human brain, and is the same as is seen on *Śivas*' head in pictures, and from which a sort of juice exudes. It is the retaining of this exudation which makes one immortal.

英譯註：後文有說月叢位於人腦千瓣蓮花中，在希瓦圖象上可以看到同樣的表示，月甘露即從中泌出。此分泌若能留用，行人即能因之而不朽。

47. Those who eat the flesh of the cow and drink the immortal liquor daily, are regarded by me men of noble family. Others are but a disgrace to their families.

日啖鮮牛肉、常飲不死酒者，其人即躋身尊貴種姓，餘則有損門風。

鮮牛肉：意喻伸入顎咽的舌頭。

不死酒：喻月叢所分泌之甘露。

48. The word "*go-* " means tongue; eating it is thrusting it in the gullet which destroys great sins.

牛肉（*go-*）意喻舌頭，將之伸入顎咽穴孔，即「日啖鮮牛肉」之真義；具此成就者，可消除往昔重罪。

49. Immortal liquor is the nectar exuding from the moon (*Chandra* situated on the left side of the space between the eyebrows). It is produced by the fire which is generated by thrusting the tongue.

不死酒是從月叢分泌的甘露，由伸入顎咽空穴舌頭的煖熱所產生。

譯按：舌入顎咽空穴舌頭的煖熱所產生，這只是外相，重要的是其後的心地法門。

50. If the tongue can touch with its end the hole from which falls the *rasa* (juice) which is saltish, bitter, sour, milky and similar to ghee

and honey, one can drive away disease, destroy old age, can evade an attack of arms, become immortal in eight ways and can attract fairies.

若此甘露流向捲抵顎咽之舌，則有鹹、辛、酸等類如奶、蜜、醍醐之味。此甘露能袪病延年，免受刀兵刧，可得長生和八種妙成就，且能吸引天女。

八種妙成就：詳本章第 8 節註。

天女：女性仙人或修行有成之女瑜伽士；此處有易得天女相助之意。

51. He who drinks the clear stream of liquor of the moon (*soma*) falling from the brain to the sixteen-petalled lotus (in the throat), obtained by means of *Práṇa*, by applying the tongue to the hole of the pendant in the palate, and by meditating on the great power (*Kuṇḍaliní*), becomes free from disease and tender in body, like the stalk of a lotus, and the *Yogí* lives a very long life.

行人以舌捲抵顎咽孔穴，內觀靈能軍荼利；藉調息法之助。顱內月叢泌出之純淨甘露滴入喉輪十六瓣蓮花中。飲甘露之瑜伽行者不受病苦，周身柔若蓮花之莖，長生久視

十六瓣蓮花：喻由喉輪控制的十六種情緒，如甜美的表達、惱人的表達等等。

52. On the top of the *Merú* (vertebral column), concealed in a hole, is the *Somarasa* (nectar of *Chandra*); the wise, [whose intellect is not overpowered by Raja and *Tama guṇas*, but in whom *Sattva guṇa* is predominant, say there is the (universal spirit) *átma* in it. It is the source of the down-going *Idá*, *Pingalá* and *Suṣumná Nádis*, which are the *Ganges*, the *Yamuna* and the *Sarasvati*.] From that *Chandra* is shed the essence of the body which causes death of men. It should, therefore, be stopped from shedding. This (*Khechari mudrá*) is a very good instrument for this purpose. There is no other means of achieving this end.

月甘露自眾脈之源彌樓山最高峰頂處泌出，唯淨智行人了知真性居於其中。此甘露乃身之精華，流失則亦為致死之因；而此上品身印可阻甘露流失，此外無有他法能達此目的。

彌樓山：泛指人身之脊椎，此處喻中脈。

譯按：英文括號內的文字是英譯對何謂淨智行人的註解，譯成中文為「其智未受變性及惰性屬性遮障，而是由悅性屬性主導之行人，可謂是人有真性居彼其中；此真性之下分出左脈、右脈和中脈，或說分出恆河、賈穆納河和薩拉斯瓦蒂河。」

53. This hole is the generator of knowledge and is the source of the five streams (*Idá*, *Pingalá*, &c.). In that colorless vacuum, *Khecharí mudrá* should be established.

此秘穴是知識的泉眼，是五河的發源地；於此清淨真空處，即明空身印安立之處。

五河發源地：地理上的五河是指恆河、賈穆納河和薩拉斯瓦蒂……等五河，實際上的界定會因流域而有所不同。靈性上是指中脈、左脈、右脈、香行脈和象舌脈；香行脈和象舌脈屬身內十四條主脈之一，見《希瓦本集》第三章 14-15 節。

54. There is only one seed germinating the whole universe from it; and there is only one *mudrá*, called *Khecharí*. There is only one deva (god) without any one's support, and there is one condition called *Manonmaṇi*.

造化種源唯只一處，亦只有一種稱作明空身印的身印；只有一位自在無倚的真神，亦只有一種名為意摩尼的定境。

自在無倚：不依倚任何支持，自在無倚之義。舊譯無著或無所緣。

意摩尼：個體心融入空寂的定境。

●揚升鎖印

55. *Uḍḍiyána* is so called by the *Yogís*, because by its practice the *Práṇa* (*Váyu*,) flies (flows) in the *Suṣumná*.

修習此式可使「生命能」於中脈內揚升，由是瑜伽師名之為揚升鎖印。

揚升鎖印：練習此鎖印時，臍腹提吊貼脊，使能量向上揚升，故又稱「吊胃鎖印」。

56. *Uḍḍiyána* is so called, because the great bird, *Práṇa*, tied to it, flies without being fatigued. It is explained below.

名喚「揚升」是因為此鎖印繫住如大鵬鳥般的生命能，如前所言，無有疲倦地於中脈內飛升而上。

57. The belly above the navel is pressed backwards towards the spine. This *Uḍḍiyána Bandha* is like a lion for the elephant of death.

將臍腹內縮貼向背脊，謂之揚升鎖印，其威猶如撲殺死亡之象的獅子。

58. *Uḍḍiyána* is always very easy, when learnt from a *Guru*. The practiser of this, if old, becomes young again.

依從業師教導，揚升鎖印即甚簡易；習此鎖印者，得獲反老還少之效。

59. The portions above and below the navel, should be drawn backwards towards the spine. By practising this for six months one can undoubtedly conquer death.

努力地將臍腹上下內縮貼脊，持續修習六個月後，習者即能克制死亡無疑。

60. Of all the *Bandhas*, *Uḍḍiyána* is the best; for by binding it firmly liberation comes spontaneously.

揚升鎖印是諸鎖印中最好的一種，一旦成就，自得解脫。

譯按：揚升鎖印功成之後，能將生命能引入中脈，通達梵竅而得成就。

● 根鎖印

61. Pressing *Yoni* (perineum) with the heel, contract up the anus. By drawing the *Apána* thus, *Múla Bandha* is made.

以足踵抵住會陰區，提攝穀道，提引下行氣往上，此謂之根鎖印。

根鎖印：「根」*Múla* 意指會陰區域，練習此鎖印時，提縮的是直腸到肛門一帶。

62. The *Apána*, naturally inclining downward, is made to go up by force. This *Múla Bandha* is spoken of by *Yogís* as done by contracting the anus.

下行氣之性趨下，須藉力促使其上行，由於是透過收縮穀道完成，瑜伽師稱之為根鎖印。

穀道：肛門的古名，此處因為是五穀殘渣排出體外的管道，故稱穀道。

63. Pressing the heel well against the anus, draw up the air by force, again and again till it (air) goes up.

踵抵穀道，大力提氣反覆提縮，直至下行氣轉而上行。

踵抵穀道：前第 61 節寫的是抵住會陰區，包括前、後陰及中間的區域，本節則指出更明確的位置。

64. *Práṇa*, *Apána*, *Náda* and *Bindu* uniting into one in this way, give success in *Yoga*, undoubtedly.

通過根鎖印，命根氣和下行氣以及明點與秘音融而為一，即可圓證瑜伽成就，毋庸置疑。

65. By the purification of *Práṇa*, and *Apána*, urine and excrements decrease. Even an old man becomes young by constantly practising *Múla Bandha*.

由於命根氣和下行氣之淨化，大、小二遺漸減，透過持續地練習根鎖印，甚至能反老為少。

大、小二遺：即是大、小二便。

66. Going up, the *Apána* enters the zone of fire,*i.e*., the stomach. The flame of fire struck by the air is thereby lengthened.

當下行氣上行進入火曼荼羅時，彼火受到該氣煽動而變得焰長火旺。

火曼荼羅：又名火壇，此處意指臍輪。

Note.—In the centre of the body is the seat of fire, like heated gold. In men it is triangular, in quadrupeds square, in birds circular. There is a long thin flame in this fire.It is gastric fire.

英譯註：於身體中央是火之坐處，色如鍛燒過的黃金。其座在人為三角形，在獸為方形，在鳥為圓形；火中有細長焰光，是為胃火。

67. These, fire and *Apána*, go to the naturally hot *Práṇa*, which, becoming inflamed thereby, causes burning sensation in the body.

由於此火與下行氣及其性煖熱的命根氣結合，激起火焰；使得通身熾熱。

68. The *Kuṇḍaliní*, which has been sleeping all this time, becomes well heated by this means and awakens well. It becomes straight like a serpent, struck by a stick.

緣此，處於沉睡中的靈能受此熾熱所逼而醒轉，狀如盤曲之蛇在受到杖擊後，直身拔起。

69. It enters the *Brahma Nádí*, just as a serpent enters its hole. Therefore, the *Yogí* should always practise this *Múla Bandha*.

如同蛇歸返其穴，靈能亦如是進入梵脈；是故瑜伽士應持恆地習此根鎖印。

● 收頷鎖印

70. Contract the throat and press the chin firmly against the chest. This is called *Jálandhara Bandha*, which destroys old age and death.

喉頸內收，下巴牢抵胸部；此為收頷鎖印，能破衰老和死亡。

收頷鎖印：亦名喉收束法，係為防止明點甘露自喉向下流失之法，屬哈達瑜伽重要的練習。

71. It stops the opening (hole) of the group of the *Nádís*, through which the juice from the sky (from the *Soma* or *Chandra* in the brain) falls down. It is, therefore, called the *Jálandhara Bandha* —the destroyer of a host of diseases of the throat.

此鎖印可收束咽喉打開的脈叢，接住自空界流下的甘露；故名收頷鎖印，具消除喉嚨各種不適之效。

空界：意指此甘露來自於「天」，入於月叢而出，非由人為之意。

72. In *Jálandhara Bandha*, the indications of a perfect contraction of throat are, that the nectar does not fall into the fire (the *Súrya* situated in the navel), and the air is not disturbed.

此式收頷鎖印，於喉輪處形成完美的收束，月甘露便不會落入胃火（位於臍部的日火），生命氣亦不受擾動。

73. The two *Nádís* should be stopped firmly by contracting the throat. This is called the middle circuit or centre (*Madhya Chakra*), and it stops the 16 *ádháras* (*i.e.*, vital parts).

透過收束喉制住左、右二脈，如同喉輪的十六支輪輻被中轂鎖住。

十六支輪輻：本節是用十六輻共一轂的牛車輪來比喻收頷鎖印的功效，十六輻象徵所指之說法不一，有的認為是心理上的，有的認為是生理上的。由於喉輪掌控十六種心緒作用，因此意指心理上的說法較準確。英譯註則有附上生理上十六個部位，唯第五項的梵文是 *sivani*，第六是 *linga*，因此第五項譯為女根較符其義。

Note.—The sixteen vital parts mentioned by renowned *Yogís* are the (1) thumbs, (2) ankles, (3) knees, (4) thighs, (5) the prepuce, (6) organs of generation, (17) the navel, (8) the heart, (9) the neck, (10) the throat, (11) the palate, (12) the nose, (13) the middle of the eyebrows, (14) the forehead, (15) the head and (16) the *Brahmarandhra*.

英譯註：有著名瑜伽師言此十六支輪幅所指的部位是——拇指、腳踝、膝蓋、大腿、女根、男根、肚臍、心臟、頸脖、喉嚨、上顎、鼻子、眉心、前額、頭部以及梵穴。

74. By drawing up the *múlasthána* (anus,) *Uḍḍiyána Bandha* should be performed. The flow of the air should be directed to the *Suṣumná*, by closing the *Idá*, and the *Pingalá*.

提縮根處，同時做揚升鎖印；再以本鎖印牢鎖住左、右二脈，促使生命能往中脈而行。

根處：即會陰區域。

75. The *Prána* becomes calm and latent by this means, and thus there is no death, old age, disease, etc.

透過此法，使生命氣逐漸沈寂，不復有死亡、老邁和疾病。

76. These three *Bandhas* are the best of all and have been practised by the masters. Of all the means of success in the *Haṭha Yoga*, they are known to the *Yogís* as the chief ones.

以上三種上品鎖印，為習哈達瑜伽者所常習練；在所有哈達瑜伽的修法中，眾瑜伽師咸認為此三種鎖印是最殊勝的。

77. The whole of the nectar, possessing divine qualities, which exudes from the *Soma* (*Chandra*) is devoured by the *Súrya*; and, owing to this, the body becomes old.

任何從月叢流出的甘露皆微妙殊勝，然因盡為日火所噬，致使身體日益蒼老。

日火：此處梵文是 *súrya*，即太陽，或與太陽神經叢有關。太陽的特質是燃燒，不斷地在耗散能量；如同水滴入火，月叢流出的甘露幾乎盡皆被日叢之火殆盡，致使身體日益老邁。本書未明寫日叢位置，歷來多認為在胸腹間。

● 倒轉身印

78. To remedy this, the opening of the *Súrya* is avoided by excellent means. It is to be learnt best by instructions from a *Guru*; but not by even a million discussions.

有妙法可避免月甘露落入日火之口，唯其要旨需得上師親授，而非從萬千典籍中得曉。

79. Above the navel and below the palate respectively, are the *Súrya* and the Chandra. The exercise, called the *Viparíta Karaṇí*, is learnt from the *Guru's* instructions.

習練時肚臍在上、喉咽在下，亦即是採取日上、月下的體位，是為倒轉身印，此式須從明師指導學習。

80. This exercise increases the appetite; and, therefore, one who practises it, should obtain a good supply of food. If the food be scanty, it will burn him at once.

常習此可增進胃火，故習此身印者需攝取足量的食物；若飲食份量不足，將立即受到胃火煎熬。

81. Place the head on the ground and the feet up into the sky, for a second only the first day, and increase this time daily.

第一天練習此式，只需頭置於地、腳舉向天倒轉片刻；從片刻起練，然後逐日延長時間。

82. After six months, the wrinkles and grey hair are not seen. He who practises it daily, even for three hours, conquers death.

六個月後，縐紋與灰髮消失；每日規律練習此式三小時者，可降伏死亡。

● 金剛力身印

譯按：瑜伽之道講究謙恭歛己，敬天知命。故以下第 83 節到 103 節介紹的三種身印，乍看似乎有違瑜伽精神，是故有些版本將之刪節，本書仍照實譯出。以譯者之了解，瑜伽並非宗教，而是提升生命的方法；是故出家人可藉之增進慧命，在家人也可從中獲得啟發。無論是在家人或出家人，兩者共同的功課就是昇華生命原始動力。只是在家人需要自己配偶的協助，使過著居家生活的人也能有機會獲得瑜伽成就。出家人則是以觀想虛擬或其他方式來達到煉化的目的。有謂這些修煉不符悅性的靈修精神，且所敘之法亦難行於今日；平心而論，確是如此，不過其中並非無可參考。又本書成於十五世紀，閱讀時應設想那時的社會民情，而不宜以現代社會的觀念來批判。

83. Even if one who lives a wayward life, without observing any rules of *Yoga*, but performs *Vajrolí*, deserves success and is a *Yogí*.

生活方式隨性且未遵循任何瑜伽規範之人，若能正確了知金剛力身印，亦可獲得瑜伽成就。

瑜伽規範：有關之規範請見《哈達瑜伽明燈》第一章所述及其他章節相關敘述。

84. Two things are necessary for this, and these are difficult to get for the ordinary people—(1) milk and (2) a woman behaving, as desired.

有兩件必要之事常人很難做到，一是牛奶，二是讓女子安順。

牛奶：此處牛奶比喻甘露，將精昇華為氣，氣化為神，再煉神還虛而形成的甘露。
安順：敬信順服之意。

85. By practising to draw in the *bindu*, discharged during cohabitation, whether one be a man or a woman, one obtains success in the practice of *Vajrolí*.

若於排尿或雙運時，如法漸次提縮收攝，無論男女皆得成就金剛力身印。

金剛力身印：音譯瓦喬里身印，屬養腎護精之法。此法今已鮮少人使用，取代之法類如女性產前練習之「凱格爾運動」。亦即於小解時收縮骨盆底肌群一段時間，然後放鬆。
意念位置：男性在乾根海綿體及後懸韌帶尾端，女性在膀胱與尿道會合處。習練前後應保持清潔。

86. By means of a pipe, one should blow air slowly into the passage in the male organ.

通過根門小管，極緩慢地吸入氣息，氣息如是漸入莖根。

譯按：此小管英譯是外置，也有可能是生理上的管道；不過切莫在無師指導之下，自行練習此法。

87. By practice, the discharged *bindu* is drawn out. One can draw back and preserve one's own discharged *bindu*.

雙運時將出之精應練習導引回攝，已出之精應攝回向上。

88. The *Yogí* who can protect his *bindu* thus, overcomes death; because death comes by discharging *bindu*, and life is prolonged by its preservation.

知曉如是節慾保精之瑜伽行人，可戰勝死亡；蓋精失則亡，精固則生。

89. By preserving *bindu*, the body of the *Yogí* emits a pleasing smell. There is no fear of death, so long as the *bindu*is well-established in

the body.

固精於身之瑜伽達士，身出妙香，無懼死亡。

90. The *bindu* of men is under the control of the mind, and life is dependent on the *bindu*. Hence, mind and *bindu*s hould be protected by all means.

精氣受制於心，命則倚賴精氣；因此，當善護內在之心意與精氣。

91. He who knows *Yoga*, and perfect in the practice, may conserves his *bindu* and the woman's *rajas* by drawing it up as explained above.

明瑜伽且有修之有成者，當依前述提攝向上之法，護守並煉化己身精血。

精血：分別指男性之精與女性之血，可煉而化之成精血之淨分，再化之而成智慧明點。

譯按：本節此英譯本未譯，參考《哈達瑜伽明燈》其他版本之英譯。

● 俱生力身印

92. *Sahajolí* and Amarolí are only the different kinds of *Vajrolí*. Ashes from burnt up cowdung should be mixed with water.

俱生力身印、不老泉身印只是金剛力身印的兩種別相。把晒乾的牛糞燒成細灰與淨水混勻備用。

不老泉身印：請見本章第 96 至 103 節下節。

別相：意指這兩種身印方法雖與金剛力身印有別，但性質上仍屬於金剛力身印。

93. Being free from the exercise of *Vajrolí*, man and woman should both rub it on their bodies.

以金剛力心法雙運後，男女取細灰塗身吉祥處。

以細灰塗身吉祥處：即以灰塗抹身體吉祥悅性的部位，如頭頂、額、雙眼、胸口、雙肩、手臂等處，然後澄心安歇。

94. This is called *Sahajolí*, and should be relied on by *Yogís*. It does good and gives *mokṣa*.

此謂之俱生力身印，瑜伽人對之應心懷正信；不僅有其饒益，且能帶來解脫。

95. This *Yoga* is achieved by courageous wise men, who are free from sloth, and cannot he accomplished by the slothful.

勇猛精進無有懈怠之上根行人，必可獲得瑜伽成就；而懶散苟安者，難有所成。

● 不老泉身印

96. In the doctrine of the sect of the *Kapálikas*, the *Amarolí* is the drinking of the mid stream; leaving the 1st, as it is a mixture of too much bile and the last, which is useless.

棄尿液之前段與後段，取其中段飲用；因前段多含膽汁，後段於身無益。此為卡帕利卡派對不老泉身印的觀點。

取其中段飲用：中醫學認為人尿無毒。中段尿液性涼，可以入藥，其用途從肺痿到痔瘡不一而足。唐代名醫孫思邈在其著作《千金翼方》中有言「人尿乃傷科中之仙藥也」。日本近代也有醫生提倡尿療法，據稱可以抗癌。

卡帕利卡派：印度古傳苦行派一支，修法類似佛教白骨觀。

不老泉身印：梵文 *Amaroli* 的字源來自 *Amara*，意思是不朽的、不滅的、不死的；*Amaroli* 意為不死甘露，也是本節尿療法的美稱。尿，水泉也；不老，不死之代稱。故譯之為不老泉身印。

譯按：由找到的尿療文獻來看，最早尿療可能源於於印度，中外古今都有案例記錄，但從未成為主流；最著名的是 1977 年以 84 歲高齡擔任印度總理的莫拉吉德賽，於 1978 年實行過長期的尿療法，他表示：對於數百萬無法負擔醫療費用的印度人來說，尿液治療是一種完美的醫療解決方案。

97. He who drinks *Amarí*, snuffs it daily, and practices *Vajrolí*, is called practising *Amarolí*.

每日自鼻吸飲，並練習金剛力身印之人，是謂不老泉身印的練習者。

自鼻吸飲：只此四字，便知此法非可自行嘗試，定須有經驗者引領；需知此法應是非必要且有針對性之階段性鍛鍊。

98. The *bindu* discharged in the practice of *Vajrolí* should be mixed with ashes, and the rubbing it on the best parts of the body gives divine sight.

練習過程中，以身所出之精露與細灰調和，塗於身體最上勝的位置，可得靈視能力。

最上勝的位置：此處梵文關鍵字是「*uttam*」，其義有二：一是指「最好的」，一是指「身體首要之處」；身體首要之處的塗灰位置係指額頭或包括喉、胸和上臂；若單指一處，通常指的即是前額。

99. If, a woman, making herself expert through sufficient practice, draws up the own through(the practice of) *Vajroli*, she also becomes a *Yogini*.

若女子能嫻熟金剛力身印，以之攝化自他精氣，即是瑜伽女。

100. Without any doubt, even the least part of her seminal fluid is not lost. In her body, *Náda* becomes the *bindu* itself.

無疑地，瑜伽女若能習練至精不漏失，身內秘音與明點亦能融而為一。

101. That *bindu* and that rajas, become united and remaining in the body by the practice of *Vajroli* confer all *Siddhis*.

藉修金剛力身印之助，將紅白明點匯融於一身，即能獲得圓滿成就。

紅白菩提：精氣與血氣或白明點和紅明點。白明點是精之淨分，紅明點是血之淨分。血氣與精氣可昇華為紅、白智慧明點，或是下化為物質明點（精液）。

102. She who preserves by upward contraction her rajas is a *Yogini*. She knows the past and the future and certainly attains perfection in *Khechari*.

精氣煉化之瑜伽女可知過去、未來，亦能取得明空成就。

明空成就：意指融入心寂意滅的空性境界。

103. By the oractice of *Yoga* consisting of the practices of *Vajroli*, bodily perfection is obtained (beauty, grace and great strength). This *Yoga* confers merit (*punya*), and though there is sensual experience, it leads to emancipation.

修習金剛力身印者，身美體健，增添福德；雖是以欲勾牽，目的仍是為導向解脫。

● 力動身印

104. *Kutilángí* (crooked-bodied), *Kuṇḍaliní*, *Bhujangí* (a she-serpent) akti, I hwarí, *Kundalí*, *Arundhatí*,—all these words are synonymous.

靈能、蜷曲的靈蛇、龍母、靈能、自在母、軍荼利、日持等，所有這些都是同義詞。

105. As a door is opened with a key, so the *Yogí* opens the door of *mukti* by opening *Kuṇḍaliní* by means of *Haṭha Yoga*.

如同開門需藉鎖鑰之力，瑜伽修士藉哈達之法喚醒蜷曲的靈蛇，開啟解脫之門。

106. The *Parameśvarí* (*Kuṇḍaliní*) sleeps, covering the hole of the passage by which one can go to the seat of *Brahma* which is free from pains.

沉睡中的至上女神，盤踞於通往超越苦厄的梵座隘口。

至上女神：靈能女神、軍荼利女神的名字。

梵界隘口：身內之梵、本體或道體所在處之通道口。

107. *Kuṇḍalí Śakti* sleeps on the bulb, for the purpose of giving *moksa* to *Yogís* and bondage to the ignorant. He who knows it, knows *Yoga*.

靈能軍荼利沉睡於根輪之內，此大能是瑜伽士的解脫之鑰，也是無知者的束縛之根，了知此能力者即了知瑜伽。

根輪：梵文 *Kanda*，字義為根，其形如卵，位於海底輪與臍輪之間。據本章第 113 節描述，類似丹家所言之下丹田位置，是諸脈之源，亦為人身動力所在，故借丹田為 *Kanda* 之譯名。本節所述係指根持輪，位置在脊椎底端，前後陰之間。

108. *Kuṇḍalí* is of a bent shape, and has been described to be like a serpent. He who has moved that *Śakti* is no doubt *Mukta* (released from bondage).

軍荼利形如冬眠蜷曲之蛇，已將此靈能喚醒提升之人，無疑是脫黏解縛之開悟者。

開悟者：入有餘依三摩地之人，心靈融入宇宙心靈之瑜伽行者，不受世縛所擾之行人。

109. Youngster *Tapasvini* (a she-ascetic), lying between the Ganges and the *Yamuná*, (*Idá* and *Pingalá*) should be caught hold of by force, to get the highest position.

年輕寡女蜷臥在恆河與賈穆納河之間；須強力抓住她，才能通達維世努的至上境地。

年輕寡女：此處以年輕寡婦比喻少了另一半（至上意識意）的軍荼利。

恆河與賈穆納河：梵恆河是印度的聖河，賈穆納河是恆河的最大支流。

維世努：印度三大神祇之一，通譯遍在天或妙毗天。哲學上的意義是指那遍在於宇宙間每一表現中的真性，也是至上意識稱呼。

110. *Idá* is called goddess Ganges, *Pingalá* goddess *Yamuná*. In the middle of the *Idá* and the Pingalá is the infant widow, Kuṇḍalí.
神聖的恆河喻左脈，賈穆納河喻右脈；蜷臥在左右脈之間的年輕寡女，即蜷伏的軍荼利。

111. This sleeping she-serpent should be awakened by catching hold of her tail. By the force of *Haṭha*, the *Śakti* leaves her sleep, and starts upwards.
習者應抓住靈蛇之尾，將她從沉睡中喚醒，藉哈達之力使甦醒的靈能上行。

112. This she-serpent is situated in *Múládhár*. She should be caught and moved daily, morning and evening, for ½ a *prahar* (1½ hours), by filling with air through *Pingalá* by the *Paridhana* method.
此靈蛇蜷伏在海底根持輪，須每日握緊搖動；晨昏二時，以右鼻孔吸氣，然後藉持氣法執握住靈蛇搖轉一個半小時。
一個半小時：右印度時間一修時（*prahar*）為三小時，此處半修時即為一個半小時。

113. The bulb is above the anus, a *vitasti* (12 *angulas*) long, and measures 4 *angulas* (3 inches) in extent and is soft and white, and appears as if a folded cloth.
丹田約在穀道之上一掌高，四指寬，質軟色白有若以布裹覆。

114. Keeping the feet in Vajra-ásana (Padma-ásana), hold them firmly with the hands. The position of the bulb then will be near the ankle joint, where it should be pressed.
以金剛坐之姿跪坐，雙手持握左右腳踝處，收縮丹田。
金剛坐：詳第一章第 37 節。取此坐式，則丹田位置會正好在腳踝上方。於此處鍛煉，有助喚醒軍荼利。

115. The *Yogí*, sitting with *Vajra-ásana* and having moved *Kuṇḍalí*, should perform *Bhastriká* to awaken the *Kuṇḍalí* soon.

瑜伽行人以此金剛坐式引動軍荼利，再進行風箱式持氣法，促使軍荼利醒轉上升。

116. *Bhánu* (*Súrya*, near the navel) should be contracted (by contracting the navel) which will move the *Kuṇḍalí*. There is no fear for him who does so, even if he has entered the mouth of death.

依此法收縮日叢，引動軍荼利之修士，即使面對死亡亦無所懼。

日叢：位置胸腹一帶。

117. By moving this, for two *muhúrtas*, it is drawn up a little by entering the *Suṣumná* (spinal column).

如是無有怖畏地引動靈能九十六分鐘，使入中脈並往上提升少許。

九十六分鐘：原梵文音譯牟呼栗多，漢譯須臾。一晝夜三十個須臾，此處意指兩個須臾，故為九十六分鐘。

118. By this *Kuṇḍaliní* leaves the entrance of the *Suṣumná* at once, and the *Práṇa* enters it of itself.

循此方式，得使軍荼利自中脈口離開，如是生命能便得自入中脈。

119. Therefore, this comfortably sleeping *Arundhatí* should always be moved; for by so doing the *Yogí* gets rid of diseases.

依是法勤習，使酣睡的軍荼利常得啟動，瑜伽士因之免諸疾患。

120. The *Yogí*, who has been able to move the *Śakti* deserves success. It is useless to say more, suffice it to say that he conquers death playfully.

已然如是啟動靈能之瑜伽行人，成就在身；勿需多言，彼能輕易地戰勝死亡。

121. Only one who delights in the life of celibate (*Brahmacharya*), and always conforms to a moderate and salutary diet, and who practices *Yoga* in the form of stimulating *Kundalini* approaches *Siddhi* within forty days.

唯有常行淨行，節度飲食，虔心喚醒軍荼利之瑜伽行人，可在四十天內獲得成就。

淨行：外在行為規範第四項，心不離道，獨身修靜之謂。

122. After moving the *Kuṇḍalí*, plenty of *Bhastrá* should be performed. By such practice, he has no fear from the god of death.

軍荼利啟動後，須加意地習練風箱式持氣法；能如是持恆修習者，不畏死神閻摩。

123. There is no other way, but the practice of the *Kuṇḍalí*, for washing away the impurities of 72,000 *Nádís*.

除此軍荼行修煉法之外，無有他法可滌淨七萬二千經脈。

124. This middle *Nádí* becomes straight by steady practice of postures; *práṇáyáma* and *mudrás* of *Yogís*.

持恆修習體位法、呼吸法和身印法之瑜伽士，將使中脈日益通直。

125. Those whose sleep has decreased by practice and mind has become calm by *samádhi*, get beneficial accomplishments by *Sámbhaví* and other *Mudrás*.

那些心懷警惕，一意修定之瑜伽士，藉希瓦吉祥身印或其他身印能裨益法成就。

希瓦吉祥身印：請參考第四章之 36-37 節。

126. Without *Rája Yoga*, this earth, the night, and the *Mudrás*, be they howsoever wonderful, do not appear beautiful.

大地若無勝王瑜伽，寂夜若無勝王瑜伽，各式身印若無勝王瑜伽，無論它們有多麼殊勝，皆無是處。

譯按：大地喻體位法的安穩；夜晚喻持氣法帶來的的寂靜。少了勝王瑜伽，大地得不到滋養，夜晚無有月光，身印亦無所相應。

127. All the practices relating to the air should be performed with concentrated mind. A wise man should not allow his mind to wander away.

所有呼吸練習均應心思專一，慧智行人不會允許其心游移不定。

譯按：聖經智慧書箴言第四章23節「你要保守你心，勝過保守一切，因為一生的果效是由心發出。」亦是類似的觀念。

128. These are the *Mudrás*, as explained by *Ádinátha* (*Śiva*). Every one of them is the giver of great accomplishments to the practiser.

最勝主希瓦所說的這十種身印訣，任何其中一法，習之皆能獲大成就。

129. He is really the *Guru* and to be considered as *Íśvara* in human form who teaches the *Mudrás* as handed down from *Guru* to *Guru*.

代代如法承傳此身印訣的導師是真正的上師，是以人身應世的自在主。

自在主：又名至上主；此處意指恆處自在，不受五大元素形成的世界所拘的宗範師。

130. Engaging in practice, by putting faith in his words, one gets the *Siddhis* of *Anima*, etc., as also evades death.

信受上師話語，虔心修習各式身印得定之人，可獲致「能小」等成就，且不受死亡欺誑。

不受死亡欺誑：原梵文用詞 *kálavañcanam*，*kála* 意指死亡，*vañcana* 為誑惑之意，瑜伽哲學認為人之死生猶若換衣，現代量子物理學也有研究者提出「死亡只是人類意識造成的幻象」的觀點。

第四章

三摩地

Samádhi

1. Salutation to the *Guru*, the dispenser of happiness to all, appearing as *Náda*, *Vindú* and *Kalá*. One who is devoted to Him, obtains the highest bliss.

   頂禮上師希瓦，祂即是秘音、明點與作用力的化身；臣服於祂的人，將進入清淨無染之境。

   分賜眾生大樂者：此句英文係英譯添加。故中譯省略。

   秘音：意指宇宙最初的聲音或身內相應的屬靈音聲。

   明點：就形而上來說明點是宇宙音聲 *Oṁ* 的起始點，或代表宇宙勢能和宇宙意識的起點。就形而下來說，密學和哈達瑜伽中明點常代表身中精華液。最精細之明點為智慧明點，其次為風明點，再其次為物明點，乃形而下之物。

   作用力：梵語 ***Kalá***，阿南達瑪迦梵英字典的解釋是作用力（***the actional force***）；宇宙循環在變性力量主導下的有曲度之流階段。重音若在前（***Kála***），意思是時間，亦表死亡。

   清淨無染之境：清淨、離垢之境，形容最終抵達的悟境。

2. Now I will describe a regular method of attaining to *Samádhi*, which destroys death, is the means for obtaining happiness, and gives the *Brahmánanda*.

   現在，我將解說達到三摩地的上勝法門。此法能超越生死，得喜自在，生起本體大樂。

   三摩地：修行所呈現的結果，個體心靈融入所觀之謂。三摩地品類眾多，而以有餘依三摩地和無餘依三摩地最為主要。有餘依三摩地是個體心靈融入宇宙心靈，無餘依三地摩是個體我覺融入至上意識，不再有二元對待的境地。

   本體大樂：了悟終極實相大樂的靈性喜悅。

3. *Rája Yoga*, *Samádhi*, *Unmani*, *Manonmaní*, *Amarativa*, *Laya*, *Tattva*, *Súnya-aśúnya*, *Parama Pada*；

   勝王瑜伽、三摩地、心寂、意摩尼、不死地、深定、真如、空有一如、無上境；

心寂：一種心行寂滅之空如定境。

意摩尼定：詳第二章 42 節經句。

深定：甚深禪定；融於所觀定境之中。

空有一如：意指非空非有，既空既有；空有不二，空有一如之境。

4. *Amanaska*, *Advaitama*, *Nirãlamba*, *Nirañjana*, *Jívana Mukti*, *Sahajá*, *Turyá*, are all synonymous.

忘我、不二、無著、命解脫、本然、空明，都是三摩地的同義詞。

空明：意指心靈的第四種狀態——融入宇宙意識的狀態，其他三種是醒、夢、深眠。

5. As salt being dissolved in water becomes one with it, so when *Átmá* and mind become one, it is called *Samádhi*.

鹽粒入水即與水融而為一，如是心靈與自性本我融而為一，即名三摩地。

自性本我：意指靈魂、意識、真我、神聖的本我；相對字詞是假我、小我、個體我。

6. When the *Práṇa* becomes lean (vigourless) and the mind becomes absorbed, then their becoming equal is called *Samádhi*.

當氣息懸止，心念不生時之無差別境界，即名三摩地。

無差別：梵語 *Samarása*，此字和 *ekarása* 同義，意思是一味、等味、無差別，即無二元對待之意。

7. This equality and oneness of the self and the ultra self, when all *Saḿkalpas* cease to exist, is called *Samádhi*.

當個體意識與至上意識一如，所有思維分別俱泯，即名三摩地。

個體意識：個體靈魂、個體意識、個體小我。

至上意識：宇宙靈魂、宇宙本我、至上意識、至上本我。

思維分別：分別、思維、思想；心靈連結物質客體朝向外在世界的傾向。

8. Or, who can know the true greatness of the *Rája Yoga*. Knowledge, *mukti*, condition, and *Siddhís* can be learnt by instructions from a *Guru* alone.

誰能如實了知勝王瑜伽之功德？唯有從上師教誨中方能獲致深慧、解脫、安止和成就。

功德：修身修性，能助人超越濁世乃至三界的功用德行。

深慧：意指勝智、妙智、正智等屬靈的知識之謂，通譯知識。

安止：心靈安然寂止之處。謂於內心失念散亂時，仍能警醒反攝，安止善處。

9. Indifference to worldly enjoyments is very difficult to obtain, and equally difficult is the knowledge of the Realities to obtain. It is very difficult to get the condition of *Samádhi*, without the favour of a true *Guru*.

若無真上師之慈憫，若未出離世間享樂，甚難得證真如實相，更不易悟達本然三摩地。

本然三昧：梵語 *Sahajávasthá*，悟達本心境地之三摩地。

10. By means of various postures and different *Kumbhakas*, when the great power (*Kuṇḍalí*) awakens, then the *Práṇa* becomes absorbed in *Súnya* (*Samádhi*).

透過修習種種體位法、持氣法和身印法，喚醒巨大的靈力後，生命氣消融於空性中。

巨大的靈力：靈能軍荼利的別稱。

空性：一種非常深邃靈明的空寂境界。

11. The *Yogí* whose *śakti* has awakened, and who has renounced all actions, attains to the condition of *Samádhi*, without any effort.

一位喚醒靈力，且業累盡消的瑜伽行者，自能隨順生起本然三摩地。

行業盡消：行為之果已盡捨無餘之行人。

12. When the *Práṇa* flows in the *Suṣumná*, and the mind has entered *śúnya*, then the *Yogí* is free from the effects of *Karmas*.

當生命能行於中脈，心也消融在空性中，如是行人一切業累之根即除。

一切業累之根即除：意即獲得「不受一切業累影響」之果。

13. O Immortal one (that is, the *Yogí* who has attained to the condition of *Samádhi)*, I salute thee! Even death itself, into whose mouth the whole of this movable and immovable world has fallen, has been conquered by thee.

禮敬不朽者，宇宙動靜萬象都難逃其口的時間之輪，亦為汝所降伏。

不朽者：意指成道之瑜伽行者。

時間之輪：意表時間、時輪、死神等；此字英譯為死亡，中譯採更廣義之「時間之輪」。

14. *Amarolí*, *Vajrolí* and *Sahajolí* are accomplished when the mind becomes calm and *Práṇa* has entered the middle channel.

心若已達等持定境，氣息亦安行於中脈，其人已成就不老泉身印、金剛力身印和俱生力身印。

等持：梵語 *Samatva*，字義平等，此處意指平等維持，蓋心能住於一境故。

15. How can it he possible to get knowledge, so long as the *Práṇa* is living and the mind has not died? No one else can get *mokṣa*, except one who can make one's *Práṇa* and mind latent.

只要是心尚未寂止，出入息仍具動相，自性正智如何浮現心中？除非心、息俱止，無由能得真解脫。

16. Always living in a good locality and having known the secret of the *Suṣumná*, which has a middle course, and making the *Váyu* move in it., (the *Yogí*) should restrain the *Váyu* in the *Brahmarandhra*.

常坐處上善之地，循開通中脈之法，令生命氣行入其中，而後寂止於梵竅。

梵竅：一名梵穴，即頂輪或千瓣蓮花輪位置，至上意識與人身的接觸點。

17. Time, in the form of night and day, is made by the sun and the moon. That, the *Suṣumná* devours this time (death) even, is a great secret.

日月分時成晝夜，然時間卻為中脈所噬，此是一大奧密。

譯按：時間是一種量度，是頭腦二元思考的概念，亦是生與死的推手，然不存在於一元境界的範疇。

18. In this body there are 72,000 openings of *Nádis*; of these, the *Suṣumná*, which has the *Śámhhaví Śakti* in it, is the only important one, the rest are useless.

人身內部有七萬二千開啟的經脈，居首之中脈藏有純意識的陰性力量，是唯一重要之脈，其餘諸脈無甚大用。

純意識的陰性力量：靈能之別稱，覺醒後能予瑜伽行者妙喜悅。

19. The *Váyu* should be made to enter the *Suṣumná* without restraint by him who has practised the control of breathing and has awakened the *Kuṇḍali* by the (gastric) fire.

出入息調伏後，當運用發起之煖熱即時喚醒拙火，使其直入中脈。

出入息：泛指風、風大、風息，衍申義有呼吸、內息、出入息、生命氣等。

煖熱：此處指呼吸調伏後身內產生出的正能量，亦有版本譯作胃火或消化之火。

20. The *Práṇa*, flowing through the *Suṣumná*, brings about the condition of *manonmaṇí*; other practices are simply futile for the *Yogí*.

當生命氣通達中脈，行者自然入於意摩尼定境；若不圖此，鍛煉便只是無謂的努力。

21. By whom the breathing has been controlled, by him the activities of the mind also have been controlled; and, conversely, by whom the activities of the mind have been controlled, by him the breathing also has been controlled.

已調伏其氣者，亦能調伏其心；已調伏其心者，必能調伏其氣。

22. There are two causes of the activities of the mind: (1) *Vásaná* (desires) and (2) the respiration (the *Práṇa*). Of these, the destruction of the one is the destruction of both.

動念之因有二，是為熏習與風息；止寂其一，餘亦停歇。

動念之因：梵語 **hetu**，字義依處、因處，意即支持起心動念之因處。

熏習：意指染久成習之觀念、思想、作為，形成業行種子。

風息：此處指呼吸、氣息及身內一切來去如風的感受。

23. Breathing is lessened when the mind becomes absorbed, and the mind becomes absorbed when the *Práṇa* is restrained.

心止風即止，風止心亦止。

24. Both the mind and the breath are united together, like milk and water; and both of them are equal in their activities. Mind begins its activities where there is the breath, and the *Práṇa* begins its activities where there is the mind.

當心與息如水乳般交融時，心息動向相依；心動處即有息相，息動處即有心行。

息：泛指呼吸；古云「一出一入謂之息」，故以「息」之一字表之。

動：心息動態流轉、相續之相狀。

25. By the suspension of the one, therefore, comes the suspension of the other, and by the operations of the one are brought about the operations of the other. When they are present, the *Indriyas* (the senses) remain engaged in their proper functions, and when they become latent then there is *moksa*.

此止彼亦止，此動彼亦動，彼此動止相依。二者若未止歇，所有知作根便會忙於各自功用；一旦心息歸寂，即真解脫。

知作根：意指五種感覺器官與五種行動器官之總稱。

26. By nature, Mercury and mind are unsteady: there is nothing in the world which cannot be accomplished when these are made steady.

譬如水銀與心，其性皆動轉不定；若能使之安定凝止，世上何事不成？

27. O *Párvati!* Mercury and breathing, when made steady, destroy diseases and the dead himself comes to life (by their means). By their (proper) control, moving in the air is attained.

噢！帕瓦蒂，水銀般之心風若寂止，即能除一切病，死地亦得新生；彼若得控制，即能融入虛空。

帕瓦蒂：上主希瓦的法侶，別號雪山女神，常向希瓦提問一些靈修者關心的問題，並且把希瓦的回答整理出來，即成學人學習之依歸。

28. The breathing is calmed when the mind becomes steady and calm; and hence the preservation of *bindu*. The preservation of this latter makes the *sattva* established in the body.

內心安靜風息亦靜，如是明點亦得固守，明點固守者即能常保穩定悅性之身。

明點：詳第二章 78 節譯註。

29. Mind is the master of the senses, and the breath is the master of the mind. The breath in its turn is subordinate to the *laya* (absorption), and that *laya* depends on the *náda*.

心是感官之主，息是心之主，甚深定境是息之主，而深定則取決於秘音。

30. This very laya is what is called *mokṣa*, or, being a sectarian, you may not call it *mokṣa*; but when the mind becomes absorbed, a sort of ecstasy is experienced.

這種甚深禪定之境即名真解脫，或有宗派不作此名，但在心歸湛寂之後，確能經驗到難以言喻的靈性喜悅。

靈性喜悅：梵語 *Ánanda*，意為清淨、神聖的喜悅；無有消長起伏的絕對喜悅。

31. By the suspension of respiration and the annihilation of the enjoyments of the senses, when the mind becomes devoid of all the activities and remains changeless, then the *Yogí* attains to the *Laya* Stage.

不耽著感官欲樂，呼吸懸止若亡，如是內心放下一切外緣而安止不動；是為瑜伽士成就深定之相。

32. When all the thoughts and activities are destroyed, then the *Laya* Stage is produced, to describe which is beyond the power of speech, being known by self-experience alone.

當一切身心活動俱寂，甚深定境於焉生起；此境無法言傳，只能親自領會。

33. Where vision is directed, spiritual reality occurs. That in which the elements and the senses, as well as that *Shakti* which is in all living things, both are dissolved in the characteristicless.

一朝見性，實相現前；那隱於五大元素和感官之中，亦隱於所有生靈之中的造化力，都在甚深禪定中消弭於無形。

五大元素：形成物質世界的基礎元素，通常是指地、水、火、風、空等五大元素，亦稱固態、液態、光或熱、氣態、乙太元素。

34. They often speak of Laya, Laya; but what is meant by it? *Laya* is simply then forgetting of the objects of senses when the *Vásanás* (desires) do not rise into existence again.

人常言及深定、深定，但何謂深定？深定是無念塵緣，宿業餘習亦不復現之意。

宿業餘習：意指熏染久了以後所形成的習氣或欲望。

35. The *Vedas* and the *Śástras* are like ordinary public women. *Śámhhaví mudrá* is the one, which is secluded like a respectable lady.

吠陀、經論和往世書，有如鄉里淑女；而吉祥身印則如名門閨秀。

鄉里淑女：意喻較易親近之對象。

吉祥身印：也稱作希瓦身印。*Sámbhu* 意表希瓦，而希瓦一詞源自比梵語更早的印度先民達羅維荼語，意味著吉祥、完美，故譯為吉祥身印。

名門閨秀：出身高尚的閨秀，意喻即便熱情以對，然得親近者仍寡。

譯按：本節內容與《葛蘭達本集》第三章65節相似，是以大眾心理學觀點，藉淑女、閨秀之名比較知識和實修間的反差，無褒貶之意，事實上兩者成就的機會是均等的。

吉祥身印

36. Aiming at *Brahman* inwardly, while keeping the sight directed to the external objects, without blinking the eyes, is called the *Sámbhaví mudrá*, hidden in the Vedas and the *Sástras*.

內照真常，雙眼定睛若視外物，目不稍瞬，即是秘載於吠陀與典籍中的吉祥身印。

內照真常：往內觀照，專注在師授的集中點或脈輪上；而本節所指之觀照對象是真如自性，亦可謂至上本體，故英譯用詞是以內在之至上本體為專注目標。

雙眼定睛：一種入定後的神態——雙眼目不稍瞬，眼神內攝，見物如鏡映。

37. When the *Yogí* remains inwardly attentive to the *Brahman*, keeping the mind and the *Práṇa* absorbed, and the sight steady, as if seeing everything while in reality seeing nothing outside, below, or above, verily then it is called the *Sámbhaví mudrá*, which is learnt by the favour of a *Guru*. Whatever, wonderful, Súnya or *Asúnya* is perceived, is to be regarded as the manifestation of that great *Śambhú* (*Śiva*).

當瑜伽行人住於內在所觀，心息若止，眼瞳不動，雖視而不見，此為真吉祥身印。是法需蒙上師恩典授習，方得領悟此空有一如妙境實是至上意識之呈現。

空有一如：非有非空、空有不二的非二元境界。

38. The two states, the *Sámbhaví* and the *Khecharí*, are different because of their seats (being the heart and the space between the eyebrows respectively); but both cause happiness, for the mind becomes absorbed in the *Chita-sukha-Rupa-átmana* which is void.

吉祥身印與明空身印兩者雖然心、眼專注之處有別，然俱能生起大樂，蓋皆能使心融入真如本體之空性喜悅。

39. Fix the gaze on the light (seen on the tip of the nose) and raise the eyebrows a little, with the mind contemplating as before (in the *Śambhaví mudrá*, that is, inwardly thinking of *Brahma*, but apparently looking outside.) This will create the *Unmaní avasthá* at once.

雙眉微揚，兩眼繫意鼻端白光；以前述吉祥身印法存神內觀，可速登達心寂定境。

譯按：英文次行括號內文字為英譯註腳，中文意為「修持吉祥身印之重點在：眼半闔外視如鏡，心內觀思惟真常。」

救度者（The *Táraka*）

40. Some are devoted to the *Vedas*, some to *Nigama*, while others are enwrapt in Logic, but none knows the value of this *mudrá*, which enables one to cross the ocean of existence.

有囿於聖教羅網者，有惑於經論之言者，有迷於邏輯詰辯者，然無人識此堪為解脫津樑之身印。

聖教羅網：聖教或權威之言，喻權威之言錯綜如網。

經論之言：有關修行事理的言論。

識此津樑：原梵文 *jánanti tárakam*，直譯「識此能夠橫渡世海之橋樑」。

41. With steady calm mind and half closed eyes, fixed on the tip of the nose, stopping the *Idá* and the *Pingalá* without blinking, he who can see the light which is the all, the seed, the entire brilliant, great *Tattvama*, approaches Him, who is the great object. What is the use of more talk?

繫意鼻端，雙眼半闔，凝心不動，如是降伏日月兩脈而入定者，可親見萬象本源、如如真性之大光明；臻此實相，何用多言。

42. One should not meditate on the *Linga* (*i.e.*, *Átman*) in the day (*i.e.*, while *Súrya* or *Pingalá* is working) or at night (when *Idá* is working), but should always contemplate after restraining both.

禮拜萬象主不在於晝或夜，二六時中俱應心繫萬象主。

萬象主：印度聖地或廟宇常見的雕塑，形似男根，音譯靈根或林伽。靈性上象徵萬象的本源。

晝與夜：英譯於括號內的說明是—— 白晝是日脈或右脈工作時間，夜晚是月脈或左脈工作時間。

明空身印

43. When the air has ceased to move in the right and the left nostrils, and has begun to flow in the middle path, then the *Khecharí mudrá*, can be accomplished there. There is no doubt of this.

當活躍於左、右脈的生命氣轉寂而進入中脈，即是明空身印成就無疑。

44. If the *Práṇa* can be drawn into the *Súnya* (*Suṣumná*), which is between the *Idá* and the *Pingalá*, and make motionless there, then the *Khecharí mudrá* can truly become steady there.

生命氣若能沒入左右脈中間的空境而不動，於此境地明空身印方真穩定。

45. That *mudrá* is called *Khecharí* which is performed in the supportless space between the *Súrya* and the *Chandra* (the *Idá* and the *Pingalá*) and called the *Vyoma Chakra*.

此身印習者謂之「明空」，係因在日、月脈之間稱作空輪的無所緣處用功。

無所緣處：意指在無思、無作的空性上用功。

46. The *Khecharí* which causes the stream to flow from the *Chandra* (*Soma*) is beloved of *Śiva*. The incomparable divine *Suṣumná* should be closed by the tongue drawn back.

因明空身印引發月叢所分泌的甘露最為主希瓦所喜，故此殊妙無比的中脈口，須以反捲之舌從後覆蓋。

譯按：本節經句重點是——「從月叢流出的甘露最為主希瓦所喜，應將此甘露注入殊妙無比的中脈。」怎麼注入呢？本節次句提出的方法是以反捲之舌覆住中脈口，意為先阻其流失，而後再談及注入。

47. It can be closed from the front also (by stopping the movements of the *Práṇa*), and then surely it becomes the *Khecharí*. By practice,

this *Khecharí* leads to *Unmaní*.

此口若是自前覆蓋（即以舌抵上顎來阻止生命氣流動），亦是明空身印；勤習此身印，也能導入心寂定境。

48. The seat of *Śiva* is between the eyebrows, and the mind becomes absorbed there. This condition (in which the mind is thus absorbed) is known as *Túrya*, and death has no access there.

兩眉之間是主希瓦安坐之處，亦為心行寂滅之處；臻此即入空明之境，時間或死亡於此境中不復存在。

空明之境：意識的第四種狀態—— 個體意識融入宇宙意識；於此境中，意識的其他三種狀態——醒、夢和深眠（無夢的睡眠狀態），無有作用。

49. The *Khecharí* should be practised till there is *Yoga-nidrá* (*Samádhi*). One who has induced *Yoga-nidrá*, cannot fall a victim to death.

明空身印直須修煉至瑜伽眠境，於此境中，無有死亡（時間）之存在。

瑜伽眠：物質身處於深眠狀態，但意識是清醒的，然尚非空明境界。

50. Freeing the mind from all thoughts and thinking of nothing, one should sit firmly like a pot in the space (surrounded and filled with the ether).

宴坐時，令心無依無著，無思無作；如同壺置虛空，內外皆空。

51. As the air, in and out of the body, remains unmoved, so the breath with mind becomes steady in its place (*i.e.*, in *Brahmarandhra*).

當外在息相消停若亡，內息亦必轉趨平寂，屆時心、息都將安住本處。

息相：意指呼吸之外相，止觀法門謂息（呼吸）有「風、喘、氣、息」四相，靜坐時，前三種為不調相，第四種方為調相。

安住本處：安住於本所從來之處，亦即心、息未發前之清淨處。

52. By thus practising, night and day, the breathing is brought under control, and, as the practice increases, the mind becomes calm and steady.

如是日夜修煉制氣之道，待修至生命氣控制自如，如是漸增，其心亦將寂而不動。

53. By rubbing the body over with *Amrita* (exuding from the moon), from head to foot, one gets *Mahákáyá*, *i.e.*, great strength and energy.

從頭至足，讓甘露彌漫全身；習者可獲得相好大身，擁有勇健力和大能力。

相好大身：梵文直譯為大身，大於群輩之身；金剛經觀點，佛說非身，即名大身，亦有說「法身即名大身」。

三摩地

54. Placing the mind into the *Kuṇḍalini*, and getting the latter into the mind, by looking upon the *Buddhi* (intellect) with mind (reflexively), the *Param Pada* (*Brahma*) should be obtained.

將心置於造化力中，亦將造化力持於心中；靜心觀照此覺性，如是當證究竟地。

造化力：原經句梵文 *Śaktimı*，意指有大能力的，亦指造化勢能；有時亦為靈能軍荼利的同義詞，故英譯將之譯為軍荼利，中譯取其原意。

觀照此覺性：靜心觀照此菩提覺性。

究竟地：梵語 *paramam* 字義為至上、圓滿、究竟，*pada* 義為處、地；內心冥想、觀想欲融於其中的境地。

55. Keep the *átmá* inside the *Kha* (*Brahma*) and place *Brahma* inside

your *átmá*. Having made everything pervaded with *Kha* (*Brahma*), think of nothing else.

將真常本性住於空中，亦將空存於真常本性中；觀一切造化皆空，內心湛然清淨。

真常本性：真常的靈魂或本性。

空：意指至上本體或大梵之空性。

56. One should become void in and void out, and voice like a pot in the space. Full in and full outside, like a jar in the ocean.

內、外皆虛空，如壺置虛空；內、外皆實滿，如壺置海中。

內、外皆虛空：此句意旨為觀內、外無物，有如六祖惠能之言：本來無一物，何處惹塵埃。

壺：意喻人身。

內、外皆實滿：此句意旨頗有道家抽坎填離的觀念，以先天陽正之炁取代身內陰邪之氣。

57. He should be neither of his inside nor of outside world; and, leaving all thoughts, he should think of nothing.

外離諸相境色，內心亦復如是；棄捨一切念想，內心湛然清淨。

58. The whole of this world and all the schemes of the mind are but the creations of thought. Discarding these thoughts and taking leave of all conjectures, O *Ráma*! obtain peace.

所有胸中籌劃乃至整個世界唯心所造，但捨此心，離諸臆測，依止喜悅之源，即獲祥和平安。

喜悅之源：梵文 *Ráma*，音譯羅摩，上主名號之一；表超越一切念想的至上意識、喜源的源頭。

祥和平安：祝福平靜、寂靜、祥和平安之語。

59. As camphor disappears in fire, and rock salt in water, so the mind united with the *átmá* loses its identity.

有如樟腦融於火焰，鹽粒化於海水，心思在親嘗真諦後亦消融其中。

60. When the knowable, and the knowledge, are both destroyed equally, then there is no second way (*i.e.*, Duality is destroyed).

所知、已知和可知皆此一心，若已知和所知俱泯，即無二元之路。

皆此一心：意指所知、已知和可知皆為一心所現。

譯按：本節首句梵文 *jñeyaṃ sarvaṃ pratítaṃ cha jñánaṃ cha mana uchyate*，英譯缺譯，中譯補上。

61. All this movable and immovable world is mind. When the mind has attained to the *unmaní avasthá*, there is no *dvaita* (from the absence of the working of the mind.)

一切世間之動與不動，皆此一心；在心融於心寂定境後，二元亦不復存。

62. Mind disappears by removing the knowable, and, on its disappearance, *átmá* only remains behind.

盡棄所知，心即不存；心若不存，所餘者唯不共之真常。

所餘者唯不共之真常：即至上意識究竟之境。

63. The high-souled *Ácháryas* (Teachers) of yore gained experience in the various methods of *Samádhi* themselves, and then they preached them to others.

故知覺證之法有多門，俱是根據往昔大宗師們己身之三摩地經驗傳承下來。

秘音圓通

64. Salutations to Thee, O *Suṣumná*, to Thee O *Kuṇḍaliní*, to Thee O *Sudhá*, born of *Chandra*, to Thee O *Manonmnaní*! to Thee O great power, energy and the intelligent spirit.

禮敬彼中脈、軍荼利、月甘露、意摩尼、大造化力、純淨意識。

65. I will describe now the practice of *anáhata náda*, as propounded by *Gorakṣa Nátha*, for the benefit of those who are unable to understand the principles of knowledge—a method, which is liked by the ignorant also.

我現在要講述由葛拉克夏尊者所傳授的秘音法門。那些無暇學習經典，無法理解真如實義之人，也可以受持修習。

葛拉克夏尊者：本書作者的導師，見《哈達瑜伽明燈》第一章第 4 節。

66. *Ádinátha* propounded 1¼ crore methods of trance, and they are all extant. Of these, the hearing of the *anáhata náda* is the Only one, the chief, in my opinion.

至尊主希瓦曾傳授過一千二百五十萬種尚存的入定法，我認為只有秘音圓通法門是其中最好的。

一千二百五十萬：梵文 *crore*，又名 *koti*，音譯俱胝，字義千萬。

67. Sitting with *Mukta Ásana* and with the *Sámbhaví mudrá*, the *Yogí* should hear the sound inside his right ear, with collected mind.

習者取自在坐式進行吉祥身印，凝神靜慮，傾聽右耳內出現的秘音。

自在坐式：成就坐別名，見《哈達瑜伽明燈》第一章 37 節。
譯按：秉持正念，如法修持者，不必太在意秘音是否從右耳出。

68. The ears, the eyes, the nose, and the mouth should be closed and then the clear sound is heard in the passage of the *Suṣumná* which has been cleansed of all its impurities.

雙手按住眼、耳、鼻、口，若中脈已得淨化，將聽聞到中脈內清晰的秘音。

69. In all the *Yogas*, there are four states: (1) *árambha* or the preliminary, (2) *Ghata*, or the state of a jar, (3) *Parichaya* (known), (4) *niṣpatti* (consummate).

一切瑜伽修法中，都包含初修、充實、內化和圓成等四個階段。

初修階段

70. When the *Brahma granthi* (in the heart) is pierced through by *Práṇáyáma*, then a sort of happiness is experienced in the vacuum of the heart, and the *anáhat* sounds, like various tinkling sounds of ornaments, are heard in the body.

梵結貫通後，即有妙喜自空境生起，且能聽到身內有如各種鈴聲般的秘音。

梵結：據瑜伽傳統觀念，在人的精細身上有三道結位於中脈之上，三道結常態下都阻礙著人體生命能的自由流動。梵結是其中第一道結，束縛住海底輪和生殖輪，使人擔心健康、害怕死亡，過於依賴物質需求。

譯按：原梵文經句有 *anáhat* 一字，英譯認為是指心輪，故譯為「體驗到自真空之心輪生出的妙喜和心輪之聲。」而比哈瑜伽學院的 *Swami Muktibodhanan* 解釋梵結位於海底根持輪，本節 *anahata* 聲指的是一種非由樂器或器具產生的秘音。故這部分中譯有別於英譯。

71. In the *árambha*, a *Yogís* body becomes divine, glowing, healthy, and emits a divine smell. The whole of his heart becomes void.

當行人於初修階段內見自心空性，身體純淨健康，透出光澤及聖潔妙香。

充實階段

72. In the second stage, the airs are united into one and begin moving in the middle channel. The *Yogís* posture becomes firm, and he

becomes wise like a god.

達到第二個充實階段後，生命內息匯入中脈；彼時行人坐式安穩，智慧如神。

73. By this means the *Viṣṇu knot* (in the throat) is pierced which is indicated by highest pleasure experienced, And then the *Bherí* sound (like the beating of a kettle drain) is evolved in the vacuum in the throat.

當維世努結貫通後，將體驗到甚深的喜悅；於此空境，會聽到有如罐鼓的鼓聲。

維世努結：維世努結是第二道結，位在心輪一帶，有時也稱作心結；藉由我執以及個人的權力來阻礙軍荼利沿中脈上行。

罐鼓聲：*Bherí* 是一種印度鼓，形如罐，音似銅鼓或定音鼓。

內化階段

74. In the third stage, the sound of a drum is known to arise in the *Súnya* between the eyebrows, and then the *Váyu* goes to the *Maháśúnya*, which is the home of all the *siddhís*.

若進入第三個內化階段，於眉心空界升起有如牟陀羅鼓的聲音，內在風息融入此一切成就依止處的極勝空境。

牟陀羅鼓：梵語 *mardala*，一種印度的雙面筒狀鼓，至今仍常使用（本節英譯未指鼓名，查梵文經句為此鼓）。

75. Conquering, then, the pleasures of the mind, ecstasy is spontaneously produced which is devoid of evils, pains, old age, disease, hunger and sleep.

此結貫通，內心將經驗到俱生的本然喜悅，自得遠離邪惑、苦惱、老衰、疾病、飢餓和睡眠等要能失調之患。

要能：一種與身生俱有的重要生物能，梵語 *dosha*，要能失調即會罹患不同的疾病。請參考第一章第三十一節。

圓成階段

76. When the *Rudra granthi* is pierced and the air enters the seat of the Lord (the space between the eyebrows), then the perfect sound like that of a flute is produced.

魯德羅結貫通進入圓成階段後，一切內在風息歸趨本座，將聆聽到有如橫笛和維那琴合鳴的妙聲。

魯德羅結：此為第三道結，又稱額結，位置一般認為是在眉心輪處；欲穿越此結縛身須得無有眷戀塵世之心，且視眾生一如，隨緣以大愛行入世之事。

歸趨本座：融入原來之起始處，亦即至上主或造化主或自在主的坐處。

77. The union of the mind and the sound is called the *Rája Yoga*. The (real) *Yogí* becomes the creator and destroyer of the universe, like God.

當內心一切種種歸於一境，即名勝王瑜伽成就；瑜伽師如同自在主，成為能生滅者。

內心一切種種歸於一境：此語即原經句梵文 *ekíbhútaṃ tadá chittaṃ* 之直譯，英文版譯文之意是「心與內在音聲合一」，由於音聲或內在秘音亦內心種種之一，為貼近原意，中譯略作修訂。

自在主：梵語 *íśvara*，字義控制者，瑜伽哲學中意指心靈的控制者，亦即心靈的主人。又因一切唯心造，故亦稱之為能生滅者。

78. Perpetual Happiness is achieved by this; I do not care if the *mukti* be not attained. This happiness, resulting from absorption [in *Brahma*], is obtained by means of *Rája Yoga*.

無論有無解脫，行人已覺證此永恆大樂，如是大喜悅係勝王瑜伽之修行成就。

79. Those who are ignorant of the *Rája Yoga* and practise only the

Haṭha Yoga, will, in my opinion, waste their energy fruitlessly.

僅練習哈達瑜伽而未明勝王瑜伽之人，我認為修習者是白費力氣，難有成果。

80. Contemplation on the space between the eyebrows is, in my opinion, best for accomplishing soon the *Unmani* state. For people of small intellect, it is a very easy method for obtaining perfection in the *Rája Yoga*. The *Laya* produced by náda, at once gives experience (of spiritual powers).

我以為繫心眉間修定能速證心寂定境，亦是少智行人達悟勝王瑜伽境地之直捷行法，信受奉行者立可體驗到從秘音生起的甚深定境。

81. The happiness which increases in the hearts of *Yogiśvaras*, who have gained success in *Samádhi* by means of attention to the *náda*, is beyond description, and is known to *Śri Gur Nátha* alone.

從深聞秘音而入三摩地之觀自在瑜伽士，內心漸增無法言喻之大樂成就；如是進境，唯有了悟之上師能明。

觀自在瑜伽士：以自在主或以降伏心靈為成就目標的瑜伽行人。

大樂成就：純淨的靈性大喜悅。

82. The sound which a *muni* hears by closing his ears with his fingers, should be heard attentively, till the mind becomes steady in it.

以兩手捂住雙耳，牟尼如是傾聽內在秘音；須是十分留心諦聽，直至不動境地。

牟尼：字義寂靜、能默，亦指聖者、仁人，一心追求智慧的賢者或修行人。

83. By practising with this náda, all other external sounds are stopped. The *Yogí* becomes happy by overcoming all distractions within 15 days.

如是持續聞修秘音，一切外在音聲逐漸寂止，瑜伽行人將在十五天內克服一切散亂而生喜樂。

84. In the beginning, the sounds heard are of great variety and very loud; but, as the practice increases, they become more and more subtle.

修習初期，會聽到各種明顯的秘音；然而隨著修習的進展，其所聽聞到的也將愈趨精細。

85. In the first stage, the sounds are surging, thundering like the beating of kettle drums and jingling ones. In the intermediate stage, they are like those produced by conch, *Mridanga*, bells, etc.

初期可能聽到海潮聲、雲湧聲、罐鼓聲、鈸鼓聲，中期可能聽到牟陀羅鼓聲、海螺聲、鈴聲、和號角聲等類似的聲音。

譯按：本節八種聲音對應的梵文依次是 ***jaladhi***、***jimuta***、***bheri***、***jharjharaı***；***mardala***、***śankha***、***ghantá***、***Káhala***。

86. In the last stage, the sounds resemble those from tinkles, flute, *Víṇá*, bee, etc. These various kinds of sounds are heard as being produced in the body.

後期則會聽到像脆鈴、橫笛、維那琴和蜂鳴等聲音，如是種種所聞秘音俱來自身內。

譯註：本節四種聲音對應的梵文依次是 ***kinkini***、***vamśa***、***viná*** 和 ***bhramara***。

87. Though hearing loud sounds like those of thunder, kettle drums, etc., one should practise with the subtle sounds also.

即便聽到如雲湧聲、罐鼓聲等廣大音聲，修持時仍應專注於內在精細之秘音。

譯按：意即莫耽著所聞之音聲。

88. Leaving the loudest, taking up the subtle one, and leaving the subtle one, taking up the loudest, thus practising, the distracted mind does not wander elsewhere.

傾聽時或捨細聲而擇粗聲，或棄粗聲而擇細聲，然修持時決不可分心留連於其他。

89. Wherever the mind attaches itself first, it becomes steady there; and then it becomes absorbed in it.

無論內心最先受何秘音吸引，即專注於彼音，隨之直至融入定境。

90. Just as a bee, drinking sweet juice, does not care for the smell of the flower; so the mind, absorbed in the *náda*, does not desire the objects of enjoyment.

猶如蜂採花蜜不受花香所擾，心從秘音入三摩地之後，亦不受塵境欲樂所惑。

91. The mind, like an elephant habituated to wander in the garden of enjoyments, is capable of being controlled by the sharp goad of *anáhata náda*.

心意如同遊於塵境之醉象，秘音堪比功能馴象之刺棒。

馴象刺棒：一種帶有尖刺與倒鉤的短棒。

92. The mind, captivated in the snare of *náda*, gives up all its activity; and, like a bird with clipped wings, becomes calm at once.

一旦心為秘音之索調伏，一切躁動歸於平寂，不動若收攏雙翼之雀鳥。

93. Those desirous of the kingdom of *Yoga*, should take up the practice of hearing the *anáhata náda*, with mind collected and free from all cares.

志慕瑜伽無上成就者，當捨一切掛念，用心諦聽秘音。

94. *Náda* is the snare for catching the mind; and, when it is caught like a deer, it can be killed also like it.

秘音有如補捉心鹿之獵網，有如獵殺心鹿之獵戶。

心鹿：比喻心中之妄念。

95. *Náda* is the bolt of the stable door for the horse (the minds of the *Yogís*). A *Yogí* should determine to practise constantly in the hearing of the *náda* sounds.

亦有如控制意馬之銜轡，是故瑜伽行人應持恆地諦聽秘音。

意馬：以馬喻心意，形容其不易控制。

96. Mind gets the properties of calcined mercury. When deprived of its unsteadiness it is calcined, combined with the sulphur of *náda*, and then it roams like it in the supportless *ákáśa* or *Brahma*.

在有如硫磺之秘音的煅燒下，性若水銀之攀緣心遂失其動性，而能悠遊於無依倚之空性中。

97. The mind is like a serpent, forgetting all its unsteadiness by hearing the *náda*, it does not run away anywhere.

心思如毒龍，一旦內聞秘音後，即忘卻一切心妄，不再外馳。

98. The fire, catching firewood, is extinguished along with it (after burning it up); and so the mind also, working with the *náda*, becomes latent along with it.

燒柴生火，柴盡火熄；內觀秘音，心亦如是隨聲消融。

99. The *antahkaraṇa* (mind), like a deer, becomes absorbed and motionless on hearing the sound of hells, etc.; and then it is very easy for an expert archer to kill it.

心之作用猶如鹿性，會受鈴音吸引而止步，是時即易為善射者獵補。

鈴音：比喻秘音。

善射者：靈性上意指嫻熟反聞秘音之瑜伽行人。

100. The knowable interpenetrates the *anáhata* sound which is heard, and the mind interpenetrates the knowable. The mind becomes absorbed there, which is the seat of the all-pervading, almighty Lord.

所觀隱於所聞之秘音中，心入於所聞秘音即入所觀，如是心亦深定於遍在主維世努之至上寶座。

所觀：英譯所用之 knowable 是對應梵文 *upalabhyate* 一字，查梵漢字典 *upalabhyate* 一字之解釋有所知、所得、所見、所觀等，而細審句義，譯為所觀，更可以表現經句文義。所觀之標即至上意識或至上主。

維世努之至上寶座：比喻融入見至上意識存於一切遍在中之定境，維世努通譯遍在天或妙毗天，是俱屬性世界的維持者。

101. So long as the sounds continue, there is the idea of *ákáśa*. When they disappear, then it is called *Param Brahma*, *Paramátmana*.

吠陀有言：有聲作用處，即存有空識；唯彼俱寂，方得融入至上本體或無上自性。

吠陀有言：原經句梵文 *gíyate* 一字之字義為榮耀，然亦有用作「吠陀之言」之義。

至上本體：舊譯大梵或至上大梵，同義詞有本初、本體、道體、至上實相等譯名。

無上自性：即清淨無染之淨識；常用之譯名有 - 至上靈魂、至上意識乃至至上真我等譯名。

102. Whatever is heard in the form of *náda*, is the *śakti* (power). That which is formless, the final state of the *Tattvas*, is tile *Parameśvara*.

一切所聞音聲俱為造化力之用，唯彼無形無相之終極真性，方是無上自在主。

終極真性：梵文 *tattvánta*，*tattva* 字義真諦、真實義、真如理，*ánta* 為盡、端、末、邊際等義；故直譯為終極真性。

無上自在主：舊譯大自在天，字義是萬象心靈最高的控制者。

三摩地中的瑜伽行者

103. All the methods of *Haṭha* are meant for gaining success in the *Rája Yoga*; for the man, who is well-established in the *Rája Yoga*, overcomes death.

所有哈達瑜伽之修法都是為了勝王瑜伽成就，安住勝王瑜伽之人即可欺瞞死亡。

欺瞞死亡：梵語 *kála-vañcakaḥ*，*kála* 也表示時間，因為一切生命俱在時間推移下消亡。*vañcakaḥ* 字義為惑、誑、欺、詐等。

104. *Tattva* is the seed, *Haṭha* the field; and Indifference (*Vairágya*) the water. By the action of these three, the creeper *Unmaní* thrives very rapidly.

真性如種子，哈達如田土，離欲如淨水；合此三者修行，心寂定境將如願湧現。

真諦：真實義諦，關於本體實相方面的真理。

哈達：哈達瑜伽之簡稱。

離欲：意指離欲心，心無執著方可為灌溉真性之水。

105. All the accumulations of sins are destroyed by practising always with the *náda*; and the mind and the airs do certainly become latent in the colorless (*Paramátmana*).

常修持秘音可滅除所積累之罪業，心與息亦必消融於清淨無染之中。

清淨無染：梵語 *nirañjana*，字義是無瑕、離垢、無染，意指無染無縛無有屬性的純意識狀態。

106. Such a one. does not hear the noise of the conch and *Dundubhi*. Being in the *Unmaní avasthá*, his body becomes like a piece of wood.

如是修之有成者，在心寂定境中，身形安止若枯木，彼時不復聽聞海螺、法鼓等聲。

107. There is no doubt, such a *Yogí* becomes free from all states, from all cares, and remains like one dead.

如是瑜伽行人，外離一切諸相，內心無有掛礙，死生一如無別，無疑已臻自在解脫。

無疑已臻自在解脫：原經句末梵文 *mukto nátra saṃśayaḥ* 之中譯，英譯遺漏。

108. He is not devoured by death, is not bound by his actions. The *Yogí* who is engaged in *Samádhi* is overpowered by none.

三摩地中的瑜伽行者，不被死亡吞噬，不受業力繫縛，亦不受任何人事影響。

109. The *Yogí*, engaged in *Samádhi*, feels neither smell, taste, color, touch, sound, nor is conscious of his own self.

三摩地中的瑜伽行者，於色、聲、香、味、觸等不生執念，亦無自、他之分別。

110. He whose mind is neither sleeping, walking, remembering, destitute of memory, disappearing nor appearing, is liberated.

其心處於非醒非眠，非憶非忘，非有念非無念之人，是為真自在解脫者。

111. He feels neither heat, cold, pain, pleasure, respect nor disrespect. Such a *Yogí* is absorbed in *Samádhi*.

三摩地中的瑜伽行者，無有冷、熱、樂、苦及榮、辱之分別。

112. He who, though awake, appears like one sleeping, and is without inspiration and expiration, is certainly free.

安穩無病，醒夢一如，呼吸似有而若無，無疑是真自在解脫者。

113. The *Yogí*, engaged in *Samádhi*, cannot be killed by any instrument, and is beyond the controlling power of beings. He is beyond the reach of incantations and charms.

三摩地中的瑜伽行者，一切刀兵不能傷，眾生不能勝，亦不被符文、呪術所拘。

114. As long as the *Práṇa* does not enter and flow in the middle channel and the *vindu* does not become firm by the control of the movements of the *Práṇa*; as long as the mind does not assume the form of *Brahma* without any effort in contemplation, so long all the talk of knowledge and wisdom is merely the nonsensical babbling of a mad man.

只要生命氣尚未通達中脈，只要明點尚未經由調伏生命能而堅固，只要心尚未經由禪法澈見實相，則所有關於靈修知識的談論，都是癡人夢語。

附錄

瑜伽日常
修行指引

這篇〈瑜伽日常修習指引〉總有二十一條，原附於由潘強辛英譯的《哈達瑜伽明燈》第二章50節之後。審其編排未知是否《哈達瑜伽明燈》原典所有，亦未通見於其他版本。不過逐條弄清楚內容後，發現這其實是一篇很具參考價值的日常實修指引，反映了正統瑜伽士日課的細節。緣此，特別迻譯如下。

1. I am going to describe the procedure of the practice of *Yoga*, in order that *Yogís* may succeed. A wise man should leave his bed in the *Uṣá* Kála (i.e., at the peep of dawn or 4 o'clock) in the morning.

   為利修行者成就，現在我要談談瑜伽練習的過程。慧智行人宜於清晨四點起床。

2. Remembering his *Guru* over his head, and his desired deity in his heart, after answering the calls of nature, and cleaning his mouth, he should apply *Bhaṣma* (ashes).

   起床後，於其頂首憶念上師，並在如廁漱洗後，以灰塗身。

   以灰塗身：見塗灰二字，即連想到塗灰外道，不過非洲某些部族亦有塗灰於身的習慣，所以不能認定塗灰就是外道。印度天熱，且因物質條件關係，瑜伽行人一般習慣只著下裳。塗灰於身可防蚊蟲叮咬，並具防止晒傷之效，有其實用功能；是否外道，還需於心地求之。

3. In a clean spot, clean room and charming ground, he should spread a soft ásana (cloth for sitting on). Having seated on it and remembering, in his mind his *Guru* and his God.

   擇靜室平坦潔淨之處，鋪於坐處；盤坐其上，虔心憶念其上師和本尊。

4. Having extolled the place and the time and taking up the vow thus: 'To day by the grace of God, I will perform *Prànàyàmas* with *ásanas* for gaining samádhi (trance) and its fruits.' He should salute the infinite *Deva*, Lord of the *Nàgas*, to ensure success in the *ásanas* (postures).

每回靜坐前，默念如下誓言：「今日承主恩典，我將虔心調息宴坐入三摩地以達成就果。」習者應禮敬永恆的宇天龍王，以確保坐式能有成就。

宇天龍王：此處指的是維持宇宙之神——妙毗天、維世努或遍在天。

5. Salutation to the Lord of the *Nágas*, who is adorned with thousands of heads, set with brilliant jewels (ma is), and who has sustained the whole universe, nourishes it, and is infinite. After this he should begin his exercise of *ásanas* and when fatigued, he should practise *Śava ásana*. Should there be no fatigue, he should not practise it.

頂禮坐於光輝寶座，頭飾千首的宇天龍王，祂無有止盡地維繫、滋育著浩瀚的宇宙。之後即可開始體位法式的習練，若覺疲倦，可以大休息式躺下，未恢復前，不宜繼續練習。

大休息式：又名攤屍式，可迅速消除疲勞。詳見第一章第三十四節。

6. Before *Kumbhaka*, he should perform *Viparíta Karaṇí mudrá*, in order that he may be able to perform *Jálandhar bandha comfortably*.

進行持氣法之前，應先練習倒轉身印，俾能舒適地練習收頷鎖印。

倒轉身印：類似肩立式，詳見第三章第七十八節。

收頷鎖印：持氣法常做的鎖印，屬三種上品鎖印之一，詳見第三章第七十節。

7. Sipping a little water, he should begin the exercise of *Práṇáyáma*, after saluting *Yogindras*, as described in the *Karma Paráńa*, in the words of iva.

啜飲些水，習者即可開始練習生命能控制法（調息法）。首先依如下希瓦教法作禮本師。

8. Such as "Saluting *Yogindras* and their disciples and *Guru Vináyaka,*

the *Yogí* should unite with me with composed mind."

「作禮瑜伽主及其傳承與除障上師之後，瑜伽修行者應潛心與我作連結。」

除障上師：梵文 *Guru Vináyaka*，擅掃除信眾道途障礙，是印度最受歡迎的神祇之一象神的別名。

我：此處是上主希瓦的第一人稱。

9. While practising, he should sit with Siddhásana, and having performed bandha and Kumbhaka, should begin with ten *Práṇáyámas* the first day, and go on increasing five daily.

   本修習應採完美坐式來鍛煉鎖印和持氣法，第一天從十次調息開始，之後每日增加五息。

   完美坐式：詳見第一章第三十五節。

10. With composed mind 80 *Kumbhakas* should be performed at a time; beginning first with the *chandra* (the left nostril) and then *súrya* (the right nostril).

    直到能夠靜心調息至一坐八十次持氣為止，第一息以月脈（左鼻孔）入息，然後以日脈（右鼻孔）出息。

11-12. This has been spoken of by wise men as *Aṇuloma and Viloma*. Having practised *Súrya Bhedan*, with *Bandhas*, the wise rust) should practise *Ujjáyí* and then *Sítkárí Śítalí*, and *Bhastriká*, he may practice others or not.

智者在解釋左右脈交替呼吸法時曾說過，每次隨鎖印練習日脈通達法時後，識者應繼續進行勝利呼吸法，然後接著嘶聲持氣法及風箱調息法，這些以外的可根據需求選擇是否練習。

左右脈交替呼吸法：意即順逆交替深呼吸法，與第二章第七節所述的左右脈淨化呼吸法是同一呼吸法，但在語意上要求呼吸的更深。

13. He should practise mudrás properly, as instructed by his *Guru*. Then sitting with *Padmásana*, he should hear *anáhata náda* attentively.
習者應當依照上師指示，正確地練習身印。然後取蓮花坐式靜坐，專心一意傾聽內在秘音。

14. He should resign the fruits of all his practice reverently to God, and, on rising on the completion of the practice, a warm bath should be taken.
每次完成修習，應將所有的修持成果虔心地回向給上師或本尊。修畢之後，宜以溫水沐浴。

15. The bath should bring all the daily duties briefly to an end. At noon also a little rest should be taken at the end of the exercise, and then food should be taken.
浴後進行當日所有的工作直至告一段落。午課修習結束，應稍事休息再進食。

16. *Yogís* should always take wholesome food and never anything unwholesome. After dinner he should eat *Ilháchí or lavanga*.
瑜伽修行者始終應該選取有益健康的飲食，切忌攝取無益健康的飲食。用完晚餐，宜吃點綠荳蔻或丁香。

17. Some like camphor, and betel leaf. To the *Yogís*, practising *Práṇáyáma*, betel leaf without powders, i, e., lime, nuts and *kátha*, is beneficial.
有些人喜歡樟木香，有些人喜歡蒟醬葉；對瑜伽行者而言，修習生命能控制法期間，不添加石灰粉、堅果碎和兒茶粉的蒟醬葉是有益的。

蒟醬葉：亦名荖葉、蔞葉、蓽芠等，常用來包檳榔。味辛微甘，性溫；富含鐵、鈣、維化命 B 群，具有祛風散寒、行氣化痰、消腫止癢之效。外用有助傷口癒合，口嚼保持口腔衛生；內用有助消化，葉搗汁加入鮮奶可利尿；加蜂蜜可止咳化痰，改善自律神經紊亂。

18. After taking food he should read books treating of salvation, or hear *Purá* as and repeat the name of God.

餐後宜閱讀靈性書籍，或是聆聽往世書並默誦上主洪名。

19. In the evening the exercise should be begun before finishing *Sandhyá*, as before, beginning the practice 3 *ghatiká* or one hour before the sun sets.

晚課修行應始於晚供之前，亦即應於日落前一小時開始練習。

譯按：梵文 *Sandhyá* 指的是日夜交會之時，如黎明或黃昏。這是左右脈與中脈在眉心輪融會的時辰，此時的氣場有利於生命氣融入中脈。

20. Evening *sandhyá* should always be performed after practice, and *Haṭha Yoga* should be practised at midnight.

晚供始終應在修習之後完成，而哈達瑜伽應在午夜之前完成練習。

譯按：印度保留有在黎明及黃昏之時進行早、晚供的習慣。而午夜時分則是內、外在能量轉換之際，萬籟沉寂，有助喚醒靈能軍荼利。

21. *Viparíta Karṇí* is to be practised in the evening and at midnight, and not just after eating, as it does no good at this time.

倒轉身印宜在傍晚與午夜之間練習，不宜在餐後即練，這是不恰當時間。

葛蘭達本集

Gheraṇḍa Saṁhitá

〈中譯本前言〉

最古老的哈達瑜伽百科

《葛蘭達本集》書名的意思是葛蘭達經句集成，是瑜伽成就者葛蘭達回答旃檀迦帕里問法的記錄，內容分為七章三百五十一節。本書作者及成書年代均不詳，從現存的梵文文獻中也沒有葛蘭達與旃檀迦帕里的記載，因此本書可能是一部深入瑜伽修行的隱士之作。

葛蘭達尊者的回答包含了從身體的淨化到契入三摩地之道，呈現出瑜伽是一門昇華生命的鍛煉，而所有的古本瑜伽典籍都勾勒出相同的要旨。因此欲進一步了解瑜伽的精神，閱讀古老的瑜伽典籍不失為現代行人的方便途徑。《葛蘭達本集》除了《哈達瑜伽明燈》所敘及的四支瑜伽外，另專章論及身清淨法、心收攝法及禪定法，含括了勝王瑜伽八支功法的後六支，並帶進了一些密續的修法。在身清淨法一章中列舉了許多清淨身體的技巧與療效，三摩地一章則對三昧定境作了知性的分類。在古典瑜伽文本中《葛蘭達本集》的內容被認為最為豐富也最詳盡，因此有著「瑜伽百科」的美名。

勝王瑜伽的修持建基在內外在規範，哈達瑜伽的修持建基在清淨身心，故需從清淨身心起修，這一部分在《葛蘭達本集》中敘述的最完整。傳統的哈達瑜伽行人即是試圖透過身心淨化、生命能控制、身印、禪定等的鍛煉來達到更深邃的定境，進而登入勝王瑜伽的殿堂，以期了悟最高的自性真我。

本書介紹了許多瑜伽常見的以及不常見的修法，但讀者應避免因好奇而隨意修習。依傳統規矩，學習瑜伽通常會依止一位信得過的明師，在沒有富經驗者的指導下，不宜冒然自習，以免生害。本書前言之後有一篇英譯導讀，是了解哈達瑜伽的捷徑，非常值得一讀。

《葛蘭達本集》的梵文抄本在十七世紀被發現，累計各地發現的手抄本有十四本之多。本書梵英譯本現有四種版本，第一位翻譯者是十九世紀印度知名的學者室利薩．旃德羅．婆藪（*Srisa Chandra Vasu*, 1861-1918），他是當時知名的數學和梵文學者，譯作頗豐，包括印度大學者帕里尼的古梵語文法《八章書》、《希瓦本集》、《吠檀多經》等，因此英譯的內容當無疑義；若有矛盾處，問題較可能出在梵文抄本，像是本書第三章 77 節和第五章 39 節對於心輪風元素顏色不一致的譯文。不過室利薩．旃德羅．婆藪所英譯的瑜伽典籍仍是流傳最廣的版本，本書中譯即是採用他的英譯本，有疑處再參照梵文羅馬拼音之經句解釋。原英譯本附註有限，中譯本則增加了大量的註釋，希望有助讀者了解。本書雖細心迻譯，或仍不免疏漏，還請同好指教。

《哈達瑜伽明燈》和《葛蘭達本集》都介紹了許多體位法和身印，前者研究者較多，有關的出版品多附有圖片可供參考；後者研究者較少，加之有些描述過簡，可供參考的圖像便相對不足。一八八六年德國的印度學者理查．蓋柏在印北聖城瓦那納西買下一組關於《葛蘭達本集》內所述體位法、淨化法和身印的手繪圖稿，這些手繪圖雖然不及照片詳盡，但亦饒富古趣。可在後列網址看到這些手繪圖 http://www.payer.de/quellenkunde/quellen072.htm

〈英譯本導讀〉

如法修習，可除一切病

《葛蘭達本集》是一部論述哈達瑜伽的密學事典，由古瑜伽大師葛蘭達和參學者旃檀迦帕里以對話的方式呈現。書的內容分成七個主題或說七篇章節，共三百五十一節經句，其內容和知名的哈達瑜伽典籍《哈達瑜伽明燈》相似；事實上，《葛蘭達本集》中有許多與《哈達瑜伽明燈》裡近乎雷同的經句，因此兩者有可能相互借鏡，或是兩者取材自共通的來源。

本書藉靈性修持的七個篇章來教導瑜伽。第一章教導身清淨法，第二章聚焦體位法，第三章身印法，第四章感官內攝法，第五章生命能調息法，第六章瑜伽禪定法，第七章三摩地。這些教導循序漸進，篇章相互呼應（見第一章 9 至 11 節）。

哈達瑜伽的理論，泛言之，就是專注執持或三摩地是可以透過身清淨法及某些身體的鍛煉來達成。身、心之間的關係是如此的周密與細緻，相互的作用是如此的微妙以及籠罩著這麼多的神秘，因此哈達瑜伽修習者認為身體經過一定的鍛煉就會產生一定的心理轉換毫不足怪。

晚近哈達瑜伽的另一種解釋是：瑜伽意指「哈」（ह-*ha*）和「達」（ठ-*tha*）的結合，「哈」表日，「達」表月；或表示命根氣和下行氣的結合，這也是一種提升到更高層面的生理轉化過程。

細讀本書後，若是一位客觀的研究者，第一個浮現的問題通常會是：這一切有可能嗎？這些練習，能產生書中所說的效果嗎？

關於這些練習的可能性，可以不用懷疑。書中所述並不違反任何解剖或生理上的事實。這些練習，至少其中某些方法，或許令人反感和噁心，但這些練習並非不可能。甚至，許多讀者也可能遇到過能夠演練這些功法的人，這樣的人在印度絕不少見。每一朝聖之地，像是瓦拉納西和阿拉哈巴德，都有這些處在不同進展階段的修士。我的上師亦曾向我示範過所有遊客們在阿拉哈巴德和密洛特見到的幾種練習，也告訴過一些人如何自我練習。比較困難的功法，像是水洗法（第一章 17 節）、火洗法（第一章 20 節）、根莖清潔法（第一章 37 節）、布清潔法（第一章 40 節）等等，他都示範過；還示範過各種淨腸法、淨鼻法、體位法等等。其中不少可歸類為健身的體操，他們的演練並非得像聖徒一般，有些人藉表演各種體位法和身印來謀求生計。一些較困難的體式對於肌肉緊繃和因為老化而骨骼僵硬的人，確實難以做到，但也不必因年齡因素做不到而失望。習法中規律的生命能調息法、心思集中法和瑜伽禪定法可以適用於所有人。

至於這些練習的功效，也有人抱持著懷疑，且認為有許多練習看起來好像還滿冒險的，即使沒有正面的害處，但也可能是沒有用的。雖然我知道要在短短的篇幅裡合理化所有的練習是不可能的，不過為了向心存懷疑的讀者證明，我仍將扼要地說明其中的一些好處。我且先從風洗法（第一章 15 節）開始。這是一種飲氣入腹，從穀道排出的過程。人體內最大的管道是消化道，它從食道開始，結束於直腸，垂直長度約八十公分；功用是消化、吸收食物然後幫助廢物排出身體。生理的自然機制會定期的清理廢物，而瑜伽練習使得清理更暢通、自發。如果清理不完全，在胃與腸之間的糞便就會腐爛，產生出有害及有毒氣體，引發疾病。藉風洗法使腸道通氣，氧化體內糞便，從而有益健康以及增加消化能力；事實上，它有協調整個系統的作用。同樣的，水洗法是以水代風沖洗腸道，徹底地清洗整付胃腸；和通便劑與瀉藥的作用相同，但效益更增十倍且沒有藥害。通曉風洗法和水洗法的人，即不再需要瀉藥。另外腸洗法（第一章 22 節）和火洗法也具有相同的作用，可使腸胃的神經和肌肉接受意志的控制。藉由溫和的滾動胃腹及腸道，活化這些器官原本的呆滯不振，以更大的活力履行其責。第一章二十三節、二十四節介紹的腸洗法二，是有點危險，或可能導致直腸脫垂。能做水洗法的人不需要做 23 節、24 節介紹的腸洗法二。清潔牙齒和舌頭的優點是顯而易見的，無需多言。展延舌頭（第一章 32 節）對修習瑜伽定境的人有其必要。之所以這樣做，是模仿冬眠動物，像青蛙等；牠們在蟄伏時，舌頭回捲向上，將呼吸道封住。也許，在所有淨胃法中最有趣的是布清潔法（第一章 41 節），此法令不了解的人以為一個瑜伽士可以把腸子從口中拉出來清洗，再吞回去歸位。其實這個淨胃方法是非常簡單的過程，透過此法，能清除附著在消化道上粘液、痰濕等濁物。水洗法和風洗法都不能清除這些牢附在管壁上的粘性物質。

淨鼻法是一種清潔鼻腔的簡單過程，可防治感冒和鼻粘膜炎的形成。淨腦法（第一章 55 節）是淨化前額竇的方法，據說此處是智慧之所在。這處竇腔部位不能從外部直接處理，然而藉由淨腦法，圍繞額竇與遍佈前額的神經會被激活而起作用。

第二章論及不同的體位法，是身瑜伽的練習，對一般的健康、內心的平靜和沉澱情緒有益。本書介紹了三十二種體式，其功效和重要性不盡相同。蓮花坐是最受普遍認可的體式，有些並不常見，只是為了變換口味和增加趣味。有的體式藉減弱特定部位的神經作用可以幫助抑制本能的激情，有的則透過特定肌肉群的張力和伸展引生出某種力量增強和清新舒暢的愉悅感。體位法是幫助瑜伽冥想坐姿穩定持久的良藥，否則不良的習慣也有可能導致心理幻覺和神經失調。

身印法在動作姿勢和功效上與體位法類似。淨目法有時具有誘發催眠之效。而鎖印或收束法是封閉所有出入息門戶，俾在身體系統內產生一種張力，藉之引發一股名為靈能軍荼利的強力電能。而能使瑜伽師行使奇行異事的就是這股靈力。明空身印（第三章 25-27 節）可令身懸浮於空，現在已被確認這種懸浮是可能的。只是西方科學尚不完全清楚那要在什麼特定條件下才會發生，唯止息持氣是其條件之一，這毋庸置疑。力動身印是種神秘的修煉，直到行人親證前都是很難被相信的。身印法是混合了生理和心理的鍛煉，是體位法和生命能調息法間的橋樑。

第四章只有五節經句，講述感官內攝之法，重點是把外馳的心靈收歸於內，並將之導入一不變的理念。所有五種感官都必須受到控制，且不得移轉失焦。

生命能調息法或呼吸法是哈達瑜伽中很殊勝的一環，練習時如果沒有稱職的導師指引有其危險性，但若是在老師的督導下練習則是很有幫助的。曾有這方面豐富經驗的專家說過：「如法修習，可除一切病；但若修習不如法，則生一切病，諸如打嗝、哮喘、咳嗽、頭痛、耳朵痛、眼疾等等！」所以跟從一位切實的明師學習呼吸功法是絕對必要的。本書所提供的指引是頗有用的輔助規則，只要能嚴守這些規則，那麼，就能夠避開許多的錯誤和危險。修習場所當擇獨居之斗室，季節宜於春、秋兩季，飲食應選輕淡悅性之食品；這都是一些重要的前置準備。過度的勞累與禁食等均應避免（第五章相關諸節）。這清楚地表明了哈達瑜伽不該和苦行主義混為一談，兩者實際相差頗遠。猶如不能視運動選手的培訓為苦行，所以也不能如是看待哈達瑜伽的修行。的確，獨身生活對兩者而言都是必要的條件，然而獨身本身並不構成苦行。食物上的指示似乎偏向西孟加拉人的飲食習慣，顯然本書作者是西孟加拉邦的維世努派修士，然而對於其他國家及學人，這些指示可能並不全都適用。不過動物性食物、煙酒和麻醉毒品，在所有地方都應嚴格禁止。

生命能調息有三個部分：吸氣或入息、持氣或住息與呼氣或出息。這三者的比例應該是一比四比二，亦即若吸氣用了十二秒，那麼就持氣四十八秒，再用二十四秒呼氣。該比率應保持不變，但吸氣長度可酌量增減，往復循環次數也可以逐漸增加。初學者練習時應謹慎，別超過十六秒比六十四秒比三十二秒。修習期間，習者應仔細地觀察各種心理和生理上的變化。汗水應該使用乾毛巾擦拭，若發生有渾身抖動的感覺也不用害怕。有時習者可能猛地從坐席拔起，有時可能會不自主地像青蛙一樣在房間裡跳動；別用這些來嚇唬他，其實並不一定會有這些生理現象。有時也會產生一些心理上的反應，習者可能聽到某些聲音，看見某些異象，聞到奇特的香味，或是嚐到令人愉悅的美味等等。這些大都是幻覺，顯示出神經系統的某種興奮狀態，只要不去在意，這些現象很快就會自行消退。除此之外，真理的靈光也會不時地在習者心中發亮。有時心處空境時，習者內心可能反映出遠地的景象或事件，或者人們會在心中見到祂，他自己也可能會出神離身，以不可思議的速度漫遊太空。這些都是伴隨著呼吸或調息法可能有的現象。明師必須能時刻從旁給予協助與督導，否則可能產生精神錯亂而非洞悉千里的能力。這些是調息法更高境界的現象。每個人都可以練習兩三分鐘調息法，親身體驗一下它的效果。有些微恙，像是頭痛、腹痛、忽熱忽冷、身心疲憊等，在練習兩三次持氣之後就會緩解或消失。有些人天生就具備修習調息法的能力，西方的史威登堡 * 是一個實際的例子。我們每一個人專注深層思考的時候，也都不自覺地在練習著調息法。十種生命氣（第五章 60 節）是人體內各種的神經脈衝或能量流，各有其特定的作用。

第五章講解各種持氣法，並不需要太多的闡釋。蜂鳴持氣法（第五章 78 節），或許略帶神秘，它可以使習者聽到稱作秘音的各種內在聲音。這些聲音據說是流經動脈和靜脈的血液在體內造成的，一心專注於此內在秘音，能很快的進入定境。

禪定法與三摩地純是心地法門，是專心內觀一處以生三昧定境之法。在某種層面上，催眠術的實驗也證明了這一點。將心專注於一境或一個理念也可以使心智能力提高。

室利薩・旃德羅・婆藪（*Srisa Chandra Vasu*, 1861-1918）

---

* 譯按：史威登堡（Swedenbourg, 1688-1772），瑞典科學家、神秘主義者、哲學家和神學家；著有神秘學巨著《天堂與地獄》。

第一章

身清淨法

The Training of the Physical Body

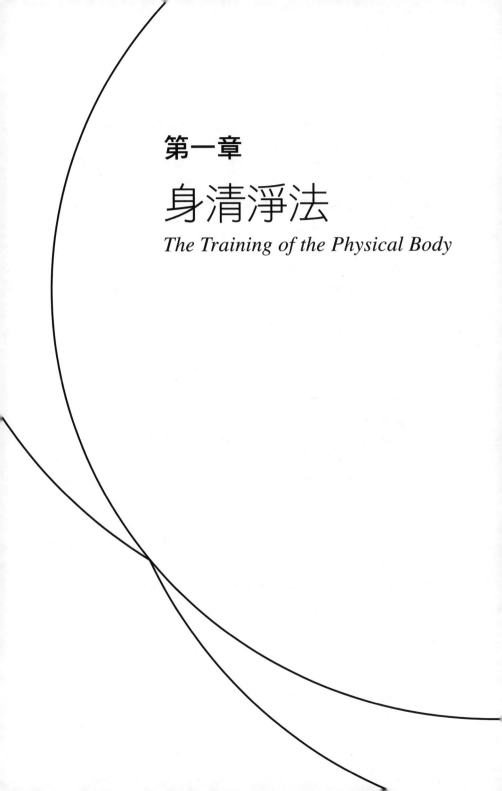

I bow to that Lord Primeval who taught in the beginning the science of the Training in Hardiness (*Haṭha Yoga*) — a science that stands out as the first rang on the ladder that leads to the supreme heights of Royal Training (*Rája Yoga*).

我向教導哈達瑜伽之道的先師致敬，此法門誠為晉身至高勝王瑜伽的階梯。

1. Once *Canḍrakápali* going to the cottage of *Gheranḍa* saluted him with reverence and devotion.

   一日旃檀迦帕里前往葛蘭達修舍，以至誠心向師禮敬，如是請求：

   旃檀迦帕里：問法者，有謂其為一邦之君，而從其名推測亦為希瓦宗的行人。

   葛蘭達：哈達瑜伽導師，教導弟子旃檀迦帕里七種瑜伽身心修法的隱士，生平不詳。

2. O Master of *Yoga* ! O best of the *Yogins* ! O Lord ! I wish now to learn the Physical Discipline (*Yoga*), which leads to the knowledge of truth (or *Tattva- jñána*).

   噢，瑜伽師！噢，瑜伽尊！噢，上主！弟子以至誠，求教趣向真智之身瑜伽法。

   真智：世出世間的智慧真理。

   身瑜伽法：非僅指體位法，而是本章 10-11 節所說的七支修法。

3. Well asked, indeed, O mighty armed, I shall tell thee, O child, what thou askest me. Attend to it with diligence.

   葛蘭達言：善哉問！雄臂子，諦聽之，吾將語汝之所問。

   雄臂子：長而壯健的手臂，透露出問道者旃檀迦帕里的身形特徵與善射本領，或是武士階級。

4. There are no fetters like those of Illusion (*Máyá*), no strength like

that which conies from discipline (*Yoga*), there is no friend higher than knowledge (*Jñána*), and no greater enemy than Egoism (*Ahaḿkára*).

網罟無如世幻，勇力無如瑜伽，良友無如真知，寃親無如我執。

5. As by learning the alphabets one can, through practice, master all the sciences, so by thoroughly piactising first the (physical) training, one acquires the Knowledge of the True.

欲明經典之教，須從字母起學；欲悟真智之道，當自身瑜伽起修。

身瑜伽：開展及平衡身心的鍛練方法。

6. On account of good and bad deeds, the bodies of all animated beings are produced, and the bodies give rise to works (*Karma* which leadn to rebirth) and thus the circle is continued like that of a Persian Wheel.

緣善惡業行，形成眾生報身；報身復造新殃，如是若水車轆轤般循環不止。

7. As the Persian Wheel in drawing water from a well goes up and down, moved by the bullocks (filling and exhausting the buckets again and again), so the soul passes through life and death moved by its Deeds.

水車汲水周而復始，轆轤循環上下不止，個體靈魂也隨業浮沉於生死之中。

8. Lake unto an unbaked earthen pot thrown in water, the body is soon decayed (in this world). Bake it hard in the fire of Training in order to strengthen and purify the body.

將未窯燒的胚瓶盛水，瓶身難以久；欲令身淨體健，亦須經修持之火鍛煉。

9. The seven exercises which appertain to this Training of the body are the following Purificatory, strengthening, steadying, calming, and those leading to lightness, perception, and isolation.

清淨、強健、穩定、沉著、輕捷、定靜、自在等法是有關修身的七種方法。

七種方法：七種親近目標的修持法，亦名七支修法。

10-11. First.— The purification is acquired by the regular performance of six practices (to be mentioned shortly); Second —*Ásana* or posture gives *Dṛḍhatá* or strength ; Third —*Mudrá* gives Sthirata or steadiness; Fourth—*Pratyáhára* gives *Dhairyata* or calmness; Fifth—*Pránáyáma* gives lightness or *Laghimá*; Sixth—*Dhyána* gives perception (*Pratyakṣatva*) of Self; and Seventh—*Samádhi* gives isolation (*Nirliptatá*), which is verily the Freedom.

瑜伽七支修法特點：

第一支—身淨化六法，規律行之可令身清淨；第二支—體位法，習之令身強健；第三支—身印法，習之令身安穩；第四支—內攝法，習之令心沉著；第五支—調息法，習之令身輕捷；第六支—禪定法，習之能入定靜；第七支—三摩地法，可得自在。

七支修法：七支修法中淨化六法的梵文是 *Ṣaṭkarmáṁ Śodhanám*，其餘六支梵文名稱如英文所示。

12. (1) *Dhauti* ; (2) *Basti* ; (3) *Neti* ; (4) *Laukikí* ; (5) *Trátaka* ; (6) *Kapálabháti* are the *Ṣaṭkarmáṁ*s or six practices, known as *Śadhana*.

淨胃法、淨腸法、淨鼻法、滾腹法、淨目法、淨腦法，是所謂的身淨化六法。

六之一：淨胃法

13. The *Dhautis* are of four kinds, and they clear away the impurities of the body They are—(a) *Antardhauti* (internal washing); (b)

Dantadhauti (cleaning the teeth) ; (c) *Hṛiddhauti* (cleaning the heart); (d) *Múlaśhodhana* (cleaning the rectum).

淨胃法分四種，能去除體內不純淨的雜質；它們是：內部清洗法，淨齒法，洗心法，直腸清洗法。

14. *Antardhauti* is again sub-divided into four parts : *Vátasára* (wind purification), *Várisárá* (water purification), *Vahnisárá* (fire purification), and *Bahiṣkṛita*.

內部清洗法又細分成四個部分：風洗法，水洗法，火洗法，腸洗法。

15. Contract the mouth like the beak of a crow and drink air slowly, and filling the 6tomach slowly with it, move it therein, and then slowly force it out through the lower passage.

風洗法：撮唇如烏喙，徐飲氣入腹，攪動其中，然後徐緩地促使其由穀道排出。

穀道：後陰、直腸口。

16. The *Vátasára* is a very secret process, it causes the purification of the body, it destroys all diseases and increases the gastric-fire.

風清洗法之術甚秘，行之有淨化身體之效；能增活力，除一切疾。

活力：身體裡的火、風、膽汁、動力、消化力的統稱。

17. Pill the mouth with water down to the throat, and then drink it slowly, and then move it through the stomach, forcing it downwards expelling it through the rectum.

水洗法：飲水及喉，徐徐嚥下，然後攪動肚腹，使水下行至穀道排出。

18. This process should be kept very secret. It purifies the body. And by practising it with care, one gets a luminous or shining body.

此法能淨化身體，細心習之可使身色光采宛若天人，當善守其秘。

身色似天人：有若天人之身，如和悅、光采、吸引人等。

19. The *Várisárá* is the highest *Dhauti*. He who practises it with ease, purifies his filthy body and turns it into a shining one.

水清洗法為上品淨化法，行之嫻熟，不淨之身亦得煥發光采。

20. Press in the naval knot or intestines towards the spine for one hundred times. This is *Agnisára* or fire process. This gives success in the practice of *Yoga*, it cures all the diseases of the stomach (gastric juice) and increases the internal fire.

火洗法：將臍腹往脊椎方向壓按一百次，是為火洗法；此法能增胃火，去胃疾；有助瑜伽士成就。

一百次：習者宜由少次漸增，循序漸進。

21. This form of *Dhauti* should be kept very secret, and it is hardly to be attained even by the gods. By this *Dhauti* alone one certainly gets a luminous body.

此修法天人亦難大成，然持恆習之者必獲光明身，當慎守其秘。

22. By *Kákacañcu* or crow-bill *mudrá*, fill the stomach with air, hold ii there for one hour and a half, and then force it down towards the intestines. This *Dhauti* must be kept a great secret, and most not be revealed to anybody.

腸洗法一：以鳥喙身印飲氣入腹，持氣一個半小時，然後使氣下行至腸。此法之秘旨須慎守，切莫輕示於人。

鳥喙身印：詳第三章第 86 節。本節與下節所述腸洗之法，讀者切莫輕易嘗試，冒然試之，恐危及健康！絕非戲言。

23. Then standing in navel-deep water, draw out the *Śaktináḍí*(long intestinee), wash the *Náḍí* with hand, and so long as its filth is not all washed away, wash it with care, and then draw it in again into the abdomen.

腸洗法二：立於深及臍腹的淨水中，拉出直腸，以手小心地洗出污穢後沖淨，再放回腹中。

腸洗法二：此法非絕無可能，但肯定需要相關的配合條件；在習者主客觀條件未成熟前，不可嘗試。

24. This process should be kept secret. It is not easily to be attained even by the gods. Simply by this *Dhauti* one gets *Devadeha* (Godlike body.)

此法須隱密行之，然雖諸天亦不易有成，一意行之者當可身淨如神。

譯按：此法可用他法取代，重點在於保持腸內清淨，如道門所言「若要不老，腹中不飽；若要不死，腸中無屎。」

25. As long as a person has not the power of retaining the breath for an hour and a half (or retaining wind in the stomach for that period), so long he cannot achieve this grand *Dhauti* or purification, known as *Bahiṣkṛtadhauti*.

未能持氣一個半小時不亂者，即無法成就此體外腸洗法。

26. *Danta-Dhauti* is of five kinds : purification of the teeth, of the root of the tongue, of the two holes of the ear, and of the frontal-sinuses.

淨齒法有五：洗牙法、洗舌根法、清耳竅法、清顱腔法。

淨齒法：五種淨齒法之梵語依序為洗牙法（*danta-múla-dhauti*）、洗舌根法（*jihvá-dhauti*）、清耳竅法（*karna-dhauti*）、清顱腔法（*kapála-randhra-dhauti*）。

27. Rub the teeth with *catechu*-powder or with pure earth, so long as dental impurities are not removed.

洗牙法：取兒茶樹灰或淨泥土擦齒，直至牙垢盡除。

兒茶樹：為豆科金合歡屬植物，藥性：苦、澀、涼，歸心、肺、脾經。功能收濕斂瘡、生肌止血。另外印度人也常用苦楝樹枝來潔牙。

28. This teeth-washing is a great *Dhauti* and an important process in

the practice of *Yoga* for the *Yogís*. It should be done daily in the morning by the *Yogís*, in order to preserve the teeth. In purification this is approved of by the *Yogís*.

此洗齒法是重要的清潔法，對於修習瑜伽之人尤其重要；為了護牙，習者每日清晨均應行之。

29. I shall now tell you the method of cleansing the tongue. The elongation of the tongue destroys old age, death and disease.

洗舌根法：現在述說淨舌之法，其重點在於增加舌之延展度，以達防老、延年與祛病之效。

30. Join together the three fingers known as the index, the middle and the ring finger, put them into the throat, and rub well and clean the root of the tongue, and by washing it again throw out the phlegm.

合併食指、中指和無名指伸入喉嚨，如是搓淨舌根；藉如是搓洗，可以防止水能失衡。

水能：三種體質要能之一，對應的病素為黏液素，組成元素為水和土，故亦有地能之譯。身體的水份都和水能有關，水能失衡導致胃寒、多痰、嗜睡、便秘、貪執、嫉妒、抑鬱等等的不適。

31. Having thus washed it, rub it with butter, and milk it again and again; then by holding the tip of the tongue with an iron instrument pull it out slowly and slowly.

如是滌洗，復塗以乳脂，如擠牛奶般反覆搓揉；然後定持舌端，用刮舌器順著舌面從裡向外慢慢的往外刮。

乳脂：鮮奶油。

32. Do this daily with diligence before the rising and setting sun. By so doing the tongue becomes elongated.

每日晨昏規律地勤行此法，即可展延舌長。

33. Clean the two holes of the ears by the index and the ring fingers. By

practising it daily, the mystical sounds are heard.

清耳竅法：以食指或無名指來清淨左右耳竅；日行此法，得聞秘音。

34. Rub with the thumb of the right hand the depression in the forehead near the bridge of the nose. By the practice of this *Yoga*, diseases arising from derangements of phlegmatic humours are cured.

清顱腔法：以右手姆指摩擦眉間印堂。行此瑜伽之術，可防治水能失調。

35. The vessels become purified and clairvoyance is induced. This should be practised daily after awakening from sleep, after meals, and in the evening.

此法淨化脈道，助發直覺洞見；宜於每日醒後、餐後及傍晚行之。

直覺洞見：一種靈視或直覺的遙視能力。

36. *Hṛd-Dhauti*, or purification of heart (or rather throat] is of three kinds, viz., by a stick (*Daṇḍa*), vomiting(*Vamana*), and by cloth (*Vastra*) .

洗心法有三：根莖清潔法、漱喉清潔法及布清潔法。

洗心法：也稱洗喉法；三種洗心法梵語見英譯括弧所示。

37. Take either a plantain stalk or a stalk of turmeric (*Haridra*) or a stalk of cane, and thrust it slowly into the aesophagus and then diaw it out slowly.

根莖清潔法：取粗長適中之薑黃根或甘蔗莖或蕉藤洗淨，小心地伸入食道中，再慢慢地抽出來。

譯按：嘗試此法時需心細手穩，注意用材之尺寸口徑及安全，循序漸進。

38. By this process all the phlegm, bile and other impurities are expelled out of the mouth. By this *Daṇḍa -Dhauti* every kind of heart disease is surely cured.

由此過程，水能、火能及其它不淨分泌從口中排出，依此法各種心臟疾病皆得防治。

火能：三種體質要能之一，對應的病素為膽汁素，組成元素為火和水，主導元素是火。火能主責體內的轉化及荷爾蒙，包括消化、吸收、代謝。火能失衡導致體溫偏高、肝功能降低、胃酸過多、易怒、氣餒、煩躁等等的不適。

39. After meal, let the wise practitioner drink water full up to the throat, then looking for a short while upwards, let him vomit it out again. By daily practising this *Yoga*, disorders of phlegm and bile are cured.

漱喉清潔法：餐後，識者飲淨水滿喉，引首向上漱喉片刻吐出。每日行此瑜伽法，可防治水能、火能失衡。

40. Let him swallow slowly a thin cloth, four fingers wide, then let him draw it out again. This is called *Vástra-Dhauti*.

布清潔法：習者取一寬四指之細淨紗布，徐徐自口吞嚥而下；之後再慢慢抽出，此為布清潔法。

譯按：此法可除食道痰液。紗布入口下嚥前，須先以水洗淨，浸濕後再一點一點嚥下。

41. This cures *Gulma* or abdominal diseases, fever, enlarged spleen, leprosy, and other skin diseases and disorders of phlegm and bile, and day by day the practitioner gets health, strength, and cheerfulness.

此法可防治腹疾、熱病、脾腫、痲瘋以及其他膚疾，平衡水能和火能之失調；日行之，可強身健體，心情愉悅。

42. The *Apánaváyu* does not flow freely so long as the rectum is not purified. Therefore with the greatest care let him practise this purification of the large intestines.

直腸清洗法：直腸不淨，下行氣不暢者，應極細心地以此法滌淨洗大腸。

43. By the stalk of the root of *Haridra*(turmeric) or the middle finger, the rectum should he carefully cleansed with water over and over again.

取薑黃之根莖或中指沾水，小心地以之反覆清潔穀道。

44. This destroys constipation, indigestion, and dyspepsia, and increases the beauty and vigour of the body and enkindles the sphere of the fire (i.e., the gastric juice).

此法消除便秘、消化不良，改善氣色及增添活力，引燃脾胃消化之火。

引燃脾胃消化之火：字義引燃或激活腹內脾胃的消化能力。

六之二：淨腸法

45. The *Bastis* are described of two kinds, viz: *Jala Basti* (or water *Basti*) and *Śuṣka Basti* or dry *Basti*). Water *Basti* Is done in water and dry *Basti* always on land.

淨腸法分水洗和乾洗二種，水洗法於水中進行，乾洗法在陸上為之。

46. Entering water up to the navel and assuming the posture called *Utkatásana*, let him contract and dilate the sphincter-muscle of the anus. This is called *Jala-basti*.

水洗淨腸法：浸於臍高之水中，以椅子式蹲下，縮放肛門括約肌，此為水洗淨腸法。

椅子式：又名幻椅式，詳第二章第二十七節。

47. This cures *Prameha*(urinary disorders), *Udávarta* (disorders of digestion) and *Krúraváyu* a (disorders of the wind). The body becomes free from all diseases and becomes as beautiful as that of the God Cupid.

此法可防治尿失禁、消化不良和風能失衡；令身諸病不侵，美若愛神。

風能：三種體質要能之一，對應的病素為體風素，組成元素為風和乙太，主導元素是風。風能主責體內運作的輸送與催化，包括心跳、肺部、橫膈肌等等。風能失衡導致血行不良、心悸、關節炎、腹脹、失眠、猶豫、健忘等不適。

48. Assuming the posture called *Paśchimottána*, let him move the intestines slowly downwards, then contract and dilate the sphincter-muscle of the anus with *Aśviní-mudrá*.

乾洗淨腸法：採背伸展式坐姿，推腸下移，然後以提肛身印縮放肛門括約肌。

背伸展式坐姿：詳第二章第二十四節。

提肛身印：詳第三章第八十二節。

49. By this practice of *Yoga*, constipation never occurs, and it increases gastric fire and cures flatulence.

習此瑜伽體式，得免便秘之患，且可促進胃火 ，防治胃脹氣。

六之三：淨鼻法

50. Take a thin thread, measuring half a cubit, and insert it into the nostrils, and passing it through, pull it out by the mouth. This is called *Neti-Kriyá*.

取腕尺長細線，使從一鼻孔穿入，再自口中拉出；此為淨鼻法。

淨鼻法：清除鼻腔黏液的有效方法，梵語 *Neti-Kriyá*。線長英譯經句寫的是半腕尺長，可能誤植；標準應要有一腕尺長五十公分上下，現在多使用橡皮繩。

51. By practising the *Neti-Kriya*, one obtains *Khecarí Siddhi*. It destroys the disorders or phlegm and produces clairvoyance or clear sight.

習此淨鼻法可得明空成就，助發直覺洞見力，防治水能失衡。

明空成就：詳第三章第二十八節起對明空身印成就的闡述。

六之四：滾腹法

52. With great force move the stomach and intestines from one side to the other. This is called *Laukikí-Yoga*. This destroys all diseases and increases the bodily fire.

左右滾動或轉動胃腸，是為滾腹法。此法破諸疾，提升身體活力。

滾腹法：有意識地滾動腹腔肌群，強力地按摩腸胃，需空腹練習。練習步驟應先練熟將腹部貼往脊背，再練習左右分離腹肌，前法嫻熟後最後再練習滾腹法。

六之五：淨目法

53. Gaze steadily without winking at any small object, until tears begin to flow. This is called *Tráṭaka* by the wise.

目不眨眼地凝視任一小點，直至淚出，識者謂之淨目法。

淨目法：又稱一點凝視法，常以燭光做為凝視標的，重點是將光輝映入腦海，凝視時間可由數秒逐漸加長至十五分鐘。

54. By practising this *Yoga*, *Śámbhaví Siddhis* are obtained; and certainly all diseases of the eye are destroyed and clairvoyance is induced.

勤習此瑜伽之法，破諸眼疾，助發直覺洞見，可得希瓦身印成就。

希瓦身印成就：詳第三章第六十四至六十七節。

六之六：淨腦法

55. The *Kapálabháti* is of three kinds : *Váma-krama*, *Vyut-krama*, and *Sít-krama*. They destroy disorders of phlegm.

淨腦法分三種：調和呼吸法、引流法、逆引流法，皆能防治水能失衡。

淨腦法：此處葛蘭達所說之淨腦法和《瑜伽明燈》所說的淨腦法雖梵文相同，但做法有相當差異。「有如鐵匠抽送風箱般地快速呼氣和吸氣，是為淨腦法」瑜伽明燈第二章 35-1。

56. Draw the wind through the left nostril and expel it through the right, and draw it again through the right and expel it through the left.

調和呼吸法：先以左鼻孔吸氣，再從右鼻孔呼氣；復自右鼻孔吸氣，再從左鼻孔呼氣。

左鼻孔：即月脈口，月脈又稱左脈，通向左鼻孔。

右鼻孔：即日脈口，日脈又稱右脈，通向右鼻孔。

57. This inspiration and expiration must be done without any force. This practice destroys disorders of phlegm.

呼吸時不可用強，宜從容為之，習之可改善水能的失衡。

58. Draw the water through the two nostrils and expel it through the mouth slowly and slowly. This is called *Vyut-krama* which destroys disorders of phlegm.

引流法：自鼻孔吸入淨水，然後令自口中吐出，此為引流法，可改善失衡之水能。

59. Suck water through the mouth and expel it through the nostrils. By this practice of *Yoga* one becomes like the god Cupid.

逆引流法：飲淨水入口，復俯首令水自鼻出；藉此鍛煉，可使己身若愛神。

60. Old age never comes to him and decrepitude never disfigures him. The body becomes healthy, elastic, and disorders of phlegm are destroyed.

此法令身不老，形不衰，身形健康富彈性，並回復失衡之水能。

第二章

瑜伽體位法

Ásanas

1. *Gheraṇḍa* said: There are eighty-four hundreds of thousands of *Ásanas* described by *Śiva*. The postures aie ae many in number as there are numbers of species of living creatures in this universe.

葛蘭達言：「希瓦敘述了八萬四千種體式，其數有如世界含靈之種類。」

希瓦：七千年前住世印度的密宗上師，亦被尊稱為瑜伽之父。他透過歌曲、舞蹈、醫道和靈修靜坐及社會倫理，將靈性的觀念帶給世人，所以也被視為現代文明之父。在信仰上，由於他在世俗層面及及靈性層面帶給世人的貢獻，咸認為他是上主的化身；因此他的名字也是清淨識、純意識或至上意識的同義詞。

體式：又譯坐式、體位法，瑜伽八支功法中的第三支，作用是保持身體的安穩舒適。體位法可以調節身心，尤其是那些會干擾靈修的身心問題。

2. Among them eighty-four are the best ; and among these eighty-four, thirty-two have been found useful for mankind in this world.

其中最好的有八十四種，八十四種體式中對世人最有用的有三十二種，列名如後。

3-6. The thirty-two *Ásanas* that give perfection in this mortal world are the following :

1. *Siddhásana* (Perfect posture)
2. *Padmásana* (Lotus posture)
3. *Bhadrásana* (Gentle posture)
4. *Muktásana* (Free posture)
5. *Vajrásana* (Adamant posture)
6. *Svastíkásana* (Prosperous posture)
7. *Siṃhásana* (Lion posture)
8. *Gomukhásana* (Cow-mouth posture)
9. *Virásana* (Heroic posture)
10. *Dhanurásana* (Bow posture)
11. *Mṛitásana* (Corpse posture)
12. *Guptásana* (Hidden posture)

17. *Utkaṭásana* (Chair Posture)
18. *Sankatásana* (Dangerous posture)
19. *Máyúrásana* (Peacock posture)
20. *Kukkutásana* (Cock posture)
21. *Kukuṭásana* (Tortoise posture)
22. *Uttánakúrmásana* (stand Tortoise posture)
23. *Maṇḍukásana* (Frog posture)
24. *Uttánamaṇḍukásana* (stand Frog posture)
25. *Vṛkṣásana* (Tree posture)
26.*Garuḍásana* (Engle posture)
27. *Vṛṣásana* (Bull posture)
28. *Salabhásana* (Locust posture)

13. *Matsyásana* (Fish posture)
14. *Matsyendrásana* (Lord of the Fishes Pose)
15.*Paścimottánásana* (Intense Dorsal Stretch)
16. *Gorakṣásana* (*Gorakṣá* posture)
29.*Makarásana* (Dolphin posture).
30. *Uṣṭrásana* (Camel posture)
31. *Bhujangásana* (Snake posture)
32. *Yogásana* (*Yoga* posture)

以下是完整流傳人世間的三十二種體式：

1. 完美坐
2. 蓮花坐
3. 普賢坐
4. 自在坐
5. 金剛坐
6. 吉祥坐
7. 獅子式
8. 牛面式
9. 勇士式
10. 弓式
11. 攤屍式
12. 笈多坐
13. 魚式
14. 瑪辛卓式
15. 背部伸展式
16. 葛拉克夏式
17. 椅子式
18. 跨鶴坐
19. 孔雀式
20. 公雞式
21. 龜式
22. 龜立式
23. 蛙式
24. 蛙立式
25. 樹式
26. 金翅鳥式
27. 牡牛式
28. 蝗蟲式
29. 鯨豚式
30. 駱駝式
31. 眼鏡蛇式
32. 瑜伽式

7. The *Siddhásana*: The practitioner who has subdued his passions, having placed one heel at the anal aperture should keep the other heel on the root of the generative organ; afterwards he should affix his chin upon the chest, and being quiet and straight, gaze at the spot between the two eye-brows. This is called the *Siddhásana* and leads to emancipation.

   完美坐：習者攝心端坐，將一足踵抵於會陰，復置另一足踵於前陰之上；然後下巴觸胸，正身靜意，神凝眉間；是名完美坐，依之可得解脫之果。

   完美坐：此式有助能量自下層往上導入脊椎，刺激腦部，緩和神經系統；是最被推薦的瑜伽體式之一，宜常練習。

解脫：此字梵文為 *mokśa*，意指真解脫、究竟解脫，融入無屬性本體真空之境。

8. The *Padmásana*: Place the right foot ou the left thigh and similarly the left one on the right thigh, also cross the hands behind the hack and firmly catch hold of the great toes of feet so crossed. Place the chin on the chest and fix the gaze on the tip of the nose. This posture is called the *Padmásana* (or Lotus posture). This posture destroys all diseases.

蓮花坐：右腳置於左腿上，復將左腳置於右腿上；雙手背後交叉，於腰側分別牢握左、右兩腳大足趾；微收下巴，繫意鼻端；是名蓮花坐，依之可除一切病。

蓮花坐：此式有助身體長時間的穩定。式名蓮花坐，取其出淤泥而不染，喻人處紅塵濁世因常依此坐式修持而離雜染。從體式說明看，本式今稱鎖蓮式。現在通行的蓮花坐多為雙手疊於腹前。

9-10. The *Bhadrásana*: Place the heels crosswise under the testes attentively; cross the hands behind the back, and take hold of the toes of the feet. Fix the gaze on the tip of the nose, having previously adopted the *mudrá* called *Jálandhara*. This is the *Bhadrásana* (or happy posture) which destroys all sorts of diseases.

普賢坐：將兩腳足踝反向置於前陰下，雙手再從背後交叉握住大腳趾；內觀鼻端，行收頷身印。此為普賢坐，可除各類疾患。

普賢坐：此式又有優雅式、賢王式之譯，亦是受到瑜伽學人重視的瑜伽坐式之一，不過在做法上有些分歧。本節所述為足踝反向置於會陰近生殖器官處，意思應是雙膝併攏跪地，足背向下，如此雙手才能從背後握住大腳趾。《哈達瑜伽明燈》中本式的做法是：兩足腳掌相合，足趾朝前，足跟儘量拉近前陰之下，雙手牢握相合之腳掌。注意練習過程中須隨時根據習者自身條件調整難易度。
收領身印：詳見第三章第十二節。

11. The *Muktásana*: Place the left heel at the root of the organ of generation and the right heel above that, keep the head and the neck straight with the body. This posture is called the *Muktásana*. It gives *Siddhi* (perfection).

自在坐：左足置前陰根處，右踵疊於其上，保持身頸中正，此謂之自在坐；習之可得屬靈成就。

自在坐：兩手可掌心朝下結智慧印分置於左右膝腿上，繫意眉心，呼吸宜細長。

屬靈成就：音譯悉地，指任何超越物質之靈性成就。

12. The *Vajrásana*: Make the thighs tight like adamant and place the legs by the two sides of the anus. This is called the *Vajrásana* a. It gives psychic powers to the *Yogí*.

金剛坐：兩腿穩若金剛，跪置於後陰兩側；此謂之金剛坐，惠予行者解脫成就。

金剛坐：手掌可分置左右大腿上，掌心朝下輕貼於腿面，呼吸宜細長。

13. The *Svastíkásana*: Drawing the legs and thighs together and placing the feet underneath them, keeping the body in its easy condition and sitting straight, constitute the posture called the *Svastikasana*.

吉祥坐：左右大小腿內收盤坐，復將兩足置於其下；舒身端坐，如是謂之吉祥坐。

吉祥坐：本坐式是將大小腿內盤靠攏，然後將左腳掌置於右大小腿之下，右腳掌置於左大小腿之下。本式手掌可置膝上結智慧印，亦即拇指、食指環扣，餘指自然鬆開；亦可上下交握或交疊於小腹前。

14-15. The *Siṃhásana*: The two heels to be placed under the scrotum contrariwise (i.e., left heel on the right side and the right, heel on the left side of it) and turned upwards, the knees to be placed on the ground, (and the hands placed on the knees), mouth to be kept open ; practising the *Jálandhara mudrá* one should fix his gaze on the tip of the nose. This is the *Siṃhásana* (Lion-posture), the destroyer of all diseases.

獅子式：左右腳跟反向置於會陰下，足心向上，雙膝觸地；張口收頷，目視鼻端。此為獅子式，習之能除所有身疾。

獅子式：獅子有叢林王之譽，本式取獅子之氣勢故名。此式足腿之擺放，原經句意思是「左右腳跟與平常相反置於會陰下」，英譯括號內加註（左腳跟置於右側，右腳跟疊於左側），意即兩腳踝交叉之意；實際進行時或交叉或不交叉，兩種做法都有人做。本式兩腿跪地開膝，雙手置膝或置地，收腹含胸；「張口收頷」是指「嘴巴張開，下巴內收進行收頷身印」。若雙手置地，可將雙手置於兩膝腿之間，手指轉向身體，腳趾相觸而不相交。

16. The *Gomukhásana*: The two feet to be placed on the ground, and the heels to be placed contrariwise under the buttocks; the body to be kept steady and and the mouth raised, and sitting equably; this is called the *Gomukhásana*, resembling the mouth of a cow.

牛面式：兩足置地，兩腳跟方向相反置於對向臀側；保持身形安穩，嘴微上揚。此式形若牛面，故以牛面式名之。

嘴微上揚：應非抬頭而為保持微笑之意。

牛面式：此式兩膝上下交疊，右腳跟置於左臀側，左腳跟置於右臀側。上肢做法，兩手可交握於小腹前，或是兩臂一上一下於背後扣指相連。

17. The *Virásana*: One leg (the right foot) to be placed on the other (left) thigh, and the other foot to be turned backwards : This is called the *Virásana* (Hero-posture).

勇士式：一腳置於另一腿上，另一腿向後彎曲，此為勇士式。

勇士式：又名英雄式。本節所述之勇士式頗不同於今習見之勇士式，文述做法臀部著地，後屈之腳跟置於臀下或臀側。雙手結印置於腿面，左右交替行之。而現今習見之勇士式有二，一為取跪坐姿，臀坐於兩腿之間；一為屈左腳，左腳置於左臀側或坐於左腳跟上，右腳立屈腳跟近身腳板置地，左手於臍前握住右腕；或是右肘置右膝頭反手支頤，左手覆於左膝腿上。

18. The *Dhanurásana*: Spreading the legs on the ground, straight like a stick, and catching hold of (the toes of) the feet with the hands, and making the body bent like a bow, ie called by the *Yogís* the *Dhanurásana* or Bow-posture.

弓式：兩腿分開直伸如杖，兩手分別握住左右腳趾，然後彎身拉足如拉弓；行者名之為弓式。

弓式：此式左右交替練習，左腿伸直時，左手握右大趾拉向左耳處；右腿伸直時，右手握左大趾拉向右耳處。此式梵文名稱與現通行的弓式相同，因做法有別，故又有「拉弓式」之名。而習見之弓式做法為：俯身平臥，雙手後伸握住左右腳踝或腳趾，徐徐弓身上彎，彎身時腳跟靠近臀部，腳大趾相互輕觸。本節亦或為更困難之做法，預備式為俯臥伸腿如杖，餘如《哈達瑜伽明燈》第一章 25 節第二種弓式之做法。

19. The *Mṛitásana*: Lying flat on the ground like a corpse is called the *Mṛitásana*(the Corpse-posture). This pasture destroys fatigue, and quiets the agitation of the mind.

攤屍式：仰面平躺於地有如攤屍，是為攤屍式；此式消除疲憊，平靜心思之紛擾。

攤屍式：本式即瑜伽人所熟知之大休息式，而本式之梵語 *mritá* 意為死亡；式名攤屍，除形似外，更重要的皆是取身心如屍般，放鬆、放空，另名大休息式。

20. The *Guptásana*: Hide the two feet under the two knees, and place the anpa on the feet. This is known as the *Guptásana* (Hidden-postute).

笈多坐：雙腳隱於對側膝腿之下，上對後陰，是為笈多坐。

笈多坐：字義為秘藏，義譯秘藏式，藏心於密，音譯笈多坐。此式定式：雙膝左右打開端坐，雙腳交疊隱於對側大小腿間，雙手結印分置兩膝蓋上。

21. The *Matsyásana*: Make the *Padmásana*-postare (as stated in verse 8) without the crossing of the arms; lie on the back, holding the head by the two elbows. This is the *Matsyásana*(Pish-postuie), the destroyer of diseases.

魚式：採蓮花坐式坐定，雙臂不需背後交叉；仰躺拱背，頭項枕於兩肘之間。此為魚式，能除諸病。

魚式：本式拱背時，背需徐徐拱起，臀腿不可離地，呼吸保持慢長。無法雙盤者可單盤腳或是兩腳合攏平伸。本式亦有兩手握住腳趾之做法，採此方式時，將背徐徐拱起，直至後腦上緣著地。

22-23. The *Matsyendrásana*: Keeping the abdominal region at ease like the back, bending the left leg, place it on the right thigh; then place en this the elbow of the right hand, and place the face on the palm of the right hand, and fix the gaze between the eye-brows. This is called the *Matsyendrásana*-poeture.

瑪辛卓式：保持胸腹舒展如背，彎曲左小腿置於右大腿上；然後右手肘置於右膝之上，再將頭面輕置於右手掌，意守眉心；此謂之瑪辛卓式。

瑪辛卓式：梵語之意為魚王，故本式又稱魚王式，音譯瑪辛卓式。在瑜伽史上，瑪辛卓為哈達瑜伽大成就者之一，為大瑜伽師葛拉克夏之師。本節所述瑪辛卓式之姿勢與現今熟知之作法頗有差異。依文所述，其細節應是：採坐姿，左腳置於右腿近胯處，右足屈膝近置臀部地面；右肘置於右膝上，右手或支頤或下巴抵手背，輕托頭面；練習時，兩側需交替行之。本式現今之做法為：左腳橫屈於右臀側，右腳縱跨於左腿外側，腳趾向前；右臂反手繞背，手背貼腰左腰側，左手肘外側緊抵右膝外側，手掌或立或握住右腳大趾。左右交替進行，上身向右扭轉後視，故又簡稱扭轉式。姿勢可視習者身體條件來做調整。

24. The *Paścimottánásana*: Spread the two legs on the ground, stiff like a stick (the heele not touching), and place the forehead on the two knees, and catch with the hands the toes. This is called the *Paścimottánásana*.

背伸展式：兩腿如杖向前平伸於地面，然後前額向雙膝靠近，雙手前伸握住腳趾；此謂之背伸展式。

背伸展式：此式兩腳直伸而不相觸。注意句中「前額向雙膝靠近」非指前額努力地貼近膝蓋頭，重點在使胸肋從胯往膝腿貼近；由於此式伸展的重點在背脊及後腿，故上背及頭頸切忌緊張用力。

25-26. The *Gorakṣásana*: Between the knees and the thighs, the two feet tamed upward and placed in a hidden way, the heels being carefully covered by the two hands outstretched ; the throat being contracted, let one fix the gaze on the tip of the nose. This is called the *Gorakṣásana*. It gives success to the *Yogís*.

葛拉克夏式：兩腳盤屈足心朝上隱於膝腿之間，然後以雙手小心地輕覆足跟；下巴內收，凝目鼻端；此謂之葛拉克夏式，行者習之可得屬靈之成就。

葛拉克夏式：印度大瑜伽師及密續上師之一，有《葛拉克夏本集》等著作傳世，本式冠以其名紀念，著重的是凝神內斂。依本節句意，此式為兩腿相盤，兩足夾於對側大小腿之間，然後雙手掌心朝上遮覆足跟；兩手亦可掌心朝上交疊置於足跟之上。

27. The *Utkaṭásana:* Let the toes touch the ground, and the heels be raised in the air ; place the anus on the heels : this is known as the *Utkaṭásana*.

椅子式：腳趾抵地，腳跟踮起，後陰對腳跟蹲下，是為椅子式。

椅子式：式名取其如坐椅子之形。本式可強化膝、腿、腰腹，下蹲時腳趾抵地之力度與下蹲程度成正比。

28. The *Sankatásana:* Placing the left foot and the leg on the ground, surround the left foot by the right leg ; and place the two hands on the two knees. This is the *Sankatásana*.

跨鶴坐：左足腿置於地面，將右腿繞纏左腿，然後把雙手置於兩膝上。此為跨鶴坐。

跨鶴坐：梵文式名有合同、收合之意，中譯名取其形命名。做法為左足屈膝，腳跟近右側臀；右腿疊於左腿上，腳跟近左側臀；兩膝蓋頭上下相對，雙手交疊於在上之膝蓋頭。

29. The *Máyúrásana*: Place the palms of the two hands on the ground, place the umbilical region on the two elbows, stand upon the hands, the legs being raised in the air, and crossed like *Padmásana*. This is called the *Máyúrásana* (Peacock-posture).

孔雀式：雙掌按地，臍腹緊抵雙肘上，然後以手撐地而起，使兩腿懸於空中，並相盤如蓮花坐之腿姿。此式名孔雀式。

孔雀式：本式須經相當時間練習，練習時可先盤起雙腿。步驟為：雙盤兩腿，雙掌撐地，身前傾，令臍腹緊抵兩肘；然後以雙掌撐起身體，將盤起之雙腿徐徐離地升起，再平衡全身。本式亦可雙腿平伸懸空來練習。

30. The Peacock-posture destroys the effects of unwholesome food ; it produces heat in the stomach; it destroys the effects of deadly

poisons; it easily cures diseases, like *Gulina* and fever ; such is this useful posture.

孔雀式能增生胃火，緩解有害食物的影響，甚至能緩解致命毒素的傷害；有助脾腫、發燒等疾病之康復，是很有裨益的體式。

胃火：此處「 生胃火」是指能強化脾胃消化機能，非指食用煎炒燥熱出現的口渴、口臭、口乾、口苦等之胃燥現象。

31. The *Kukuṭásana*: Sitting on the ground, cross the legs in the *Padmásana* posture, thrust down the hands between the thighs and the knees, stand on the hands, supporting the body on the elbows. This is called the Cock-posture.

公雞式：以蓮花坐盤足坐地，將雙手自膝、腿之間穿入，然後雙手撐地，以雙肘支持身體；此謂之公雞式。

公雞式：本式除支撐身體之雙掌外，餘皆離地懸起；可增強臂力與核心肌群，有助喚醒靈能軍荼利。

32. The *Kúrmásana*: Place the heels contrariwise under the scrotum, stiffen (or keep at ease) the head, neck and body. This is called the Tortoise-posture.

龜式：兩腳足踝反向置於會陰下，保持頭、頸及身體安舒中正，此謂之龜式。

兩腳足踝反向：此節梵文首句和本章第九節及第十四節首句皆相同亦即足踝相疊置於會陰下。此式與自在坐相似，不同處是自在坐之足踝置於前陰下，龜式是置於會陰下。足踝擺放之位置還有一說是：腳掌外轉足跟相對，筆者採用較適合靜坐且容易進行的方式。

龜式：本式上身不前彎，重點是取龜不動時的靜定精神。今通行之做法是兩腿左右分開前伸，身軀前俯，兩臂前伸或自膝下向左右貼地平伸，掌心朝下；進一步，雙手往後靠近臀腿或相觸於臀後。練習時，可視自身狀況做調整，避免受傷。簡單的龜式是跪坐開膝，向內曲膝腳掌相合，身驅前俯，兩臂前伸，掌心向下。

33. The *Uttánakúrmásana*: Assume the Cock-posture (as stated in verse 31), catch hold of the neck with the hands, and stand stretched like a tortoise. This is the *Uttánakúrmásana*.

龜立式：以公雞式坐定，然後用雙手托頸，以坐姿如龜立起；此為龜立式。

龜立式：這是一個高難度的體式，定式是以臀部著地坐立；通常會從背觸地、胸腹朝上的仰龜式開始練習。

34. The *Maṇḍukásana*: Carry the feet towards the back, the toes touching each other, and place the knees forwards, This is called the Frog-posture.

蛙式：兩腳屈向後，足趾相觸，兩膝朝前；此謂之蛙式。

蛙式：此式所述與習見之做法不同。此處做法有二：一是兩膝旁開，脊背保持中正，手結印膝上或兩手腕交叉胯處；二是，兩膝合攏，大足足相觸，兩手腕交叉胯處。變形做法：雙手握拳置於臍兩側，虎口朝上，然後向前俯身，則握拳處可有按摩腹部器官之效。

35. The *Uttánamaṇḍukásana*: Assume the Frog-posture (as in verse 34), hold the head by the elbows, and stand up like a frog. This is called the *Uttánamaṇḍukásana*.

蛙立式：以蛙式坐定，以兩肘穩定頭項，膝立如蛙；此謂之蛙立式。

蛙立式：本式定式兩膝如蛙式坐定後，兩肘上舉交叉抱肘，後腦貼於交抱之小臂內側，以膝為支點向上立起。如無法立起，做立起之勢，臀腿有收縮即可。另一方式是打開兩腿成V形，雙肘上舉靠近頭兩側，手腕交叉於頸後，手指輕貼兩肩，向上伸展身軀，呼吸宜細。

36. The *Vṛkṣásana*: Stand straight on one leg (the left), bending the right leg, and placing the right foot on the root of the left thigh ; standing thus like a tree on the ground, is called the Tree-posture.

樹式：左腿立直，彎曲右腿，置右腳於左腿胯部；穩立如大地樹，此謂之樹式。

樹式：本式左右交替進行。站穩後兩手可合十於胸前，或垂於身體兩側；熟練者兩臂可進一步伸展，向天合掌。

37. The *Garuḍásana*: Place the legs and the thighs on the ground pressing it, steady the body with the two knees, place the two hands on the knees: this is called the *Garuḍá*-posture.

金翅鳥式：兩腳大小腿緊抵於地，以兩膝穩定身體；雙手置於雙膝上，此謂之金翅鳥式。

金翅鳥式：神話中金翅鳥是妙毗天的坐騎。本式做法「兩腳大小腿緊抵於地」，如果要同時觸抵於地，應是採取併膝跪坐，臀坐於左右腳跟之間，足外翻（即大小腿內側著地，腳背與腳腕約成九十度，兩足腳弓側觸地），姿勢著重身穩心靜。從定式外形看，類似勇士式或半閃電式。此處金翅鳥式與現今習見的做法大為不同，習見的做法是：單腳直立，另一腿纏繞其上；雙臂曲肘交疊，手腕相纏掌心相對，指尖向上；肘尖與身體成九十度，然後上身保持中正，沉身下蹲。

38. The *Vṛṣásana*: Place the anus on the right heel, on the left of it place the left leg crossing it opposite way, and touch the ground. This is called the Bull-posture.

牡牛式：後陰置於右踵上，再將左腳向右跨過右腿觸地；此謂之牡牛式。

牡牛式：又名公牛式；兩手可交疊於左膝上或任何舒適之處。

39. The *Salabhásana*: Lie on the ground face downwards, the two hands being placed on the chest, touching the ground with the

palms, raise the legs in the air one cubit high. This is called the Locust-posture.

蝗蟲式：面朝下平躺，雙掌置於胸部兩側，然後兩足向空中舉起一腕尺高；此謂之蝗蟲式。

一腕尺高：本節舉起高度原梵語是用一搩手（*vitasti*），這是古印度的長度單位，一搩手是指手掌展開拇指與小指間的距離，相當於十二指寬，約合 21-22 公分左右，又稱一掌尺。英譯一腕尺約等於兩搩手。實際可舉高些或低些，視習者自身之狀況而有不同。

蝗蟲式：此處所述之蝗蟲式與現今通行的做法不同；此處手肘靠近兩脅，因此上背及頭頸向上抬起較為舒適。而現今做法是兩臂置於身體兩側，掌心朝下觸地，然後兩腿併攏舉起（膝蓋不彎），舉腿時可稍藉手掌下按之力。亦可雙手握拳，拳背朝下置於小腹下，然後舉腿。

40. The *Makarásana*: Lie on the ground face downwards, the chest touching the earth, the two legs being stretched : catch the head with the two arms. This is *Makarásana*, the increaser of the bodily heat.

鯨豚式：俯面平躺，胸部觸地，兩腳向後伸展；以雙臂支持頭項，此為鯨豚式，可增加身體熱能。

鯨豚式：梵語 *Makara* 是神話中的海中神獸，古譯巨鰲、摩竭魚；英譯鯨豚或鱷魚。現今多譯鱷魚式，取鱷魚靜止之態。為休息式之一，支持頭項之手肘觸地，手臂近腕之內側輕貼頭兩側；下巴可輕觸地，兩腳合攏，呼吸宜緩並於吸吐氣間稍做停頓，每回以五息為度。

41. The *Uṣṭrásana*: Lie on the ground face downwards, turn up the legs and place them, towards the back, catch the legs with the hands, contract forcibly the mouth and the abdomen. This is called the Camel-posture.

駱駝式：俯面平躺，兩膝腿上屈，朝向腰背；雙手後伸抓住兩腳，收腹閉口；此謂之駱駝式。

駱駝式：做法有異習見之駱駝式；反而是像常見的弓式，胸離地可開展胸肺，兩腿亦可交叉後用手握住。現今習見之駱駝式有二：一為跪立姿勢，手扶腰背，然後臍以上向後上方徐徐彎身；稍停，然後回至跪立姿式。另一種是採取併腳仰臥，然後收腹舉腿，每次舉三十度高，分三次舉至九十度；放下時亦分三次，每次三十度將腿放回地面。

42-43. The *Bujangásana*: Let the body, from the navel downwards to the toes, touch the ground, place the palms on the ground, raise the head (the upper por- tion of the body) like a serpent. This is called the Serpent-posture. This 1 always increases the bodily heat, destroys all diseases, and by the practice of this posture the Serpent-Goddess (the kundalini force) awakes.

眼鏡蛇式：令身從臍到足俯貼地面，雙掌平置地面，昂首如蛇，此謂之眼鏡蛇式。常習之能增強體能，消除諸病，並有助於甦醒靈能軍荼利。

眼鏡蛇式：常習體式之一。俯躺時下巴觸地，兩腿平伸合攏；吸氣同時引身向上，臍腹至足貼地，滿息後繼續向上一些，稍停再徐徐復位。

44-45. The *Yogásana*: Turn the feet upwards, place them on the knees; then place the hands on the ground with the palms turned upwards; inspire, and fix the gaze on the tip of the nose. This is called the *Yoga*-posture, assumed by the *Yogí*s when practising *Yoga*.

瑜伽式：兩腳足心朝上盤於膝腿之上，兩手掌心向天、指尖觸地；誠心悅意，繫緣鼻端，此謂之瑜伽式；於行者鍛煉瑜伽時行之。

瑜伽式：進行此式保持身體中正，或單盤或雙盤，手背觸於小腿近膝處，手不能及地者可置於膝上。本式與通行的需向前俯身的瑜伽身印不同。句中明言此式「於行者鍛煉瑜伽時行之」，意即此式是適用於所有心瑜伽的鍛煉。

第三章

身印法

Mudrás

1-3. *Gheraṇḍa* said: There are twenty-five *Mudrás*, the practice of which gives success to the *Yogís*. They are：(1) *Mahá-mudrá*, (2) *Nabhomudrá*, (3)*Uḍḍiyánabandha*, (4) *Jálandharabhanda*, (5) *Múlabandha*, (6) *Mahábandha*, (7) *Mahávedha*, (8) *Khecarímudrá*, (9) *Viparítakaraṇímudrá*, (10) *Yonimudrá*, (11) *Vajroṇímudrá*, (12) *Śakticálanamudrá*, (13) *Taḍágimudrá*, (14) *Mándukimudrá*, (15) *Śámbhavímudrá*; *Pañcadháraṇá*(five *dháṛanás*),(16) *Párthivídháraṇámudrá*, (17) *Ámbhasídháranámudrá*, (18) *Ágneyídháraná mudrá*, (19) *Váyavídháraná mudrá*, (20) *Ákáshídháraná mudrá*, (21) *Ashvinimudrá*, (22) *Páśinímudrá*, (23) *Kákímudrá*, (24) *Mátanginímudrá*, (25) *Bhujanginímudrá*.

葛蘭達言：「有二十五種身印，瑜伽人習之可獲成就。」這些身印是：

(1) 大身印，(2) 虛空身印，(3) 揚升鎖印，(4) 收頷鎖印，(5) 根鎖印，(6) 大鎖印，(7) 大穿透印，(8) 明空身印，(9) 倒轉身印，(10) 胎藏身印，(11) 金剛力身印，(12) 力動身印，(13) 腹貼脊身印，(14) 蛙眠身印，(15) 希瓦身印；五大執持身印：(16) 地大執持身印，(17) 水大執持身印，(18) 火大執持身印，(19) 風大執持身印，(20) 空大執持身印；(21) 提肛身印，(22) 套索身印，(23) 鳥喙身印，(24) 大象身印，(25) 龍飲身印。

修習身印利益

4-5. *Maheśwara*, when addressing his consort, has recited the advantages of *mudrás* in these words: O *Devi*! I have told you all the *mudras*; their knowledge leads to adept-ship (those who practice in obtaining *siddhi*). It should be kept secret with great care, and should not be taught indiscriminately to everyone. This gives happiness to the *Yogí*, and is not to be easily attained by the *Maruts*(gods of air) even.

大自在者語其妻，以如是言說身印利益：「德妃！我曾語汝一切身印法門，其法可使習者得大成就。應善護持此法秘要，不當輕意示人。此法帶給瑜伽士之喜樂，即使風神亦難輕易獲得。

大自在者語其妻：大自在者為後世表彰希瓦的眾多名號之一，其妻帕瓦蒂後人尊為雪山女神；經常為瑜伽行人向希瓦請問有關靈修上的問題，而希瓦的回答即成為瑜伽行人學習的準繩。

德妃：梵語 *devi*。從宇宙核心發出的波動，在哲學上名為 *Deva*，故有神、天等翻譯；而 *devi* 是陰性詞，亦為對女性的尊稱。

身印：具有意涵的手勢或姿勢，又名手印；習法如體位法，是結合了能量與理念的一種鍛煉，作用兼及於神經和肌肉。

風神：能控制風元素之人或神。

譯按：《葛蘭達本集》常有「應善護持此法秘要，不當輕意示人」之語，意在提醒瑜伽師們，除非習者已達進階修持階段，否則不得教以身印之修法；因為在初修階段練習身印，因體內阻塞仍多，可能會帶來傷害。

6-7. *Mahámudrá*: Press carefully the anus by the left heel. Stretch the right leg, and take hold of the great toe by the hands. Contract the throat(not expelling the breath), and fix the gaze between the eyebrows. This is called *Maha-mudrá* by the wise.

大身印：小心地將左腳跟抵住後陰，伸直右腿，以雙手握住右大腳趾；收頷住氣，意念凝注於眉心。智者稱此為大身印。

大身印：結合根鎖印和收頷身印的練習，是身瑜伽中主要的鍛煉之一，可去體內濕氣及淨化身內經絡。

8. The practice of *Mahá-mudrá* cures consumption, the obstruction of the bowels, the enlargement of the spleen, indigestion and fever, in fact it cures all diseases.

練習大身印可防治如結核病、腸阻塞、脾腫、消化不良和發燒，事實上它甚至能對治百病。

9. *Nabhomurdrá*: In whatever business a *Yogí* may be engaged, wherever he may be, let him always keep his tongue upward (toward the soft palate), and restrain the breath. This is called *Nabho-mudrá* ; it destroys all the diseases of the *Yogís*.

   虛空身印：無論瑜伽行人在從事何種工作，無論身處何地，常保持舌頭上抵（向軟顎的方向），調和氣息；此印名為虛空身印，能除瑜伽士一切身疾。

   虛空身印：一種簡易版的明空身印。

10. *Uḍḍiyánabandha*: Contract the bowels equably above and below the navel towards the back, so that the abdominal viscera may touch the back. He who practices this *Uddiyana*(Flying up), without ceasing, conquers death. The Great Bird(Breath), by this process, is instantly forced up into the *sushumnas*, and flies(moves) constantly therein only.

    揚升鎖印：均勻地往背脊收縮臍腹中的大小腸，以使腹內臟器貼近背脊；持續不斷地習此揚升身印者，能克服死亡。依此法，能促使如鵬鳥般的氣息迅速地被迫入中脈，只在其中揚升。

    揚升身印：又名吊胃身印。

    克服死亡：在古本瑜伽典籍中，常見到克服死亡、降伏死亡或無有死亡等敘述，其實俱是指克服、降伏或是不再有對肉身死亡的恐懼，所得到的是洞悉器世間的無常，悟及生死真諦的屬靈成就。

11. Of all Bandhans, this is best. The complete practice of this makes emancipation easy.

    在所有鎖印中，此鎖印是最好的；善加修習此法，自得成就解脫。

    鎖印：可強化神經的特別體式，並藉此來影響體內的生命活力。

12. *Jálandharabandha*: Contracting the throat, place the chin on the chest. This is called *Jálandara*. By this *Bandha* the sixteen *Adharas* are closed. This and the *Maha-mudrá* destroy death.

收頷鎖印：收縮喉嚨並將下頷收抵胸口，此稱為收頷鎖印；透過此鎖印封住十六種基本習性，此鎖印與大手印能降伏死亡。

收領身印：直譯喉鎖印，中譯取其外觀之形。

十六種基本習性：意指喉輪的十六種情緒傾向，包括唵聲、吽聲及七種音階和其他七種有關表達的精細傾向。另有說這是指身體的十六個重要部位。

13. The *Jálandhara* is a success-giving and well-tried *Bandha*; he who practices it for six months, becomes an adept without doubt.

收頷鎖印是行之有效以及能助瑜伽士成就的鎖印，連續修習此鎖印六個月即能嫻熟，毋庸置疑。

14-15. *Múlabandha:* Press the heel of left foot the region between the anus and the scrotum, and contract the rectum; carefully press the intestines near the navel on the spine; and put the right heel on the organ of generation or pubes. This is called *Múlabandha,* destroyer of decay.

根鎖印：以左腳跟置抵會陰，提肛內縮直腸，小心地將臍腹內大小腸向背脊處收縮；右腳跟置於前陰，此為根鎖印，能抗逐衰老。

根鎖印：本式以所束鎖的部位命名，此鎖印女性收縮位置在子宮頸後方。

16-17. The persons who desires to cross the ocean of Existence, let him go to a retired place, and practice in secrecy this *Mudrá*. By the practice of it, the *Vayu*(*Prana*) is controlled undoubtedly; let one silently practice this, without laziness and with care.

渴望橫渡生死海之人，應覓僻靜之地，秘修此身印；通過修習此身印，生命能必得控制。故當以精勤謹慎之心靜修此印。

18-19. *Mahábandha:* Close the anal orifice by the heel of the left foot, press the heel with the right foot carefully, move slowly the muscles of the rectum, and slowly contract the muscles of the yoni or perineum (space between anus and organ); restrain the breath by *Jálandhara*. This is called *Mahábandha*.

大鎖印：以左足跟置抵後陰，再小心地把右足跟交疊其上；慢慢地將直腸肌上提，同時緩緩地收縮會陰，以收頷身印持氣。此稱之為大鎖印。

大鎖印：結合收頷、揚升及根等三鎖印於一身的鎖印，故宜先熟悉前述三種鎖印。孕婦或罹患胸腹臟腑疾病者，忌練習本鎖印。

20. *Mahábandha* is the Greatest *Bandha*; it destroys decay and death; by virtue of this *Bandha* a man accomplishes all his desire.

大鎖印是鎖印之最，能克服衰老和死亡；憑藉此鎖印，習者得遂所願。

21-22. *Mahávedha:* As the beauty, youth and charm of woman are in vain without a men, so are *Múlabandha* and *Mahábandha* without *Mahávedha*. Sitting first in *Mahábandha* posture, then retain breath by *Uḍḍána Kumbhaka* (retention of breath with lungs empty uddiyana-bandha). This is called *Mahávedha*- the giver of success to the *Yogís*.

大穿透印：猶如貌美、年青、迷人的女子，若無男子青睞亦是枉然，缺少大穿透印的根鎖印和大鎖印亦如是。首先以大鎖印姿勢坐好，再以優檀那持氣法，此謂之大穿透印—瑜伽士成就的賜予者。

優檀那持氣法：意譯是「向上持氣法」，即以以揚升鎖印吐氣完後暫懸氣息。

大穿透印：此處所述做法不同於其他哈達瑜伽經典。本式有助收攝心靈及喚醒靈能軍荼利。

23-24. The *Yogí* who daily practices *Mahábandha* and *Mulábandha*, accompanied with *Mahávedha*, is the best of *Yogís*. For him there is no fear of death, and decay does not approach him; this *Vedha* should be kept carefully secret by the *Yogí*.

每日修習大鎖印、根鎖印以及大穿透印等三鎖印之瑜伽士是最優秀的瑜伽士；老邁和死亡的恐懼不能近其身，瑜伽士應妥善保守此大穿透身印之秘。

25. *Khecarímudrá:* Cut down the lower tendon of the tongue, and move the tongue constantly; rub it with fresh butter, and draw it out(to lengthen it) with an iron instrument.

明空身印：分次細割舌下繫帶，經常攪動舌頭；抹上新鮮的乳脂，並用鋼製的工具拉長舌頭。

分次細割舌下繫帶：原英譯註建議每次切開十二分之一吋，《哈達瑜伽明燈》的方式是每次切開髮絲細，餘差異不大。

英註：這是明空身印的準備階段，目的是為了延展舌頭；希望舌頭能延長到舌尖可以觸及眉心，這可以由切開舌繫帶來達成。繫帶全部切開約莫需要六個月至三年的時間，我曾見師父做過。每週星期一他便將舌繫帶切開髮絲細深，灑上鹽，這樣切開之處就不會黏在一塊兒，再抹上黃奶油。他經常將舌頭向外伸長。

26. By practicing this always, the tongue become long, and when it reaches the space between the two eyebrows, then the *Khechari* is accomplished.

持續地鍛煉此法，舌頭遂逐漸拉長；當舌尖能夠觸及眉心之時，明空身印即完成準備。

明空身印：原字義是空行身印，行者藉此身印安定身心，解悟空性。切斷舌下繫帶若操作不慎，後遺症可能影響說話的流暢，今已少人採行，一般將舌頭常抵上顎即可。

27. Then (the tongue being lengthened) practice, turning it upwards and backwards so as to touch the palate, till at length it reaches the holes of the nostrils opening into the mouth. Close those holes with the tongue (thus stopping inspiration), and fix the gaze on the space between the two eyebrows. This is called *Khechari*.
將切完繫帶的舌頭向上反捲伸向上顎，直到觸及鼻咽通往口腔的咽孔；以舌頭封閉此咽孔（以中止紛飛的念頭），繫意兩眉之間；此為明空身印。

28. By this practice there is neither fainting, nor hunger, nor thirst, nor laziness. There comes neither disease, nor decay, nor death. The body becomes divine.
通過這樣的練習，習者既不會惛沉也不會飢餓，既不會口渴也不會懶散，既無疾病亦無老死，身體逐漸變得光潔。

29. The body cannot be burned by fire, nor dried up by the air, nor wetted by water, nor bitten by snakes.
如是身體火不能燒，風不能燥，水不能濕，蛇不能傷。

30. The body becomes beautiful; *Samadhi* is verily attained, and the tongue touching the holes obtains various juices (it drinks nectar).
體貌因之更為俊秀，亦必通達三摩地，且因舌頭觸及顎咽口之故而獲各色甘露。

31-32. Various juices being produced, day by day the man experiences new sensations; first, he experiences a salty taste, then alkaline, then bitter, then astringent, then the feels the taste of butter, then of ghee, then of milk, then of curd, then of whey, then of honey, then of palm juice, and lastly, arises the test of nectar.
各色甘露由是泌出，習者每天經驗到新的覺受；首先體驗到的是鹹味，跟著是辛味，再來是苦味，之後是澀味，然後是乳脂味，接著是醍醐味、牛乳味、凝乳味、乳清味、蜂蜜味、棗汁味，最後浮現的是甘露味。

33-35. *Viparítakaraṇímudrá*: The sun (solar *nádí* or plexus) dwells at the root of the navel, and the moon at the root of the palate; the process by which the sun is brought upward and the moon carried downward is called *Viparítakaraṇí*. It is a secret *mudrá* in all the Tantras. Place the head on the ground, with hands spread, raise the legs up, and thus remain steady. This is called *Viparítakaraṇí*.

倒轉身印：日脈叢位於臍根，月脈叢位於顎根；使日脈叢向上，月脈叢向下之體式謂之倒轉身印，是一切密續中的秘密身印。仰躺於地，兩手分置身側；舉雙腿向上，保持姿勢穩定，即名倒轉身印。

倒轉身印：此式定式臍部在下顎之上，故稱倒轉身印。練習結束後，宜接一個反向體式如魚式來平衡。有頸椎、腰椎不適者，患有高血壓及心臟病者，不宜冒然練習本式。兩臂動作是肩肘置抵於地，兩手支撐於後腰，視線可向著腳趾。

36. By the constant practice of this *mudrá*, decay and death are destroyed. He becomes an adept, and does not perish even at *Pralaya*.

持恆地修習此身印，能克服衰老和死亡；習者得大成就，即使毀劫現前亦能不滅。

大成就：功法修證有成之謂。

毀劫：印度傳統哲學認為有多種時長不一的大小生滅循環，名之為劫；毀劫之時，大地化為水，水化為火，火化為風，風復歸虛空。

37. Yoni *mudrá*: Sitting in *Siddhásana*, close the two ears with the two thumbs, the eyes with the index fingers, the nostrils with the middle fingers, the upper lip with the four fingers, and the lower lip with the little fingers.

胎藏身印：以完美坐式坐下，以拇指封閉兩耳，食指封閉雙眼，中指封住鼻孔，無名指封住上唇，小指封住下唇。

38. Draw in the *Práṇa-váyu* by *Káki-mudrá* (as in verse 86) and join it with the *Apána-váyu;* contemplating the six chakras in their order, let the wise one awaken the sleeping serpent-Goddess *Kundalini*.

以鳥喙身印吸入持命氣並將之與下行氣結合，依序觀想六個脈輪，智者循此喚醒沉睡的軍荼利女神。

鳥喙身印：詳本章第八十六節文句。

持命氣：泛指提供活力的生命能；若為五種內在生命能之一，則名為持命氣或命根氣；作用於聲帶與腹臍之間，負責生命體之呼吸作用。

下行氣：五種內在生命能之一，作用於腹臍與後陰之氣，控制大小二便。

39. By repeating the mantra *Huṅ*, and *Haṁsaḥ,* and raising the *Śakti*(Force kundalini) with the *jiva*, place them at the thousand-petal lotus.

持誦心咒 *Huṅ* 與 *Haṁsah*，以靈識提升造化靈能，將之安置於千瓣蓮花輪。

Huṅ 與 *Haṁsaḥ*：此節略述瑜伽靜坐心要，心咒前者為靈能軍荼利升起之聲，後者為靈性修持之梵咒，此咒音聲之外尚有奧義，僅因好奇心而習者無大裨益。按傳統具體修法須從師授，方見真功用。

靈識：梵語 *jiva* 或 *jiiva*，其義有人、命、神我、靈魂、神識、靈識、靈魂意識等翻譯。

造化靈能：又名造化力、造化勢能；而靈能是指沉睡在根持輪亦即海底輪，受造化力束縛住的悅性意識。一般認為她是一股神秘的靈性能量，又名軍荼利或靈能軍荼利、拙火等名稱。

40. Being himself full of *Sakti*, being joined with the great *Śiva*, let him think of the various pleasures and enjoyments.

讓自己滿盈造化靈能，使之與至上希瓦結合，觀想己身浸於各種喜樂與大樂之境。

至上希瓦：原英譯之用語是 *great Śiva*。此處至上希瓦意喻「至上意識」；意識與造化力是本體或宇宙本體之一體兩面，而造化勢能與至上意識的結合，即是靈性修持的終點，意謂著生命最終的圓成。

41. Let him contemplate on the union of *Śiva* and *Śakti* in this world. Being himself all bliss, let him realize that he is the *Brahma*.

於此世間靜慮至上意識與造化勢能合一，習者融入無比大樂中，循此習者了悟他即是至上本體。

至上本體：含容宇宙的本體，舊譯梵或大梵。古印度哲學中的梵或大梵是超越一切名相的，無法用思辨來體驗，是只能透過瑜伽漸悟或頓悟的終極、無始存在。本節文含藏著「梵我一如」的奧義，也是瑜伽中的最勝成就。

42. This *Yoni-mudrá* is a great secret, difficult to be obtained even by *Devas*. By once obtaining perfection in its practice, one enters verily into *Samàdhi*.

此胎藏身印是一大秘密，即使諸天亦難窺其秘義；一旦於修習中證得要旨，即入三摩地實相。

胎藏身印：亦稱胎藏鎖印，與《哈達瑜伽明燈》中的根門身印梵名相同，然作法、心法有別。此式做法是以十指封閉頭面七竅，默誦梵咒或聆聽聖音。同樣的做法，也有書籍稱作閉七竅身印。

諸天：神聖的存在，泛指天界諸神或具有神性特質者。

43-44. By the practice of this *mudrá*, one is never polluted by the sins of killing a *Bráhman*, killing a fetus, drinking liquor, or polluting the bed of the Preceptor. All the mortal sins and the venal sins are completely destroyed by this practice of *mudrá*. Let him therefore practice it, if he wishes for emamcipation.

通過修持此身印，永不為殺僧、殺胎、飲酒或褻瀆上師坐床等諸罪染污。緣修此身印，所有輕、重等罪盡皆滌除；願望自在解脫者，當如是修習此身印。

45. *Vajroṇímudrá*: Place the two palms on the ground, raise the legs in the air upward, the head not touching the earth. This awakens the *Śakti*, causes long life, and is called *Vajroṇí* by the sage.

金剛力身印：兩手掌按地而坐，雙腿向上舉於空中，注意頭不要碰觸地板；此式能喚醒造化靈能，增長世壽，賢者稱之為金剛力身印。

金剛力身印：此身印梵文字根意為杵、金剛、霹靂等，音譯瓦喬里身印。此式預備式是取坐姿兩手輕按地，兩腿前伸合攏；吐氣時藉腰腹之力上舉兩腿，膝蓋不彎，提縮尿道，身體略成 V 形。尿道發炎者暫不宜練習。

46-48. This practice is the highest of *Yogas*; it causes emancipation, and this beneficial *Yoga* gives perfection to the *Yogís*. By virtue of this *Yoga*, the *Bindu-Siddhi* (retention of seed) is obtained, and when that *Siddhi* is obtained what else can be not attain in this world. Though immersed in manifold pleasures, if he practices this *mudrá*, he attains verily all perfections.

此為最高階之瑜伽練習，能引領習者得解脫；此身印具有大利益，能助瑜伽士成就圓滿。由於此瑜伽之功，習者得明點成就，既得此成就，世間還有何事不能達成？身處世間逸樂之人習此身印，亦能如實達到一切成就。

明點成就：意指精氣不漏成就。密續觀念明點漏失表示人之身心有不圓滿之處，得明點成就表示精氣化神歸一，為所有進階成就之發端。

49-50. *Śakticálana mudrá*: The great goddess *Kundalini*, the energy of self, the *Atma-Shakti*, sleep in *Múladharachakra*; she has the form of a serpent thaving three coils and a half. So long as she is asleep in the body, the jiva is a mere animal, and true knowledge does not arise, though he may practice ten millions of *Yoga*.

力動身印：至尊女神軍荼利是內在真我的靈性能量，深眠於海底輪，其形有如一條蜷曲三圈半之蛇。只要她在身內處於深眠狀態，個體生命就仍停留在動物階段；即使彼已修習瑜伽千萬年，真知仍然蒙昧。

真我的靈性能量：內在真我的造化靈能，此靈性能量蟄伏於人身，因受到至上真我或至上意識的吸引而甦醒。

蜷曲三圈半：有說三圈代表生、住、滅，半圈代表再生循環。

51. As by a key a door is opened, so by awakening the *Kundaliní* by *Haṭha Yoga*, the door of *Brahman* is unlocked.

猶如鑰匙開門，哈達瑜伽喚醒靈能軍荼利，由是開啟至上本體之門。

52. Encircling the loins with a piece of cloth, seated in a secret room, not naked in an outer room, let him practice the *Shakticalana*.

莫裸身戶外，腰間圍布，於密室中安坐，潛修力動身印。

力動身印：攪動身內沉睡造化力或原力的身印。

53. One cubit long, and four fingers(3 inches) wide, should be the encircling cloth, soft, white and of fine texture. Join this cloth with the Kati-Sutra(a string worn round the loins).

圍布約一肘長，寬四指，觸感要軟，色白且質地良好，然後以腰繩繫固。

一肘長：從肘尖到中指尖的距離為一肘長，以圍布的長寬來看，圍遮範圍應是自臍繞過胯下至後腰，然後用腰帶固定。印度有種傳統的稱作 *lauńgota* 的褲兜，或為進化版，為瑜伽行者所喜用。

54-55. Rub the body with ashes, sit in *Siddhasana*-posture, drawing the *Prana-vayu* with the nostrils, forcibly join it with the *Apana*. Contract the rectum slowly by the *Ashvini-mudrá*, so long as the *Vayu* does not enter the *Sushumna*, and manifests its presence.

以灰塗身，取完美坐式，以鼻吸入命根氣並導引使與下行氣結合；徐徐以提肛身印收腹提肛，持續練習直至氣入中脈。

以灰塗身：梵語 *bhasmaná*，在印度傳統阿育吠陀醫學中，*bhasma* 是一種鍛燒礦植物後所提煉的藥用粉末，用以治療許多類型的疾病。在日常生活裡，古代有以澡豆磨粉來塗拭去身垢的習慣。在精神層面上，*bhasma* 象徵著將自我燒成灰燼，而與空性連結，又有提醒此身有一天也會回歸灰燼之意。故知以灰塗身在那個時代的生活及精神上均有其用意。

提肛身印：一種收縮後陰的身印，詳本章第八十二節文句。

56. By restraining the breath by *Kumbhaka* in this way, the Serpent Kundalini feeling suffocated, awakes and rises upward to the *Brahmarandhra*.

以此方式行持氣法懸止呼吸，蜷伏的靈能軍荼利因感窒息而往梵穴提升。

持氣法：字義為瓶、甕，故又名瓶氣法或寶瓶氣，以瓶喻人身故；是一暫懸氣息的功法，分為兩種：吸氣後的停息與呼氣後的停息。

梵穴：頂輪的別稱。

57. Without *Śakticálana*, the *Yonimudrá* is not complete or perfected; first the *Cálana* should be practiced, and then the *Yonimudrá* should be learnt.

若無力動身印搭配，胎藏身印難臻完全；首先練習力動身印，而後練習胎藏身印。

58. O *Chaṇḍa Kápáli!* thus have I taught thee the *Śakticálana*. Preserve it with care, and practice it daily.

旃檀子啊！以上所言即是力動身印，當細心護持並每日行持。

59. This *mudrá* should be kept carefully concealed. It destroys decay and death. Therefore the *Yogí*, desirous of perfection, should

practice it.

此身印能克服衰老和死亡，應謹慎守護；有心成就的瑜伽士，當勤習之。

60. The *Yogí* who practices this daily, acquires adeptship, attains *Vigraha-siddhi* and all his diseases are cured.

日習此身印之瑜伽士，嫻熟之後，得身成就，能治一切病。

身成就：獲得調控小宇宙身的能力。

61. *Táḍágimudrá*: Sitting in *Paśćimottánásana* posture, make the stomach like a tank(hollow). This is *Taḍágimudrá*(Tank-*mudrá*), destroyer of all decay and death.

腹貼脊身印：採取背部伸展式坐好，然後內縮臍腹；此為腹貼脊身印，能克服一切衰老及死亡。

背部伸展式：取坐姿伸腿前俯手握腳趾，然後令胸腹貼近膝腿，做法見第二章第二十四節所述。

腹貼脊身印：行此身印時先放鬆臍腹，以背部伸展式之姿吸氣後稍停息，吐氣時提肛縮腹如臍向內貼向背脊。本式有強化腹腔器官之效。由於重點在於腹部之作用，此身印亦可採曲膝仰躺之姿進行；進行時腳跟近臀，手扶腿胯之處，吸氣預備，吐氣同時將肚腹下拉貼脊。

62. *Mándukimudrá*: Closing the mouth, move the tip of tongue towards the palate, and taste slowly the nectar(flowing from the Thousand-petals Lotus); This is Frog-*mudrá*.

蛙眠身印：雙唇輕闔，舌尖反轉輕抵上顎，細品千瓣蓮花輪泌出的甘露，是為蛙眠身印。

蛙眠身印：此身印取名蛙眠，在於習者如蛙冬眠般身形安止，繫心最勝空性或至上主或至上意識，細品因之泌出的甘露法味。

63. The body never sickens or become old, and it retains perpetual youth; the hair of him who practices this never grows white.

色身因此永不罹病或變老，青春長駐，習此身印者鬢髮永不灰白。

64. *Śámbhavímudrá*: Fixing the gaze between the two eyes-brows, behold the Self-existent. This is *Shambavi* , secret in all the Tantras.

希瓦身印：內觀兩眉之間，安住真我法喜，此為希瓦身印，乃一切密續之秘密。

安住真我法喜：意指安住於內在真我喜悅之源。

希瓦身印：此為「充分體現希瓦精神的身印」，是密續和哈達瑜伽中最重要的身印之一。

65. The *Vedas*, the scriptures, the *Puranas* are like public women, but this *Sambhavi* should be guarded as if it were a lady of a respectable family.

四吠陀、聖教經典、往世書有如風塵女，然此希瓦身印應如護佑名門淑女般對待。

四吠陀：本義為真正的知識，亦是傳承靈性知識的鉅著；學術上則視之為源於阿利安人並由其傳入印度的一門宗教或思想學派，著重在透過儀軌來獲得神的應許。吠陀內容是五千至一萬年前知識累積的結集，分成四吠陀。依成書時間分別是黎俱吠陀、夜柔吠陀、阿闥婆吠陀及沙摩吠陀，沙摩吠陀是擷取前三部吠陀中與音樂主題相關的別冊，而阿育吠陀是吠陀中的養生和醫療知識。

聖教經典：教導世人當為之事與不當為之規範，以達解脫目的的聖教典籍。

往世書：古老的梵語故事書，或說是具有重大教育價值的故事書。《摩訶婆羅多》的作者毗耶薩寫下了十八卷具有教育意義的往世書傳世，靈性導師雪莉．雪莉．阿南達慕提曾說：在毗耶薩十八卷的往世書中，歸結最重要的兩句話就是「從事善行即美德，從事惡行即邪惑」。

66. He, who knows this *Sambhavi,* is like the *Adinatha*(*Śiva*), he is a

Narayana (*Vishnu*), he is *Brahmá* the Creator.

明此希瓦身印之士，即如本初主，彼即造化主，彼即創造主。

本初主：梵語 ***Ádinátha*** 由 ***ádi+nátha*** 組成，***ádi*** 字義原初的，***nátha*** 字義是主宰、上主；***Ádinátha*** 一詞意指本初之天主，在印度普遍認為 ***Ádinátha*** 即是指一切的控制者希瓦。

造化主：梵語 ***Náráyaṇa***，***nára*** 有水、虔誠及宇宙運作法則等義，***ayana*** 為庇護之意；在此處 ***Náráyaṇa*** 意指宇宙運作法則的庇護者，亦是指無所不在、遍及一切的維世努或妙毗天。

創造主：梵語 ***Brahmá*** 指的是至上本體創造、維繫及毀滅等三個面向中的創造者。在梵文中，要注意 ***Brahmá*** 和 ***Brahma*** 的分別；後者是指超越一切分別的絕對存在，如下一節經文所述。

67. Maheiś hvara has said：Truly, truly, and again truly, he who knows the *Sambhavi*, is *Brahma*. There is no doubt of this.

大自在主嘗言：「真真實實、的的確確，明此希瓦身印者，即如至上本體，毋庸置疑。」

68. The *Śámbhavi* has explained; hear now five *Dháranás*. Learning these five *Dháranás*, what cannot be accomplished in this world?

希瓦身印已述明如上，現在諦聽五大執持身印法，習此五執持身印之士，世間無有不能成就之事。

五大執持身印法：梵語 ***Pañcadháraṇámudrá***，***Pañca*** 字義是「五」，表示五大元素，而五大元素是器世間或宇宙一切組成之根本。***dháraṇá*** 字義是「制心一處」；***dháraṇá*** 譯名有執持、受持或總持，白話譯文為專注或集中。此處第六十八節至八十一節是敘述五大元素的觀修身印。

69. By this, with the human body one can visit and revisit *Svarga-loka*, he can go wherever he likes, as swiftly as mind, he acquires

the faculty of walking in the sky. These five *Dharanas* are: *Párthivi*(eEarthy), *Ámbhasi*(Watery), *Váyavi*(Aerial), *Ágneyi*(Fiery), and *Ákási*(Ethereal).

觀修五執持身印之士，可以到訪或重臨天界；習者獲得空行的能力，可前去任何想往之處，其速迅捷如心。這五種執持身印分別是：地大執持身印、水大執持身印、火大執持身印、風大執持身印與空大執持身印。

五大執持身印：控制及開展身內地、水、火、風、空等五大元素的身印。

70. *Párthiví-dháraná mudrá:* The *Prithivi-tattva* has the color of orpiment(yellow), the letter(*la*) is its secret symbol or seed, its form is four-sided, and *Brahmá*, its presiding deity. Place this Tattva in the heart, and fix by *Kumbhaki* the *Prána-váyu* and the *chitta* there for the period of five *ghatikas*(2.5 hours). This is called *Adhodháraná*. By this, one conquers the Earth, and no earthy-elements can injure him; and it causes steadiness.

地大執持身印：地元素色若雄黃，音根種子字是 *la*（ल），其形四方，大梵天為其主神。將此元素持觀於心，以瓶氣法安住心息於此五炷香時間，是為地大觀修法。依此觀修，習者征服地大，不受地元素之傷害，身益堅穩。

地元素：又名土元素或固體元素，具有形塑、撐持地上萬有著的特性，在人體內起著支撐、成形等作用，其形亦是穩固、安定的象徵。

大梵天：又名創造主，也就是至上本體的創造面，代表創造之神或創造之作用。

瓶氣法：意指「將氣息留持於身內」，亦指出、入息中間的這段時間。

五炷香時間：根據古印度的時間計算單位，一 *ghatiká* 表示一炷香時間，約合二十四分鐘，五炷香共計是兩小時。

71. He who practices this dharana, becomes like the conqueror of Death; as an adept he walks over this earth.

如法觀修之士，成為死亡的征服者，可以成就者之姿行走大地。

大地：指器世間、物界世界、於此地表、於此星球等……。

72. *Ámbhasi-dháraná mudrá* This Water-*tattva* is white like the kunda-flower or a conch or the moon, its form is circular like the moon, the letter (*va*) is the seed of this ambrosial element, and Vishnu is its presiding deity. By *Yoga*, produce the water-tattva in the heart, and fix there the *Prana* with the *chitta*(consciousness), for five ghatikas, practicing *Kumbhaka*. This is Watery *Dharana*; it is the destroyer of all sorrows. Water cannot injure him who practices this.

水大執持身印：水元素色白若茉莉，形似彎月，音根種子字是 *va*（व），妙毗天為其主神。依瑜伽法，於心中持觀水元素，以瓶氣法安住心息於此五炷香時間。此是水大觀修法，能去一切惱苦，習者得不受水大之傷害。

水元素：又名液體元素，具有擴散、淨潤、流通的特性，在人體內起著代謝、滋養、潤澤等作用。其彎月之形乃是廣納水元素的象徵。

妙毗天：亦即維世努，又名遍入天或遍在天，是護持宇宙的神或作用，佛教裡稱那羅延天。

73-74. The *Ambhasi* is a great *mudrá*; the *Yogí* who knows it, never meets death even in the deepest water. This should be kept carefully concealed. By revealing it success is lost, verily I tell you the truth.

水大執持身印係上勝身印，明此之瑜伽士遇深水亦不溺亡。此法應細心護持，實言相告，若輕意泄漏其功亦失。

75. *Ágneyi-dháraná mudrá:* The Fire-*tattva* is situated at the navel, its color is red like the Indra-gop insect, its form is triangular, its seed is (*ra*), its presiding deity is *Rudra*. It is refulgent like the sun,

and the giver of success. Fix the Prana along with the chitta in this Tattva for five *ghatikas*. This is called Fire-*Dharana*, destroyer of the fear of dreadful death, and fire cannot injure him.

火大執持身印：火元素位於臍輪，色若紅絲絨蟎，其形三角，音根種子字是 *ra*(र)，主神是魯卓天；其光輝若太陽，能賦予人成就。以瓶氣法安住心息於此五炷香時間。此是火大觀修法，能粉碎憂心死亡的恐懼，且習者得不受火大之傷害。

火元素：又名光元素，物質界的能量成分，表示溫暖和力量，在人體內起著煖熱、熟化等作用。其形有盛裝宇宙力量的象徵。

魯卓天：是黎俱吠陀中力量最強大的神，令人怖畏！人稱魯卓天為使人哭泣者，藉使人流淚來教導人以達教化的目的。隨著後代觀念的改變，魯卓天進化為主希瓦。

76. If the practitioner is thrown into burning fire, by virtue of this *mudrá* he remains alive, without fear of death.

若習者身陷火場，緣修習此身印之功而得活命，無有死亡之恐懼。

77. *Váyavi-dháraná mudrá:* The Air-*tattva* is black as unguent for the eyes(collirium), the letter (*ya*) is its seed, and *Iśvara* its presiding deity. This Tattva is full of *Sattva* quality. Fix the Prana and the *chitta* for five *ghatikas* in this *Tattva*. This is *Vayavi-Dharana*. By this, the practitioner walks in the air.

風大執持身印：風元素色如灰煙，音根種子字是 *ya* (य)，主神是自在天。風元素富含悅性特質，安住心息於此五炷香時間。此是風大觀修法，由此，習者能於空中行走。

風元素色如灰煙：亦名氣態元素，具移轉性，有方向無形質，兼具柔和與狂暴的特性；在人體內起著推動循環、血行及增長能量等作用，思想、情緒亦如風。其形慣以代表往復循環不絕的圓作象徵。原英譯謂此元素色黑若眼膏，然在本書第五章第三十九節言：風元素其色如烟，而在施化難陀所著的《軍荼利瑜伽》一書中，謂此元素形如六芒星色如烟。故此處改黑色為烟色。

自在天：宇宙萬有一切作用或念想的控制者；超越一切的束縛，故稱自在天。

78-79. This great *mudrá* destroys decay and death. Its practitioner is never killed by any aerial disturbances; by its virtue one walks in the air. This should not taught to the wicked or those devoid of faith. By so doing success is lost; Oh *Chaṇḍa*! this is verily the truth.

此勝妙身印能滅衰老與死亡，習者永不為任何風災所亡；緣此法之功，習者能空行。此法不得授予心術不正或缺乏信心之人，否則亦必徒勞。旃檀子！此乃真實之言！

80. *Ákási-dháraná mudrá:* The Ether-*tattva* has the color of pure sea-water, (*ha*) is its seed, its presiding deity is *Sádaśiva*. Fix the *Prana* along with *Chitta* for five ghatikas in this *Tattva*. This is Ether-*Dharana*. Its open the gates of emancipation.

空大執持身印：空元素色若淨海水，*ha*（ह）為其音根種子字，主神是永恆的希瓦。安定心息於此元素五炷香時間。此是空大觀修法，能打開解脫之門。

空元素：又名乙太元素，提供一切所需的空間；無方向無形質無有邊際，唯聲音可藉之傳遞。在人體內起著平衡生機、連結微妙空性等的作用。

色若淨海水：此處未言其形，在施化難陀所著的《軍荼利瑜伽》一書中，謂此元素形圓色藍。

永恆的希瓦：是傳統印度信仰三大主神之一，與梵天、妙毗天或維世努並稱。希瓦之名有吉祥、慈悲之意，但一般觀念認為希瓦是毀滅之神，而在印度哲學中毀滅即意味著再生，實際上代表著重生或新的契機。

81. He who knows this *Dharana* is real *Yogí*. Death does not approach him, nor does he perish at the *pralaya*.

明此空大執持身印者為真瑜伽士，死亡不能侵，毀劫不能滅。

82. *Aśhvinimudrá:* Contract and dilate the anal aperture again and again, this called *Aśvini-mudrá*. It awakens the *Śakti*(*Kuṇḍalini*).

提肛身印：反覆縮放後陰的括約肌，此謂之提肛身印，能喚醒靈能軍荼利。

提肛身印：原梵文字義是馬陰身印，類似馬縮肛之動作。

83. This Asvini is a great *mudrá*; its destroys all diseases of the rectum; its gives strength vigor, and prevents premature death.

提肛身印是很重要的身印，能剷除所有直腸的疾病，賦予習者強大的活力，並防止早逝。

84. *Páśinímudrá:* Throw the two legs on the neck towards the back, holding them strongly together like a *Pasa*(a noose). This is called *páśinímudrá*; its awakens the *Śakti*(*Kuṇḍalini*).

套索身印：舉腿往後向上於頸後交叉，像套索般緊緊的圈在一起；此為套索身印，能喚醒靈能軍荼利。

套索身印：此身印雙腿如套索般圈住軀體，因而得名。練習時可先採取仰臥姿，嫻熟後再試著以坐姿進行。

85. This grand *mudrá* gives strength and nourishment. It should be practiced with care by those who desire success.

此一重要身印能長養身力，有心成就之人應注意修習。

86. *Kákímudrá:* Contract the lips like the beak of a crow, and drink(draw in) the air slowly and slowly. This is *Kákí* (crow) *mudrá*, destroyer of all diseases.

烏喙身印：撮唇如烏喙，緩緩自口吸氣下嚥，此為烏喙身印，能除一切病。

鳥喙身印：此身印撮唇如鳥喙，故名鳥喙身印。此身印亦可捲舌如鳥喙，略伸出口唇，再緩緩吸氣下嚥。

87. The *Kákímudrá* is a great *mudrá*, kept secret in all Tantras. By virtue of this, one become free from disease like a crow.

鳥喙身印亦為重要身印，其秘藏於一切密續中；憑藉此身印，習者能如烏鴉般不為疾病所侵。

88-89. *Mátanginímudrá:* Stand in neck-deep water, draw in the water through the nostrils, and throw it out by the mouth. Then draw in the water through(the mouth and expel it through) the nostrils. Let one repeat this again and again. This is called Elephant-*mudrá*, destroyer of decay and death.

大象身印：立於深及頸項之水中，以鼻吸水入喉，再由嘴口吐出；復由嘴吸水入口再由鼻送出，反覆若干次。此為大象身印，能克服衰老及死亡。

大象身印：大象於水塘中常以鼻吸水或噴水，故名大象身印。古早瑜伽士會在溪河或池塘中練習此身印，口鼻雖相通，不過由鼻吸水由口吐出易，由口入水由鼻送出較難，需有良好的鼻咽控制力。就清潔鼻腔而言，單向為之已足夠。

90-91. In a solitary place, free from human intrusion, one should practices with fixed attention this Elephant *mudrá*; by so doing, he becomes strong like Elephant. Whatever he may be, by this process the *Yogí* enjoys great pleasure; therefore this *mudrá* should be practiced with great care.

於僻靜無擾處，專注練習此身印，如是習者將健壯如象。任何修習此身印之士，得享大喜樂，故當以虔敬心修此身印。

92. *Bhujanginímudrá:* Extending the neck a little forward, let him drink(draw in) air through the esophagus; This is called Serpent-mudra. Destroyer of decay and death.

龍飲身印：微向前伸頸，以食道飲氣嚥下；此為龍飲身印，能克服衰老及死亡。

龍飲身印：印度有靈蛇飲氣為生的說法，此身印取其意而名之。本式有防治胃功能失調之效，然宜在空氣清新處練習。

93. This Serpent-*mudrá* quickly destroys all stomach diseases, especially indigestion, and dyspepsia, etc.

此龍飲身印能迅速消除一切胃疾，尤其是消化不良和胃弱等方面的疾病。

身印的功效

94. O *Chaṇḍa Kápáli*! thus have I recited to thee the chapter on *Mudras*. This is beloved of all adepts, and destroys decay and death.

哦，旃檀子！以上所言即是能克服老死，受一切成就者所珍視之身印篇章。

95. This should not be taught indiscriminately, nor to a wicked person, nor to one devoid of faith; this should be preserved secret with great care; it is difficult to be even by the deva.

莫輕意示人身印之法，亦不可授予心術不正及信力不堅之士；此法門縱或諸天亦行之不易，當秘守之。

譯按：瑜伽行法如修道，輔以身印則有助道之功；然恐理法不明，反生輕慢心，故古之瑜伽選擇弟子素來謹慎。

96. These *mudrás* which give happiness and emancipation should be taught to guileless, calm and peace-minded person, who is devoted to his Teacher and comes of good family.

如是賦予法喜與心寂之諸身印法，應授予品性樸實、內心平和、敬信上師以及家教良好之人。

寂心：梵語 *sántacittáya*，*sánta* 意為寂靜、寂滅，*cittá* 意為心，故中譯寂心；英譯 emancipation，意為解脫；中譯名從梵語之意。

97. These *Mudras* destroy all diseases. They increase the gastric fire of him who practices them daily.

日習諸身印法之士，能增強胃火，除一切病。

增強胃火：意為增強消化能力，非指胃熱或胃燥熱。

98. To him death never comes, nor decay, etc; there is no fear to him from fire and water, nor from air.

成就者無有老死等諸苦，於火災、水災及風災亦無所懼。

99. Cough, asthma, enlargement of spleen, leprosy, being diseases of twenty sorts, are verily destroyed by the practice of these *Mudras*.

修持諸身印之士，能防治咳嗽、氣喘、脾腫、痲瘋等二十餘種疾病。

100. O *Chaṇḍa*! What more shall I tell thee? In short, there is nothing in this world like the *Mudras* for giving quick success.

噢，旃檀子！還有什麼我該告訴你的？要言之，世間沒有比身印法更好的成就捷徑了。

第四章

感官內攝法

Pratyáhára

1. *Gheraṇḍa* said: Now I shall tell thee, *Pratyáhára-Yoga* the best. By its knowledge, all the passions like lust, etc., are destroyed.
   葛蘭達言：現在講述上乘瑜伽內攝之法，依此修持，能滅一切慾想。
   內攝之法：瑜伽八支功法中的第五支——將心靈從外在客體收回，再將收回的心靈導向無上空性、至上本體或至上意識。

2. Let one bring the Chitta(thinking principle) under his control by withdrawing it, whenever it wanders away drawn by the various objects of sight.
   每當心馳外境，當即收視返聽；必使之內攝而將心意收於控制之下。

3. Praise or censure; good speech or bad speech; let one withdraw his mind from all these and bring the *chitta* under the control of the Self.
   令心自褒貶之詞、善惡之言收回；攝心於真我控制之下。
   真我：同美詞有靈魂、意識、真我、真性、純淨識、無染識，未沾染的本來自性；用於大宇宙靈魂稱為至上靈魂，用於個體稱作個體靈魂。

4. From sweet smells or bad smells, by whatever odor the mind may be distracted or attracted, let one withdraw the mind from that, and bring the thinking principle under the control of Self.
   令心自香氛或臭味等任何會使心靈迎拒之氣味收回，攝之於真我控制之下。

5. From sweet or acid tastes, from bitter or astringent tastes, by whatever teste the mind may be attracted, let one withdraw it from that, and bringing it within the control of his Self.
   令心自酸、甜、苦、澀等任何會使心靈迎拒之口味收回，攝之於真我控制之下。

第五章

調息法

Práṇáyáma

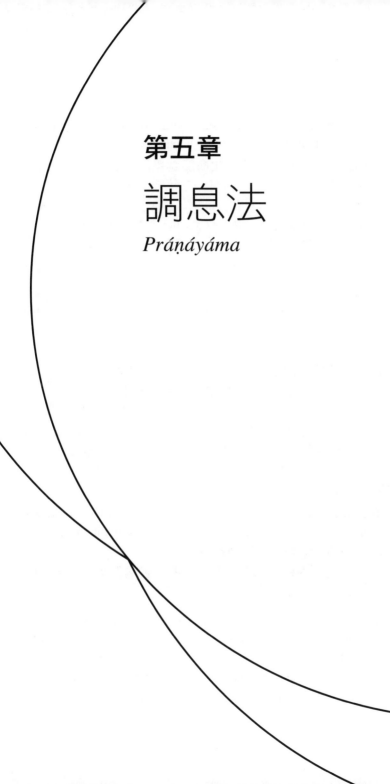

1. *Gheraṇḍa* said: Now I shall tell thee the rules of Pranayama or regulation of breath. By its practice a man become like a god.

   葛蘭達言：現在我將講述生命能調息法，依此修持，常人亦能有如神。

   生命能調息法：瑜伽八支功法中的第四支：藉助控制呼吸及有理念的呼吸來控制生命能以幫助心靈集中與靜坐。

   有如神：意指依調息法修持有成，在精神上、力氣上都有如神助。

2. Four things are necessary in practice pranayama. First, a good place; second, a suitable time; third, moderate food; and lastly, the purifications of the *Nádís*.(vessels of the body, *i.e.*, .alimentary canal, etc.,)

   練習生命能調息法時須注意四事：一為良好的地點；次為適當的時間；三是有節制的飲食；四是經脈的淨化。

   經脈：身內精細的能量管道，《哈達瑜伽明燈》提及身內經脈總有七萬兩千條，尤其重要的是從根持輪或海底至眉心輪間，靈能軍荼利所經的中脈及繞於其上的左脈與右脈。

良好的地點

3. The practice of *Yoga* should not be attempted in a far off country (from home), nor in a forest, nor in a capital city, nor in the midst of a crowd. If one does so, he loses success.

   莫於遠地、森林、都市裡和群眾間修習瑜伽；若然，易敗於垂成。

4. In a distant country, one loses faith (because of the *Yoga* not being known there); In a forest, one is without protection; and in the midst of a thick population, there is danger of exposure (for then the curios will trouble him). Therefore, let one avoid these three.

   處遠地，易失信心（因為沒有瑜伽善知識可資親近）；居森林中，人無保護；而於人口稠密處，易曝光陷危（易受到好奇人士的滋擾）。是故習者應避開這些地方。

人口稠密處：有各種避開都市修行的因素，主要理由還有噪音及空氣污染。

5. In a good country whose king is just, where food is easily and abundantly procurable, where there are no disturbances, let one erect there a small hut, around it let him raise walls.

宜築修舍於有道之邦，周圍以矮牆護之；如是邦君公義仁正，資糧易辦，無虞侵擾。

6. And in the centre of the enclosure, let him sink a well and dig a tank. Let the hut be neither very high nor very low，let it be free from insects.

護牆之內，鑿井修池，修舍大小適度，能防蟲蟻。

7. It should be completely plastered over with cow-dung. In a hut thus constructed and situated in such a hidden place, let him practice Pranayama.

外牆應滿塗牛糞，修舍宜築於幽靜處，方便修習生命能調息法。

外牆應滿塗牛糞：印度鄉間善用牛糞，除作為燃料外，還具有保溫、隔音及防蟲之效。

適當的時節

8. The practice of *Yoga* should not be commenced in these four seasons out of six: winter, cold, hot, rainy. If one begins in these seasons, one will contract diseases.

莫於六季中的初冬、嚴冬、熱季、雨季等四季練習瑜伽，若在此四季節開始練習，易招引疾病。

9. The practice of *Yoga* should be commenced by a beginner in

Spring(*Vasanta*); and Autumn(*Śarad*). By so doing, he attains success; and verily he does not become liable to diseases.

初習者應在春、秋兩季開始練習瑜伽；順應時節練習，習者得獲成就，且不易招引疾病。

10. The six seasons occur in their order in the twelve months beginning with Chaitra and ending with Phalguna; two months being occupied by each season. But each season is experienced for four months, beginning with Magha and ending with Phalguna.

一年十二個月分成六季，其序始於三月，終於二月，每季長兩個月；但每季經歷達四個月，始於元月，終於二月。

譯按：前者以每季以基期兩個月計，始於三月，終於二月；後者計入每季氣候的交替期，故基期長四個月，始於元月，終於二月。詳如以下第 11 節、12 節所述。

印度的六季

11. The six seasons are as follows:

六季切分順序如下：

春季（*Vaṣánta*）：3~4 月（*Chaitra* and *Varṣáka*）

夏季（*Griṣmán*）：5~6 月（*Áṣádha* and *Jeṣhtha*）

雨季（*Varṣá*）：7~8 月（*Śravaṇa* and *Bhádra*）

秋季（*Śarada*）：9~10 月（*Áśvina* and *Kártika*）

初冬（*Hemanta*）：11~12 月（*Agraháyana* and pausha）

嚴冬（*Śiśirá*）：1~2 月（*Mágha and Phálguna*）

12-14. Now I shall tell thee the experiencing of seasons. They are as follows:

六季交替月份切分如下：

一月至四月（*Mágha-Vaiśáka*）

三月至六月（*Chaitra-Áṣádha*）

六月至九月（*Áṣádha-Áśvina*）

八月至十一月（*Bhádra-Agraháyana*）
十月到一月（*Kártika-Mágha*）
十一月到二月（*Agraháyana-Phálguna*）

15. The practice of *Yoga* should be commenced either in *Vaṣánta*(Spring) or *Śarad*(Autumn). For in the season success is attained without much trouble.

修習瑜伽宜始於春、秋兩季，如是季節可較無干擾地獲致成就。

節制飲食

16. He who practices *Yoga* without moderation of diet, incurs various diseases, and obtains no success.

修習瑜伽而未節制飲食，反易招致各種疾病，難以成就。

17. A *Yogí* should eat rice, barley (bread), or wheaten bread. He may eat mudga beans, asha beans, gram, etc. These should be clean, white and free from chaff.

瑜伽行者應攝食米飯、大麥麵包、小麥麵包，也可以食綠豆、鷹嘴豆等豆類，所有食料須潔淨及去殼。

18-19. A *Yogí* may eat *patola* (a kind of cucumber), jackfruit, taro, *kakkola* (a kind of berry), the jujube (Chinese date), the bonduc nut (Bonducella guilandina), cucumber, all plantains (including stems and roots), figs, eggplant, and medicinal roots and fruits.

瑜伽行人可食櫛瓜、波蘿蜜、芋頭、畢澄茄、棗子、灰榛子、胡瓜、芭蕉(含根莖)、無花果、茄子和藥草根及水果。

灰榛子：豆科蘇木屬植物，中文名稱有老虎心、刺果蘇木、肉葉刺等。葉、莖、種子味苦性涼，可入藥，能行氣袪瘀、清熱解毒、治療急慢性胃疾、腸道積蟲、便秘等等。種子色灰質硬，故名灰榛子。

20. He may eat green, fresh vegetables, black vegetables, the leaves of patola, the *Vastuka-saka,* and *hima-lochiká Saka*. These are the five *sakas* (vegetable leaves) praised as fit food for *Yogís*.

亦可食用新鮮的綠色及深色蔬菜、櫛瓜葉、菠菜、水田芥等任何五種時蔬，這是最適合瑜伽行人的食物。

21. Pure, sweet and cooling food should be eaten to fill half the stomach: eating thus sweet juices with pleasure, and leaving the other half of the stomach empty is called moderation in diet.

應攝取純淨、甘甜和性涼的食物，攝取量宜為胃納量的一半；以愉悅的心情啜飲甘甜的果汁，另一半的胃留空，是為節制飲食。

性涼的食物：身心的發展與食物密切相關。根據阿育吠陀的飲食觀念，某些食物令身體發熱，某些食物令身體清涼；發熱的例如肉類，清涼的如薑黃。因此一般會引起身體發汗、會引起口鼻或眼睛熱灼的食物或香料均宜避免。

22. Half the stomach should be filled with food, one quarter with water: and one quarter should be kept empty for practicing *Práṇáyáma*.

二分之一的胃裝食物，四分之一裝湯水，餘四分之一留空，方便練習調息法。

禁止的食物

23. In the beginning of *Yoga*-practice one should discard bitter, acid, salt, pungent and roasted things, curd, whey, heavy vegetables, wine, palm nuts, and over-ripe jack-fruit.

瑜伽練習之初應避免過苦、過酸、過鹹、香辛及焦烤的食物、凝乳、乳清、不易消化的蔬菜、麻醉飲料、檳榔和過熟的波蘿蜜。

練習之初：百日築基，至少持續三個月，再視狀況調整。

24. So also *kulattha* and pandu fruit, pumpkins and vegetable stems,

gourds, berries, *katha-bel*, (*feronia elephantum*), *kanta-bilva* and *palasa* (*Butea frondosa*).

也應避免食用馬豆、小扁豆、爛熟水果或南瓜、菜梗、瓢瓜、漿果、象橘、曼陀蘿花、膠蟲樹花。

25. So also *Kadamba* (*Nauclea cadamba*), citron, *bimba*, *lukucha* (a kind of bread fruit tree), onions, lotus, *Kamaranga*, *piyala*(*Buchanania latifolia*), asafoetida, *salmali*, *kemuka*.

復應避免迦曇婆果、香櫞、蘋婆、麵包果、蔥蒜、蓮花、大高良薑、楊桃、山檨子、阿魏、木綿花、螺旋薑。

迦曇婆果：又稱團花，印度喬木，雨季開花，花白有香氣，花序及果可食。

蓮花：蓮花全株可食，但此處不明指蓮花哪一部位；在蓮花、蓬子、蓮心、蓮葉和蓮藕中，蓮心最寒涼，胃弱體虛者不宜生食。

26-27. A beginner should avoid much travelling, company of women, and warming himself by fire. So also he should avoid fresh butter, ghee, thickened milk, sugar and date-sugar, etc., as well as ripe plantain, cocoa-nut, pomegranate, dates, lavani fruit, *amlaki* (myrobalans), and everything containing acid juices.

初習者應避免奔波遊方、伴隨婦女和偎火取暖，也應避免鮮奶油、醍醐、濃奶、蔗糖、棗糖等，以及過熟的芭蕉、椰肉、石榴、乾棗、釋迦果、醋栗和一切酸味果汁。

28. But cardamom, *jaipha,* cloves, aphrodisiacs or stimulants, the rose-apple, *haritaki*, and palm dates, a *Yogí* may eat while practising *Yoga*.

然而在練習瑜伽期間，可取食綠荳蔻、肉荳蔻、丁香、無花果、酪梨、蓮霧、訶子和椰棗。

29. Easily digestible, agreeable and cooling foods which nourish the humors of the body, a *Yogí* may eat according to his desire.

若需要，瑜伽行人可適意地攝取一些順口、容易消化並能滋養身體的食物。

30. But a *Yogí* should avoid hard-to-digest food, sinful food, or putrid food, or very hot, or very stale food, as well as very cooling or very much exciting food.

然瑜伽行人應避免粗硬、不潔、陳腐、難消化的食物，或是太熱、太冷及刺激性強的食物。

31. He should avoid bathing before sunrise, fasting (and severe austerities in general), or anything giving pain to the body; so also is prohibited to him eating only once a day, or not eating at all. But he may remain without food for 3 hours.

避免日出前沐浴，斷食（和嚴格的苦行）或是任何令身體疼痛之情事。亦不建議只日食一餐或是整日不食，兩餐間至少相隔三小時。

32. Regulating his life in this way, let him practice Prá áyáma. In the beginning before commencing it, he should take a little milk and ghee daily, and take his food twice daily, once at noon, and once in the evening.

如是規範日常作息後，可修習生命能調息法。練習之初，習者應每天攝取一些牛奶和醍醐，日進兩餐；日中一餐，傍晚一餐。

譯按：修習生命能調息法過程之中，很耗體能，故此時需注意攝取充分營養。

經脈的淨化

33. He should sit on a seat of *Kuśa*-grass, or an antelope skin, or tiger skin or a blanket, or on earth, calmly and quietly, facing east or north. Having purified the *nádis*, let him begin *Práṇáyáma*.

習者應以吉祥草為席，或以羚羊皮、虎皮、毛毯或大地為席，心靜語默，面向東或向北；在淨化經脈之後，開始修習生命能調息法。

吉祥草：禾本科羽穗草屬，為多年生草本植物，印藏視為聖草，可編織為席。

34. *Chaṇḍa Kápáli* said: O ocean of mercy! How are *náḍis* purified, what is the purification of *náḍis*; I want to learn all this; recite this to me.

旃檀子言：慈悲的海洋啊！什麼是經脈淨化？要如何淨化經脈？弟子想要了解這一切，祈請為我述說。

慈悲的海洋：此處未稱上師名，而以深不可測之海洋代名深不可測的上師。

35. *Gheraṇḍa* said: The *Váyu* does not (cannot) enter the nadis so long as they are full of impurities. How then can *Práṇáyáma* be accomplished? How can there be knowledge of *Tattvas*? Therefore, first the *Nádís* should be purified, and then *Práṇáyáma* should be practised.

葛蘭達言：只要經脈充滿不淨，內氣即不能進入經脈，行人豈能成就生命能功法？又怎會生出真實智慧？是故，行人需先淨化經脈，而後才能鍛煉調息功法。

內氣：泛指身內運行作用於身心的精細能量。

真實智慧：明了世俗諦、勝義諦如幻起滅的智慧。

36. The purification of *Náḍi* is of two sorts: *Samanu* and *Nirmanu*. The *Samanu* is done by a mental process with *Bíja-mantra*. The *Nirmanu* is performed by physical cleanings.

經脈淨化有兩類：心脈淨化法和身脈淨化法，心脈淨化法是透過種子梵咒來完成內心淨化，身脈淨化法是透過身體的淨化來完成。

心脈淨化法：透過音根梵咒及心意的轉換達成內心的淨化。

身脈淨化法：透過哈達瑜伽六淨化法來達成生理的淨化。

37. The physical cleanings of *Dhautis* have already been taught. They consist of the six *Sadhanas*. Now, O *Chaṇḍa,* listen to the *Samanu* process of purifying the vessels.

身脈淨化法如淨胃法等如前已說，其法含括於六淨化法中。現在，旃檀子，諦聽心脈淨化法。

淨胃法：其法有四，詳見第一章第十三節文句。

六淨化法：詳見第一章第十二節文句。

38. Sitting in the *Padmásana* posture, and performing the adoration of the *Guru*, etc., as taught by the Teacher, let him perform purification of *Nádís* for success in *Práṇáyáma*.

作禮上師，以蓮花坐式盤坐，願習者依師教誨通過生命能調息法成功淨化諸脈。

39-40. Contemplating on *Váyu-Bíja* (*yám*), full of energy and of a smoke-color, let him draw in breath by the left nostril, repeating the *Bija* (*yám*) sixteen times. This is *Púraka* (inhalation). Let him restrain the breath for a period of sixty-four repetitions of the *Mantra* (*yám*). This is *Kumbhaka* (retention). Then let him expel the air by the right nostril slowly during a period occupied by repeating the *Mantra* (*yám*) thirty-two times (this is *Rechaka*-exhalation).

觀想風元素種子音根滿含能量，其色如煙；習者以左鼻吸氣，複誦種子音咒「यं-*yám*」一十六次，此時入息；接著停息複誦種子咒六十四次，此時瓶息持氣；然後徐徐以右鼻呼氣，複誦種子咒三十二次，此時出息。

風元素種子音根：風元素座於心輪，故亦指心輪的音根。

41-42. The root of the navel is the seat of *Agni-Tattva*.Raising the fire from that place, join the *Pṛithiví-Tattva* with it; then contemplate on this mixed light. Then repeating sixteen times the *Agni-Bíja* (*rám*), let him draw in breath by the right nostril, and retain it for the period of sixty-four repetitions of the *mantras*, and expel it by the left nostril for a period of thirty-two repetitions of the *Mantra*.

火元素坐於臍輪，由此處生起能量之火，使與地元素之光相接，觀此接合之光；繼之複誦火大種子音咒「रं- *rám*」一十六次，同時以右鼻吸氣，復停息默誦種子咒六十四次，再以左鼻呼氣，複誦種子咒三十二次。

43-44. Then fixing the gaze on the tip of the nose and contemplating the luminous reflection of the moon there, let him inhale thorough the left nostril, repeating the syllable *thám* sixteen times; let him retain it by repeating the syllable (*thám*) sixty-four times; in the meanwhile contemplate that the nectar flowing from the moon at the tip of the nose runs through all the vessels of the body, and purifies them. Thus contemplating, let him expel the air by repeating thirty-two times the *Pṛithivi* syllable *lám*.

然後繫意鼻端，觀想月光映於其上，同時以左鼻吸氣，複誦種子咒「ठं-*thám*」一十六次；接著停息複誦種子咒六十四次，同時觀想鼻端月有甘露流注全身經脈，將之淨化；續此觀想，然後徐徐以右鼻呼氣，複誦地元素種子咒「लं-*lam*」三十二次。

繫意鼻端：鼻端是對應眉心輪的一個集中點，其所誦種子咒即眉心輪音根，故為靜坐修行的專注點之一，楞嚴經第五卷有世尊教導孫陀羅難陀觀鼻端白的敘述。

譯按：三種心淨脈法如第 38 至 44 節所述，然具體修持次第不建議冒然練習，宜依循阿闍黎之教導。

45. By these three *Práṇáyáma* the *nádis* are purified. Then sitting firmly in a posture, let him begin regular *Práṇáyáma*.

依此三種生命能調息法，身內諸脈可得淨化；如是淨化後，習者靜心安坐，開始生命能調息法的例行修習。

持氣法種類

46. The *Kumbhakas* or retentions of breath are of eight sorts: *Sahita, Surya-bheda, Ujjayi, Sitali, Bhastrika, Bhramari, Murchha* and *Kevalí*.

持氣法或瓶氣法有八種：益隨持氣法、貫通日脈持氣法、勝利持氣法、清涼持氣法、風箱式持氣法、蜂鳴持氣法、意醺持氣法和本然持氣法。

益隨持氣法：梵語 *Sahita-kumbhaka*，字義為助益、伴隨等，為連結吸氣、住氣、呼氣令身心得益的持氣法。

貫通日脈持氣法：梵語 *súrya bheda-kumbhaka*，*súrya* 即太陽，*bheda* 意為破、穿、貫穿；此法是以右鼻吸氣以激活並貫通日脈的呼吸練習。

勝利持氣法：梵語 *ujjáyi-kumbhaka*，字義為克服、征服、贏得；是藉壓縮喉部聲門發出氣摩擦聲，以克服老病取得勝利的呼吸法，又名喉呼吸法。

清涼持氣法：梵語 *śítalí-kumbhaka*，清涼使冷之意，其法是藉捲舌或由舌面吸氣以降低體溫、減少渴意的呼吸法。練習時宜選清晨、傍晚或午夜時分的清涼空氣。

風箱式持氣法：梵語 *bhastriká-kumbhaka*，字義風箱；此法是運用類似鐵匠鼓動風箱的呼吸法來淨化身心。

蜂鳴持氣法：梵語 *bhrámarí-kumbhaka*，字義蜜蜂；此法是藉模仿黑蜂振翅共鳴之聲的呼吸技巧來協助入定。

意醺持氣法：梵語 *múrchá-kumbhaka*，有幻、迷、昏暈等義；是藉控制入息、停息節奏以產生醺然喜悅的呼吸法。

本然持氣法：梵語 *kevalí-kumbhaka*，*kevalí* 一字來自 *kevala*，為不共、唯獨、絕對之義；這是一種終極的或說是最高層次的呼吸形式，行人的息相進入自發性的、極為細慢長且若有若無的狀態，呼吸中伴隨著天然的咒音理念。

一、益隨持氣法

47. The *Sahita-kumbhaka* is of two sorts: *Sagarbha* and *Nirgarbha* (with sound and without sound). The *Kumbhaka* performed by the repetition of *Bija-mantra* is Sagarbha; that done without such repetition is *Nirgarbha*.

益隨持氣法分為隨咒持氣與不隨咒持氣兩種：持氣同時複誦種子梵咒是隨咒持氣，持氣時不伴隨梵咒是屬不隨咒持氣。

48. First I shall tell thee the *Sagarbha Práṇáyáma*. Sitting in *Sukhásana* posture, facing east or north, let him contemplate on *Brahmá* full of *Rajas* quality of a blood-red color, in the form of the Sanskrit letter "अ- *a*".

首先述說「隨咒持氣法」，面向東方或北方，以方便坐式坐下，觀想從梵文字母「अ- *a*」中生起變性屬性的血紅色梵天全像。

方便坐式：又名安樂坐，即一般所謂的散盤坐式。

अ- *a*：梵語 अ 發音如 another 之 *a*。

血紅色梵天：是至上本體的創造作用，創造變化萬千，故以變性屬性的紅色表示。

49. Let the wise practitioner inhale by the left nostril, repeating the letter "*a*" sixteen times. Then before he begins retention (but at the end of inhalation), let him perform *Uḍḍíyánabandha*.

睿智行人此時會以左脈鼻孔入息，同時複誦「अँ-*an*」十六次；在持氣之前（入息之後），進行揚升鎖印。

अँ-*an*：原英譯對應梵文 अँ 的發音與前句相同，一樣是 *a*；但梵文字母較之前句梵文字多了一個 ँ，而成為 अँ，若為 अँ 則發音應為 *an*，音如 umbrella 之 um。

50. Then let him retain breath by repeating "उ- *u*" sixty-four times, contemplating on *Hari*, of a black color and of *Sáttva* quality.

繼之持氣複誦「उ- *u*」六十四次，觀想悅性屬性的黑色訶利全像。

उ- *u*：梵語उ發音如 flute 之 u。

黑色訶利：上主名號，意為暗中取走信眾罪業或傷悲者，亦是維世努或克里希那的名號之一。黑色有如黑洞，具吸引一切顏色的屬性，克里希那意為吸引著眾生朝他前進的存在，故又名大黑天。維世努是至上本體維持受造物存在的維繫作用，受造物在存續期間若仍能以上主為念，則即使生存不易，其結果還是悅性光明的。

51. Then let him exhale the breath through the right nostril(*pingalá*) by repeating the Sanskrit letter " मँ- *maṅ* "(*makara*) thirty-two times, contemplating Siva of a white color and of *Támas* quality.

繼之習者以右脈鼻孔出息，複誦梵字「मँ- *maṅ*」三十二次，作意觀想惰性屬性的白色希瓦全像。

मँ- *maṅ*：梵語 *maṅ*，發音如 *ma*+*ṅ*= *maṅ*，尾音 *ṅ* 發短音。

白色希瓦：希瓦名號之一是毀滅之神，是至上本體結束受造物的毀滅作用。受造存續告終之際若仍以上主為念，則雖然死亡是惰性表現，但所觀是白色希瓦卻是悅性重生的契機。

譯按：上述第 50 節的觀想悅性屬性的黑色訶利，此處第 51 節的觀想惰性屬性的白色希瓦；然依印度傳統，一般是以白色表悅性屬性，以黑色表惰性屬性，以紅色表變性屬性。

52. Then again inhale through *Pingalá*(right nostril), retain by *Kumbhaka*, and exhale by *Idá* (left), in the method taugh above, changing the nostrils alternately.

然後再度用右脈鼻孔入息，以瓶息持氣，通過左脈鼻孔出息；其法如前所述，以左右脈鼻孔交替出入息。

53. Let him practice, thus alternating the nostrils again and again. When inhalation is completed, close both nostrils, the right one by the thumb and left one by the ring- finger, never using the index and

middle finger. The nostrils to be closed so long as *Kumbhaka* is.

習者如法以兩脈鼻孔反覆交替出入息。當入息滿息時，以右手拇指封閉右鼻，無名指封閉左鼻，絕不可用食指和中指做壓按動作。只要是持氣法進行中，即應封閉兩鼻孔。

譯按：瑜伽修持的觀念裡，食指代表自我，舉中指則是帶有冒犯的不雅手勢，故此處不取。

54. The *Nirgarbha*(or simple or mantraless) *Práṇáyáma* is performed without repeating of *Bija-mantra*; and the period of *Púraka*(inhalation or inspiration), *Kumbhaka*(retention) and *Rechaka*(expiration) may be extended from one to hundred *mátrás*.

不隨咒持氣調息法（又稱簡易或無咒法）是修習時不持種子梵咒，且入息、持息和出息的長度得自一拍延長到一百拍。

拍：梵語 *mátrá*，字面義為分、量、份量，一個單位。

55. The best is twenty *Mátrás*: i.e., *Púraka* 20 seconds, *Kumbhaka* 80, and *Rechaka* 40 seconds. The sixteen *matras* is middling, ie, 16, 64 and 32. The twelve *matra* is the lowest, *i.e*, 12,48,24. Thus the *Práṇáyáma* is of three sorts.

持氣調息最好的是以二十拍為基的調息，即入息二十秒，持息八十秒及出息四十秒；中級的是以十六拍為基的調息，即入息十六秒，持息六十四秒及出息三十二秒；基礎級的是以十二拍為基的調息，即入息十二秒，持息四十八秒及出息二十四秒；以上是為調息的三個類型。

56. By practicing the lowest *Práṇáyáma* for sometime, the body begins to perspire copiously; by practicing the middling, the body begins to quiver(especially, there is a feeling of quivering along the spinal cord.). By the highest *Práṇáyáma*, one leaves the ground, *i.e.,* there is levitation. These signs attend the success of these three sorts of *Práṇáyáma*.

修習基礎級調息一段時間，身體會大量出汗；修習中級調息，身體會產生顫動（尤其是沿著脊柱的顫動感覺）；修習最好的調息，習者或能離地升起。這是三個類型調息修習有成的徵象。

57. By *Práṇáyáma* is attained the power of levitation (*khecharí-Śhakti*), by *Práṇáyáma* disease are cured, by *Práṇáyáma* the *Shakti* (spiritual energy) is awakened, by *Práṇáyáma* is obtained the calmness of mind and exhalation of mental powers (clairvoyance, etc.,); by this, mind becomes full of bliss; verily the practitioner of *Práṇáyáma* is happy.

透過生命能調息得明空成就，透過生命能調息疾病得治，透過生命能調息能喚醒造化靈力，透過生命能調息獲得內心寧靜以及心靈定境，由此心靈幸福滿溢；是故修習調息之行人如是常得身心喜樂。

明空成就：即明解空義的修行成就。

心靈定境：梵語 ***manonmaní***，字面意思為如意寶或意摩尼寶，為心靈定境之名，中譯意摩尼定；《哈達瑜伽明燈》第二章 42 節「內息順達中脈後，可使心意寂然安止；這種心靈定境，謂之意摩尼定」。

二、貫通日脈持氣法

58-59. Gheranda said: I have told thee the *Sahita kumbhaka*, now hear the *Súryabheda*. Inspire with all your strength the external air through the sun-tube(right nostril)，retain this air with the greatest care, performing the *Jálandaramudra*. Let the *Kumbhaka* be kept up so long as the perspiration does not burst out from the tips of the nails and the root of the hair.

葛蘭達言：益隨持氣法已述說如前，現在諦聽貫通日脈持氣法。以右脈鼻孔全力吸入外氣，悉心持氣於內，然後進行收頷身印，續維持瓶息勿使汗水從指尖和髮根滲出。

譯按：貫通日脈持氣法是透過日脈的孔竅—右鼻孔吸氣、持氣的功法。此法《哈達瑜伽明燈》未提及使汗水滲出，所述為「續持氣於身內，直到感覺氣息透達髮根和指尖；然後再由左鼻孔極緩慢的呼氣。第二章 48 節」。

●生命氣

60. The *vayus* are ten, namely- *Práńa, Apana, Samána, Udána and Vyána; Naga, Kúrma, Kṛikara, Devadatta and Dhanañjaya.*

體內生命氣有十種，即命根氣、下行氣、平行氣、上行氣、遍行氣及彈伸氣、收縮氣、呵欠氣、飢渴氣、惓眠氣。

命根氣：一名持命氣，作用於喉、臍之間，有助於心肺呼吸功能和生命能量循環的內在生命能。

下行氣：作用於肚臍以下，有助於大、小二便排出的內在生命能。

平行氣：位於臍部，平衡命根氣與下行氣的內在生命能。

上行氣：位於喉部，有助於控制聲帶和思想表達的內在生命能。

遍行氣：作用遍及全身，有助於體液和血液循環以及經驗是否感知的內在生命能。

彈伸氣：梵文字義為蛇、龍等；存在於關節中，協助身體跳躍、伸展和投擲的對外生命能。

收縮氣：字義為龜；存在於不同的腺體裡，協助身體收縮作用的對外生命能。

呵欠氣：梵文字義是鷓鴣；散佈全身，藉體內氣壓的增減來表現；有助於一般睡前呵欠和醒後伸展的對外生命能。掌控打呵欠的對外生命能。.

飢渴氣：梵文字義為天授，也就是上天的賜予；根據胃中食物和水的增減壓力，反應出飢餓或口渴訊號的對外生命能。

惓眠氣：梵文字義為降伏、得勝；身體因疲累或睏惓而生睡意，這種惓眠的感覺即來自偏布全身的惓眠氣，亦屬於對外生命能。

譯按：坊間通行的十種生命氣解釋，無論是阿育吠陀生命學或是《瑜伽明燈》、《葛蘭達本集》、《希瓦本集》等，大都本於奧義書所述的觀念。而此處筆者採用的是近代靈性導師暨國際阿南達瑪迦靈性服務組織創建人雪莉．雪莉．阿南達慕提的詮釋。由於先生對於人類生心理及靈性修持有著超常的洞悉，故分享於此。對照於以下本章第六十三節至六十八節的原本譯文，讀者當可察覺出兩者的不同，特別是呵欠氣（*kṛikara*）和飢渴氣（*devadatta*）的部分。此節筆者將 *kṛikara* 中譯為呵欠氣，*devadatta* 中譯為飢渴氣；而第六十三到第六十五節，筆者依原文句意，將 *kṛikara* 中譯為飢渴氣，*devadatta* 中譯為呵欠氣，特此說明。

•諸氣分佈之所

61-62. The *Práṇa* moves always in the heart; the *Apána* in the sphere of anus; the *Samána* in the navel region; the *Udána* in the throat; and the *Vyána* pervades the whole body. These are the five principal *Váyu*, known as *Práṇádí*, They belong to the Inner body. The *Nágádí* five *Vayus* belong to the Outer body.

命根氣主行於心臟，下行氣範圍及於後陰，平行氣行於臍腹，上行氣行於喉嚨，遍行氣行於全身，此五種主要的生命氣，名為內向生命能，作用於體內。而五種外向的生命氣，屬於向外的作用。

63-64. I now tell thee the seats of these five external *Vayus*. The *Nága-váyu* performs the function of eructation; the *Kúrma* opens the eyelids; the *Kṛikara* causes sneezing; the *Devadatta* does yawning; the *Dhanañjaya* pervades the whole gross body, and does not leave it even after death.

現在敘述這五種向外作用的生命氣：彈伸氣執行噯氣等功能，收縮氣開張眼瞼，呵欠氣引發噴嚏，飢渴氣導致呵欠；惓眠氣遍佈此粗重之身，甚至死後仍遲不消散。

譯按：梵學者徐梵澄先生（1909~2000）在其 1984 年所譯就出版的《五十奧義書》中名此五種向外作用的生命能為：呻氣、瞬氣、生飢氣、欠伸氣和本氣。

65. The *Nága-váyu* gives rise to consciousness, the *Kúrma causes* vision, the *Kṛikara* hunger and thirst, the *Devadatta* produces yawning and by *Dhanañjaya* sound is produced; this does not leave the body ever.

彈伸氣引生知覺，收縮氣使人見物，飢渴氣傳達飢渴之感，呵欠氣導致呵欠，惓眠氣產生聲音且幾不離身。

66-67. All these *Váyus*, separated by *Súrya-nádi*, let him raise up from the root of the navel; then let him expire by the *Idá-nádi*, slowly and with unbroken, continuous force. Let him again draw the air through the right nostril, retaining it, as taught above, and exhale it again. Let him do this again and again. In this process, the air is always inspired through the *Súrya-nádi*.

所有前述生命氣，透過日脈分離出來，並由臍根升起，然後平緩綿續地從月脈鼻孔呼出；復自右鼻孔吸氣，如前述之法持氣，再將之呼出，反覆如是練習。此法過程中，始終由日脈鼻孔吸入氣息。

68. The *Súryabheda-kumbhaka* destroys decay and death, awakens the *Kuṇḍalini-Śhakti* , increases the body fire. Oh, *Chaṇḍa*! Thus have I taught thee the *Súryabheda-kumbhaka*.

此日脈貫通持氣法能克服老死，喚醒靈能軍荼利，並增添身體活力。旃檀子啊！此即我所語汝之日脈貫通持氣法。

三、勝利持氣法

69. Close the mouth, draw in the external air by both the nostrils, and pull up the internal air from the lungs and throat; retain them in the

mouth.

口唇輕閉，自鼻吸氣，然後從胸、喉抽引出肺氣，含之於口。

譯按：原英譯文句甚簡，於此略作解釋——此法如若窒息中吸氣般，略開聲門從兩鼻孔吸氣；呼氣時如從將氣息抽出肺喉，呼出之氣由是摩擦聲門而於胸喉之間發出類似嘶哮之聲；呼出之氣息暫留持口中，是所謂的「從胸、喉抽引肺氣，含之於口」。呼氣時也可以輕按右鼻孔，單以左鼻孔出息。

70. Then having washed the mouth (*i.e.*, expelled air through mouth) perform *Jálandhara*. Let him perform *Kumbhaka* with all his might and retain the air unhindered.

自口徐徐漱出氣息，繼而專心收頷身印；盡力依瓶氣法持氣，保持氣息和諧無違。

漱出氣息：即由口呼出氣息，而後進行收頷身印。出息時如同吸氣一樣，輕閉聲門，伴隨胸喉間的嘶哮聲徐徐呼氣。

收頷身印：做法詳第三章 12 節；行此身印時，感覺若良好可儘量持住氣息。

71-72. works are accomplished by *Ujjáyi-kumbhaka*. He is never attacked by phlegm diseases, or indigestion, or dysentery, or consumption, or cough; or fever or [enlarged] spleen. Let a man perform *Ujjáyi* to destroy decay and death.

依此勝利持氣法一切所作皆得成就，身不受痰濕或神經失調、消化不良、痢疾、咳嗽、發燒及脾腫等疾患之侵擾，如法行持者得克服衰老和死亡。

痰濕：意指黏液型或水型體質疾病。印度阿育吠陀生命學將人的體質分成風、火、水三類，*kapha* 即是由水元素和土元素主導的體質，主要反映的是胸喉一帶造成的疾病，如黏液或痰濕積聚、畏冷、舌苔白、水腫、代謝緩慢、腹脹、便稠、容易抑鬱等不適。

四、清涼持氣法

73. Draw in the air through the mouth (with the lips contracted and tongue thrown out), and fill the stomach slowly. Retain it there for a short time. Then exhale it through both the nostrils.

縮口伸舌，由舌面經口徐徐納息入腹，稍事停息，然後自兩鼻呼出氣息。

縮口伸舌：口唇微收，舌頭伸出唇外，可捲舌者可將舌頭從兩側往中間捲成管狀，口唇包住舌外緣，由舌尖開口處吸入空氣；滿息後持住氣息，再緩緩呼出氣息。捲舌有困難者，由舌面吸入即可。

74. Let the *Yogí* always practice this *Śitalí-kumbhaka*, giver of bliss; by so doing, he will be free from indigestion, phlegm and bilious disorders.

經常修習清涼持氣法之瑜伽士，散發喜悅；由是行之，習者將免受消化不良與痰濕、膽疾的侵擾。

膽疾：意指膽汁型或火型體質疾病，火能型是由火元素和水元素主導的體質；主要反映的是胃腹一帶造成的疾病，如體溫偏高、汗多異味、頭易禿或少年白、肝功能下降、胃酸過多、腹瀉、便稠、容易發怒、氣餒或煩躁等不適。

五、風箱持氣法

75. As the bellows of the ironsmith constantly dilate and contracts, similarly let him slowly draw in the air by both the nostrils and expand the stomach; then throw it out quickly (the wind making sound like bellows).

如同打鐵匠連續開闔的鼓風箱，習者以鼻徐徐納息鼓腹，隨即縮腹以鼻出聲噴息。

以鼻出聲噴息：意即使氣息如颶風般噴出鼻腔。

76-77. Having thus inspired and expired quickly twenty times, let him perform *Kumbhaka*; then let him expel it by the previous method. Let the wise one perform this *Bhastriká* (bellow-like) *kumbhaka* thrice; he will never suffer any disease and will always be healthy.

習者依此法出入息二十次後，以瓶息持氣於內，再依前述之法呼出氣息；智行人日行此風箱持氣法三回，將永不罹病，長保健康。

依前述之法呼出氣息：意指持氣後徐徐出息，再進行第二回，如是三回。

六、蜂鳴持氣法

78. At past midnight, in a place where there are no sounds of any animals, etc., to be heard, let the *Yogí* practice *Púraka* and *Kumbhaka*, closing the ears by the hands.

午夜之後，於無任何蟲獸等雜音入耳之處，瑜伽行人以雙手貼覆兩耳，修習入息和瓶息法。

以雙手閉塞兩耳：通行之蜂鳴持氣法是以鼻腔之共鳴發出類似黑雄蜂的嗡嗡聲，而本節所述之蜂鳴持氣法不主動發聲，是由雙手摀耳閉塞耳根的方式令耳根反聞內在的音聲。

79-80. He will heard then various internal sounds in his right ear. The first sound will be like that of crickets, then that of a flute, then that of a thunder, then that of a drum, then that of a beetle, then that of bells, then those of gongs of bell-metal, trumpets, *kettle*-drums, *miṛidaṅga*, military drums, and *Dundubhi*, etc.

行人右耳或將聽到若干內在的音聲，首先可能聽到蟋蟀聲，再來可能聽到吹笛聲，再來可能聽到雷鳴聲，再來可能聽到擊鼓聲，再來可能聽到蜂鳴聲，再來可能聽到銅鈴聲，再來可能聽到銅鑼、小號、定音鼓、舞鼓、戰鼓和大鼓等等的聲音。

舞鼓：在印度常用來配合靈性詠舞的一種大小頭雙面鼓。

譯按：所述音聲皆為仿聲，或對應不同層次的定境，為修持過程中的一瞥，習者也不一定會經驗所有的聲音。

81-82. Thus various sounds are cognized by daily practice of this *Kumbhaka*. Last of all is heard the *Anáhata* sound rising from the heart; of this sound there is a resonance, in that resonance there is a Light. In that Light the mind should be immersed. When the mind is absorbed, then it reaches the Highest seat of *Viṣhnu*(*Parama-pada*). By success in this *Bhrámarí-kumbhaka* one gets success in *samádhi*.

日行此持氣法即能體認到這些不同的聲音，最後將聽到來自心輪的內在聲音。於此聲音共振之中有明光，心靈當浸沐於此明光中；當心靈與此光相融，習者即達勝妙果位。能於此蜂鳴持氣法成就者即能成就三摩地。

勝妙果位：妙毗天或維世努的最高寶座，喻覺悟到存在於每一生命中的至上意識。

三摩地：又名三昧、等持或等至，自心融入所緣或所觀之謂，八支瑜伽中的第八支。在瑜伽修行的過程中或能體驗到不同層次的三摩地，最高的兩種是個體心靈融入大宇宙心靈或是融入本體自性（至上意識）。

七、意醺持氣法

83. Having performed *Kumbhaka* with comfort, let him withdraw the mind from all objects and fix it in the space between the two eyebrow. This causes fainting of the mind, and gives happiness. For, by thus joining the *Manas* with *Átmá*, the bliss of *Yoga* is certainly obtained.

以安適之心修習瓶息持氣，將心識從一切外境收回，凝定於兩眉之間；如是將使心靈昇華而醺然，生大喜樂。緣此心意與自性結合，定獲瑜伽三昧大樂。

心意：唯識哲學中八識的第七識末那識，在一般應用上可為心意的同義詞。

自性：泛指自性、靈魂、神識或神我，在本質上個體自性和宇宙本體自性無有二致。

瑜伽三昧大樂：梵語 *Yogá-ánanda*，*yoga* 字義為相應、連結，*ánanda* 意指不受外在影響的屬靈喜悅，亦即融入本體自性的無上喜悅。

八、本然持氣法

84. The breath of every person in entering makes the sound of "*sah*" and in coming out, that of "*ham*". These two sounds make "*soham*(I am That)" or "*haḿsa* (the great swan)". Throughout a day and a night there are twenty-one thousand and six hundred such respirations (that is, 15 respirations per minute). Every *jiva*(living being) perform this *japa* unconsciously, but constantly. This is called *Ajapá Gáyatri*.

每一個人在入息時會發出「*sah*」的聲音，在出息時會發出「*ham*」的聲音，這兩個聲音組成了「सोऽहम-*soham*- 吾即彼」或「हंसः-*haḿsa*- 天鴻」之義。常人出入息一日夜兩萬一千六百息（每分鐘約十五息），每一生靈都一直不自覺地持誦著這組音聲，這稱作「自發性持咒」。

吾即彼：「吾即彼」是奧義書中常提及的觀念，「彼」是指大我、真我、大梵、本體或至上靈魂等最高的存在；「吾」即小我、個體我或個體靈魂，兩者本質是一如不二的 - 我就是祂，祂就是我。

天鴻：亦名天鵝。根據密乘，此音聲亦是生命能量之音根。印度傳統上視天鴻為神聖的象徵，常為天神的坐騎；達到瑜伽最高成就的人也被尊稱為「至尊天鴻 -*Paramahaḿsa*」，亦即融入至上大我之人。

自發性持咒：意為無需努力自發性地念誦，即自發但不自知地持著導向解脫的梵咒。*Gáyatri* 為黎俱吠陀中祈求上主引領走向至上意識的梵咒。故自發性持咒意指伴隨著呼吸不自覺地持誦著「吾即彼」理念的咒聲。

譯按：梵咒重點在意涵，必得將之深化內化，才有宏效；若只鸚鵡學聲，難得大用。

85. This *Ajapa japa* is performed in three places, *i.e.*, in the *múládhára*chakra, in the *Anáhata* lotus(heart) and in the *Ájña* lotus(the space where the two nostrils joint).

此「自發性持咒」可在三處進行，亦即海底輪處、心輪和眉心輪三處。

86-87. This body of Vayu is ninety-six digits length (*i.e*., six feet as a standard). The ordinary length of the air-current when expired is twelve digits (9 inches); in singing, its length becomes sixteen digits (one foot); in eating. It is twenty digits(15 inches); in walking, it is twenty-four digits (18 inches); in sleep, it is thirty digits(22.5 inches); in copulation, it is thirty-six digits(27 inches), and in taking physical exercise, it is more that.

身體氣場的範圍為九十六指寬（約 6 英呎），呼氣時氣流的一般長度是十二指寬（9 英吋）；吟唱時，長度為十六指寬（1 英呎）；吃東西時，長度為二十指寬（15 英吋）；行走時，長度為二十四指寬（18 英吋）；睡眠時，長為三十指寬（22.5 英吋）；敦倫時，長為三十六指寬（27 英吋）；若是從事運動，長度還會增加。

指寬：即一指的寬度，等於公制的 1.875 公分，合英制是 0.75 英吋。

88. By decreasing the natural length of the expired curry from nine inches to less and less, there takes place increase of life; and by increasing the current, there is decrease of life.

藉由減少呼氣時氣流的自然長度，即從九英吋長往下遞減，可以延長壽命；若增加氣流，歲壽就會縮短。

譯按：本節句意是指呼吸若趨細慢長則可益壽延年，反之則可能折損世壽。

89. So long as breath remains in the body there is no death. When the full length of the wind is all confined in the body, nothing being allowed to go out, it is *Kevala-kumbhaka*.

只要命氣住身，死亡即不能勝；當周身真氣充滿無漏，即處於本然持氣法中。

死亡即不能勝：本句參照原梵文 *maraṇaṁ naiva jáyate* 中譯：*maraṇaṁ*- 死亡；*naiva*- 非、無；*jáyate*- 勝、得勝。

90-91. All *Jivas* are constantly and unconsciously reciting this *Ajapa Mantra*, only for a fixed number of times every day. But a *Yogí* should recite this consciously and counting the numbers. By doubling the number of *Ajapa* (*i.e*, by 30 respirations per minute), the state of *Manonmani*(fixedness of mind) is attained. There are no regular *Rechaka* and *Púraka* in this process. It is only (*Kevala*) *Kumbhaka*.

隨著每日固定的命息次數，眾生一直不自覺地進行著此種自發性持咒；但是身為瑜伽行者則應有意識地以數息法來進行，透過加倍次數的自發性持誦，即可達意摩尼定境；在此定境中沒有常態的出入息，獨存本然的先天之息。

意摩尼定境：請見本章第 57 節註釋。

92. By Inspiring air by both nostrils, let him perform *Kevala kumbhaka*. On the first day, let him retain breath from one to sixty-four times.

以鼻納息，修習本然持氣法；第一天，習者住氣一到六十四息。

93-94. This *Kevalí* should be performed eight times a day, once in every three hours; or one may do it five times a day, as I shall tell thee. First in the early morning, then at noon, then in the twilight, then at midnight, and then in the fourth quarter of the night. Or one may do it thrice a day, *i.e.,* in the morning, noon and evening.

本然持氣法一日應修習八回，每隔三小時修習一回；習者亦可每日修習五回，首回時辰在清晨，其次在中午，其次在黃昏，其次在午夜，其次是意識處在超然狀態之際；也可以每日修習三回，即早晨、中午、傍晚各一回。

超然狀態：意識的第四種狀態。吠檀多不二論將人之意識分為四種狀態，前三態分別是醒、夢、眠（無夢狀態），第四種狀態是一種超意識狀態或說是定境狀態，故應非為某一時段，原梵文亦未有時段文字。

95-96. So long as success is not obtained in *Kevalí*, he should increase the length of *Ajapa-japa* every day, one to five times. He who knows *Práṇáyáma* and *Kevalí* is real *Yogí*. What can he not accomplish in this world who has acquired success in *Kevalí-kumbhaka*?

只要尚未自本然持氣法中成就道果，習者即應日增自發性持咒一至五回。通曉生命能調息法與本然持氣法者是為真瑜伽士。而能於本然持氣法中成就道果之行人，則於世間何愁不能成就？

第六章

禪定瑜伽

Dhyána Yoga

1. *Gheraṇḍa* said: The *Dhyána* or contemplation is of three sorts: gross, subtle and luminous. When a particular figure, such as one's *Guru* or Deity is contemplated, it is *Sthúla* or gross contemplation. When *Brahma* or *Prakṛiti* is contemplated as a mass of light, it is called *Jyotiṣ* contemplation. When *Brahma* as a *Bindu*(point) and *Kuṇḍaliní* force are contemplated, it is *Súkṣhma* or subtle contemplation.

葛蘭達言：禪觀之道有三，曰：初品禪法、上品禪法和光明禪法。觀想所敬重的上師或神明等特定的圖像，是為初品禪法；以宇宙本體或造化勢能的光明相作冥想，是為光明禪法；以本體實相的明點或靈能軍荼利作冥想，是為上品禪法。

初品禪法：係以世間之莊嚴形象或聖物為所觀的禪法。

宇宙本體：宇宙本體或至上本體，作為至上本體的創造面時，名大梵天。

造化勢能：宇宙本體一體兩面中的一面，是至上意識演化成大千世界的催化劑，又名造化力、造化勢能或宇宙力量。

光明禪法：冥想或專念法體光明的禪法。

明點：瑜伽中認為明點是生命力的昇華。明點分物質明點、氣脈明點、智慧明點及咒明點等數種，此處特指本體實相的光明點。

上品禪法：是不著外相，超越二元對待，心繫無屬性本體的觀空禪法。而就瑜伽修持而言，喚醒靈能軍荼利使之提升至頂輪，則是瑜伽圓成的表徵。

初品禪法

2-8. (Having close the eyes), let him contemplate that there is a sea of nectar in his heart; that in the midst of that sea there is an island of precious stones, the very sand of which is pulverized diamonds and rubies. That on all sides of it, there are *Kadamba* trees, laden with sweet flowers; that , next to these, like a rampart, there is a row of flowering trees, such as *málatí*, *Mallika*, *játí*, *Kesara*, *champaka*, *párijáta* and *padmas*, and that the fragrance of these flowers is spread all round, in every quarter. In the middle of this garden, let the *Yogí* imagine that there stands a beautiful *Kalpa* tree, having four branches, representing the four *Vedas*, and it is full of flowers and fruits. Insects are humming there and cuckoos singing. Beneath that tree, let him imagine a rich platform of precious gems, and on that a costly throne inland with jewel, and that on that throne sits his particular Deity, as taught to him by his *Guru*. Let him contemplate on the appropriate form, ornaments and vehicle of that Deity. The constant contemplation of such a form is *Sthúla-dhyána*.

雙眼輕闔，行人觀想心中有甘露海，海中有七寶之島，以細鑽與紅寶石為沙灘；島上遍栽迦曇婆樹，香花錦簇，其後花樹成行如護牆；有大花素馨、茉莉、柚子花、萬壽菊、玉蘭花、刺桐花以及蓮花，香氛瀰漫全島。續觀想，花園中央挺立著美麗的滿願樹；樹有四分枝，象徵四吠陀，花果纍纍。飛蟲鳴舞，布穀鳥歌唱。觀想樹蔭下，寬厚寶石台上有七寶之座；座上有與彼相應之本尊端坐，景況歷歷如同上師之所言示。觀想彼本尊法相清淨，瓔珞嚴飾，坐騎在旁。如是觀照不輟，即名初品禪法。

迦曇婆樹：別名團花樹、黃梁木、大葉黃梁木；茜草科團花屬植物，花香果甜。

滿願樹：印度神話及宗中滿足人願望的聖樹，非為單一樹種；維基百科稱印度榕、金合歡、椰子樹、黃油樹、珊瑚樹等都被稱作滿願樹。

本尊：所觀想的神明，此處意指行人所修法門或傳承的肇始者；心誠之時，本尊或會以不同方式顯現。在進階的修法中，有修行者與本尊合一的修法。

9-11. Another Process : Let the *Yogí* imagine that in the pericarp of the great thousand- petals lotus (Brain) there is a smallest lotus of twelve petals. Its color is white, highly luminous, having twelve *bij*a letters, named (*ha, sa , kṣa, ma, la, va, ra, yum, ha, sa, kha, phrem*). In the pericarp of this smaller lotus there are three lines forming a triangle (*a, ka, tha*), having three angles called (*ha, la, kṣa*); and In the middle of this triangle is the, there is the *Praṇava*(*Oṁ*).

復有另法：瑜伽行人觀想於頂輪千瓣蓮花中有一小蓮具十二花瓣，色白光潔，其上依次有十二種子字，分別為ह、स、ध、म、ल、व、र、यु、हु、सु、खु、फ्रें。小蓮花芯之中有अ、क、थ三條線，形成一三角形；三角形的三個角有梵字ह、ल、ध；而位 此三角形中央的是本初聖音 *Oṁ*- ओम्。

十二種子字：對應此十二梵文種子字的羅馬拼音依序為 *a*、*sa*、*kṣa*、*ma*、*la*、*va*、*ra*、*yuṁ*、*haṁ*、*saṁ*、*khaṁ*、*phreṁ*。

अ、क、थ三條線：對應此三條線的三個梵文種子字的羅馬拼音依序為 *a*、*ka*、*tha*，分表創造、水元素、月亮的音根。

三個角有梵字：對應此三個角的三個種子字的羅馬拼音依序為 *ha*、*la*、*kṣa* 分表太陽、地元素、世諦的音根。

本初聖音：是聖音「*Oṁ*- 唵」的稱名，梵文 ओम् 是 *a*（生）、*u*（住）、*ma*（滅）三義的合字，其符以 ॐ 為代表；此聲是創造之初外顯的第一道振動，也是顯現宇宙生住滅循環現象的音根。生滅有時，循環無窮，故被喻為永恆之聲，在印度被認為是宇宙中最有力量的聲音。瑜伽經中謂 *Oṁ* 為一切智種子的象徵。

12. Then let him contemplate that in that there is a beautiful seat having *Náda* and *Bindu*. On that seat there are two swans, and a pair of wooden sandals or shoes.

復次觀想有秘音、明點之樸美坐床置於其內，中有天鵝一對和檀木聖屐一雙。

秘音：精細的音波，是內在修證有成所內聞到的永恆之聲。

檀木聖屐：足部在印度傳統文化中是最受尊敬的部位，觸足禮至今仍然存在。本節所觀檀木聖屐之意涵如同上主之足印。

13-14. There let him contemplate his *Guru Deva*, having two arms and three eyes, and dressed in pure white, anointed with white sandal-paste, wearing garlands of white flowers; to the left of whom stands *Śakti* of blood-red color. By thus contemplating the *Guru*, the *Sthúla Dhyána* is attained.

續觀想上師之神格形象，有兩臂三眼，身著純淨白衣，額抹白檀聖記，項戴白色花環；血色造化力母立於左側。依此法觀想上師，可成就初品禪法。

光明禪法

15. *Gheraṇḍa* said: I have told thee of the *Sthúla Dhyána*; listen now to the contemplation of Light, by which the *Yogí* attains success and sees his Self.

葛蘭達言：初品禪法已說如前，現在諦聽光明禪法，瑜伽行人可由此法成就並親見自性真我。

16. In the *Mulådhára* is *Kundaliní* of the form of a serpent. The *Jívátman* is there like the flame of a lamp. Contemplate on this flame as the Luminous *Brahma*. This is the *Tejo-Dhyána* or *Jyotir-Dhyána*.

於海底輪中有靈能軍荼利蜷伏，個體靈魂於彼處有如燈焰；觀想此燈焰猶光明本體，是為光明禪法。

個體靈魂：個體生命的小我、自性、意識或靈魂。

光明本體：至上本體的光明相。

17. Another process : In the middle of the eyebrows, above the Manas, there is the Light consisting of *AUM*. Let him contemplate on this flame. This is another method of contemplation of Light.

復有另法：兩眉之間，意根之上，有明光顯現之本初聖音；瑜伽行人可專注觀照彼處明光，此亦為光明禪法。

本初聖音：即 ॐ 唵聲，羅馬拼音為 *Auṃ* 或 *Oṃ*。

上品禪法

18-19. O *Caṇḍa*! thou hast heard the *Tejo-Dhyána*, listen now to the *Súkshma Dhyána*. When by a great good fortune, the *Kundalí* is awakened, it joins with the *Átmán* and leaves the body through the portals of the eyes; and enjoys itself by walking in the royal road. It cannot be seen on account of its subtleness and great changeability.

旃檀子啊！汝已聽聞光明禪法，現在諦聽上品禪法。當因緣具足之時，靈能軍荼利甦醒，與至上真我結合並通過眼門離開身體，復因行走在勝王道上而享自身大樂。彼性精微恍惚，故不可見。

眼門：眼、耳、鼻、舌、身、意是謂六根，入色、聲、香、味、觸、法六塵境時，是謂六門；如是相應而生六識，成就者對境生識後能不生煩惱故得享大樂。

20. The *Yogí*, however, attains this success by performing *Sámbhaví mudrá*, i.e. by gazing fixedly at space without winking. (Then he will see his *Súkshma Śaríra*.) This is called *Súkshma Dhyána*, difficult to be attained even by the Devas, as it is a great mystery.

修此希瓦身印有成之瑜伽行人，眼注於空，目不稍瞬，（如是內見己之精微身），是名上品禪法。此法深密，雖諸天亦難成。

希瓦身印：又名吉祥身印一種繫心眉間，凝神觀空，安住自性喜悅的身印法，詳見第三章六十四節所述。

精微身：或指自性光，或指色身轉化後，顯現出的某種舍利或體性光輝；*Súkshma Śaríra* 直譯是極微或深細身。

上品禪法：此法非是與物質身相應，是在精微的特殊真知智慧層內（五心靈層中的真知層或識成身）完成的。

21. The contemplation on Light is a hundred times superior to contemplation on Form; and a hundred thousand times superior to *Tejo-Dhyána* is the contemplation of the *Súkshma*.

光明禪法勝於初品禪法百倍，而上品禪法又勝於光明禪法十萬倍。

22. O *Caṇḍa*! thus have I told thee the *Dhyána Yoga*- a most precious knowledge; for, by it, there is direct perception of the Self. Hence *Dhyána* is belauded.

旃檀子！這就是我所講述的禪定瑜伽，此法極為珍貴，是直悟至上真我之津梁，為殊勝非常之法要。

第七章

三摩地瑜伽

Samádhi Yoga

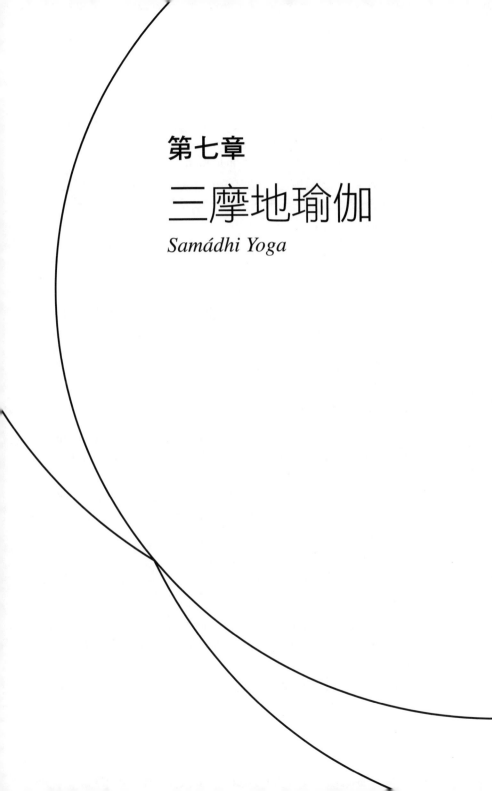

1. *Gheraṇa* said:The *Samádhi* is a great *Yoga*; it is acquired by great good fortune. It is obtained through the grace and kindness and of the *Guru*, and by intense devotion to him.

葛蘭達言：三摩地是瑜伽之究竟，福緣俱足者方能得之；亦即需透過上師的恩典、慈悲，以及對上師非常之虔誠才能獲得。

三摩地：同義詞有入定、三昧、等持、正定、正受，泛指心識融入所觀，如「人心融入天心、小我融入真我、個體意識融入至上意識」等。

2. That *Yogí* quickly attains this beautiful practice of *Samádhi*, who has confidence (or faith) in knowledge, faith in his own *Guru*, faith in his own Self and whose mind (*manas*) awakens to intelligence from day to day.

瑜伽學人欲速證三摩地法之微妙，須相信所學，信任上師，對內在真我不疑且日增內心覺智。

3. Separate the *Manasa* from the body, and unite it with the *Paramátman*. This is known as *Samádhi* or *Mukti,* liberation from all states of consciousness.

將心意抽離自身，與至上真我融合，是即三摩地或自在解脫，亦即從所有的意識狀態中解脫出來。

至上真我：即至上意識、宇宙意識、宇宙靈魂；不受宇宙力量影響能見證個體小我起心動念者。

自在解脫：個體心靈融入宇宙心靈之謂，指心得自在，不受造化力束縛之境。

4. I am *Brahman*, I am nothing else, *Brahman* is certainly I, I am not participator of sorrow, I am Existence, Intelligence and Bliss; always free, of one essence.

我即至上本體，我非其他，至上本體即是我；我非此哀傷者，我即無上喜悅之意識實相；始終自在，本質一如。

我即至上本體：梵語 *Ahaṁ Brahma*，文法上 *Brahman* 為 *Brahma* 的呼格，故英譯為 I am *Brahman*。*Brahma* 傳統上常譯作大梵，本句舊譯常為「吾即大梵」。哲學上 *Brahma* 意指絕對的、無限的、永恆的、無上的真理，也是無限意識、至上意識或含括了宇宙意識及宇宙力量的至上本體。另一句奧義書哲學的精髓是「*Tat Tvam Asi*- 彼即汝」，晚唐洞山良价禪師過水睹影頓悟無情說法之旨，言：「切忌從他覓，迢迢與我疏；我今獨自往，處處得逢渠；渠今正是我，我今不是渠；應須恁這麼會，方得契如如。」此偈可與本節併參。

無上喜悅之意識實相：梵語 *Sac-cid-ánandá*，吠檀多哲學中描述究竟本體實相的三種性質的頌詞；*sat* 意思是神、真理或絕對的實相，*chit* 是意識、淨識，*ananad* 之義為極樂、法喜、無上的喜悅、絕對的喜悅。

5-6. The *Samádhi* is four-fold, *i.e. Dhyána*, *Náda*, *Rasánanda*, and *Laya Samádhi* respectively accomplished by *Śámbhaví mudrá*, *Khecarí mudrá*, *Bhrámarí mudrá* and *Yoni-mudrá*. The *Bhakti-Yoga Samádhi* is fifth, and *Rája Yoga Samádhi*, attained through *Mano-Múrcchá Kumbhaka*, is the sixth form of *Samádhi*.

三摩地有四支，即禪定三摩地、秘音三摩地、極樂味三摩地和深定三摩地，分別透過希瓦身印、明空身印、蜂鳴身印和胎藏身印成就；虔誠瑜伽三摩地是第五支，而勝王瑜伽三摩地係透過意醺持氣法成就，是為三摩地的第六支。

禪定三摩地：內見不動自性，令心定於彼處而獲得之定境。

秘音三摩地：藉明空身印使心專注於空性，得聞內在秘音而獲之定境。

極樂味三摩地：透過蜂鳴持氣法制心入靜，內心順天心之流而入寂得定。

深定三摩地：甚深禪定三摩地，瑜伽行人之心受所觀吸引而深融其中之定境。（以上四支或指哈達瑜伽三摩地）

虔誠瑜伽三摩地：行人因虔誠之心行，獲得本尊或上師之加持而得定。

勝王瑜伽三摩地：通過意釀持氣法精進修持至心意與自性合一而入之定境。

禪定瑜伽三摩地

7. Performing the *Śámbhaví mudrá* perceive the *Átman*. Having seen once the *Brahman* in a *Bindu* (point of light), fix the mind on that point.

   修習希瓦身印以達悟真我，一旦於明點中得見至上本體，即定心於彼處。

8. Bring the *Átma* in *Kha* (Ether), bring the *Kha* (Ether or Space) in the *Átma*. Thus seeing the *Átma* full of *Kh*a (Space or Brahman), nothing will obstruct him. Being full of perpetual bliss, the man enters *Samádhi* (Trance or Ecstasy).

   納至上真我於虛空中，納虛空於至上真我中；如是見真我遍滿虛空，無有障礙；從而法喜滿溢，行者入於三摩地。

秘音瑜伽三摩地

9. Turn the tongue upwards, closing the wind-passages, by performing the *Khecharí-mudrá*; by so doing, *Samádhi*(trance asphyxiation) will be induced; there is no necessity of performing anything else.

   捲舌向上，封抵顎咽氣門，進行明空身印；如是行之，將觸生三摩地定境，無需再修其他。

   明空身印：凝意眉間，心契空性之修法身印，詳見第三章二十五節句解。現代習者可以第三章第九節之虛空身印代之。

極樂味瑜伽三摩地

10-11. Let him perform the *Bhrámari Kumbhaka*, drawing in the air slowly；expel the air slowly and slowly, with a buzzing sound like that of a beetle. Let him carry the *Manas* and place it in the centre of this sound of humming beetle. By so doing, there will be *Samádhi* and by this, knowledge of *So'ham* (I am That) arises, and a great happiness takes place.

行蜂鳴持氣法，徐徐入息；緩緩出息，出息時伴隨著有如蜂鳴般的聲音；引導心意念想化入蜂鳴聲中心，如是行之可得三摩地，「吾即彼 - *so'ham*」之覺境現前，大樂油然而生。

蜂鳴持氣法：以手閉耳，反聞內音，使心與心光相應之持氣法，詳見第五章七十八節句解。

吾即彼：英譯 I am That，聖經記載耶和華對摩西說 "I am that I am"，很有趣的巧合。

深定瑜伽三摩地

12-13. Perform the *Yoní-mudrá,* and let him imagine that he is *Śákti*, and *Paramátman* is *Puruṣa*; and that both have been united is one. By this he becomes full of bliss, and realizes *Ahaṁ Brahma* I am *Brahman*. This conduces to *Advaita Samádhi*.

進行胎藏身印，行人觀想自己即造化力母，而至上真我即無限的宇宙意識，兩者於觀想中融而為一；如是行者生圓滿大樂，得悟「我即至上本體」，此法有助成就不二三摩地。

胎藏身印：喚醒提升靈能軍荼利，契入頂輪之修法身印，詳見第三章三十七節句解。

造化力母：又稱造化勢能或宇宙力量；此力能在無限宇宙意識的允許下影響意識，幻化出此浩瀚無垠的大千世界。

至上真我：宇宙靈魂，見證小宇宙內心意動的至上意識。

宇宙意識：個體意識和宇宙意識之統稱，亦一切意識之統稱；此意識是一切活動的中心及見證者。

不二三摩地：主客雙泯，無有二元對待或分別之三摩地。

虔誠瑜伽三摩地

14-15. Let him contemplate within his heart his special Deity; let him be full of ecstasy by such contemplation; let him shed tears of happiness, and by so doing he will become entranced. This leads to *Samãdh*i and *Manonmaní*.

於心中觀想本尊神明，緣此觀修大樂滿溢，喜淚盈眶！緣如是行，行人心生大樂，而入三摩地及意摩尼定。

意摩尼定：生命氣通達中脈，心意安寂之心靈定境。

勝王瑜伽三摩地

16. Performing *Manomurcchá Kumbhaka*, unite the *Manas* with the *Átman*. By this Union is obtained *Rája Yoga Samádhi*.

行意釀持氣法，心意與真我融而為一，瑜伽行人緣此融合得入勝王瑜伽三摩地。

意醺持氣法：收心眉間，昇華心意而生喜樂之持氣法，詳見第五章八十三節句解。

17. O *Caṇḍa*! thus have I told thee about *Samádhi* which leads to emancipation. *Rája Yoga Samádhi, Unmaní, Sahajávasthã* are all synonyms, and mean the Union of *Manas* with *Átman*.

旃檀子！以上所言三摩地皆可引領行者開悟解脫；勝王瑜伽三摩地、心寂定、本然定等皆同義詞，皆表心意與真我或真如自性之結合。

心寂定：一種無有對待、心融於空寂的大樂定境。

本然定：指悟達本心境地之三摩地。

18. *Viṣṇu* is in water, *Viṣṇu* is in the earth, *Viṣṇu* is on the peak of the mountain; *Viṣṇu* is in the midst of the volcanic fires and flames; the whole universe is full of *Viṣṇu*.

妙毗天在水中，妙毗天在大地，妙毗天在山顛，妙毗天在火山噴出的光焰中，整個宇宙全是妙毗天。

妙毗天：至上本體遍在一切、維繫一切的作用。本節表示祂無處不在的特質。又名遍在天、維世努。

19. All those that walk on land or move in the air, all living and animate creation, trees, shrubs, roots, creepers and grass, etc, oceans and mountains-all, know ye to be *Brahman*. See them all in *Átma*.

一切陸上行走或空中飛行的，一切生靈與受造萬物，高矮樹木，根莖、攀緣植物和花草以及海洋與叢山等等，一切唯是至上本體，一切皆映現於真我中。

20. The *Átman* confined in the body is *Caitanya* or Consciousness, it is without a second, the Eternal, the Highest; knowing it separate from body, let him be free from desires and passions.

真我以大覺意識之形態存於身中，祂是獨一無二、永恆和最上的，深入內心領悟到祂的人，即不為欲望和激情所牽絆。

意識：梵語 *Caitanya*，意識別名，特指覺醒的意識。

21. Thus is *Samádhi* obtained free from all desires. Free from attachment to his own body, to son, wife, friends, kinsmen, or riches; being free from all, let him obtain fully the *Samádhi*.

如是入三摩地之行人從一切欲望中解脫，不再執著於己身，乃至子女、夫妻、親友、貧富等亦不執著，於一切中得自在，得證圓滿三摩地。

22. *Śiva* has revealed many *Tattvas*, such as *Layámṛita*, etc., of them, I have told thee an abstract, leading to emancipation.

主希瓦曾揭示許多如甚深禪定甘露法等實法要義，大要如我所言，俱是解脫指津。

實法要義：真實不虛之義理，分真、俗二種，此節所言屬真諦之義理。

23. O *Caṇḍa*! thus have I told thee of *Samádhi*, difficult of attainment.

By knowing this, there is no rebirth in this Sphere.

旃檀子！如是所言三摩地法，達成不易，經由通曉前述法要，即能不再流轉於生死世界。

希瓦本集

Śiva Saṁhitá

〈中譯本前言〉

密乘瑜伽修行指津

《希瓦本集》是被公認的三本古典哈達瑜伽梵文經典之一，成書於十五世紀或更晚些，作者不詳。從這本書的內容推敲，作者自身就是一位實修的瑜伽行者，修習的傳承可能是希瓦密宗或維世努密宗的一支，因此本書著重之處與《哈達瑜伽明燈》及《葛蘭達本集》明顯有別。

《哈達瑜伽明燈》是較為人知的瑜伽指南，介紹了十六種體位法、十二種身印和八種持氣法。《葛蘭達本集》敘述淨化法最詳盡且被譽為最早的瑜伽百科，介紹了三十二種體位法、二十五種身印以及八種和《哈達瑜伽明燈》不盡相同的持氣法。《希瓦本集》的文體是以希瓦為第一人稱的方式，述說許多瑜伽哲學主題和密乘的修行觀念。書內提及常見的體位法有八十四種，卻只說明了三種坐式和一種體位法；但其他有關學習瑜伽的心態、呼吸法、身印法、修行次第、在家人應如何修行、弟子與上師間的關係，甚至包括一些不常見的修行密法，都有更深入的解說。顯示出作者對於心瑜伽的重視更甚於身瑜伽，故而花了許多篇幅介紹了身心靈瑜伽的整體鍛煉之道，這補足了《瑜伽經》未著墨的部分。

因此與其說《希瓦本集》屬於哈達瑜伽經典，不如說它更像是一本密乘瑜伽修行手冊；不論是在學術上或是實際鍛煉上，對於了解整體的瑜伽修法，《希瓦本集》都有很高的參考價值。可以說，雖然本書是被歸類於哈達瑜伽的經典，然而從其內涵觀之，實已超越了哈達瑜伽的領域。

「現在我們所要陳述的這卷瑜伽法要，是門非常深秘的教導，只向三界中具高尚胸懷的虔誠信士揭露。」(I:19)

《希瓦本集》一書內分五章五百四十節經句，原典目錄未書章題，考量讀者辨識方便，筆者依各篇主旨附上章題。全書內容為藉由上主希瓦和法侶帕瓦蒂間的問答，開示瑜伽正學，釐清不實之見，是三部哈達瑜伽經典中內容最豐富的。

在《瑜伽經》中，大哲帕檀迦利揭示了勝王瑜伽之道。《希瓦本集》第五章 181 節則述明哈達瑜伽是階及勝王瑜伽的踏腳石：「沒有勝王瑜伽，哈達瑜伽無法有成；少了哈達瑜伽，勝王瑜伽也難以奏功；是故，行人宜先從明師指示修習哈達瑜伽。」《希瓦本集》在第五章中除了勝王瑜伽的修法外，還提出了「王中之王瑜伽」的概念和修法；雖不很詳盡，但可以知道原作者是有接觸這門修法的，亦可得知作者是位勝王瑜伽行者甚或是王中之王瑜伽行者。

由於古人受限書寫工具之短缺不便，傳承多賴口授心傳。本書以《希瓦本集》命名，固是假託希瓦之名的著作，但審視其文，其中確實是有許多正統傳承的希瓦法要，是一部值得重視的密乘之作，在修行上很具參究價值。誠如本書經句所言「此法是為那些內心不疑且一意向我之人的靈性解脫而說」(I:3)，願廣大讀者亦能從中獲益，在瑜伽道上更上層樓。

〈中譯本導讀〉
希瓦教誨的結集

希瓦誕生於七千年前，是印度歷史上實有的人物，他為世間打下堅實的靈修基礎，被尊為瑜伽始祖，從其所傳承下來的密乘瑜伽修持至今不輟。由於他對印度文化與社會的整體貢獻無人能出其右，因此他在古今印度人心目中的地位也最為崇高，在瑜伽哲學上希瓦之名和宇宙最高意識已成為同義詞。《希瓦本集》書名的意思是「希瓦教誨的結集」，以希瓦第一人稱之教誨為名存在了數百年，至今仍受到瑜伽行人的推崇，表示其內容確實保留有為瑜伽學人肯定且有助實質修行的希瓦法要。

《希瓦本集》是一部有關密乘瑜伽法要的集要，內容是指引行人如何從自身起修，漸次覓得身心作用的神秘源頭以及了解形而下的虛幻與形而上的真實，乃至洞悉空與有的本質。原著佚名，著作年代也不詳；學者從有限的線索推敲，著書地點可能在印北的瓦拉納西，作者則有可能是瑪茲央卓尊者，由於機緣安排，他把上主希瓦對夫人帕瓦蒂訴說的瑜伽之道記錄下來成為本書。筆者推測撰寫者本人或是希瓦派密乘瑜伽修行人，把自己所學的重要教導筆記下來而後成書的。

近代最早的英譯是一八八四年由印度數學暨梵文學者室利薩・旃德羅・婆藪（*Srisa Chandra Vasu*, 1861-1918）翻譯，發表在當時雅利安月刊上的文本；一九一四年全本英文版正式出書，這本中文《希瓦本集》即是以他的英譯為藍本。

《希瓦本集》第一章以說理為主，說明修行的基礎哲理。

內容包括知識的真相、當時存在的各種信仰取向、唯一真理的探索、修行之道的事與理、神性的本質、瑜伽對幻象的看法、宇宙生成的過程、人生的見地以及歸真之道等。在短短的九十六節經句裡，論述了豐富的哲學主題，娓娓道出古印度顯密二乘哲學的精華；直言莫執著於行為之果，靈性是永恆不朽的，只有靈性知識和虔心修持才是出脫輪迴苦惱的倚仗。讀來頗如醍醐灌頂，清涼人心。

「猶如空性遍滿瓶罐的內外，同樣在此無常大千世界的內外，存在著一如的宇宙神性。」（1:50）

第二章從人身切入，揭示人體系統是與宇宙系統相互呼應及關聯的，這在當時是非常前衛的論述。然而自從量子物理學成為主流以來，對通過經脈作用的精細能量生理心理學也是今日許多人有興趣的領域。本章對身內的能量網路作了深入淺出的介紹，敘及體內脊柱和十四條重要的經脈，從此處衍生出無數的經絡和分支，而十四條經脈中，左脈、右脈與中脈是其中最重要的三條。除此之外，本章更花了不少篇幅分析個體靈魂或真我如何受到禁錮以及解禁之道，點出生命的虛幻與真實以及去幻入真的方向，是饒有趣味的一章。

「如同認珠蚌為銀的錯見，人們受到己身宿業的熏染，誤認此物質宇宙為本體實相。」（2:43）

第三章論述生命能調息的功法、次第作用和功能，還有修習應有的心態和明師的角色與重要性。由於生命能調息法在瑜伽修煉中對平衡身心的作用至關重要，因此本章在這方面的論述頗多；包括氣息的分類、修習場所的條件、推薦的坐姿、修習期間的注意事項、精進的方法、不同階段的成就表徵等等。並指出宿世的習氣伏藏於心表現於外，引生種種過患，而滌除之道盡在瑜伽，值得瑜伽行人探究。

「此生命能控制法消除惡業，猶似大火燒盡棉花堆，使瑜伽行者不為惡業牽絆，進而還能解除一切善業的束縛。」（3:51）

第四章專論靈能軍荼利及各種身印的作法與功用，本章講述了十種身印法及一種以觀想為主的胎藏身印的微妙作用。身印是具有意涵的姿勢或手勢，可作用於神經及肌肉，有助喚醒靈能軍荼利。本章敘述了一些身心開展過程中可能產生的神秘經驗，這些神秘經驗和身心蛻變的現象是對應的，只是過程，不必貪著。身印練習如同體位法，但需加入更多的觀想；因為身印也有將內在意念外顯化的作用，只有少數幾種身印不具此外化的作用。

「此法（大身印法）帶給身體無瑕之美，滅除老死；獲得所有欲望和快樂之果，並控制感官諸根。」（4:18）

第五章經句從帕瓦蒂祈請希瓦指點「什麼是瑜伽道上的障礙與阻撓」開始，是本書內容最廣泛也最多樣化的一章。希瓦的回答由剖析世間苦樂、宗教儀式、知識障礙為引子，講到瑜伽的分類、靈修者的品級、什麼屬性的修行者適合那一類的瑜伽，以及各種修持方法。尤為特別的是在這一章用了上百節的經句講解三脈七輪及其轉變後生起的妙用，從中可以窺見古瑜伽的脈輪觀。篇末講到什麼是勝王瑜伽，什麼是王中之王瑜伽，最後以相關修行的一些梵咒修法作收，可謂是顯密修法兼備的一章，不論出家、在家人，修習之後都能裨益人生。

「雖居家生活於妻兒間，於內心無有執著，且密行瑜伽不輟之在家居士，甚至可為成就之典範；如是信受奉行吾之教導者，得永住於無上喜悅之境。」（5:212）

瑜伽可以全面地提升人類身心的各個層面。在有限的幾本古典瑜伽文導獻中，《希瓦本集》內文所述是可以和瑜伽鍛煉與教學連結的知識；這些知識告訴學人如何藉由察覺神性來擺脫無明業行的糾纏，讓學人從行持中逐漸蛻變，而達無上喜悅的幸福之境。沒有瑜伽，人容易只為感官的享受而生活；而瑜伽道上若缺乏適當的指導，亦可能偏離瑜伽的本質。期盼透過本書，不論是瑜伽老師或是瑜伽學人，可以更深入的了解瑜伽，減少摸索的時間。

第一章

觀念篇

Conception

唯一的存在

1. The *Jńána* alone is eternal; it is without beginning or end; there exists no other real substance. Diversities which we see in the world are results of sense-conditions; when the latter cease, then this *Jńána* alone, and nothing else, remains.

真智是永恆的，無有開始或結束。真智的存在非具實質，我們眼睛所見世界之多樣性乃是官能條件形成的結果；當後者歸寂，所存者唯此天真靈智，無有其他。

真智：Jńána 原義是屬靈的知識，此處特指本自具足的般若智慧。

2-3. I, *Iśhvara*, the lover of my devotees, and Giver of spiritual emancipation to all creatures, thus declare the science of *yogánuśásana* (the exposition of *Yoga*). In it are discarded all those doctrines of disputants, which lead to false knowledge. It is for the spiritual disenthralment of persons whose minds are undistracted and fully turned towards Me.

我，自在者，為吾信眾所摯愛者，一切眾生靈性解脫的施予者，如是開示瑜伽之學；從中釐清了所有那些導向錯見、引人爭議的教條；此法是為那些內心不疑且一意向「我」之人的靈性解脫而說。

自在者：常見之譯名有自在主、自在天，為其不受世俗苦惱、煩惱所侵襲及不受作用力與反作用力的侵襲；又名控制者、宇宙的控制者，因其能控制萬有一切之作用；亦名至上主，意指其擁有能小等八大神通法力；以其無需任何其他庇護，也有薄伽梵、自在如來等名。靈性哲學上意指致因世界的見證者、宇宙思想波的控制者。此處取「自在者」為其自稱之名。

我：此處既指 *Śiva* 亦指 *Ishvara*，意喻大宇宙的控制者、宇宙思想波的控制者、所有控制者的控制者、超越所有約束縛的存在。

紛紜的見解

4. Some praise truth, others purification and asceticism; some praise forgiveness, others equality and sincerity.
有人稱頌真理，有人推崇淨化和苦行；有人讚美寬容，有人頌揚平等與真誠。

5. Some praise alms-giving, others laud sacrifices made in honor of one's ancestors; some praise *karma*, others think *vairágya* to be the best.
有人稱許佈施，有人褒揚讓祖先榮耀的犧牲；有人誇獎業行，有人認為離欲或不執著是最好的。
業行：來自業力的思想、言語和行為；現在的業行是過去的業果和未來的業因。
離欲或不執著：對世俗世界種種無有貪著之意。

6. Some wise persons praise the performance of the duties of the householder; other authorities hold up fire-sacrifice &c., as the highest.
有些智者稱揚一家之主的責任，有些權威則說舉行火祭最為崇高。
火祭：吠陀火祭是向上主遍在天行供養，祈求人類的療癒及其居住環境的淨化。

7. Some praise *mantrayoga*, others the frequenting of places of pilgrimage. Thus are the ways which people declare emancipation.
有人推崇梵唱瑜伽，有人則鼓勵常往聖地朝聖；這些都是人們宣稱能獲得解脫的途徑。
梵唱瑜伽：梵唱是有助解脫心靈束縛的梵語詠唱，又名真言瑜伽；然此處係指有助心靈回攝的梵唱，故名梵唱瑜伽。

8. Being thus diversely engaged in this world, even those who still know what actions are good and what are evil, though free from sin, become subject to bewilderment.

在此眾說紛紜的世界裡，即便是知曉善惡業行之人，縱已不受罪縛，卻仍感困惑。

9. Persons who follow these doctrines, having committed good and bad actions, constantly wander in the worlds, in the cycle of births and deaths, bound by dire necessity.

服膺這些教條之人，都曾有過或好或不好的行為，如是不斷地徘徊世間，流轉生死，亟待出脫。

10. Others, wiser among many, and eagerly devoted to the investigation of the occult, declare that the souls are many and eternal, and omnipresent.

亦有世間聰敏者，熱衷究訪神祕之學，聲稱靈魂有許多並且是永恆和遍在的。

譯按：熱衷秘學者，迷於造化力作用，執於控制五大元素；聲稱靈魂有許多，則偏信天堂地獄，皆非瑜伽正旨。

11. Others say, “Only those things can be said to exist which are perceived by the senses and nothing besides them; where is heaven or hell?” Such is their firm belief.

另有人認為：「只有為感官所覺察的東西方存在，此外無他，何有天堂和地獄？」他們所堅信的就是這樣。

譯按：持此觀點，不信有神，認為人死如燈滅，偏向唯物思想。如印度順世派（*Cárváka*）的哲學主張。

12. Others believe the world to be a current of consciousness and no material entity; some call the void as the greatest. Others believe in two essences –*prakriti* and *purusa*.

還有人認為世界就是當下的意識，並無物質實體；有人稱許「空」是最大的，有人則相信意識和造化力兩種本質。

空：此處意指空性。

意識：別譯神我、原人、普魯沙（*puruśa*）等；亦指精神的本質，本然的認知力。

這化力：別譯冥性、原質、普拉克提（*prakrti*）等；亦指造化勢能，本然認知力的作用力。

譯按：本節舉出三種觀點，一是不明相對的真實，認為「一切皆幻」；二是「空觀思想」，三是「數論學派」的論點。

13-14. Thus believing in widely different doctrines, with faces turned away from the supreme goal, they think, according to their understanding and education, that this universe is without God; others believe there is a God, basing their assertions on various irrefutable arguments, founded on texts declaring difference between soul and God, and anxious to establish the existence of God.

這些差異懸殊的教義信仰背離了至上目標，他們心想：根據他們的所知和所學，宇宙間並沒有上帝。其餘信有上帝存在之人，基於種種確鑿的論據和載於文獻上有關個體靈魂和上帝之間相異的聲明，則亟想望確立上帝存在。

15-16. These and many other sages with various different denominations, have been declared in the *Shastras* as leaders of the human mind into delusion. It is not possible to describe fully the doctrines of these persons so fond of quarrel and contention; people thus wander in this universe, being driven away from the path of emancipation.

這些以及許多其他不同教派的賢哲，在其著述中的主張導致人心愈趨困惑。由於很難全面解析這些善辯之士的教義，人們因而徘徊所處世間，日漸遠離解脫之道。

瑜伽：唯一的真理

17. Having studied all the *Śhastras* and having pondered over them well, again and again, this *Yoga Sastra* has been found to be the only true and firm doctrine.

由是飽覽群經，反覆思索參究，終在這卷瑜伽經典中發現了唯一真實的教旨。

18. Since by *Yoga* all this verily is known as a certainty, all exertion should be made to acquire it. What is the necessity then of any other doctrines?

而透過瑜伽修習，明一切本來現成，如是悉心領會，何需任何其他教言？

19. This *Yoga Shastra*, now being declared by us, is a very secret doctrine, only to be revealed to a high-souled pious devotee throughout the three worlds.

現在我們所要陳述的這卷瑜伽法要，是門非常深秘的教導，只向三界中具高尚胸懷的虔誠信士揭露。

事部

20. There are two systems (as found in the *Vedas*). *Karmakanda* (ritualism) and *jnanakanda* (wisdom). *Jnanakanda* and *karmakanda* are again each subdivided into two parts.

吠陀聖典分兩種體系：事部和理部，事部和理部中又可各細分為兩個部分。

事部：又名業行部，教導可取和不可取的行為。

理部：又名智慧部，有關知識的教導。

21. The *karmakanda* is twofold – consisting of injunctions and prohibitions.

事部的兩支，包括當為之事和不當為之事。

22. Prohibited acts when done, will certainly bring forth sin; from performance of enjoined acts there certainly results merit.

行不當為之事，必然招致罪愆；而行當為之事，肯定帶來善果。

23. The injunctions are threefold – *nitya* (regular), *naimittika* (occasional), and *kamya* (optional). By the nonperformance of *nitya* or daily rites there accrues sin; but by their performance no merit

is gained. On the other hand, the occasional and optional duties, if done or left undone, produce merit or demerit.

當為之事有三：日常行、特定行和揀擇行。未踐履日常行，累積過失，無有善果；另一方面，特定行和揀擇行的責份是——為則有功，不為則無功。

日常行：每天需要做的事情，如決漱洗、禮拜、靜坐、用餐、工作、為善等等。

特定行：不需常做，但一年總會有幾次，如慶典、婚喪、特殊聚會或特別慶祝等等。

揀擇行：可依情況或意志選擇做或不做，如勸募活動、靈性假期、個人或團體朝聖等等。

24. Fruits of actions are twofold – heaven or hell. The heavens are of various kinds and so also hells are diverse.

行為之果有二：天堂或地獄；天堂有若干層，地獄也有若干層。

25. The good actions are verily heaven, and sinful deeds are verily hell; the creation is the natural outcome of *karma* and nothing else.

行諸善定入天堂，為諸惡必墜地獄；造化乃是業行的自然結果，別無其他。

造化：造化有二義，一指個人之福分、命運，一指自然界發展繁衍的功能；此處前者多些，故有「造化弄人」之語。

業行：特指相生相因自因果業力的好、壞行為。

26. Creatures enjoy many pleasures in heaven; many intolerable pains are suffered in hell.

眾生在天堂可享受許多的喜樂，處地獄需承受許多難忍的痛苦。

譯按：天堂和地獄是相對的觀念，樂境即天堂，若心覺不足，即非天堂；苦境即地獄，若心無怨懟，即非地獄。故天堂和地獄只在一念之間，非真有其國土。

27. From sinful acts pain, from good acts happiness, results. For the sake of happiness, men constantly perform good actions.
罪行之果招苦惱，善行之果生喜樂；為求幸福喜樂，人當持續從事良好的行為。

28. When the sufferings for evil actions are gone through, then there take place re-births certainly; when the fruits of good actions have been exhausted, then also, verily, the result is the same.
當經歷了惡行之苦後，必再投生；當善行之果耗盡，結果也是如此。

29. Even in heaven there is experiencing of pain by seeing the higher enjoyment of others; verily, there is no doubt of it that this whole universe is full of sorrow.
即使在天堂，也可能因見到其他更好的享樂而覺痛苦；是故，這整個宇宙無疑都充滿著苦惱。

30. The classifiers of *karma* have divided it into two parts; good and bad actions; they are the veritable bondage of embodied souls each in its turn.
業行的種類略分為善行和惡行兩類，它們是靈魂每次投胎轉生後的真正束縛。

31. Those who are not desirous of enjoying the fruits of their actions in this or the next world, should renounce all actions which are done with an eye to their fruits, and having similarly discarded the attachment for the daily and the *naimittika* acts, should employ themselves in the practice of *Yoga*.
那些不欲受享此生或來世行為之果的行人，應捨棄對一切行為之果的關注；放下對日常行和特定行的執著，發心從事瑜伽的修習。

理部

32. The wise *Yogí*, having realized the truth of *karmakanda* (works), should renounce them; and having left both virtue and vice, he must engage in *jnanakanda* (knowledge).

智瑜伽行人在體會到「事部」之真諦後，即當捨棄它們；善惡一併捨棄，並從事「理部」之修學。

33. The Vedic texts, – "The Spirit ought to be seen," – "About it one must hear", &c., are the real saviors and givers of true knowledge. They must be studied with great care.

吠陀經文如：「清淨自性直須見」、「如是至理須聽聞」等，乃是真正的救贖者及實相智的給予者；一定要細細參研。

清淨自性：梵語 *Átmá*，意為宇宙間不二不異、圓滿喜樂之真性，又名真如本性，至上靈魂、神性、真我之同義詞。

34. That Intelligence, which incites the functions into the paths of virtue or vice, am I. All this universe, moveable and immovable, is from me; all things are preserved by me; all are absorbed into me (at the time of *pralaya*); because there exists nothing but the spirit and I am that spirit – there exists nothing else.

心智具有激發人步入善或惡途的作用。這個宇宙中的一切，會動的和不會動的，皆從「我」而出；且透過「我」維持一切事物，一切毀滅之後亦回歸於「我」。因為彼處無有其他，唯只是神性；而「我」即彼神性——無有其他存在。

35. As in innumerable cups full of water, many reflections of the sun are seen, but the substance is the same; similarly individuals, like cups are innumerable, but the vivifying spirit, like the sun, is one.

如同無數盛滿水的杯子，可以反映出無數所見的太陽，其質不二；同樣的每一個體，就像無數的杯子；其中生機勃勃的神性，猶如太陽，就是一個。

36. As in a dream the one soul creates many objects by mere willing; but on awaking everything vanishes but the one soul; so is this universe.

好似夢中，個體靈魂據其意願幻化出許多事物；一旦甦醒便都消散，唯存靈魂；這個宇宙亦復如是。

37. As through illusion a rope appears like a snake, or a pearl-shell like silver; similarly, all this universe is superimposed in the *Paramátmá* (the Universal Spirit).

如同因想像故，認繩作蛇，或認貝殼作白銀；同理，這個宇宙的一切都是在無上自性中的假立。

無上自性：同義詞有有上主、至上意識至上靈魂、清淨自性、真常自性等，意指見證自己大宇宙心理意願的至上神性。

38. As, when the knowledge of the rope is obtained, the erroneous notion of its being a snake does not remain; so, by the arising of the knowledge of self, vanishes this universe based on illusion.

然若了知繩索的知識，即不會誤認繩索作蛇；是故，自性智升起，此建基於想像的宇宙即塌滅。

39. As, when the knowledge of the mother-of-pearl is obtained, the erroneous notion of its being silver does not remain; so, through the knowledge of spirit, the world always appears a delusion.

當掌握了珍珠母貝的知識，就不會誤認貝殼為白銀；是故，若然了知自性清淨，即知此世界恆為幻。

40. As, when a man besmears his eyelids with the collyrium prepared from the fat of frogs, a bamboo appears like a serpent, so the world appears in the *Paramátma*, owing to the delusive pigment of habit and imagination.

猶如吾人若用蛙脂做成的眼藥塗眼，竹子也會看成蛇；同理，這個從至上真性中顯現的世界，亦是習氣和想像的虛幻形色。

41. As through knowledge of rope the serpent appears a delusion; similarly, through spiritual knowledge, the world. As through jaundiced eyes white appears yellow; similarly, through the disease of ignorance, this world appears in the spirit – an error very difficult to be removed.

猶如通過對繩子的了解，頓悟蛇影為妄想；透過靈性的知識，世界亦如是。又有如黃疸患者見物，視白若黃；同理，緣無明病，此由自性所展現出的世界，是甚難祛除的幻化。

42. As when the jaundice is removed the patient sees the colour as it is, so when delusive ignorance is destroyed, the true nature of the Spirit is made manifest.

然若黃疸消除，患者所見即為本色；如是一旦無明幻化滅除，自性的真實本質便即顯露。

43. As a rope can never become a snake, in the past, present or future; so the spirit which is beyond all *gunas* and which is pure, never becomes the universe.

如同繩索在過去、現在、未來皆永難成蛇，故而超越一切束縛的清淨自性，亦永遠超然於萬象。

44. Some wise men, well-versed in Scriptures, receiving the knowledge of spirit, have declared that even *Devas* like *Indra*, etc., are non-eternal, subject to birth and death, and liable to destruction.

有些熟諳經典的智者，聲稱即便如因陀羅等諸神，亦非永恆；彼有生有死，且有其覆滅。

因陀羅：即帝釋天，全名釋提桓因陀羅，代表展現的宇宙力量。吠陀經中謂其為空界主宰，眾神的領袖；後吠陀時期地位逐漸弱化，上首地位被希瓦、維世努、梵天三神所取代。

45. Like a bubble in the sea rising through the agitation of the wind, this transitory world arises from the Spirit.

猶如海中浮漚因風鼓盪而上升；此無常世界亦如是從清淨自性或神性中誕生。

46. The Unity exists always; the Diversity does not exist always; there comes a time when it ceases: two-fold, three-fold, and manifold distinctions arise only through illusion.

一真永恆存在，多樣性則非永存；當因幻妄而生的二重、三重乃至多重分別消散時，此理自現。

一真：原梵文 *Abheda*，字義不可分的，英文 Unity，是無有生滅、無有增減的本然境界。佛教有一真法界之說，禪宗亦有萬法歸一之問；愛因斯坦在提出相對論以後，也致力於尋找一種統一的理論……。故謂萬象復歸一源之說始終不墜。

47. Whatever was, is or will be, either formed or formless, in short, all this universe is superimposed on the Supreme Spirit.

無論是曾經、現在或將來，無論是具象或抽象，都是短暫的，大千世界中的一切俱是假立於最高的神性上。

48. Suggested by the Lords of suggestion comes out *avidyá*. It is born of untruth, and its very essence is unreal. How can this world with such antecedents (foundations) be true?

無明係從上主之想像演化而出，因地不真，則其質亦不實；依此生起的世界，如何為真？

無明：不通達真理或不能明白事相之狀態，為一切苦之來由。本節意旨在於「大千世界只是宇宙本體呈現的想像，亦即只是本體之相用，既非本體，故為無明之所從出也」。

神性

49. All this universe, moveable or unmovable, has come out of Intelligence. Renouncing everything else, take shelter in it (Intelligence).

大千世界中的一切，有情或無情，皆從大覺而來；當捨離一切，以彼覺為庇護。

大覺：意指從混沌中初醒有我的大覺狀態，然後續隨想像而演化，形成大千世界。

50. As space pervades a jar both inside and out, similarly within and beyond this ever-changing universe, there exists one Universal Spirit.

猶如空性遍滿瓶罐的內外，同樣在此無常大千世界的內外，存在著一如的宇宙神性。

51. As the space pervading the five false states of matter does not mix with them, so the Spirit does not mix with this ever-changing universe.

猶如空性虛通五大卻不與之相混，宇宙神性於此無常世界亦如是恆保湛然。

52. From *Deva*s down to this material universe all are pervaded by one Spirit. There is one *satchitananda* (Being, Consciousness, and Bliss) all-pervading and secondless.

從天界到器世間，無不遍滿此一如之神性；其所遍滿者唯彼「無上喜悅的真實意識」，無有二致。

器世間：世間如器，生命體所居之物質環境及生活環境，又名物質界。

無上喜悅的真實意識：梵語 *sat-chit-ananda*，吠陀經裡形容至上本體特質的頌詞；*sat* 意思是神、真理或絕對的實相，*chit* 是意識、淨識，*ananad* 之義為極樂、法喜、無上的喜悅、絕對的喜悅。

53. Since it is not illuminated by another, therefore it is self-luminous; and for that self-luminosity, the very nature of Spirit is Light.

彼自始不由他明，為彼自明故；緣彼自明，神性本質即是大光明。

54. Since the Spirit in its nature is not limited by time, or space, it is therefore infinite, all-pervading and entirety itself.
由於神性本質不為時間或空間所侷限，因此祂是無限、遍在及圓滿的。

55. Since the Spirit is unlike this world, which is composed of five states of matter, that are false and subject to destruction, therefore, it is eternal. It is never destroyed.
神性從來迥異於此五大幻化元素所構成的會朽壞的世界，故彼永恆常住而不壞。

56. Save and beyond it, there is no other substance, therefore, it is one; without it everything else is false; therefore, it is True Existence.
除神性之外，此間無有其他實質，唯此一實相；無此實相，一切皆幻；是故唯彼方為真實的存在。
實相：宇宙萬法的真實本相。

57. Since in this world created by ignorance, the destruction of sorrow means the gaining of happiness; and, through Gnosis, immunity from all sorrow ensues; therefore, the Spirit is Bliss.
大千世界既由無明所造，終結惱苦意味著獲得幸福大樂；透過直覺真智，可免於一切紛至沓來的惱苦；因此神性即幸福大樂。
直覺真智：相應真如本體，直覺而出的智慧；非析理、非線性思考而得。

58. Since by Gnosis is destroyed the Ignorance, which is the cause of the universe; therefore, the Spirit is Gnosis; and this Gnosis is consequently eternal.
透過直覺真智可以滅除無明，彼無明即宇宙化生之因；所以神性即直覺真智，且此直覺真智亦為永恆。

59. Since in time this manifold universe takes its origin, therefore, there

is One who is verily the Self, unchanging through all times. Who is one, and unthinkable.

此多重的宇宙因時間而有其起源，故而必有一至上真我恆貫於一切時間而不變。祂是唯一且不可思議的。

60. All these external substances will perish in the course of time; (but) that Spirit which is indescribable by word (will exist) without a second.

一切外在之物都會隨著歲月推移而消逝，唯彼言語所不及之神性無有二致。

61. Neither ether, air, fire, water, earth, nor their combinations, nor the *Devas*, are perfect; the Spirit alone is so.

圓滿者非空、非風、非火、非水、非地，非五大之假合，亦非天界諸神；圓滿者唯彼神性。

瑜伽與幻相

62. Having renounced all false desires and abandoned all false worldly chains, the *Yogí* sees certainly in his own spirit the Universal Spirit by the self.

捨棄一切妄想雜念，拋卻一切世俗鎖鏈；瑜伽行者必得於己心中自見宇宙神性。

世俗鎖鏈：或鐵鎖鏈或金鎖鏈。

63. Having seen the Spirit, that brings forth happiness, in his own spirit by the help of the self, he forgets this universe, and enjoys the ineffable bliss of *Samádhi* (profound meditation.)

既見自性與宇宙神性無有差別，心中生大安樂；行人忘卻宇宙塵囂，於三摩地中得甚深妙樂。

64. *Máyá*(illusion) is the mother of the universe. Not from any other principle has the universe been created; when this *máyá* is destroyed, the world certainly does not exist.

幻力為宇宙生母，宇宙非由其他而生；幻力若止，世界當即不存。

幻力：宇宙心靈的想像力、幻化力，又名創造法則；創造階段中令所造置於束縛下的作用。

65. He, to whom this world is but the pleasure-ground of *maya*, therefore, contemptible and worthless, cannot find any happiness in riches, body, etc., nor in pleasures.

對祂而言，這個世界只是幻力的遊戲場，無足掛齒且無實際價值；是故於財富、身體等等之中，既找不到幸福也找不到喜樂。

66. This world appears in three different aspects to men – either friendly, inimical, or indifferent; such is always found in worldly dealing; there is distinction also in substances, as they are good, bad or indifferent.

對人而言，這個世界是以善的、惡的或是不善不惡的三重不同面貌顯現；此三者常於世事中得見，即便如物質界也常有好、壞或是不好不壞的分別。

67. That one Spirit, through differentiation, verily becomes a son, a father, etc. The Sacred Scriptures have demonstrated the universe to be the freak of maya (illusion). The *Yogí* destroys this phenomenal universe by realizing that it is but the result of *adhyaropa* (superimposition) and by means of *aparada* (refutation of a wrong belief).

此一神性，透過造化，如實地化為子女、父母等等，密續經典嘗言此宇宙乃是幻力的異想。瑜伽修士了悟到宇宙萬象只是幻力增益和妄想交織的結果，而看破了這個幻化的遊戲。

幻力增益：梵語 *adhyaropa*，原義為增益，常用來解釋物性的疊加，如乙物的性質被加諸或增益於甲物之上，甲物本身並不為乙物的體性所改變，但使甲物類若乙物或具有乙物的性質。又譬如意識或心性本淨，然受幻力增益的結果，使本自清淨的意識或心性產生扭曲，雖體性未變，但誤認為自他是無常如幻的。

妄想交織：梵語 *aparada*，原英譯的解釋是「refutation of a wrong belief」(錯誤信念的辨解)，有點錯錯相因的意味」。《楞嚴經》有「……想澄成國土」之句，意謂著萬象實由想像所生。

至尊天鴻的定義

68. When a person is free from the infinite distinctions and states of existence as caste, individuality etc., then he can say that he is indivisible intelligence, and pure Unit.

當一個人不再惑於無盡的分別以及如種姓、個性等存在的狀態，那麼可以說他已是悟得平等性智的清淨人。

種姓：原指印度一種世襲的階級制度，今泛指一切社會地位的等地差別。

幻化或進化

69. The Lord willed to create his creatures; from His will came out *avidyá* (Ignorance), the mother of this false universe.

上主意願創造眾生，從其意願隨生無明，遂成此虛幻宇宙之母。

70. There takes place the conjunction between the Pure *Brahma* and *avidyá*, from which arises *Brahma*, from which comes out the *ákasá*.

其間清淨本體和無明兩相並存，從中生起梵境，從中顯露虛空。

清淨本體：同義詞有：清淨大梵、清淨宇宙本體等。

梵境：傳統多譯為大梵或梵天，考其意涵實與本體、法身等同義，此處指法身之清淨相。

虛空：泛指空、空相、空界、真空等義。

71. From the *ákasá* emanated the air; from the air came the fire; from fire – water; and from water came the earth. This is the order of subtle emanation.

從空元素幻化出風元素，從風元素幻化出火元素，從火元素幻化出水元素，從水元素幻化出地元素，此為精細幻化的次序。

譯按：希臘哲學、印度哲學認為此五大元素是構成物質世界的基本材料，小至細胞大至星辰皆是如此。

72. From ether, air; from the air and ether combined came fire; from the triple compound of ether, air and fire came water; from the combination of ether, air, fire and water was produced the (gross) earth.

從空元素中出風元素，風與空結合成火，復從空、風與火三者合成為水，最後從空、風、火和水的和合中形成地元素。

73. The quality of ether is sound; of air motion and touch. Form is the quality of fire, and taste of water. And smell is the quality of earth. There is no gainsaying this.

空的介質是聲，風的介質是觸，火的介質是色，水的介質是味，地的介質是香（嗅）；以上已無可批駁。

74. *Akasa* has one quality; air two, fire three, water four, and earth five qualities, viz, sound, touch, taste, form and smell. This has been declared by the wise.

空大介質有一，風大有二，火大有三，水大有四，地大有五，是為聲、觸、色、味、香；此理往昔智者已然宣說。

75-76. Form is perceived through he eyes, smell through the nose, taste through the tongue, touch through the skin and sound through the ear. These are verily the organs of perception.

色由眼見，香由鼻嗅，味由舌嚐，觸由身知，聲由耳聞；這些都是實在的感覺器官。

77. From Intelligence has come out all this universe, movable and immovable; whether or not its existence can be inferred, the "All Intelligence" One does exist.

宇宙的一切，無論是有情、無情，皆由心造；無論其可證量與否，此天心之作用確實存在。

天心：宇宙心之意，人心則是天心的全息再現。

返樸歸真

78. The earth becomes subtle and is dissolved in water; water is resolved into fire; fire similarly merges in air; air gets absorption in ether, and ether is resolved in *avidyá* (Ignorance), which merges into the Great *Brahma*.

地元素轉細則融於水，水元素融於火，火元素融於風，風元素融於空，空元素融於無明，然後融入於無限本體。

無限本體：大梵、宇宙本體。

79. There are two forces – *vikśepa*, (the out-going energy) and *ávarańa* (the transforming energy) which are of great potentiality and power, and whose form is happiness. The great *máyá*, when non-intelligent and material, has three attributes *sáttva* (rhythm) *rájas* (energy) and *támas* (inertia).

大幻力有二勢力——離散力與遮障力，皆具大力與甚深潛力，且以幸福大樂為貌。當其處於昏昧及物質性之時，具有悅性、變性和惰性三種屬性。

大幻力：宇宙造化勢能開始創造時的名稱，是不同階段的宇宙力量。

離散力：離心外向之力，使生命體遠離至上核心的力量。

遮障力：使所遮變化或變形之力，此力在心中促發妄想，而逐漸遠離道心；這種遮障作用，造成見性障礙。

悅性：覺性，舊譯喜德，精細的屬性或作用力，其力能喚醒從束縛轉向解脫的欲望。

變性：行動原則，舊譯憂德，促使行動的作用力，保持心思參與行動的力量。

惰性：舊譯闇德，惰性作用力，造成所有慣性的力量。

80. The non-intelligent form of *máyá* covered by the *ávaraňa* force (concealment), manifests itself as the universe, owing to the nature of *vikśepa* force.

從幻力而出的昏昧狀態為遮障力所覆，復由於離散力之性質，展現自身為宇宙萬象。

81. When the *avidyá* has an excess of *támas*, then it manifests itself as *Durgá*; the intelligence which presides over her is called *Isvara*. When the *avidyá* has an excess of *sáttva*, it manifests itself as the beautiful *Lakshimi*; the Intelligence which presides over her is called *Viśhńu*.

當無明中之惰性居主導時，彼現身為難近母，主管她的神明為自在天；當無明中之悅性居主導時，彼現身為美麗的吉祥女神，主管她的神明為妙毗天。

難近母：印度降魔女神，被視為是希瓦妻雪山女神帕瓦蒂的降魔相。

自在天：宇宙本體的人格化神，心靈的控制者。

吉祥女神：幸福與財富女神，神話中也是遍在天妻室。

妙毗天：又譯維世務、毗濕奴等，主管創造後的維護之神，因其無所不在的特質，也譯遍在天。

82. When the *avidya* has an excess of rajas, it manifests itself as the wise *Saraswati*; the intelligence which presides over her is known as *Brahmá*.

當無明中之變性居主導時，彼現身為聰慧的辯才女神，主管她的神明為大梵天。

辯才女神：又名妙音天女，梵天妻，代表著醫療、子嗣、智慧、美貌、音樂之女神。

梵天：印度的創造之神，神話中與表毀滅的希瓦、表維持的遍在天並稱三主神。

83. Gods like *Śiva*, *Brahmá*, *Vishnu*, etc., are all seen in the great Spirit; bodies and all material objects are the various products of *avidya*.

諸神如希瓦、大梵天、妙毗天等等，處處可見其偉大神性；而身體和所有的物質體皆是無明的各種產物。

希瓦：約七千年前實際存在的大宗師，瑜伽法門之父。《希瓦本集》即是以其為第一人稱的修行指津。

84. The wise have thus explained the creation of the world – *tattwas* (elements) and non-*tattwa*s (non-elements) are thus produced – not otherwise.

智者如是解釋世界的創造，元素和非元素係為創造而產生，非由其他。

85. All things are seen as finite, etc. (endowed with qualities, etc.), and there arise various distinctions merely through words and names; but there is no real difference.

一切事物看起來都是有限的（皆有其被賦予的種種特質），然浩瀚萬象的不同只是名相上的區分，實質上沒有真正的差別。

86. Therefore, the things do exist; the great and glorious One that manifests them, alone exists; though things are false and unreal, yet, as the reflection of the real, they, for the time being, appear real.

因此，如實存在的事物，其中含藏著的偉大與榮耀的真一，始終存在著；雖然事物是如幻、不實的，然而就像是真實的映射，它們暫時有如真實的呈現。

87. The One Entity, blissful, entire and all-pervading, alone exists, and nothing else; he who constantly realizes this knowledge is freed from death and the sorrow of the world-wheel.

此一真法界，極樂、圓滿且遍及一切，始終存在，別無其他。時時有此慧見之人，不為世輪的死亡和悲傷所拘。

88. When through the knowledge that all is illusory perception(*aropa*) and by intellectual refutation(*apaváda*) of other doctrines, this universe is resolved into the one, then, there exists that One and nothing else; then this is clearly perceived by the mind.

藉由慧見了解到一切俱是不實的認知，以及透過相關教理的智辨，了知此宇宙是一，也存於此一中，別無其他；此是透過心靈的明澈了悟。

業識藉身體裹覆著個體靈魂

89. From the *Annamaya Kosa* (the physical vehicle) of the father, and in accordance with its past karma, the human soul is re-incarnated; therefore, the wise consider this beautiful body as a punishment, for the suffering of the effects of the past karma.

從父之身，依據其過去的業力，人類靈魂轉世投生；是故，智者認為這付美麗的軀體是一種懲罰，是為承受過去業行作用的苦果。

身：字義為食物所成的身體，亦即人的物質肉身。

90. This temple of suffering and enjoyment (human body), made up of flesh, bones, nerves, marrow, blood, and intersected with blood vessels etc., is only for the sake of suffering of sorrow.

這座由肌肉、骨骼、神經、骨髓與血管等交織組成的苦樂殿堂（人身），只是為了承擔悲苦的煎熬。

91. This body, the abode of *Brahma*, and composed of five elements

and known as *Brahmándá* (the egg of *Brahma* or microcosm) has been made for the enjoyment of pleasure or suffering of pain.

而此由五大元素假合而成，人稱作梵胎或宇宙縮影的大梵所居之身，則是為了享受快樂與煩惱苦受而造。

梵胎：亦名梵卵，喻此創造出來的宇宙，又名俱屬性本體；此處又喻宇宙縮影人身。

92. From the self-combination of the Śpirit which is *Śiva* and the Matter which is *Śakti*, and, through their inherent interaction on each other, all creatures are born.

從神性的自我組合，亦即透過純意識與造化力兩者彼此固有的相互作用，萬物於焉而生。

純意識：哲學上純意識與至上意識是同義詞，上主希瓦是此概念的神格化代名詞。

造化力：造化力或造化勢能；是希瓦的陰性力量，宇宙的原力。

93. From the fivefold combination of all subtle elements, in this universe, gross innumerable objects are produced. The intelligence that is confined in them, through karma, is called the *jiva*. All this world is derived from the five elements. The *jiva* is the enjoyer of the fruits of action.

於此宇宙間，從五大和合而成的一切微妙元素中，無以計數的萬有被創造出來；復透過業行，有心智作用於其中者，名之為生命。此世界中的一切都來自五大元素，而個體生命則是行為之果的享受者。

生命：有人、命、生靈、個體靈魂、個體意識等譯詞，視上下文而用。

94. In conformity with the effects of the past *karma* of the *jivas*, I regulate all destinies. *Jiva* is immaterial, and is in all things; but it enters the material body to enjoy the fruits of karma.

個體生命依據往世業行的影響，而「我」調控著一切命運；個體靈魂是隱藏於萬有中的非物質體，藉著棲身於物質體得享受業行之果。

「我」：梵語 *aham*，字義為我執、作意之我；此處有雙關語意味，大命運由宇宙「我」調控，小命運由個體「我」調控。

95. Bound in the chain of matter by their *karma*, the *jivas* receive various names. In this world, they come again and again to undergo the consequences of their.

個體生命因其業行得到種種不同的名相，受困於世事的鎖鏈中；為經歷己身的業果，個體靈魂在這個娑婆世界裡，一次又一次地再來。

96. When the fruits of have been enjoyed, the *jiva* is absorbed in the *Parambrahma*.

當業行之果儘皆滿足，個體靈魂便融入至上本體。

第二章

知識篇

Knowledge

微觀宇宙

1. In this body, the mount *Meru* – i.e., the vertebral column – is surrounded by seven islands; there are rivers, seas, mountains, fields; and lords of the fields too.

   身內脊柱亦名彌樓山，為七島嶼所圍繞；域內有河流、湖海、群山、田野和守護的神祇。

   彌樓山：印度各宗教宇宙論中最高的聖山，眾神的居所；又稱持地山、妙高山或須彌山。

   七島：喻體內七個脈輪或能量中心。

2. There are in it seers and sages; all the stars and planets as well. There are sacred pilgrimages, shrines; and presiding deities of the shrines.

   其中有先知與賢哲，也有星辰和行星；有虔誠的朝聖者和廟寺，以及廟寺供奉的神祇。

3. The sun and moon, agents of creation and destruction, also move in it. Ether, air, water and earth are also there.

   日月運行其間，代理著創造和毀滅；乙太、風、火和水、地亦在其中。

   乙太：即空元素。

神經中樞

4. All the beings that exist in the three worlds are also to be found in the body; surrounding the *Meru*. They are engaged in their respective functions.

   三界所有的存在皆能在此身中尋得，如是存在圍繞著彌樓山各司其事。

   三界：即一般所熟知的地界、天界、空界或是意識界、潛意識界和無意識界，是印度傳統對世界的概念。

5. (But ordinary men do not know it). He who knows all this is a *Yogí*;

there is no doubt about it.

能明此一切者唯瑜伽師（常人不知此秘），毋庸置疑。

6. In this body, which is called *Brahmándá* (microcosm, literally the mundane egg), there is the nectar-rayed moon, in its proper place, on the top of the spinal cord, with eight *Kalás* (in the shape of a semi-circle).

於此名為梵胎之身中，其脊柱頂端特定處，有月甘露隨八縷光瓣呈半圓形泌出。

脊柱頂端特定處：意指脊椎頂端，或指松果體，位在雙眉間，印堂後，百會穴之下，亦即中腦前丘和丘腦之間。

月甘露：月甘露係指由松果體分泌，能滋生靈性喜悅的內分泌。

光瓣：梵語 *Kalás*，複數形。*Kalá* 一字多義，原義係指一種具有弧度的流線體，亦可表示為月亮的月相；印度天文將暗月到滿月分成 16 *Kalás*，從之演變為衡量一個人的構成部分或生命能發展的輝度。在生命構成方面，16 *Kalás*，指的是五大基本元素加五知根加五作根加心靈。而生命能輝度方面，有說植物的輝度是 6，動物是 7，常人是 8，完人是 16，介於 9 到 16 之間便是不同的聖賢、天使或菩薩。

7. This has its face downwards, and rains nectar day and night. The ambrosia further sub-divides itself into two subtle parts:

光瓣其面向下，日夜滴灑著甘露，此甘露復一分為二細流：

8. One of these, through the channel named *Idá*, goes over the body to nourish it, like the waters of the heavenly Ganges – certainly this ambrosia nourishes the whole body through the channel of Ida.

其一經由月脈流通身體，如同神聖的恆河水，經由月脈將此神聖甘露滋養全身。

月脈：此脈終於左鼻孔，又名左脈；纏於中脈兩側，當內心參與心理導向靈性的追求時作用。

9. This milk-ray (moon) is on the left side. The other ray, brilliant as the purest milk and fountain of great joy, enters through the *suśhumná* into the spinal cord, in order to create this moon.

此是流經左側的月甘露。另一細流，光潔若純淨牛乳，是為大喜樂之源，經中脈流入脊柱，以生成此月露。

中脈：起於脊椎根底，終於頂輪，又名空脈，靈能甦醒後循此脈通往頂輪。

10. At the bottom of the *Meru* there is the sun having twelve *Kalas*. In the *Pingalá*, the lord of creatures carries (the fluid) through its rays upwards.

在彌樓山底之日脈有十二縷光瓣；於此日脈，造化主攜所泌出之元精循光瓣上行。

日脈：此脈終於右鼻孔，又名右脈；纏於中脈兩側，當內心參與心理導向物欲的追逐時作用。

元精：元精是腎之元氣厚積所生，從虛極靜篤而生者精清，從妄念淫事而生者精濁。

11. It certainly swallows the vital secretions, and ray-exuded nectar. Together with the atmosphere, the sun moves through the whole body.

行者如是飲下此一瓊漿和泌出之甘露；連同其靈氣，元陽如是流貫全身。

元陽：原句用字為 sun，從語意推敲，或指清淨元精昇華後之純陽之氣。

12. The right-side vessel, which is *pingalá* is another form of the sun, and is the giver of *nirvana*. The lord of creation and destruction (the sun) moves in this vessel through auspicious elliptical signs.

此稱作日脈之右側管道是另一種形式的太陽，是涅槃的賦予者；創造和毀滅之神(太陽）透過此一吉祥的橢圓符號，在此脈道運行著。

涅槃：意為寂滅、入滅、滅度、解脫；多用於形容超越了生死束縛的解脫境界。

橢圓符號：意指梵胎，由於其形狀似橢圓，故如是描述。

經絡

13. In the body of man there are 350,000 *nadis*; of them the principal are fourteen;

人身之內布有三十五萬經脈，其重要者有十四條。

經脈：泛指身內之神經、血脈及氣脈，此處指體內的精細能量管道。在《哈達瑜伽明燈》第一章中說到身內經脈有七萬兩千之數，然都認為中脈、左脈、右脈是最重要的。

14-15 *Suśhumná, Idá, Pingalá, Gándhárí, Hastijihviká, Kuhu, Saraswatí, Pusá, Sankhiní, Payasviní, Váruní, Alambusá, Vishvodarí,* and *Yaśasviní*. Among these *Idá, Pingalá* and *Sushumná* are the chief.

中脈、月脈、日脈、香行脈、龍舌脈、新月脈、妙音脈、普夏脈、珠母脈、波耶斯脈、皤魯脈、阿藍脈、毗達脈、耶舍脈；其中最主要的是月脈、日脈和中脈。

譯按：此十四條主脈之位置於《商枳略奧義書》第一章 15 節中有記載，大致與身體之眼耳口、前後陰、肚臍等八竅之開口以及手腳皮膚有關。

中脈：見本章經句 9 註解。

月脈：見本章經句 8 註解，起於中脈左側，故亦稱左脈。

日脈：見本章經句 10 註解，起於中脈右側，故亦稱右脈。

香行脈：自左脈背部至左眼而止。

龍舌脈：右眼角到左腳大足趾。

新月脈：從前陰到喉嚨。

妙音脈：位於舌上。

普夏脈：從喉至前陰。

珠母脈：位在香行與新月脈之間，上行至左耳止。

波耶斯脈：介於普夏脈與妙音脈之間。

皤魯脈：遍布於腹。

阿藍脈：自後陰至口。

毗達脈：位於龍舌脈和新月脈之間。

耶舍脈：右耳至右足趾。

16. Among these three, *Suśhumná* alone is the highest and beloved of the *Yogís*. Other vessels are subordinate to it in the body.

在此三脈間，唯有中脈最最主要且備受眾瑜伽師之鍾愛，身內其餘諸脈都從屬於中脈。

17. All these principal *nadis* have their mouths downwards, and are like thin threads of lotus. They are all supported by the vertebral column, and represent the sun, moon and fire.

所有這些重要的經脈之口皆向下，如若蓮蕊中的細鬚。脊柱支持著所有的經脈，而以日、月和聖火為代表。

聖火：聖火表中脈，日、月分指左右脈。

18. The innermost of these three is *chitrá*; it is my beloved. In that there is the subtlest of all hollows called *Brahmarandhra*.

三脈的最裡處名妙色脈，彼為吾所鍾愛；該處藏有一切孔脈中最微妙的梵穴。

妙色脈：梵語 *Chitrá nádi*，字義有莊嚴、嚴麗、眾妙、妙境、種種色等義，故譯為妙色。在《六脈輪實解》一書中描述中脈分三層，外層名金剛脈，妙色脈在裡層或說第二層，所包圍住的脈管空間名梵脈；故妙色脈可說是第二層脈也可說是最裡層脈。

吾：有說此為主希瓦之言，故從第一人稱。

梵穴：頂輪的別稱；有說此穴是行人涅槃時靈魂穿過之處。

19. Brilliant with five colours, pure, moving in the middle of *sushumná,* this *chitrá* is the vital part of body and centre of *Suśhumná*.

五色燦然、純淨，行於中脈中間，此妙色脈位於中脈中心，是身體最重要的部分。

20. This has been called in the *Shástras* the Heavenly Way; this is the giver of the joy of immortality; by contemplating it, the great *Yogí* destroys all sins.

經典中稱此脈為天堂之路，能予人永恆的喜樂；以之靜慮冥想，大瑜伽士能祛除一切罪過。

骨盆區域

21. Two digits above the rectum and two digits below the *linga* (penis) is the *ádhára* lotus, having a dimension of four digits.

根持蓮花輪位於後陰之前二指及前陰之後二指處，其形四指四方。

根持蓮花輪：本處意指根持輪，即通稱之海底輪。

22. In the pericarp of the *ádhára* lotus there is the triangular, beautiful yoni, hidden and kept secret in all the *Tantras*.

於根持蓮花輪之內有三角形的美麗胎藏，其秘隱藏並保守在一切密續之中。

胎藏：即女陰、女根、產處、子宮、種子等等，喻創造誕生處。

23. In it is the supreme goddess *Kuńdalini* of the form of electricity, in a coil. It has three coils and a half (like a serpent), and is in the mouth of *Suśhumná*.

彼輪內有勝妙軍荼利女神以陰性能量的形式盤蜷著，盤蜷之數三圈有半，沉睡在中脈入口。

軍荼利女神：沉睡神性之名。盤蜷三圈半代表著生、住、滅及再生循環的說法。密乘瑜伽的觀念是只有當修行者對上主或至上意識有強烈渴望時，軍荼利才會甦醒。

24. It represents the creative force of the world, and is always engaged in creation. It is the goddess of speech, whom speech cannot manifest, and who is praised by all gods.

她代表著世界的創造勢能，且一直在進行著創作；她是妙音女神，其言默默，卻為諸神所讚嘆。

妙音女神：希瓦和難近母的女兒，神話中的學習女神，散發出白色的光輝，賦予人類語言、智慧和學習的力量，又稱智慧女神、辯才女神。由於靈能軍荼利甦醒上昇帶來深廣的身心變化，故被認為和妙音女神有關聯，亦即妙音女神和根持輪是有關聯的。

25. The *nadi* called *idá* is on the left side coiling round the *Suśhumná*, it goes to the right nostril.

名為月脈的經脈位於其左，圍繞著中脈，盤捲通向左鼻孔。

26. The *nadi* called *pingalá* is on the right side; coiling round the central vessel, it enters the left nostril.

名為日脈的經脈位於其右，圍繞著中脈，盤捲通向右鼻孔。

27. The *nadi* which is between Ida and *pingalá* is certainly *Suśhumná*. It has six stages, six forces[1], six lotuses, known to the *Yogís*.

而居於月脈和日脈之間的即是中脈，瑜伽師熟知彼有六脈輪，六種力，六朵蓮花。

六種力：意指根持輪至眉心輪等六個脈輪含藏的潛力。

六朵蓮花：此處以蓮花喻脈輪，每一脈輪有不同數量的花瓣，花瓣數代表該脈輪所擁有的情緒傾向。

28. The first five stages of *Suśhumná* are known under various names; being necessary, they have been made known in this book.

中脈的前五個脈輪名稱眾多不一，必要知道的，本書皆有記載。

29. The other *nadis*, rising from '*Muládhár*', go to the various parts of the body, e.g. the tongue, penis, eyes, feet, toes, ears, the abdomen, the armpit, fingers of the hands, the scrotum and the anus. Having risen from their proper place, they stop at their respective destinations, as above described.

其餘起自根持輪的經脈走往身體不同的部位，例如舌頭、前陰、眼睛、雙腳、足趾、耳朵、腹部、腋窩、手指、前陰與後陰；如前所述，這些經絡始於其應起之處，終於其所止之處。

30. From all these (fourteen) *nadis*, there arise gradually other branches and sub-branches, so that at last they become three hundred thousand and a half in number, and supply their respective places.

從所有這十四經脈漸次再分出其他分支和次分支，最後形成了三十五萬之數，各在其位司其職。

31. These *nadis* are spread through the body cross-wise and length-wise; they are vehicles of sensation and keep watch over the movements of the air i.e., they regulate the motor functions also.

這些經脈縱橫交織遍布全身，既是感受知覺的載具亦守望著內氣的運行，亦即兼具有調節運動機能的作用。

腹部區域

32. In the abdomen there burns the fire – digester of food – situated in the middle of the sphere of the sun having twelve *Kalás*. Know this as the fire of *Vaiswanara*; it is born from a portion of my own energy, and digests the various foods of creatures, being inside their bodies.

在腹部之內燃有消化之火，坐於其中央之太陽有十二光瓣，是謂胃火；此火出自己身能量，負責消化身內種種的食物。

胃火：消化能力。與中醫因飲食辛辣、厚味，或五志過極，化火生熱等犯胃而致胃熱過盛之「胃火」不同。

33. This fire increases life, and gives strength and nourishment, makes the body full of energy, destroys all diseases, and gives health.

此胃火增強生命力，予人力量和榮養，使身體充滿活力，祛除一切疾病，使人健康。

34. The wise *Yogí*, having kindled this *Viswanaric* fire according to proper rites, should sacrifice food into it every day, in conformity with the teachings of his spiritual teacher.

循其靈性導師教示，慧智靈修者如法點燃胃火，每日自供身食。

35. This body called the *Brahmándá* (microcosm) has many parts, but I have enumerated the most important of them in this book. (Surely) they ought to be known.

此身亦名微宇宙，分有許多部分；其中應該知曉的重點，本書均有列舉。

36. Various are their names, and innumerable are the places in this human body; all of them cannot be enumerated here.

然而亦無法一一盡述它們在人體內所有不同的名稱和詳盡的部位。

個體靈魂

37. In the body thus described, there dwelleth the *Jiva*, all-pervading, adorned with the garland of endless desires and chained to the body by karma.

如前所述，生命寓居此身，此身因業行果報鑲滿著無盡欲望的花環和鎖鏈。

生命：亦表個體靈魂。

38. The *Jiva* possessed of many qualities and the agent of all events, enjoys the fruits of his various karmas amassed in the past life.
個體生命擁有許多特質且為一切事件活動的行為者，享受著過去世累積的種種業果。

39. Whatever is seen among men (whether pleasure or pain) is born of karma. All creatures enjoy or suffer, according to the results of their actions.
人間所見的任何苦樂皆從業識而生，一切眾生的快樂或痛苦，乃是根據他們行為的果報。
業識：積累前世業行之力而形成今生器識，亦為命運之藍本。

40. The desires, etc., which cause pleasure or pain, act according to the past karma of the *Jiva*.
欲望是快樂或痛苦的成因，行事係皆根據個體生命過去的業報。

41. The *Jiva* that has accumulated an excess of good and virtuous actions receives a happy life; and in the world he gets pleasant and good things to enjoy, without any trouble.
命中常行善、厚積德，即能獲得幸福的生活，在世間順利地安享美好的事物。

42. In proportion to the force of his karma, man suffers misery or enjoys pleasure. The *Jiva* that has accumulated an excess of evil never stays in peace – it is not separate from its karmas; except karma, there is nothing in this world. From the Intelligence veiled by *maya*, all things have been evolved.
按個人業力之配比，其人遭受苦難或享受快樂；命中若累積了過多的壞事，就會惡報纏身，難處平靜！除了因果循環，這個世界其實沒有什麼；一旦覺心為幻力所障，所有的事情便於焉演生。

覺心：字義是覺醒的心。

43. As in their proper season, various creatures are born to enjoy the consequences of their karma; as through mistake a pearl-shell is taken for silver, so through the taint of one's own karmas, a man mistakes *Brahman* for the material universe.

如同適當的季節一到，萬物便應時生發以享受業行的結果；如同誤認珠蚌為銀，人們受到己身宿業的熏染，錯認此物質宇宙為本體實相。

44. From desire all these delusions arise; they can be eradicated with great difficulty; when the salvation-giving knowledge of the unreality of the world arises, then are desires destroyed.

從欲望生諸妄想，得費大力氣才能根除它們；然而一旦救贖的恩典降臨，讓人了解到世界演生的不實性，如是欲望即能根除。

45. Being engrossed in the manifested (objective) world, the delusion arises about that which is the manifestor – the subject. There is no other, (cause of this delusion). Verily, verily, I tell you the truth.

若全心貫注於顯現的客體世界，妄想即自主體（表現者）內心生起；除此無他（此為妄想之因）。千真萬確，絕非虛言。

46. The illusion of the manifested (objective world) is destroyed when the Maker of the Manifest becomes manifest. This illusion does not cease so long as one thinks, "*Brahma* is not."

當造物主實相展露，此顯現之幻象（客體世界）隨即消除；而只要吾人仍認為「梵非真」，幻力就不會消失。

梵非真：意指若認為至上本體（梵）非絕對的真實，此顯現的客體世界才是絕對的真實（而非相對的真實），就不會知道這個顯現的世界只是宇宙心靈的想像成相，因之就會一直是想像世界中的一分子。

47. By looking closely and deeply into the matter, this false knowledge vanishes. It cannot be removed otherwise; the delusion of silver remains.

透過對物質仔細與深入的觀察，這種不實的知識因而消散；否則它們很難移除，鍍銀的妄想仍殘留著。

鍍銀的妄想：鍍銀亦非真銀，意指仍停留在認鍍銀為真銀的想像裡。

48. As long as knowledge does not arise about the stainless Manifestor of the universe, so long all things appear separate and many.

只要未生起恆淨不朽之宇宙創造者的真知，那麼一切事物現出的仍是分歧和紛紜。

49. When this body, obtained through karma, is made the means of obtaining nirvana (divine beatitude); then only the carrying of the burden (of the body) becomes fruitful – not otherwise.

當此報身證得涅槃時，只有福德圓滿之身能獲此豐碩果實，非是其他。

50. Of whatever nature is the original desire(*vásaná*), that clings to and accompanies the *Jiva* (through various incarnations); similar is the delusion which it suffers, according to its deeds and misdeeds.

無論何種天性都是緣自宿習的熏染，必需攀附並伴隨著輾轉投生的個體生命；同樣的，受苦的妄想也是根據其人的作為和惡行而有。

熏染：又名熏習、習氣，原義是以氣味或煙氣接觸物品，引申為長期接觸的人或事物對品行、習慣的影響。如茶葉中放入乾茉莉花即成香片或熏花茶。

51. If the practiser of *Yoga* wishes to cross the ocean of the world, he

should perform all the duties of his *áshrama*, (the condition of life), renouncing all the fruits of his works.

若是行人渴望橫渡現世之汪洋，就必須遵從其生命四行期的所有職責，放棄一切作為的果實。

生命四行期：印度傳統上將人生分成四個階段，稱作人生四行期：(1) 梵行期：以學習為主的時期，(2) 家居期：成家、立業及社會責任期，(3) 林棲期：探究生命實相、意義及目的的時期，(4) 行腳期，又名雲遊期或遁世期：捨棄所有，行腳遊方，學習臣服，印證所悟，甚至如出家僧般乞法、乞食。

52. Persons attached to sensual objects and desirous of sensual pleasures, descend from the road of nirvana, through the delusion of much talk, and fall into sinful deeds.

執著感官對象和感官享樂的人，已從涅槃路上退轉，縱然夸談妄想，仍不免墜入惡業。

53. When a person does not see anything else here, having seen the Self by the self; then there is no sin (for him if he) renounces all ritual works. This is my opinion.

若有人眼下不見他物，所見唯己自性真我，即能出離一切業行罪愆，此為我之見解。

54. All desires and the rest are dissolved through Gnosis only, and not otherwise. When all (minor) *tattwas* (principles) cease to exist, then My *Tattva* becomes manifest.

一切欲望雜想只會透過直覺智消散而非其他，當一切世諦不復存在，吾之真性即顯。

一切世諦：英譯本是「所有次要的或較小的因素」；引申為一切世法、一切世俗外緣。

吾之真性：「吾」是即希瓦自稱；原文英字母是大寫開頭，意為我的真如自性。

第三章

修持篇

Practice

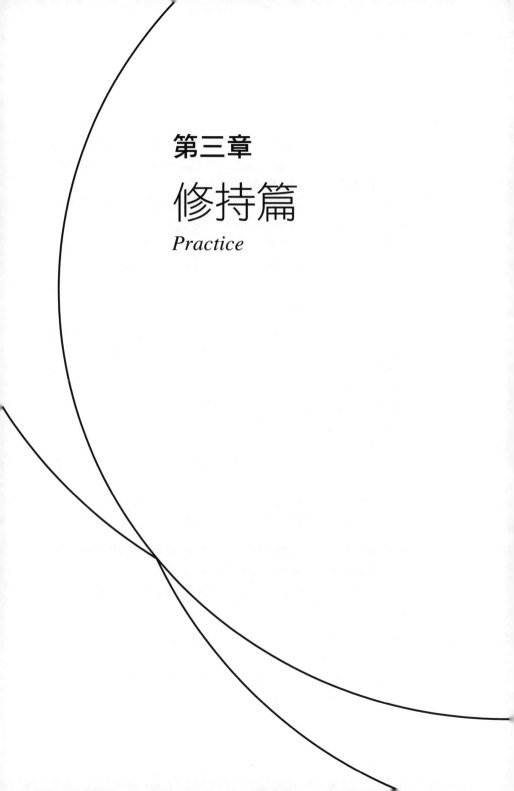

瑜伽練習之生命氣

1. In the heart, there is a brilliant lotus with twelve petals adorned with brilliant sign. It has letters from k to th (i.e., *k, kh, g, gh, n, ch, chh, j, jh, n, t, th*), the twelve beautiful letters.

   於心輪中，有光潔蓮花具十二片飾有明亮符號之花瓣，上有從「क」到「ठ」等十二個優美的字母。

   क：羅馬字拼音是 *ka*，表「希望」心裡傾向的音根。

   ठ：羅馬字拼音是 *ṭha*，表「悔意」心裡傾向的音根。

   十二個優美的字母：這裡是指代表心輪十二種心緒傾向的梵語字母，詳見第五章 83 節。

2. The *Práńa* lives there, adorned with various desires, accompanied by its past works, that have no beginning, and joined with egoism (*ahankára*).

   命根氣寓居此處，裝點著無數欲望，伴隨著自無始以來的宿業，與我執相結合。

   命根氣：又名持命氣，主責呼吸，作用於肚臍和喉頭聲帶間的生命能量。

   我執：以自我感為主心理傾向，例如我渴了，我想去，我能掌握……等等。

   Note: The heart is in the center where there is the seed यं.

   英註：心輪位於其中，彼處有種子字 यं（*yam*）。

3. From the different modifications of the *Práńa,* it receives various names; all of them cannot be stated here.

   從命根氣衍生出不同的變化，各有其名；此處不能一一盡述。

4. *Práńa, apána, samána, udána, vyána, nága, kúrma, Krikara, devadatta,* and *dhananjaya*.

   命根氣、下行氣、平行氣、上行氣、遍行氣、彈伸氣、收縮氣、呵欠氣、飢渴氣及倦眠氣。

譯按：本節前五種為內作用生命能，後五種為外作用生命能。

5. These are the ten principal names, described by me in this *Shastra*; they perform all functions, incited thereto by their own actions.

這是十種主要生命氣的名稱，我會在後文有所解釋；這十種氣透過各自的機能，刺激並推動自身的作用。

6. Again, out of these ten, the first five are the leading ones; even among these, the *práńa* and *apána* are the highest agents, in my opinion.

再者，這十種氣的前五種居主導作用；我認為其中命根氣和下行氣是最主要的媒介。

7. The seat of the *Práńa* is the heart; of the *apána*, the anus; of the *samána*, the region above the navel; of the *udána*, the throat; while the *vyána* moves all over the body.

命根氣住於心臟，下行氣住於後陰，平行氣位於臍上方，上行氣住於喉，遍行氣則遍行於全身。

下行氣：住於後陰和肚臍之間，控制大、小便的運動。

平行氣：住於肚臍，主責命根氣和下行氣之間的平衡。

上行氣：位在喉嚨主，控制聲音與聲帶。

遍行氣：遍行全身，調節血液循環及體內傳出、傳入神經的功能。

8. The five remaining *vayus*, etc., perform the following functions in the body: Eructation, opening the eyes, hunger and thirst, gaping or yawning, and lastly hiccup.

餘彈伸氣等五種外作用氣，於體內執行以下功能：噯氣、張闔眼、飢渴、張目結舌或呵欠，以及打嗝。

噯氣：由彈伸氣控制，又名龍氣，控制伸展、跳躍與投擲。噯氣是指如喝下汽水後伸展氣管引出胃中碳酸氣的情形。

張闔眼：由惓眠氣控制，舊譯瞬氣，是睡眠與睡意的成因。
飢渴：由飢渴氣控制，此氣又名生飢氣，關連體內飢渴。
張目結舌或呵欠：由呵欠氣控制，又名欠伸氣，幫助打呵欠。
打嗝：由收縮氣控制，此氣直譯名龜氣，控制身體的收縮。打嗝需收縮胃部。

9. He who in this way knows the microcosm of the body, being absolved from all sins, reaches the highest state.
   循此法認知身體即微宇宙之人，將從所有的罪愆中解脫，而達到最高的境地。

上師

10. Now I will tell you, how easily to attain success in *Yoga*, by knowing which the *Yogís* never fail in the practice of *Yoga*.
    現在我將述說如何順利地達到瑜伽成就，知曉的瑜伽行者，永遠不會在修習瑜伽時失敗。

11. Only the knowledge imparted by a *Guru*, through his lips, is powerful and useful; otherwise it becomes fruitless, weak and very painful.
    只有透過明師口傳的法要，方具力量與實效；否則將成徒勞、無力且使人苦惱。

12. He who devoted to any knowledge, while pleasing his *Guru* with every attention, readily obtains the fruit of that knowledge.
    虔心於任何法要者，凡留心處皆是以取悅其上師為念，即容易獲得該法要的成果。
    取悅上師：上師的責任是引導弟子，驅散弟子 內心的黑暗；而最能取悅上師的就只兩件事—明心見性與利益眾生。

13. There is not the least doubt that *Guru* is father. *Guru* is mother, and

Guru is God even; and as such, he should be served by all with their thought, word and deed.

毫無懸念地視上師為父，視上師為母，甚至視上師即上主；弟子應如是以其身、口、意依止侍奉。

14. By *Guru's* favor everything good relating to one's self is obtained. So the *Guru* ought to be daily served; else there can be nothing auspicious.

    經由上師恩典，弟子可得一切善法加持；是故應日日侍奉上師，否則即無真吉祥。

15. Let him salute his *Guru* after walking three times round him, and touching with his right hand his lotus-feet.

    弟子繞師三匝後，向師致敬頂禮，復以右手觸師蓮足。

初心

16. The person who has control over himself attains verily success through faith; none other can succeed. Therefore, with faith, the *Yoga* should be practiced with care and perseverance.

    已然控制自心之靈修者，透過信心可達真成就，非如此者難以成功！是故須憑藉信願，以謹慎心和堅定心修習瑜伽。

17. Those who are addicted to sensual pleasures or keep bad company, who are disbelievers, who are devoid of respect towards their *Guru*, who resort to promiscuous assemblies, who are addicted to false and vain controversies, who are cruel in their speech, and who do not give satisfaction to their *Guru* never attain success.

    執迷聲色享受或結交損友者，不信道者，對上師不敬者，耽溺頹靡聚會者，喜好虛浮爭辯者，言詞苛刻者，無心取悅上師者，永難成就。

18. The first condition of success is the firm belief that it (*vidyá*) must succeed and be fruitful; the second condition is having faith in it; the third is respect towards the *Guru*; the fourth is the spirit of universal equality; the fifth is the restraint of the organs of sense; the sixth is moderate eating, these are all. There is no seventh condition.

成功的首要條件是堅信所修必定成就且將結實豐碩，其次要對所修深具信心，三要尊敬上師，四要以平等心處世，五要約束感官諸根，六要節制飲食；以上即是所有條件，沒有第七個條件。

所修：英譯括弧註解是梵語 *vidyá*，義為直覺的科學、靈性導向的知識。知識可分為 *vidyá*、*avidyá* 兩種類型：前者是向心的知識，關注的是內在永恆的生命；後者是離心的知識，關注的是外在世俗的知識。

19. Having received instructions in *Yoga*, and obtained a *Guru* who knows *Yoga*, let him practice with earnestness and faith, according to the method taught by the teacher.

接受瑜伽的教導，歸皈一位明悉瑜伽的上師；依據上師教導，以懇切和虔信之心從事修行。

練習場所等

20. Let the *Yogí* go to a beautiful and pleasant place of retirement or a cell, assume the posture *padmásana*, and sitting on a seat (made of *kusa* grass) begin to practice the regulation of breath.

瑜伽行者宜覓一靜室或優美合度之隱密所在，採蓮花坐式安坐於吉祥草席墊上，從規律呼吸開始練習。

21. The wise beginner should keep his body firm and inflexible, his hands joined as if in supplication, and salute to the *Gurus*. He should also pay salutations to *Ganesha* on the right side, and again to the guardians of the worlds and goddess *Ambiká* who are on the left side.

明智之初習者應保持身體的穩定和端正，雙手如祈禱般合十於胸，先向上師作禮；再向右側的歡喜天作禮，接著再向左側的世界守護者安碧卡女神作禮。

歡喜天：全名大聖歡喜自在天，傳說是毀滅神希瓦和雪山女神帕瓦蒂的兒子，又名象頭神。是在印度相當受歡迎的神祇，與智慧和藝術女神莎拉斯瓦蒂同是學子必定敬拜或冥想的神。女神莎拉斯瓦蒂是智慧之神，歡喜天是袪除障礙之神或成功之神，故也被視作福德財神。

安碧卡女神：是至上意識的另一半，造化勢能在神話中的一個別名。

調息功法

22. Then let the wise practitioner close with his right thumb the *pingalá* inspire air through the i*dá*; and keep the air confined – suspend his breathing – as long as he can; and afterwards let him breathe out slowly, and not forcibly, through the right nostril.

    然後明智行人以右拇指按住右脈鼻孔，用左脈鼻孔緩緩吸氣；接著暫停呼吸，儘可能持氣於內；然後再從容地以右脈鼻孔徐徐吐氣。

23. Again, let him draw breath through the right nostril, and stop breathing as long as his strength permits; then let him expel the air through the left nostril, not forcibly, but slowly and gently.

    復次，行人以右脈鼻孔吸氣，再儘可能地持氣；然後溫和從容地以左脈鼻孔徐徐吐氣。

24. According to the above method of *Yoga*, let him practice twenty *kumbhakas*. He should practice this daily without neglect or idleness, and free from all duels (of love and hatred, and doubt and contention), etc.

    根據上述瑜伽行法，練習二十次持氣；習者應精勤不怠地每日練習，保持心情平順，無有懷疑和爭論。

持氣：吸氣後將氣保持在體內的調息法。

25. These *kumbhakas* should be practiced four times – once (1) early in the morning at sunrise, (2) then at midday, (3) the third at sun-set, and (4) the fourth at mid-night.

此持氣法應練習四次：一在清晨日出之時，二在中午，三在日落之時，四在午夜時分。

26. When this has been practiced daily, for three months, with regularity, the *náḍis* of the body will readily and surely be purified.

每日如法練習，規律地持續三個月，身內經脈必定很快地得到淨化。

I. 築基階段

27. When thus the *nádis* of the truth-perceiving *Yogí* are purified, then his defects being all destroyed, he enters the first stage in the practice of *Yoga* called *árambha*.

當領會真理的瑜伽行者經脈淨化了，那麼他的身病也會盡除，真正進入了瑜伽修持的第一個階段。

第一個階段：指的是初修築基階段。

28. Certain signs are perceived in the body of the *Yogí* whose *nádis* have been purified. I shall describe, in brief, all these various signs.

經脈已然淨化的瑜伽行者，體內會有一些可以覺察到的徵兆，我將扼要地描述這幾種徵兆。

29. The body of the person practicing the regulation of breath becomes harmoniously developed, emits sweet scent, and looks beautiful and lovely. In all kinds of *Yoga*, there are four stages of *pránáyáma*：1: *Árambha-avasthá* (the state of beginning)，2:

Ghata-avasthá (the state of co-operation of self and Higher Self)，3: *Parichaya-avasthá* (knowledge)，4: *Nishpattiavasthá* (the final consummation)

人身在規律地練習調息之後會有和諧的發展，散發出甜美的清香，看起來優雅又引人。在各種瑜伽之中，呼吸調息法可歸納為築基（初修分），充實（連結小我和更高的真我），熟化（慧智分），圓成（究竟成就分）等四個階段。

築基：調息持氣，淨化經脈階段。

充實：統合氣息、音聲和明點以及連結小我和真我的階段。

熟化：生命能進入中脈，穿過脈輪，擺脫業習影響的階段。

圓成：六輪調伏，業力拔除，融入本覺智海階段。

30. We have already described the beginning of *Árambha-avesthá* of *pránáyáma*; the rest will be described hereafter. They destroy all sin and sorrow.

我們已講過呼吸調息法的築基階段，餘在後文會提到；這些鍛練可掃除一切罪愆及悲苦。

31. The following qualities are surely always found in the bodies of every *Yogí* – Strong appetite, good digestion, cheerfulness, handsome figure, great courage, mighty enthusiasm and full strength.

下列徵兆如極佳的胃口、良好的消化能力、開朗、挺拔、無懼、熱忱和充沛的活力，總是能在每位瑜伽行者身上發現。

32. Now I tell you the great obstacles to *Yoga* which must be avoided, as by their removal the *Yogís* cross this sea of worldly sorrow.

現在我要提的是修習瑜伽必須避開的許多障礙，瑜伽行人若能排除這些牽絆，便能渡過世俗悲苦之海。

禁忌事項

33. The *Yogí* should renounce the following; 1: Acids, 2: astringents, 3: pungent substances, 4: salt, 5: mustard, and 6: bitter things; 7: much walking, 8: early bathing (before sun-rise) and 9: things roasted in oil; 10: theft, 11: killing (of animals) 12: enmity towards any person, 13: pride, 14: duplicity, and 15: crookedness; 16: fasting, 17: untruth, 18: thoughts other than those of *moksha*, 19: cruelty towards animals; 20: companionship of women, 21: worship of (or handling or sitting near) fire, and 22: much talking, without regard to pleasantness or unpleasantness of speech, and lastly, 23: much eating.

    瑜伽行者應捨棄下列事物：酸、澀、辣、鹹、芥末及苦味之物；走動過度、深夜沐浴（日出前）、炙烤的食物；竊盜、殺生、對人有敵意、自傲、心口不一、心術不正；不食、虛偽、比較悟境、對待動物殘忍；女子為伴、供奉明火（或玩火或太靠近火）、講話太多且不顧他人感受，以及飲食過度。

方法

34. Now I will tell you the means by which success in *Yoga* is quickly obtained; it must be kept secret by the practitioner so that success may come with certainty.

    現在我要講述瑜伽成就之捷徑，習者必須保守此法之秘，如是必然隨法成就。

35. The great *Yogí* should observe always the following observances – He should use 1: clarified butter, 2: milk, 3: sweet food, and 4: betel without lime, 5: camphor; 6: kind words, 7: pleasant monastery or retired cell, having a small door; 8: hear discourses on truth, and 9: always discharge his household duties with *vairágya* (without attachment), 10: sing the name of *Vishnu*; 11: and hear sweet music,

12: have patience, 13: constancy, 14: forgiveness, 15: austerities, 16: purifications, 17: modesty, 18: devotion, and 19: service of the *Guru*.

精勤的瑜伽行人應始終恪守下列事項：食用純淨的奶油、牛奶、甘甜的食物和不添加石灰的蒟醬葉，使用樟腦；說好話、常住宜人的寺院或有小門的關房；聽聞真理，以不執著心善盡一家之主之責，頌唱上主之名；聆聽悅耳的音樂，有耐心，有恆心、寬容、簡樸、純淨、謙虛、虔誠並服事上師。

36. When the air enters the sun, it is the proper time for the *Yogí* to take his food (i.e, when the breath flows through the *pingalá*); when the air enters the moon, he should go to sleep (i.e., when the breath flows through the left nostril or the *idá*).

當氣息進入日脈鼻孔，此刻是進食的適當時間；當氣息進入月脈鼻孔，則是瑜伽行人的就寢時間。

譯按：日脈指的是右脈鼻孔，月脈指的是左脈鼻孔。

37. The *Yoga* (*pránáyáma*) should not be practiced just after the meals, nor when one is very hungry; before beginning the practice, some milk and butter should be taken.

剛吃完飯不宜修習瑜伽，頗為飢餓時亦不宜；在開始修習之初，應取食一些牛奶或奶油。

剛吃完飯不宜修習瑜伽：包括體位法、身印法、生命能控制法、靜坐冥想等等。

38. When one is well established in his practice, then he need not observe these restrictions. The practitioner should eat in small quantities at a time, though frequently; and should practice *kumbhaka* daily at the stated times.

當習者之修煉已打下良好的基礎，就不需要受限這些約束。此時習者每次只應少量進食，但可增加次數；並應每日定時地修習持氣法。

39. When the *Yogí* can, of his will, regulate the air and stop the breath (whenever and how long) he likes, then certainly he gets success in *kumbhaka*, and from the success in *kumbhaka* only, what things cannot the *Yogí* command here?

當瑜伽行者能以其個人意志，隨意地調節呼吸和住氣（無論何時及多久），他自然會從持氣調息中得到成功，持氣法若得成就，還有什麼瑜伽行者不能掌握的？

第一階段

40. In the first stage of *pránáyáma*, the body of the *Yogí* begins to perspire. When it perspires, he should rub it well, otherwise the body of the *Yogí* loses its *dhátu* (humors).

修習生命能控制初期，習者的身體會排汗；當排汗之時，應妥善的擦拭，否則會流失身體的精華液。

精華液：滋養和支持身體的要素，此處意指體內的精液、淋巴液或荷爾蒙等精華液。

第二及第三階段

41. In the second stage, there takes place the trembling of the body; in the third, the jumping about like a frog; and when the practice becomes greater, the adept walks in the air.

在第二階段，習者身體會生擅抖；第三階段，身體跳動若蛙；當修持更為精深時，習者善行於空中。

42. When the *Yogí*, though remaining in *padmásana*, can raise in the air and leave the ground, then know that he has gained *váyusiddhi* (success over air), which destroys the darkness of the world.

當瑜伽行者能以蓮花坐之姿離地升起，則可知彼已得風大成就，此成就能破除世間蒙昧。

風大成就：可以調御風大或風元素的能力。莊子內篇逍遙遊中曾提及列子御風而行的故事，藏密白教祖師密勒日巴傳記也有諸脈結打通後飛行空中的記載。這種成就無關解脫，只是掌控風大後啟動的某種超然能力。

43. But so long (as he does not gain it), let him practice observing all the rules and restrictions laid down above. From the perfection of *pránáyáma*, follows decrease of sleep, excrements and urine.

然只要尚未獲得成就，行人就必需遵循所有的規則以及前述指引來用功；隨著生命能控制功成，睡眠和大、小二遺也會減少。

大、小二遺：即大、小二便。

44. The truth-perceiving *Yogí* becomes free from disease, and sorrow or affliction; he never gets (putrid) perspiration, saliva and intestinal worms.

深見真性的瑜伽行者沒有疾病、悲愁或惱苦，他從不出臭汗、不流涎，也不會有蟲寄生腸道。

45. When in the body of the practitioner, there is neither any increase of phlegm, wind, nor bile; then he may with impunity be irregular in his diet and the rest.

當習者的體內既不會添增任何的膽汁、體風，也不會增加痰濕；那麼他就無需擔心飲食、作息是否無度。

譯按：本節提及的膽汁、體風、痰濕，即是印度生命科學中身體的火能、風能和水能等三種體質要能對應的病素。

46. No injurious results then would follow, were the *Yogí* to take a large quantity of food, or very little, or no food at all. Through the strength of constant practice, the *Yogí* obtains *bhuchárisiddhi*, he moves as the frog jumps over the ground, when frightened away by the clapping of hands.

屆時隨之而來的就是瑜伽行者可以多食，可以少食，甚或不食。通過持恆修煉的力量，瑜伽行者得到地大成就；當突遇驚險時，能於拍掌間如蛙跳般騰離。

地大成就：可控制地大或地元素，類如縮地成寸，神行八方之能。

47. Verily, there are many hard and almost insurmountable obstacles in *Yoga*, yet the *Yogí* should go on with his practice at all hazards; even were his life to come to the throat.

雖然，在修煉瑜伽的過程中會有許多困難和幾乎無法逾越的障礙；然而即使命在眉睫，瑜伽行者仍應在所有困難中繼續地修行。

48. Then let the practitioner, sitting in a retired place and restraining his senses, utter by inaudible repetition, the long *pranava Oṁ*, in order to destroy all obstacles.

如是行者當於僻靜之地坐下，都攝感官諸根；為破除一切障礙，心無旁騖地反覆長誦 *Oṁ* 音。

Oṁ：神聖的音聲，中文常以「唵」字表示此神聖的音聲；創造最初的顯現波動；宇宙外在表現的音咒或音根，亦可說是創造的種子；由 *a*、*u*、*m* 三個音節組成。

49. The wise practitioner surely destroys all his *karma*, whether acquired in its life or in the past, through the regulation of breath.

透過調控出入息，明智行人必能破除自身今生或宿世所累積的一切業力。

50. The great *Yogí* destroys by sixteen *pranayamas* the various virtues and vices accumulated in his past life.

透過十六種生命能調息，大瑜伽行者能消除過去宿世種種的善業與惡業。

十六種生命能調息：自然呼吸法、瑜伽呼吸法（即完全呼吸法）、頭顱清明法、左右脈淨化法，空大、火大、水大三種清淨脈道呼吸法（第五章 39-45 節），以及持氣法八加一種（其中意隨呼吸法有兩種：第五章 46 節），共十六種。《希瓦本集》中並未一一列出這十六種，所以可能會有不同的說法。

51. This *pránáyáma* destroys sin, as fire burns away a heap of cotton; it makes the *Yogí* free from sin; next it destroys the bonds of all his good actions.

此生命能控制法消除惡業，猶似大火燒盡棉花堆，使瑜伽行者不為惡業牽絆，進而還能解除一切善業的束縛。

52. The mighty *Yogí* having attained, through *pranayama*, the eight sorts of psychic powers, and having crossed the ocean of virtue and vice, moves about freely through the three worlds.

透過生命能控制，大瑜伽士能夠成就八種妙自在，橫渡善業與惡業之海，悠遊於三界之間。

八種妙自在：梵語 *Iśvaryástakáni*，八種妙自在成就，詳《瑜伽明燈》第三章 8 節譯註。

增加修習時間

53. Then gradually he should make himself able to practice for three *ghatis* (one hour and a half) at a time(he should be able to restrain breath for that period). Through this, the *Yogí* undoubtedly obtains all the longed-for powers.

接下來逐漸地使自己每次能修習三炷香時間（行者需能在這段時間持住氣息）。循此法，瑜伽行者定可獲得所有渴望的力量。

三炷香時間：古印度以前根據恆星度量的一種六十進制時間單位，一天長六十炷香，一炷香約二十四分鐘，三炷香即七十二分鐘，英譯簡化為九十分鐘。練習持氣時間，應循序漸進，漸漸遞增，不可躐等。

成就

54. The *Yogí* acquires the following powers: *vakya siddhi* (prophecy), transporting himself everywhere at will (*kámachári*), clairvoyance (*duradristhi*), clairaudience (*durashruti*), subtle-sight (*shushma-drishti*), and the power of entering another's body (*parakaypravesana*), turning base metals to gold by rubbing them with his excrements and urine, and the power of becoming invisible, and lastly, moving in the air.

瑜伽行者獲得的力量如下：言無礙成就、神足力、天眼力、天耳力、內視力、入他身力；以二遺摩鐵成金之力，以及隱身和空行之力。

譯按：言無礙成就梵語 *vákya siddhi*，英譯括弧註文是預言力。

II. 充實階段

55. When, by the practice of *pránáyáma*, the *Yogí* reaches the state of *ghata* (water-jar), then for him there is nothing in this circle of universe which he cannot accomplish.

透過修持生命能控制法，瑜伽行者達到充實階段；如是處此天地循環之中沒有什麼是他不能完成的。

56. The ghata is said to be that state in which the *práńa* and the *apána* vayus, the *nada* and the *vindu*, the jivatma (the Human Spirit) and the *Parámátma* (the Universal Spirit) combine and co-operate.

充實階段是指命根氣和下行氣，音聲和明點，個體意識和至上意識彼此調和、協作的狀態。

個體意識和至上意識：即個體小我和至上真我、個體靈魂和至上靈魂。

57. When he gets the power of holding breath (*i.e.*, to be in trance) for three hours, then certainly the wonderful state of *pratyáhára* is

reached without fail.

當行者之定境具有可持氣三個小時的實力時，自然就達到感官內攝的妙境。

感官內攝：又稱感官回收，將對外的注意力往內收回，瑜伽八支功法之第五支。

58. Whatever object the *Yogí* perceives, let him consider it to be the spirit. When the modes of action of various senses are known, then they can be conquered.

無論行者感知到什麼，都當它是神性的展現；當不同感受的運作模式被摸清之後，就可以克服它們。

59. When, through, great practice, the *Yogí* can perform one *kumbhaka* for full three hours, when for eight *dandas* (3 hours) the breathing of the *Yogí* is suspended, then that wise one can balance himself on his thumb; but he appears to others as insane.

當透過精勤不懈地修持，瑜伽行者可以懸息達到八個檀陀，亦即能夠做到一瓶息能維持足三句鐘之時，及此之睿智行人以其拇指即能平衡自己，雖然在別人眼中他似顯顛狂。

檀陀：古印度根據吠陀系統度量時間的一種60進制計時單位；一長息24秒，60息等於一檀陀，一檀陀等於24分鐘，等同一炷香。八個檀陀等於192分鐘，約三小時又十二分鐘，所以是三句鐘時間。

瓶息：即持氣；人身如瓶，將氣息住留於身謂之瓶息。

以其拇指即能平衡自己：指及此行人能輕易地平衡自己，或是表示此時行人可以拇指支起全身。

譯按：本節所述定境，使身輕如燕，然非全無呼吸；可參考《哈達瑜伽明燈》第四章50-51節。

III. 熟化階段

60. After this, through exercise, the *Yogí* reaches the *Parichaya-avasthá*. When the air leaving the sun and moon (the right and the left nostrils), remains unmoved and steady in the ether of the tube sushumna, then it is in the *parichaya* state.

充實有成之後，通過鍛煉，瑜伽行者晉級熟化階段。當內氣逸離日脈和月脈之時，便安穩地住於中脈之空元素中，此時即進入熟化階段。

熟化階段：本章 29 節所述瑜伽修持的第三階段。

61. When he, by the practice of *Yoga*, acquires power of action (*kriya shakti*) and pierces through the six chakras, and reaches the sure condition of *parichaya*, then the *Yogí*, verily, sees the three-fold effects of karma.

當行者透過瑜伽修持獲得行為原動之力，且以此力貫穿六輪，達成熟化的一定條件；如是行者得親見業行的三重影響。

行為原動之力：梵語 *kriyá shakti*，邁向神性的行動力。

六輪：從海底輪至眉心輪等六輪。

業行的三重影響：即善、惡、不善不惡等業行的影響。

62. Then, let the *Yogí* destroy the multitude of *karmas* by the *pranava* (*Oṁ*); let him accomplish *kayavyuh* (a mystical process of arranging the various *skandas* of the body), in order to enjoy or suffer the consequences of all his actions in one life, without the necessity of re-birth.

復次，行者得以唵聲拔除累業之過，待其完成己身諸蘊的清理，便能即生燃盡所有苦樂的業行。

唵聲：即 *a-u-m* 組成之 *Oṁ* 聲。

諸蘊的清理：調理己身色、受、想、行、識等五蘊的一種神秘作用。

63. At that time let the great *Yogí* practice the five-fold *dháraňá* forms of concentration on *Vishnu*, by which command over the five elements is obtained, and fear of injuries from any one of them is removed. (Earth, water, fire, air, *ákása* cannot harm him.)

彼時讓上根上智的瑜伽行者修持五大集中法，由此獲得對五大元素的控制，如是任何緣受五大所傷之恐懼，因而袪除（亦即不為地、水、火、風、空等諸大所傷）。

五大集中法：集中也稱作執持或專注，瑜伽八支功法中的第六支；本節所述之法是在每一脈輪從事五次集中練習。（詳葛蘭達本集第三章 68 節）。

64. Let the wise *Yogí* practice *dháraňá* thus: five ghatis (2½ hours) in the ádhára lotus (*muládhára*); five ghatis in the seat of the *linga* (*svadhisthana*), five *ghatis* in the region above it, (in the navel, *maňipur*), and the same in the heart (*anáhata*); five ghatis in the throat (*visuddha*) and, lastly let him hold *dháraňá* for five *ghatis* in the space between the two eye-brows (*anjapur*). By this practice the elements cease to cause any harm to the great *Yogí*.

此時明智的瑜伽行者宜再修煉「集中」，其法如下：兩小時集中於於根持蓮花輪，兩個小時於生殖輪，兩個小時於其上的臍輪，同樣的時間於心輪，再兩個小時於喉輪，最後凝神於眉心輪兩個小時。透過這樣的鍛煉，諸元素不再對瑜伽行者有任何傷害。

兩個小時：原英譯用的時間單位是五炷香，一炷香是 24 分鐘，五炷香就是 120 分鐘，等於兩小時。

65. The wise *Yogí*, who thus continually practices concentration (*dháraňá*), never dies through hundreds of cycles of the great *Brahma*.

持續鍛煉集中的睿智瑜伽行人，縱使經歷數百梵刧亦不消亡。

IV. 圓成階段

66. After this, through gradual exercise, the *Yogí* reaches the *Nishpatti-avestha* (the condition of consummation). The *Yogí*, having destroyed all the seeds of karma which existed from the beginning, drinks the waters of immortality.

熟化之後，復漸次修習，瑜伽行者達到圓成階段；如是行者能拔除過往以來所有業力，品啜不死甘露。

圓成階段：梵語 *Nishpatti -avasthá*，本章 29 節所述瑜伽修持的第四階段。

67. When the *jivan-mukta* (delivered in the present life,) tranquil *Yogí* has obtained, through practice, the consummation of *samádhi* (meditation), and when this state of consummated *samádhi* can be voluntarily evoked, then let the *Yogí* take hold of the *chetaná* (conscious intelligence), together with the air, and with the force of (*kriya-śakti*) conquer the six wheels, and absorb it in the force called *jnana-śakti*.

當瑜伽行者通過修持獲自在三摩地，親證即身解脫之寂靜，且能夠隨意入此三摩地；如是行者當定持此覺境，並藉持氣和修持之力調伏六輪，將之融入本覺智海中。

三摩地：有入定，三昧，等持，正定，正受等諸義；泛指心識融入所觀，如：人心融入天心，小我融入真我，個體意識融入至上意識等。

即身解脫：即於今生即達成解脫的行者。

寂靜：梵語 *Saḿtasya*，釋教有言：寂靜者，離煩惱曰寂，絕苦患曰靜。老子亦有「歸根曰靜，是謂復命」之語。

修持之力：修持的功力，心想事成的能力。

覺境：靈明的意識狀態，特別是指靈性已開展的覺醒狀態。

本覺智海：梵語 *jñána-śakti*，*jñána* 本義是導向解脫的知識，本覺慧智：*śakti* 是造化勢能的作用力，句意是說修心入定，復使之融於本覺智海。

68. Now we have described the management of the air in order to remove the troubles (which await the *Yogí*); through this knowledge of *váyu-sádhaná* vanish all sufferings and enjoyments in the circle of this universe.

為消除行人惱苦，我們講述了調息之法；而藉此風大修持法，可消弭此宇宙循環圈中的一切苦受與樂受。

風大修持之法：泛稱各種生命能調息法。

69. When the skilful *Yogí*, by placing the tongue at the root of the palate, can drink the *práńa váyu,* then there occurs complete dissolution of all *Yogas* (i.e., he is no longer in need of *Yoga*).

以舌接抵上顎根處，當瑜伽行者習久功深，能接飲命根氣之時，如是行者將完全地融入一切瑜伽之聖境。

命根氣：亦名持命氣，作用於喉臍之間負責呼吸的生命氣，也是驅動其餘生命氣的根本氣息。

瑜伽之聖境：完全地融入所觀，以瑜伽作為解脫方法的任務已達成，不再需要瑜伽了（括弧英註之言）。

70. When the skilful *Yogí*, knowing the laws of action of *práńa* and *apána*, can drink the cold air through the concentration of the mouth, in the form of a crow-bill, then he becomes entitled to liberation.

當功深之瑜伽行者，已明了命根氣與下行氣之運作法要，即能以烏喙身印吸飲清涼氣息，如是行者已然踏入解脫之門。

烏喙身印：撮唇如烏喙，緩緩自口吸氣下嚥，此為烏喙身印，能滅一切病。見《葛蘭達本集》第三章 87 節。

71. The wise *Yogí*, who daily drinks the ambrosial air, according to proper rules, destroys fatigue, burning (fever), decay and old age, and injuries.

如法修持之睿智行人日飲此美味清氣，能消解疲勞、清熱潤燥，延緩衰老及避免受傷。

72. Pointing the tongue upwards, when the *yogí* can drink the nectar flowing from the moon (situated between the two eye-brows), within a month he certainly would conquer death.

當捲舌向上的瑜伽行者，能接飲從月叢（位於兩眉間內裡）泌出的甘露時，彼於一個月內必能克服死苦。

捲舌向上：靜坐中舌抵上顎的形容，喻靜坐中的瑜伽行者。

月叢：位於兩眉間之內，意指腦中松果體、腦下垂體一帶。

73. When having firmly closed the glottis by the proper *yogíc* method, and contemplating on the goddess *Kuńdalini*, he drinks (the moon fluid of immortality), he becomes a sage or poet within six months.

牢閉聲門，循適當之瑜伽修法，觀想靈能軍荼利女神，行者飲下不朽之月露，如是將於六個月內成為聖哲者或詩人。

牢閉聲門：聲門位在喉部，牢閉聲門需下巴內收如收頷鎖印，《葛蘭達本集》言：透過此鎖印封住喉輪之十六種基本習性。

靈能軍荼利女神：軍荼利為靈能之別名，具大潛力，詞性屬陰性，故稱之為女神。

不朽月露：由松果體所分泌出的荷爾蒙

74. When he drinks the air through the crow-bill, both in the morning and in the evening twilight, contemplating that it goes to the mouth of the *kuńdalini*, consumption of the lungs (phthisis) is cured.

當行者晨昏能以鳥喙身印吸飲清氣，復觀想此氣入於靈能軍荼利之口，能防治肺癆。

靈能軍荼利之口：靈能軍荼利沉睡於脊椎尾端根持輪內，軍荼利之口意指中脈位於根持輪的入口。

75. When the wise *Yogí* drinks the fluid day and night through the

crow-beak, his diseases are destroyed: he acquires certainly the powers of clairaudience and clairvoyance.

當明智之瑜伽行人日夜以烏喙身印啜飲甘露，其身疾即獲拔除，功成能得耳通與眼通之力。

76. When firmly closing the teeth (by pressing the upper on the lower jaw), and placing the tongue upwards, the wise *Yogí* drinks the fluid very slowly, within a short period he conquers death.

牙關閉合，捲舌向上，明智行者如是徐緩地啜飲甘露，如是短期間內即能克服死苦。

77. One, who daily continues this exercise for six months only, is freed from all sins, and destroys all diseases.

每日持續修習此法者，只需六個月即能離一切罪愆，除一切身疾。

78. If he continues this exercise for a year, he becomes a *Bhairava*; he obtains the powers of anima &c., and conquers all elements and the elementals.

若能持續修習此法一年，行者成為超然的密行者；得到「能小」等諸靈力，可克服一切元素及由其構成的環境。

超然的密行者：梵語 *Bhairava*，音譯拜拉瓦，對瑜伽大成就者的尊稱；達到了超越個人及世間意識的人，身具某些超然之力。

79. If the *Yogí* can remain for half a second with his tongue drawn upwards, he becomes free from disease, death, and old age.

若瑜伽行者能保持逆舌上捲半剎那，即能出離病苦、死苦和老苦。

半剎那：形容極短極短的時間。實際上出離病苦之功在於修持過程的累積，而水到渠成之時只在瞬間。

80. Verily, verily, I tell you the truth that the person never dies who

contemplates by pressing the tongue, combined with the vital fluid of *Prána*.

我真真實實的告訴你們，以逆舌上捲接飲生命甘露而入禪定之人，得永遠不死。

逆舌上捲：根據哈達瑜伽修法，舌尖應反捲伸向顎咽口；由於時代不同，今之行人多採舌抵上顎。

81. Through this exercise and *Yoga*, he becomes like *Kámadeva*, without rival. He feels neither hunger, nor thirst, nor sleep, nor swoon.

通過修習此法要及瑜伽之人，有若欲界之神，無有匹敵；既不覺有飢渴之需，亦無有昏睡之障。

欲界之神：欲界生命耽著色、聲、香、味、觸等五塵之享受，故欲界之神比喻不耽著於五塵享受之人。

82. Acting upon these methods the great *Yogí* becomes in the world perfectly independent; and freed from all obstacles, he can go everywhere.

依此法要修持之大瑜伽士，處世獨立不倚；不為一切障礙所拘，隨處自在悠遊。

譯按：如莊子「《逍遙遊》的概念一階至無己、無功、無名之境，乃能無所依憑而遊於無窮。

83. By practicing thus, he is never reborn, nor is tainted by virtue and vice, but enjoys (for ages) with the gods.

藉如是修習，行人不受後有，亦不為善惡所染著，但與諸天共享喜樂。

不受後有：不再轉世投胎於世之意。

坐姿

84. There are eighty-four postures, of various modes. Out of them, four ought to be adopted, which I mention below:-- 1, *Siddhásana*; 2,

Padmásana; 3, *Ugrásana*; 4, *Svastikásana*.

習見體式有八十四種，各有不同，其中常採用者為下列四種：(1) 成就坐，(2) 蓮花坐，(3) 威德式，(4) 吉祥坐。

體式：字義為安穩、舒適的姿勢，故舊譯為坐式，通譯體式或體位法，八支瑜伽中的第三支。

成就坐：字義成就坐，今多譯完美坐。

蓮花坐：常見坐式，各取出淤泥而不染之意。

威德式：字義威德坐式，以形為名則為坐姿前彎式。

吉祥坐：適合長時間靜坐的體式，有說佛陀成道時即是採此坐式。

成就坐

85. The *Siddhásana* that gives success to the practitioner is as follows: Pressing with care by the heel the yoni, the other heel the *Yogí* should place on the *lingam;* he should fix his gaze upwards on the space between the two eyebrows, should be steady, and restrain his senses. His body particularly must be straight and without any bend. The place should be a retired one, without any noise.

    成就坐帶給習者靈性成就，坐法如下：將足踵輕抵會陰，另一足踵需置於前陰之上（交疊其下之足）；兩眼向上定視眉心處不動，收攝六根感官，其身尤宜中正不可偏斜。靜坐之處應僻靜，無有任何噪雜之音。

86. He who wishes to attain quick consummation of *Yoga*, by exercise, should adopt the *Siddhásana* posture, and practice regulation of the breath.

    欲要速證瑜伽成就之人，應採取成就坐修持，並練習規律的呼吸。

87. Through his posture the *Yogí*, leaving the world, attains the highest end and throughout the world there is no posture more secret than

this. By assuming and contemplating in this posture, the *Yogí* is freed from sin.

經由此坐式，瑜伽行者心離塵世，達最高究竟；世上再無比此式更奧秘之體式，以此式靜坐觀想，行者可從罪惑中脫離。

蓮花坐

88. I now describe the *Padmásana* which wards off (or cures) all diseases:-- Having crossed the legs, carefully place the feet on the opposite thighs (i.e., the left foot on the right thigh, and vice versa); cross both the hands and place them similarly on the thighs; fix the sight on the tip of the nose; pressing the tongue against the root of the teeth, (the chin should be elevated, the chest expanded) then draw the air slowly, fill the chest with all your might, and expel it slowly, in an unobstructed stream.

    我現在講述可防治一切病的蓮花坐。兩小腿交盤，小心地將足交互置於對側大腿上；交叉雙手置於腹前腿上，目光諦視鼻端，舌抵上顎齒根處（下巴微收，肩胸打開）；然後慢慢吸氣，盡力吸滿後再緩緩呼氣，保持氣息平穩順暢。

89. It cannot be practiced by everybody; only the wise attains success in it.

    此法非人人可修持，唯智者能從中成就。

90. By performing and practicing this posture, undoubtedly the vital airs of the practitioner at once become completely equable, and flow harmoniously through the body.

    透過修習與鍛煉此坐式，無疑地習者之生命氣隨即徹底平順，並且在體內和諧地運行。

91. Sitting in the *Padmásana* posture, and knowing the action of the *prána* and *apána*, when the *Yogí* performs the regulation of the

breath, he is emancipated. I tell you the truth. Verily, I tell you the truth.

以蓮花式坐定，融合命根氣和下行氣入於所觀，當習者呼吸臻至深細自如時，已入自在解脫；此為我真實之語。

譯按：瑜伽坐式有穩定身心之故，至於是否成就則全看心地功夫；功夫若到，氣息脈象亦有表徵，此為本節未細表之處。

威德式

92. Stretch out both the legs and keep them apart; firmly take hold of the head by the hands, and place them on the knees. This is called *ugrásana* (the stern-posture). it excites the motion of the air, destroys the dullness and uneasiness of the body, and is also called (the posterior crossed posture.) That wise man who daily practices this noble posture can certainly induce the flow of the air up through the anus.

兩腿前伸並左右微分，雙手穩抱頭項前彎觸膝，此式稱作威德式。這個體式激活內氣的運行，消除身體的遲鈍與不適，此式又名背部前屈伸展式。每日練習此尊貴體式之明智行人，藉提攝穀道即可加強體內氣流上行。

坐式背部前屈伸展式：又名困難背伸展式，簡稱背伸展式。

提攝穀道：即提肛收腹之意，藉之可加強骨盒腔底肌肉群的張力和收縮力，活絡腹腔器官組織代謝。

93. Those who practice this obtain all the *siddhis*; therefore, those, desirous of attaining power, should practice this diligently.

習練此式之行人能得非常成就，因此欲要獲得如是力量者，應勤練此體式。

94. This should be kept secret with the greatest care, and not be given to anybody and everybody. Through it, *váyu-siddhi* is easily obtained,

and it destroys a multitude of miseries.

應悉心保守此式之秘，莫隨意示人；循此法容易取得風大成就，且能消解諸多苦難。

吉祥坐

95. Place the soles of the feet completely under the thighs, keep the body straight, and sit at ease. This is called the *Svástikásana*.

將腳掌完全地置於另一腿之下，保持身形中正，舒心安坐；此稱之為吉祥坐。

96. In this way, the wise *Yogí* should practice the regulation of the air. No disease can attack his body, and he obtains *váyu-siddhi*.

依此法，明智的瑜伽行者進行勻穩地呼吸；如是無有疾病能侵襲其身，且能獲得風大成就。

97. This is also called the *sukhásana*, the easy posture. This health-giving, good *svástikásana* should be kept secret by the *Yogí*.

此式亦名安樂坐，坐法簡易，有益健康；此一善巧之吉祥坐式，瑜伽行者當保守其密意。

譯按：修行固有種方便之法，但成就實無捷徑；須得實務和道理都了解，然後老實下功夫才能得力，否則反易生流弊。昔時法不輕傳，其意在此。

第四章

身印篇

Mudrás

胎藏身印：脊椎底端的聖甘露

1. First with a strong inspiration fix the mind in the *adhár* lotus. Then engage in contracting the *Yoni*, which is situated in the perineal space.

   首先隨著深吸氣將心定於根持蓮花中，然後收縮下腹會陰。

   根持蓮花：亦即根持輪或海底輪，由於會陰穴又名海底穴，故借名用之。

   會陰：陰經脈氣交會之處，梵語 *Yoni*，有女陰、根門、子宮或胎藏等義。此處意指前陰與後陰之間的位置，動作有如收腹提肛。

2. There let him contemplate that the God of love resides in that Brahma *Yoni* and that he is beautiful like *Bandhuk* flower (Pentapetes pheanicia)-- brilliant as tens of millions of suns, and cool as tens of millions of moons. Above this (*Yoni*) is a small and subtle flame, whose form is intelligence. Then let him imagine that a union takes place there between himself and that flame (the *Śiva* and *Śakti*).

   接著觀想上主大愛居此梵胎藏中，是愛美若金午時花，燦爛若千萬個太陽，清涼若千萬顆月亮。胎藏之上有微細火焰，其形靈妙；復想像自身與火焰融而為一（表徵靈與力的結合）。

   梵胎藏：藏密謂此為生法宮，蓋生命之一切由此而生故。

   金午時花：錦葵科黃花稔屬植物，中午盛開的花種，陽光越強，綻放越燦爛。

   自身與火焰融而為一：自身意指 *Śiva* 或靈，火焰喻 *Śakti* 或力；靈與力的結合，亦即純淨識與造化力的結合。

3. (Then imagine that) – There go up through the *sushumná* vessel, three bodies in their due order (i.e., the etheric, the astral and the mental bodies). There is emitted in every chakra the nectar, the characteristic of which is great bliss. Its colour is whitish rosey

(pink), full of splendor, showering down in jets the immortal fluid. Let him drink this wine of immortality which is divine, and then again enter the *Kula* (i.e., perineal space) .

續想像所觀循中脈上行，三種精細體各安其位；大樂甘露自每一脈輪泌出，其色白裡透紅，充滿光輝，向下噴灑著永生之水；習者飲下此聖潔的不死甘露，然後再意返脊椎底端。

三種精細體：指的是人體除肉身之外的乙太體、心智體和星光體三體，乙太體最靠近肉身，氣場與身體狀態有關，連接海底輪；心智體顯示自我的想法和精神層次，相應太陽神經叢；星光體連接物質世界和靈性領域，對應心輪。

脊椎底端：脊椎最尾端的會陰處，屬海底輪範圍；靈能或說軍荼利在未甦醒前，蜷伏沉睡在海底輪。

Note: While these subtle bodies go up, they drink at every stage, this nectar called *Kulamrita*.

英註：當這些精細體上昇時，它們在每一階段啜飲的這種甘露，名為善甘露或俱羅甘露。

4. Then let him go again to the *Kulá* through the practice of *mátrá Yoga* (i.e., *pránáyáma*). This *Yoni* has been called by me in the *Tantras* as equal to life.

通過密音調息瑜伽的修煉，使所觀再次返回脊椎底端。我曾在密續中稱此胎藏等同生命。

Note: The followers of the left hand path or *Vam* margis as they are called, may cite these verses as their authority for their demoralizing and profligate practice, which however is not actually meant by *Śiva*.

英註：左道密宗的信眾可能會因為他們鬆散無度的鍛煉而引用這些經文，但實際上並非希瓦本意。

密音調息瑜伽：梵語 *mátrá yoga*，*mátrá* 的意思是數、量、度等，傳統上用來計算各種練習的持續時間，特別是用在生命能調息。*mátrá* 亦指印度詩學和語言學中用來衡量一個音節長度的術語，如梵文字母的聲音；將這些神聖具有意義的梵文音聲作特定的組合即形成梵咒或梵唱，故而密音調息瑜伽意指結合了調理呼吸，返聞秘音或梵咒的一種精細瑜伽。

密續：密宗經典。

5. Again let him be absorbed in that *Yoni*, where dwells the fire of death – the nature of *Śiva*, &c. Thus has been described by me the method of practicing the great *Yoni-mudrá* From success in its practice, there is nothing which cannot be accomplished.

再次，習者專注於彼胎藏，希瓦之性德——懲處之火，坐於彼處。此殊勝胎藏身印修法如上所述，由此修持功成者，無有不能成就之事。

懲處之火：又有時間之火、命運之火等譯名。在《永恆的希瓦》一書中解釋希瓦有五種面容代表希瓦從慈愛到憤怒等五種感化人的面容或態度，本節梵文用詞 *kálágni* 是指令人怖畏的面容，表示希瓦懲處用罰使人心生畏而改善的一面；故衍生出具有吞噬涵義的命運之火、懲處之火或原英譯所用的死亡之火等譯詞。

胎藏身印：屬密乘瑜伽身印，依法修持者可消罪解縛乃至獲得解脫。

6. Even those *mantras* which are deformed (*chinna*) or paralyzed (*Kilita*), scorched (*stambhita*) by fire, or whose flame has become attenuated, or are dark, and ought to be abandoned, or which are evil, or too old, or which are proud of their budding youth, or have gone over to the side of the enemy, or weak and essence-less without vitality; or which have been divided into hundreds of parts, even they become fertile through time and method. All these can give powers and emancipation when properly given to the disciple by the *Guru*, after having initiated him according to proper

rites, and bathed him a thousand times. This *Yoni-mudrá* has been described, in order that the student may deserve (to be initiated into the mysteries of) and receive the mantras.

即使所持梵咒已為火所斷、所縛或中止者，亦或其火焰已衰而暗淡者、被遺棄者、作為邪惡或年邁體衰者；或初露頭角而自得者、投敵者，或是欠缺活力而虛弱者、精神不振者；或是那些曾被裂解成碎片但已透過時間與方法修復者等等。以上所有，只要能得到上師恩典，在適當的規矩下獲得啟蒙，如是經過上千次的洗滌後，都可以得到力量和解脫。故此前所述說之胎藏身印，乃是為了那些值得(啟蒙而進入堂奧）並接受持咒修行的學人而設。

梵咒：協助心靈解脫的音聲，於靜坐中引領行人契入靈性解脫的梵音、聲音或梵唱。

所斷、所縛或中止：指所有因各種狀況不再適合修習瑜伽之人，若得上師恩典悔改後，仍得入門修習。

7. He who practices *Yoni-mudrá* is not polluted by sin, were he to murder a thousand *Brahmanas* or kill all the inhabitants of the three worlds.

習練胎藏身印之人不為罪業染污，即便他謀害了千名婆羅門或是曾斬殺過一切三界的眾生。

8. Were he to kill his teacher or drink wine or commit theft, or violate the bed of his preceptor, he is not stained by these sins also, by virtue of this *mudrá*.

若有殺師、飲酒、盜竊、或褻瀆上師坐床之人，依此身印，亦不為所犯罪行染污。

譯按：世法殺人者按律服刑抵罪，然真如德性人人本具，若蒙點化，斬殺心賊，復遷惡向善，化胸中戾氣為祥和，造福人間，則亦必能有大成就。

9. Therefore, those who wish for emancipation should practice this daily. Through practice (*abhyasa*), success is obtained; through practice one gains liberation.

是故，凡欲願解脫之行人應每日練習此身印；透過精勤的修行取得成就，透過精勤的修行獲得解脫。

精勤的修行：不斷地力求心理的平衡，以達定境的努力。

10. Perfect knowledge(consciousness) is gained through practice. *Yoga* is attained through practice; success in *mudrá* comes by practice; through practice is gained success in *pránáyáma*. Death can be cheated of its prey through practice, and man becomes the conqueror of death by practice.

大圓智慧是從修行獲得，瑜伽果位亦是從修行獲得；身印成就來自修行，經由修行得御氣成就；經由修行，死神可能受其獵物欺瞞；經由修行，人亦能成為死亡之征服者。

大圓智慧：悟見一切皆來自一源，皆此一源所化，復歸之一源；於此徹見本來無有生滅、垢淨、增減，始終圓滿。

瑜伽果位：原梵語 *Yoga*，瑜伽一詞字義為連結、相應、合一、融合，皆指瑜伽修行之果。

11. Through practice one gets the power of *vach* (prophecy), and the power of going everywhere, through mere exertion of will. This *Yoni-mudrá* should be kept in great secrecy, and not be given to everybody. Even when threatened with death, it should not be revealed or given to others.

經由修行，人可得言無礙成就，且具隨心意遨遊十方之力。此胎藏身印宜守其秘奧，莫輕意傳人；即便受到死亡威脅，亦不可泄漏或交付他人。

靈能軍荼利的覺醒

12. Now I shall tell you the best means of attaining success in *Yoga*. The practitioners should keep it secret. It is the most inaccessible

Yoga.

現在我要告訴你們達到瑜伽成就最好的方法，習者應保守其秘，這也是最難達成的瑜伽。

13. When the sleeping goddess *Kundalini* is awakened, through the grace of *Guru*, when all the lotuses and the bonds are readily pierced through and through.

當沉睡的軍荼利女神甦醒，透過上師的恩典，即可徹底貫通所有的蓮花和結縛。

14. Therefore, in order that the goddess, who is asleep in the mouth of the *Brahmarandhra* (the innermost hollow of *sushumná*) be awakened, the *mudrás* should be practiced with the greatest care.

因此，為了喚醒沉睡在梵穴（中脈最內層的孔道）入口的女神，修習此身印須極其謹慎。

梵穴入口：梵穴為頂輪的別名，入口處在海底輪。

15. Out of the many mudras, the following ten are the best: (1) *Mahámudra,* (2) *Mahábandha*, (3) *Mahávedha*, (4) *Khechari*, (5) *Jalándhar,* (6) *Mulabandha,* (7) *Viparitkarana*, (8) *Uddana,* (9) *Vajrondi,* and (10) *Shaktichálana*.

在眾多的身印裡，下列十種是最好的：(1) 大身印、(2) 大鎖印、(3) 大穿透印、(4) 明空身印、(5) 收頷鎖印、(6) 根鎖印、(7) 倒轉身印、(8) 揚升鎖印、(9) 金剛力身印以及（10) 力動身印。

16. My dearest, I shall now describe to you the *Mahámudra*, from whose knowledge the ancient sages *Kapila* and others obtained success in *Yoga*.

我最親愛的，現在要向你講述大身印，這是古聖迦毗羅和其他獲得瑜伽成就者所傳授的知識。

大身印：本式功能連結海底輪和眉心輪之間的能量循環，以疏通淤積的能量。

迦毗羅：印度好幾位有名聖哲的名字，最為人所知的是數論學派的創始人；不能確定是否與本節所指是同一人。

大身印

17. In accordance with the instructions of the *Guru*, press gently the perineum with the heel of the left foot. Stretching the right foot out, hold it fast by the two hands. Having closed the nine gates (of the body), place the chin on the chest. Then concentrate the vibrations of the mind and inspire air and retain it by *kumbhaka* (so long as one can comfortably keep it). This is the *Mahámudrá*, held secret in all the *Tantras*. The steady-minded *Yogí*, having practiced it on the left side should then practice it on the right side; and in all cases must be firm in *práṇáyáma* – the regulation of his breath.

依師指示，以左腳跟輕抵會陰，右腳伸直向前，再用雙手牢握右足，封閉身體九竅，將下巴抵胸。然後集中心念吸氣，以瓶氣法持氣於胸（在不影響舒適下儘量持久）。此為大身印，其秘藏於一切密續中。心思平穩的瑜伽行者，左右側應交互練習；進行生命能調息時，呼吸無論如何都必須穩定規律。

身體九竅：嘴巴一竅，雙眼、雙耳及兩鼻孔有六竅，前、後陰有兩竅，以上共九竅。

18. In this way, even the most unfortunate *Yogí* might obtain success. By this means all the vessels of the body are roused and stirred into activity; the life is increased and its decay is checked, and all sins are destroyed. All diseases are healed, and the gastric fire is increased. It gives faultless beauty to the body, and destroys decay and death. All fruits of desire and pleasure are obtained, and the senses are conquered. The *Yogí* fixed in meditation acquires all the above-mentioned things, through practice. There should be no hesitation in doing so.

循此方式，即使最魯鈍的瑜伽士都可能獲得成就。通過此法，身內所有的經脈受到鼓舞、攪動而活絡起來；能延年益壽、中止老化及滅除一切罪，亦能治所有疾病並增加胃火。此法帶給身體無瑕之美，滅除老死；獲得所有欲望和快樂之果，並控制感官諸根。已在冥想中得定的瑜伽行者，透過修持可獲得所有上述裨益，當毫不遲疑地如法而行。

19. O ye worshipped of the gods! know that this *mudrá* is to be kept secret with the greatest care. Obtaining this, the *Yogí* crosses the ocean of the world.

受禮敬的諸神哪！獲悉此身印的人應力守其秘。修此有成，行者即能橫渡世俗之海洋。

20. This *mudrá*, described by me, is the giver of all desires to the practitioner; it should be practiced in secrecy, and ought never to be given to everybody.

以上我所言之身印法，就學人而言是所有願望的給予者；應隱密地練習，切不可公諸於人。

大鎖印

21. Then (after *Mahámudrá*), having extended the (right) foot, place it on the (left) thigh; contract the perineum, and draw the *apána vayu* upwards and join it with the *samana vayu*; bend the *prana vayu* downwards, and then let the wise *Yogí* bind them in trinity in the navel (i.e. the *prana* and the *apana* should be joined with the *Samána* in the navel). I have told you now the *Mahábandha*, which shows the way to emancipation. By this, all the fluids in the vessels of the body of the *Yogí* are propelled toward the head. This should be practiced with great care, alternately with both feet.

繼大身印之後，前伸右腳，將之置放於左大腿上；收縮會陰，提引下行氣向上，使之與平行氣結合，復回轉命根氣向下；此時明智的行者會將此三股氣息匯合於臍，此為大鎖印功法，現在我所言之大鎖印揭示了解脫的途徑。透過此法，行者身內經脈中的所有精細之流都會導向頭部。練習此式需十分注意，左右腳交替練習。

大鎖印：又名大收束印；此身印能振奮精神，強化胰臟、肝臟和脾胃，有助改善腹腔問題。

22. Through this practice, the wind enters the middle channel of *Sushumna,* the body is invigorated by it, the bones are firmly knitted, the heart of the *Yogí* becomes full (of cheerfulness). By this *Bandha,* the great *Yogí* accomplishes all his desires.

藉此練習，息入中脈，身體精氣充盈，骨骼堅固密實，習者內心滿溢喜樂；依此鎖印，精進的瑜伽行者成就一切的想望。

大穿透印、大貫穿印、大中印

23. O Goddess of the three worlds! when the *Yogí*, while performing the *Mahábandha*, causes the union of the *prána* and *apána váyus* and filling in the viscera with air drives it slowly towards the nates, it is called *Mahávedha*.

三界的女神吶！當瑜伽行者於練習大鎖印時，使命根氣與下行氣相融合並注入下腹臟腑，並將氣息徐徐導向臀部，此稱之為大穿透印。

三界女神：吠陀系統則有空界、天界、地界等三界之分，演變為後世的欲界、色界、無色界或是意識、潛意識及無意識界；三界女神實際上即是幻化女神。

大穿透印：又名大中印、大貫穿印；此式用意在穿透海底根持輪，以助靈能軍荼利升起。本節所述著重在氣息的導引，今通行的做法是取蓮花坐式，兩臂貼近身體打直，以手按地撐起身體(臀部離地)，然後以手臂控制臀部向下輕拍三次，如是三回。注意臀腿應同時觸地，尾椎不可撞擊地面。此身印宜於體位法之後，靜坐之前練習。無法採取蓮花坐者，亦可伸直兩腿練習。

24. The best of the *Yogís* having, through the help of the *váyu,* pierced with this perforator the knot which is in the path of *sushumná*, should then pierce the knot of *Brahma*.

瑜伽行者中的佼佼者，能藉內息之助，貫穿中脈內的結縛，繼而穿透梵結。

梵結：根據瑜伽生心理觀念，在人的精細身上有三道結位於中脈之上，阻礙著靈能軍荼利或人體生命能的自由流動。梵結是其中使人擔心健康、死亡及過於倚賴物質等情由，來阻礙生命能沿中脈上行的第一道結縛，一般認為梵結位於根持輪和生殖輪一帶，又名會陰結。另兩道結縛是位於心輪、喉輪一帶的維世努結和眉心輪的魯德羅結，見《哈達瑜伽明燈》第四章 73 節和 76 節。

25. He who practices this *Mahávedha* with great secrecy, obtains *vayu-siddhi* (success over the wind). It destroys decay and death.

隱秘修持此大穿透印的行者，能得風大成就，可消除衰老與死亡。

26. The gods residing in the chakras tremble owing to the gentle influx and efflux of air in 。*pránáyáma;* the great goddess, *Kunali Mahá* Máyá, is also absorbed in the mount *Kailasa*.

行調息法時居於脈輪中的神祇因柔和的出入風息而顫動，大幻女神軍荼利亦因之而融入須彌山。

大幻女神軍荼利：靈能通過不同脈輪可能生起各種超然幻力，故名之大幻軍荼利。

須彌山頂：又名妙高山或蘇迷盧山，比喻人身中的須彌山——中脈。

27. The *Mahámudrá* and *Mahábandha* become fruitless if they are not followed by *Mahávedha*; therefore, the *Yogí* should practices all these three successively with great care.

修習大身印和大鎖印之後若未能繼之以大穿透印則無有結

果，因此瑜伽行者應悉心地練習這套身印組合。

28. He who practices these three daily four times with great care, undoubtedly conquers death within six months.

以十分謹慎之心每日行此三式身印四回者，肯定能於六個月內征服死亡。

29. Only the *siddha* knows the importance of these three and no one else; knowing these, the practitioner obtains all success.

除成就者外無人知悉此這三式身印的重要性；明乎此，行者能得一切成就。

成就者：修持一種或數種要法有成之人的尊稱。

30. This should be kept in great secrecy by the practitioner desirous of obtaining power; otherwise, it is certain that the coveted powers can never be obtained through the practice of *Mudrás*.

意欲獲得所修法力之行者應善守此法密意；否則，永遠不能從身印的練習中獲得所想要的能力。

明空身印

31. The wise *Yogí*, sitting in *vajrásana* posture, in a place free from all disturbance, should firmly fix his gaze on the spot in the middle of the two eyebrows; and reversing the tongue backwards, fix it in the hollow under the epi-glottis, placing it with great care on the mouth of the well of nectar, (i.e. closing up the air passage). This *mudrá,* described by me at the request of my devotees, is the *Khecharimudrá*.

明智行人於不受任何干擾處採取金剛坐坐下，雙眼凝注眉心不動；捲舌向上，固定於顎咽下中空處，小心地以舌尖封住口中甘露井（亦即封住空氣通道）；此即明空身印，為我應弟子之請而講述。

金剛坐：一種跪姿坐式，雙足置於臀下兩側，見《葛蘭達本集》第二章 12 節。

32. O my beloved! know this to be the source of all success, always practicing it let him drink the ambrosia daily. By this he obtains *vigraha-siddhi* (power over the microcosm), even as a lion over the elephant of death.

我最摯愛的人吶！明此即握有一切成就之源，經常習此身印者得日飲仙露；藉此習者獲得身成就（調控小宇宙身的能力），猶如獅子能收服死亡之象。

身成就：獲得調控自我小宇宙身的能力。

33. Whether pure or impure, in whatever condition one may be, if success be obtained in *Khechari,* he becomes pure. There is no doubt of it.

無論是淨是染，不論一時的狀況為何，若能從明空身印中獲得成就，習者即轉垢為淨，真實不虛。

34. He who practices it even for a moment crosses the great ocean of sins, and having enjoyed the pleasures of *Deva*-world, is born into a noble family.

習者即便只練習片刻也能跨越罪惡汪洋，受享天界之樂，並誕生於高尚的家庭。

天界：類似天堂的概念，這裡是指享有神性喜樂之處。

35. He who practices this *Khechari-mudrá* calmly and without laziness counts as seconds the period of hundred *Brahmas*.

以平靜及不懈怠之心修習此身印者，則歷百梵劫猶如剎那。

百梵劫：神話中梵天司創造，一梵劫等於 3.1104 億萬地球年，百梵劫相當於 311.04 億萬餘地球年。

36. He who knows this *Khecharimudra* according to the instructions of his *Guru*, obtains the highest end, though immersed in great sins.

依師教誨通曉此身印之行者，即使身陷大罪，也能獲得最高的成果。

37. O ye adored of gods! this *mudrá*, dear as life, should not be given to everybody; it should be kept concealed with great care.

受禮敬的眾神吶！此身印珍貴如生命，切不可輕意交付他人，而應謹慎地保持隱秘。

收頷鎖印

38. Having contracted the muscles of the throat press the chin on the breast. This is said to be the *Jalandhara-Bandha*. Even gods reckon it as inestimable. The fire in the region of the navel (i.e., the gastric juice) drinks the nectar which exudes out of the thousand-petalled lotus. (In order to prevent the nectar to be thus consumed), he should practice this *bandha*.

收縮咽喉肌肉，下巴輕抵胸部，此謂之收頷鎖印。此鎖印之效即使眾神亦難估量。臍胃之火（即胃液）飲下由千瓣蓮花所泌出的甘露。（為免甘露無謂流失），應習此鎖印。

收頷鎖印：又譯喉鎖印，中譯取其定式之形。

39. Through this *bandha*, the wise *Yogí* himself drinks the nectar, and, obtaining immortality, enjoys the three worlds.

由此鎖印，睿智行人親飲甘露水，得不老長生，享三界美好。

40. This *Jalandhara-bandha* is the giver of success to the practitioner; the *Yogí* desirous of success should practice it daily.

此收頷鎖印賦予習者成就，欲成就之瑜伽行人須每日練習。

根鎖印

41. Pressing well the anus with the heel, forcibly draw upwards the *apána váyu* slowly by practice. This is described as the *Múa-bandha* – the destroyer of decay and death.

仔細地將腳跟抵住後陰，通過練習促使下行氣慢慢向上提引；此謂之為根鎖印，是衰老和死亡的毀滅者。

42. If, in the course of the practice of this *mudrá*, the *Yogí* can unite the *apána* with the *prána váyu*, then it becomes of course the *Yoni-mudrá*.

若在練習此身印的過程中，行者能將下行氣與命根氣結合，那麼此鎖印即成為胎藏身印。

43. He who has accomplished *Yoni-mudrá*, what can he not accomplish in this world. Sitting in the *padmásana* posture, free from idleness, the *Yogí*, leaving the ground, moves through the air, by the virtue of this *mudrá*.

修成胎藏身印者，世上無有彼不能成就之事。取蓮花坐式坐定，抖擻精神，藉此身印益處，瑜伽行者能離地藉氣而行。

44. If the wise *Yogí* is desirous of crossing the ocean of the world, let him practice this *bandha* in secret, in a retired place.

若有明智行人欲橫渡世海，宜於僻靜之地，秘習此鎖印。

倒轉身印

45. Putting the head on the ground, let him stretch out his legs upwards, moving them round and round. This is *Viparit-kárańa*, kept secret in all the *Tantras*.

頭頸置於地，向上伸舉兩腿，然後反覆行之；此為倒轉身印，其秘藏於所有密續中。

倒轉身印：形若背立式。具體做法：仰躺，雙腿併併攏向上伸展，讓眼睛可以看到雙腳；雙手撐於後腰，肘尖與腳儘量在一垂直線上；跟眼睛輕閉，全身放鬆。確認太陽神經叢在頭頸之上。開始練習時先以七回為度。

46. The *Yogí* who practices it daily for three hours, conquers death, and is not destroyed even in the *pralaya*.

每日習此身印三小時之瑜伽行者，能克服死亡；縱使遭遇毀劫，依然不滅。

毀劫：巨大的毀滅，一個創造循環的結束。

47. He who drinks nectar becomes equal to *Siddhas*; he who practices this *bandha* becomes an adept among creatures.

能啜飲甘露之人即如成就者，而習練此鎖印之人，即為眾生中之能人。

成就者：修習瑜伽已獲成就之行人。

揚升鎖印

48. When the intestines above and below the navel are brought to the left side, it is called *Uddána-bandha* – the destroyer of all sins and sorrows. The left side viscera of the abdominal cavity should be brought above the navel. This *Uddana-bandha*, the lion of the elephant of death.

將臍腹上下之大小腸後縮〔拉向脊柱〕，謂之揚升鎖印，能滅除一切罪過及哀傷。腹腔後側臟腑應被提挪至肚臍上方。此鎖印被喻為能收服死亡之象的獅子。

揚升鎖印：此式做法需把胃向脊椎提縮，故又稱吊胃身印，是多數胃疾的妙方。今通行之具體做法：屈膝半蹲，雙手支撐膝上方；呼氣後屏住氣息，將臍腹吸貼向脊背，停留少頃，吸氣準備下一回。

譯按：英譯之意是將腹腸向左挪移，查原梵文經句中有 *pascima* 一字，字義是西側，對應人體就是左側；但此字又有後、最後的意思，故中譯未從英文，改採符合實際的譯詞。

49. The *Yogí*, who practices it four times a day, purifies thereby his navel, through which the winds are purified.

日習四次揚升鎖印之行者，可淨化臍腹，因之內氣亦得淨化。

50. By practicing it for six months, the *Yogí* certainly conquers death; the gastric fire is kindled, and there takes place an increase of the fluids of the body.

練習此鎖印六個月後，行者即得克服死亡；胃火復燃，身內體液亦獲增加。

體液：泛指體內各種液體，包含血液、唾液、精液、尿液、腦脊髓液、淋巴液及胸、腹、心包腔液等。

51. Through this, consequently, the *vigrahasiddhi* is also obtained. All the diseases of the *Yogí* are certainly destroyed by it.

由此練習，自然獲得身成就，行者所有身病亦必因之而除。

52. Having the method from the *Guru*, the wise *Yogí* should practice it with great care. This most inaccessible *mudrá* should be practiced in a retired and undisturbed place.

睿智行人應從師所教，謹慎勤習；此為最難成就的身印之一，宜在僻靜不受干擾處練習。

金剛力身印

53. Actuated by mercy for my devotees, I shall now explain the *Vajrondi-mudrá*, the destroyer of the darkness of the world, the most secret among all secrets.

出於對我虔誠弟子之悲憫，我現在將解說金剛力身印，此身印是一切秘中之最，世間蒙昧之驅除者。

金剛力身印：音譯瓦喬里身印，自本節起至 75 節為此法之述文。文中所述方法或過於險峻，不適用定力不足之行人。而可得此身印之效且又適合多數行人的做法如後：小解時，類似凱格爾運動，收縮骨盆底肌（如忍小便）並保持一段時間，然後放鬆。練習三次，這個動作可以在尿量正常、尿液清澈時練習。小便後用淨水清潔，以保衛生。

54. Even while following all his desires, and without conforming to the regulations of *Yoga*, a householder can become emancipated, if he

practices the *Vajrondi-mudrá*.

即使順隨所有欲望也未依循瑜伽規矩之人，若習此金剛力身印，身為一家之主者亦能自在解脫。

55. This *Vajroliyoga* practice gives emancipation even when one is immersed in sensuality; therefore it should be practiced by the *Yogí* with great care.

即使有人曾縱情聲色，習此金剛力身印之後，仍能得到解脫；因此行者應善加練習。

56. First let the talented practitioner introduce into his own body, according to the proper methods, the germ-cells from the female organ of generation, by suction up through the tube of the urethra; restraining his own semen, let him practice copulation. If by chance the semen begins to move, let him stop its emission by the practice of the *Yoni-mudrá*. Let him place the semen on the left hand duct, and stop further intercourse. After a while, let him continue it again. In accordance with the instruction of his preceptors and by uttering the sound hum, let him forcibly draw up through the contraction of the *Apana Vayu* the germ-cells from the uterus.

有識之習者應先內照自身，依正確方法，觀想有蓮露自蓮瓣出，經精道向上吸提；不令精動，而習交合。若精動搖，則以胎藏身印令勿出精；續存精於左脈，停止進一步之交合。少頃，方再繼續。習者循師之指示，口出「吽」（*hum*）聲，同時提攝下行氣強力將蓮露從蓮蕊引出。

譯按：此法應是為有正常伴侶或有家室者而設。從本節述文可知此法為火中取蓮之險著，應懷中戒慎心，不宜輕易嘗試。由於所述不易拿捏掌握，出於擔心會誤導讀者及易生爭議之故，有版本不錄入金剛力身印。

57. The *Yogí*, worshipper of the lotus-feet of his *Guru*, should in order to obtain quick success in *Yoga* drink milk or nectar in this way.

行者頂禮上師蓮足，為能速證瑜伽成就，應依此法啜飲乳蜜。

58. Know semen to be moon-like, and the germ-cells the emblem of sun; let the *Yogí* make their union in his own body with great care.
知精氣若月、蓮露若日；瑜伽行者當以大戒慎心將彼二者合於體內。

59. I am the semen, *Śakti* is the germ fluid; when they both are combined, then the *Yogí* reaches the state of success, and his body becomes brilliant and divine.
吾即此精氣，造化勢能即此蓮露；當此二者相合為一，行者即入功成之境，現光明聖潔之身。
造化勢能：梵語音譯夏克提，最原初的運作勢能，造化即受此勢能影響的宇宙意識所化。萬物皆陰陽和合而生，其陽性或神聖男性形象的化身是 *Śiva*，音譯希瓦；*Śakti* 是其陰性或神聖女性形象的代表。兩者為一體之兩面，此一體即宇宙本體 *Brahma*。

60. Ejaculation of semen is death, preserving it within is life; therefore, let the *Yogí* preserve his semen with great care.
精盡則亡，精固則生；是故行者當以大戒慎心保守其精。

61. Verily, verily, men are born and die through semen; knowing this, let the *Yogí* always practice to preserve his semen.
誠然，緣彼精氣，眾生流轉生死；既明乎此，行者當常修習以護其精。

62. When through great efforts success in the preservation of the semen is obtained, what then cannot be achieved in this world? Through the greatness of its preservation one becomes like me in glory.
當通過非常之努力，成功地守護住精氣，那麼在世間還有何事不能達？緣此善護成就，習者將如我一般榮耀。

63. The *vindu* (semen) causes the pleasure and pain of all creatures living in this world, who are infatuated, and are subject to death and decay. For the *Yogí*, this preservation of semen is the best of all *Yogas*, and it is the giver of happiness.

此物質明點（精氣）是憂心老朽與死亡之世間眾生的苦樂根由。對瑜伽行者而言，此善護精氣之法是所有瑜伽中最好的，且是喜樂的施予者。

明點：明點是物質於修煉後的昇華，依其屬性有物質明點、風明點、咒明點以及智慧明點之分。明點是點燃內在光明的重要關鍵。

64. Though immersed in enjoyments, men get powers through its practice. Through the force of his practice, he becomes an adept in due season, in his present life.

或一時耽於享樂，習者仍能透過此鍛煉得到力量；通過鍛煉累積的能量，在此生適當之時亦能有助成就。

65. The *Yogí* certainly obtains through this practice all kinds of powers, at the same time enjoying all the innumerable enjoyments of the world.

透過此鍛煉，行者必能得到各種力量；於此同時，尚能享受世間種種逸樂。

66. This *Yoga* can be practiced along with much enjoyment; therefore the *Yogí* should practice it.

此為一喜樂充溢的瑜伽鍛煉，故行者得列入練習。

67. There are two modifications of the *Vajrondi*, called *Sahajoni* and *Amarani*. By all means let the *Yogí* preserve the semen.

金剛力身印另有兩種變化，名為忍法與化法；行者應透過一切方法存化精氣。

譯按：在《瑜伽明燈》中名此二法為俱生力身印與不老泉身印，然雖名稱相同，其所述作法頗有差別。

68. If at the time of copulation the *vindu* is forcibly emitted, and there takes place an union of the sun and the moon, then let him absorb this mixture through the tube of the male organ [urethra]. This is *Amarani*.

若在交合之時，明點強行而出，日月因而交融；將此融合之液由精道吸收者，是為化法。

69. The method by which the *vindu* on the point of emission can be withheld through *Yoni- mudrá* is called *Sahajoni*. It is kept secret in all the *Tantras*.

能夠於明點射出之際藉胎藏身印予以止住之法，稱之為忍法；其秘藏於一切密續中。

70. Though ultimately the action of them (*Amarani* and *Sahajoni*) is the same, there are arisen differences owing to the difference of nomenclature. Let the *Yogí* practice them with the greatest care and perseverance.

此二法最終作用相同，不同者只是名相上的差異；行者應以大戒慎心和鍥而不捨之毅力來從事練習。

71. Through love for my devotees, I have revealed this *Yoga*; it should be kept secret with the greatest care, and not be given to everybody.

出於我對弟子的鍾愛，故爾揭示此瑜伽之法；此法應以大戒慎心保守其秘，不得輕易傳人。

72. It is the most secret of all secrets that ever were or shall be; therefore let the prudent *Yogí* keep it with the greatest secrecy possible.

此法可謂一切秘中最秘之法，為此審慎之行人當盡可能地保守其秘要。

73. When at the time of voiding urine the *Yogí* draws it up forcibly through the *Apana-Vay*u, and keeping it up, discharges it slowly and slowly; and practices this daily according to the instructions of

his *Guru*, he obtains the *vindu-siddhi* (power over semen) that gives great powers.

行者於小解之時透過下行氣強行將之提引向上，並保持它向上，然後慢慢地將之排出；依師指示，每日習練此法，習者將獲得明點成就而得大能力。

74. He who practices this daily according to the instructions of his *Guru* does not lose his semen, were he to enjoy a hundred women at a time.

每日依師指示習練此法者，一時即使御百女亦不失其精。

譯按：本節經文後半句，或為昔時利誘王侯之譬喻，然已不合今日時宜。果真行之，益增心中漣漪、妄想，有若治絲益棼，反使修行之功退墜，與瑜伽本意相違。一切修行之基礎皆在「存天理，去人欲」，須先具備「無欲」或「不動心」之功，方得上乘成就，否則恐陷徒然。然若已具「無欲」或「不動心」之修為，豈有非份遐想？一有此想，即為欲牽而墜，遑論其他？凡事動機至為關鍵，經云「因地不真，果遭迂曲」，故莫為文字所欺瞞！

75. O *Parvati!* When *vindu-siddhi* is obtained, what else cannot be accomplished? Even the inaccessible glory of my godhead can be attained through it.

噢，帕瓦蒂！一旦獲得明點成就，還有什麼是不能成就的？即便是最難得的神性榮耀，也能夠藉之獲得。

力動身印

76. Let the wise *Yogí* forcibly and firmly draw up the goddess *Kundali* sleeping in the *adhar* lotus, by means of the *apána váyu*. This is *Śhakti-chalan mudrá*, the giver of all powers.

明智之行者會借助下行氣，力將沉睡於根持蓮花內的軍荼利女神穩定地吸引向上；此是力動身印，係一切力量的賦予者。

力動身印：字面含義係指造化力之運轉，是喚醒靈能軍荼利之法。

77. He who practices this *Shakti-chalan* daily, gets increase of life and destruction of diseases.

每日練習此力動身印之人，能增世壽，祛除疾病。

78. Leaving sleep, the serpent (i.e. the *Kundalini*)herself goes up; therefore let the *Yogí* desirous of power practice this.

蜷曲的靈蛇（即軍荼利）因之甦醒上行，是故欲求成就的瑜伽行者應習此身印。

79. He who practices always this best *Shakti-chalan* according to the instructions of his *Guru*, obtains the *vigraha-siddhi,* which gives the powers of *anima*, etc., and has no fear of death.

依師指示，常習此上勝力動身印之人，可得身成就，具有令身能小等等之力，且無懼死亡。

80. He who practices the *Shakti-chalan* properly for two seconds, and with care, is very near to success. This *mudrá* should be practiced by the *Yogí* in the proper posture.

以精誠心，如法練習力動身印兩須臾，亦距成功不遠；行者須以正確坐姿練習此身印。

須臾：梵語 *muhurta*，漢譯須臾、瞬息或片刻。一日夜三十須臾，一須臾合現代時間四十八分鐘。英譯「兩秒鐘」，中譯從梵語漢譯。

81. These are the ten *mudrás* whose equal there never was nor ever shall be；through the practice of any one of them. a person becomes a *siddha* and obtains success.

以上即是前無倫比、後亦難覓的十種身印；透過練習其中任何一種，習者都能入聖得果。

入聖得果：意謂勤而習之者，皆能斷惑證真，入於聖位獲得靈性上的成就。

第五章

坐禪篇

Meditation

1. *Parvati*. O Lord, O beloved *Shánka*r! tell me, for the sake of those whose minds search after the supreme end, the obstacles and the hindrances to *Yoga*.

帕瓦蒂言：「上主啊，我最摯愛的吉祥主！為了那些有心追求至上目標的人，請告訴我，在瑜伽之道上的障礙與阻撓是什麼？」

吉祥主：希瓦的尊號之一，意思是給予幸福和吉祥的人。

2. Siva. Hear, O Goddess! I shall tell thee, all the obstacles that stand in the path of *Yoga*. For the attainment of emancipation, enjoyments (*bhoga*) are the greatest of all impediments.

希瓦：「諦聽，女神！我將告訴妳一切豎立在瑜伽道上的障礙；對成就解脫而言，世俗的樂受是一切障礙之最。」

世俗的樂受：梵語 ***Bhoga***，包括因利養、境界、富樂、樂具、享受、財利、資財等引起的苦樂；一般偏向樂受解。

世俗的樂受

3. Women, beds, seats, dresses, and riches are obstacles to *Yoga*. Betels, dainty dishes, carriages, kingdoms, lordliness and powers; gold, silver, as well as copper, gems, aloe wood, and kine; learning the *Vedas* and *Shástras;* dancing, singing and ornaments; harp, flute and drum; riding on elephants and horses; wives and children, worldly enjoyments; all these are so many impediments. These are the obstacles which arise from *bhoga* (enjoyment). Hear now the impediments which arise from ritualistic religion.

女色、寢床、座席、衣著與財富形成瑜伽道上的障礙；荖藤、佳餚、車乘、王國、權勢與勢力；金銀與銅、珠寶、沉香、沉香、以及乳牛；學習四吠陀和經書；舞蹈、歌唱和裝飾；豎琴、長笛和鼓樂；乘象與騎馬；妻侶和子女、世俗的樂趣；以上總總所有都是妨礙，都是從樂受滋生的障礙。現在諦聽自儀式性宗教形成的障礙。

女色：現男女平權，所以也有可能是男色。

宗教儀式

4. The following are the obstacles which dharma interposes: ablutions, worship of deities, observing the sacred days of the moon, fire sacrifice, hankering after *moksha*, vows and penances, fasts, religious observances, silence, the ascetic practices, contemplation and the object of contemplation, mantras, and alms-giving, world-wide fame, excavating and endowing of tanks, wells, ponds, convents and groves；sacrifices, vows of starvation, *Chandrayana*, and pilgrimages.

以下是宗教法儀形成的障礙：洗禮、拜神、擇日、火祭、熱衷解脫、誓言和懺悔，齋戒禁食、宗教典儀、誓禁語、行苦行，冥想與觀想、梵唱、布施、聲譽，鑿建水塘、掘井、挖池，建廟和造林；獻祭、自誓餓苦、新月禁食和參拜朝聖等。

知識障

5. Now I shall describe, O *Párvati*, the obstacles which arise from knowledge. Sitting in the *gomukh* posture and practicing *dhauti* (washing the intestines by *Haṭha Yoga*). Knowledge of the distribution of the *nádis* (the vessels of the human body), learning of *pratyáhára* (subjugation of the senses), trying to awaken the *kundalini* force, by moving quickly the belly (a process of *Haṭha Yoga*), entering into the path of the *indriyas,* and knowledge of the action of the *nádi*s; these are the obstacles. Now listen to the mistaken notions of diet, O *Párvati*.

帕瓦蒂啊！現在我再講述從知識形成的障礙。採牛面式坐姿進行淨胃法的練習，經脈分佈的知識，學習內攝感官，嘗試喚醒靈能軍荼利之力，快速的鼓盪腹腸（哈達瑜伽的過程），進入知作根之路，以及認識經脈的循行等等；這些都是障礙。帕瓦蒂啊！現在留心傾聽飲食的錯誤觀點。

牛面式：見《哈達瑜伽明燈》第一章 20 節、《葛蘭達本集》第二章 16 節。

淨胃法：見《哈達瑜伽明燈》第二章 24 節及《葛蘭達本集》第一章 13 節。

內攝感官：瑜伽八支功法的第五支，將心思從外在客體收回轉向內在。

鼓盪腹腸：類似哈達瑜伽中的腹腔提挪法，見《哈達瑜伽明燈》第二章 23 節及《葛蘭達本集》第一章 52 節。

知作根：五種感覺器官與五種運動器官的總稱。

譯按：知識不是障礙、執著知識、搞混重點才會成為障礙。

6. That *samádhi* (trance) can be at once induced by drinking certain new chemical essences and by eating certain kinds of food, is a mistake. Now hear about the mistaken notion of the influence of company.

   認為可以藉飲用新奇或特製的藥飲或食用某些神奇的飲食就能立即誘發出三摩地是錯誤的。現在注意諦聽有關友伴影響的錯誤觀念。

7. "Keep the company of the virtuous, and avoid that of the vicious" (is a mistaken notion). Measuring the heaviness and lightness of the inspired expired air (is an erroneous idea).

   「結交益友，迴避損友」，不時察度出入息的粗細。（以上非是正確的想法）

   譯按：修行有不同的階段及不同的課題，故修法亦隨之有所變通。

8. *Brahman* is in the body or He is the maker of form, or He has a form, or He has no form, or He is everything – all these consoling doctrines are obstacles. Such notions are impediments in the shape of *Jnána* (knowledge).

   梵隱於身內，祂是形色的創造者，或說祂有形象，或說祂無形象，或說祂即是一切；所有這些撫慰性質的教義都是障礙，類似這些觀念是隱藏在知識外衣下的障礙。

梵：探其義，近代較易理解之詞為：本體、宇宙本體或至上本體。

知識：本義是指屬靈的知識，向心的知識，導引人走向自在解脫的知識。

瑜伽的分類

9. The *Yoga* is of four kinds: First *mantrayoga*, second *Haṭha Yoga* , third *layayoga*, fourth *rájayoga*, which discards duality.

瑜伽有四種：一是梵唱瑜伽，二是哈達瑜伽，三是深定瑜伽，四是勝王瑜伽；這四種瑜伽都捨棄了二元性。

梵唱瑜伽：一名真言瑜伽，但本節是指以特定的梵唱，幫助進入靈性修持之門的瑜伽法。

哈達瑜伽：調和體內陰陽、注重身心淨化的鍛煉，以心力控制能量的鍛煉，是進入勝王瑜伽的築基練習。

深定瑜伽：心住冥想目標而不動的瑜伽，其他譯名有禪定瑜伽、融入瑜伽、止寂瑜伽等。

勝王瑜伽：透過瑜伽八支法門，控制內在能量，使心靈由物質導向心理，由心理導向靈性目標的瑜伽修持。

靈修者、志道者

10. Know that aspirants are of four orders – mild, moderate, ardent and the most ardent – the best who can cross the ocean of the world.

靈修者可分為四類：下品、中品、上品以及能夠穿越塵世汪洋的上上品。

下品：意指世業較重之族群。

中品：本義為其次的、其上的。

上品：本義是少分、微少的。

上上品：義有增上、上上、上上品等。

適合梵唱瑜伽者

11. Men of small enterprise, oblivious, sickly and finding faults with the teachers; avaricious, sinful, gourmands, and attached helplessly to their wives; fickle, timid, diseased, not independent, and cruel; those whose characters are bad and who are weak – know all the above to be mild *sádhaks*. With great efforts such men succeed in twelve years; them the teachers should know fit for *mantrayoga*.

進取心薄弱、不用心、體弱多病及挑剔師長；貪心、作惡多端、講究美食、無助且需依附妻子者；三心二意、羞怯、病患、無法獨立及殘暴之人，品性不佳和軟弱之人等，所有上述之人是為下品修士。如是之人憑著不懈的努力，可在十二年內成就；為其師者應知他們適合以梵唱瑜伽修行。

適合深定瑜伽者

12. Liberal-minded, merciful, desirous of virtue, sweet in their speech; who never go to extremes in any undertaking – these are the middling. These are to be initiated by the teacher in *layayoga*.

思想開明、仁慈、渴望美德、說話甜美、任何情況不走極端，這是中品修士；應由其師啟蒙教以甚深禪定瑜伽。

適合哈達瑜伽者

13. Steady minded, knowing the *Laya-Yoga*, independent, full of energy, magnanimous, full of sympathy, forgiving, truthful, courageous, full of faith, worshippers of the lotus-feet of their *Gurus*, engaged always in the practice of *Yoga* – know such men to be *adhimatra*. They obtain success in the practice of *Yoga* within six years, and ought to be initiated in *Haṭha Yoga* and its branches.

心思堅定、熟悉深定瑜伽、獨立、活力充沛、心量寬宏、富同情心、體諒、真誠、勇敢、充滿著信心、禮敬上師蓮足、練習瑜伽不輟；這種行人可以成為上上品修士。他們持續修業六年即可獲得瑜伽成就，可於哈達瑜伽及其分支中取得進級啟蒙。

有資格修習任何一種瑜伽者

14. Those who have the largest amount of energy, are enterprising, engaging, heroic, who know the *Shástras*, and are persevering, free from the effects of blind emotions, and, not easily confused, who are in the prime of their youth, moderate in their diet, rulers of their senses, fearless, clean, skillful, charitable, a help to all; competent, firm, talented, contented, forgiving, good-natured, religious, who keep their endeavors secret, of sweet speech, peaceful, who have faith in scriptures and are worshippers of God and *Guru*, who are averse to fritter away their time in society, and are free from any grievous malady, who are acquainted with the duties of the *adhimátra*, and are the practitioners of every kind of *Yoga* --undoubtedly, they obtain success in three years; they are entitled to be initiated in all kinds of *Yoga*, without any hesitation.

那些精力充沛、積極進取、有吸引力且勇敢無懼的人；他們熟知經典，堅定不撓、不受盲目情緒的影響，不易困惑；處於年輕或鼎盛時期，飲食適度，能控制自己感官，無有恐懼、潔淨、靈巧、富憐憫心，樂於助人；能幹、堅定、有才華，知足、體諒、和善、有信仰，保守成就的秘密，言語甜美，平靜，對經典有信心且禮敬上主和上師；不喜虛耗時光在無謂的社會活動上，沒有嚴重的病症；熟悉上上品修士的本份，且可能是每一種瑜伽的修習者，則毫無疑問的，在三年之內他們會獲得成就。此時毋須猶豫，他們隨時可以接受任何一種瑜伽啟蒙。

召喚神性影現

15. The invocation of *Pratika* (shadow) gives to the devotee the objects seen as well as unseen; undoubtedly, by its very sight, a man becomes pure.

召喚神性影現賦予虔誠者見及不可見的事物；無疑地，通過所見，修習者因之淨化。

召喚神性影現：是一種通過精誠的召喚，照見內在神性的鍛煉。類如映晴空於心，見己身真性亦如朗朗虛空。

16. In a clear sun-lit sky, behold with a steady gaze your own divine reflection; whenever this is seen even for a single second in the sky, you behold God at once in the sky.

在晴朗的藍天之中，安定的凝視著自己的神性映像；不論在空中看到什麼，即便只是一秒鐘，你已在空中瞥見了神性的映現。

17. He who daily sees his shadow in the sky, will get his years increased and will never die an accidental death.

每日於空中見己神性映像者，能增世壽，而且永遠不會意外亡故。

18. When the shadow is seen fully reflected in the field of the sky, then he obtains victory; and conquering the *váyu*, he goes everywhere.

當在天空之中能照見完整的神性映像時，習者即獲勝利；並得征服風元素，其人隨處可去。

如何召喚

18b. At the time of the rising sun, or by moon, let him steadily fix his gaze on the neck of the shadow he throws; then, after sometime, let him look into the sky; if he sees a full grey shadow in the sky, it is auspicious.

在太陽或月亮升起之時，習者凝神靜觀自己所投射出的神性映像；稍待片刻，視線轉向天空，若他能於空中見著灰色全影，是為吉兆之象。

19. He who always practices this and knows the *Paramátma*, becomes fully happy, through the grace of his shadow.

常修習此法且知悉最高自性之人，透過己身神性映像的恩典，內在喜樂滿盈。

最高自性：即至上靈魂，至上真我，至上意識。

20. At the time of commencing travel, marriage, or auspicious work, or when in trouble, it is of great use. This invocation of the shadow destroys sins and increases virtue.

在旅行、婚姻、吉慶、或陷入困境時，此法有其大用，具有去惡增善之功。

21. By practicing it always, he begins at last to see it in his heart, and the persevering *Yogí* gets liberation.

常行此法之人，內心終必得見內在神性，信受奉行之瑜伽士如是而得解脫。

胎藏心印

22. Let him close the ears with his thumbs, the eyes with index fingers, the nostrils with the middle fingers, and with the reaming four fingers let him press together the upper and lower lips. The *Yogí*, by having thus firmly confined the air, sees his soul in the shape of light.

以雙手拇指封閉兩耳，兩食指封閉雙眼，中指按住兩側鼻翼，餘四指分別按壓於上下唇兩邊；瑜伽行者以此法穩定地調節氣息，得於光中內見其自性。

自性：同義詞有靈魂、淨識、真我、真性等。

譯按：本節所述以指封閉七竅之身印，亦名閉七竅身印或六頭戰神身印。

23. When one sees, without obstruction, this light for even a moment, becoming free from sin, he reaches the highest end.

當行者親見（自性）無礙，即便靈光瞬間即沒，亦能不受罪染，而達到最高目標。

24. The *Yogí*, free from sin, and practicing this continually, forgets his physical, subtle and causal bodies, and becomes one with that soul.

不受罪染且修習此法不輟之行者，漸忘卻其物質身、精細身和致因身，而與其自性合一。

25. He who practices this in secrecy, is absorbed in the *Brahman*, though he had been engaged in sinful works.

認真修習此法者，雖曾行罪業，仍得入定於本體實相。

26. This should be kept secret; it at once produces conviction; it gives *nirvana* to mankind. This is my most beloved *Yoga*. From practicing this gradually, the *Yogí* begins to hear the mystic sounds (*nádas*).

此法應予保密，它能使人立生敬信，帶給世人涅槃；是為吾所最心愛之瑜伽，漸次如法修習之行人，得聞秘密音聲。

涅槃：解脫、滅、無煩惱之意；從生死束縛中解脫。

秘密音聲：指聆聽到的內在或外在秘音，此字之本義原是指在宇宙循環圈中受悅性法則支配的無曲率音流。

虛空之聲

27. The first sound is like the *hum* of the honey-intoxicated bee, next that of a flute, then a harp; after this, by gradual practice of *Yoga*, the destroyer of the darkness of the world, he hears the sounds of ringing bells; then sounds like roar of thunder. When one fixes his full attention on this sound, being free from fear, he gets absorption, O my beloved!

初音若醉蜂發出的 *hum* 聲，其次聲若長笛，再其次聲若豎琴；之後，通過漸進的瑜伽修習，能破世間黑暗，習者聽到曉鐘之聲，復次雷鳴之聲；當行者全神貫注於此音聲時，恐懼不再，入於甚深禪定；是為吾之最愛。

28. When the mind of the *Yogí* is exceedingly engaged in this sound, he forgets all external things, and is absorbed in this sound.

當行者之心思，忘我的沉浸於此音聲中時，會忘卻一切外在情事，而融入此秘音中。

29. By practice of *Yoga* he conquers all the three qualities (i.e., good, bad and indifferent); and being free from all states, he is absorbed in *chid-ákás* (the ether of intelligence).

通過瑜伽修習，行人克服所有善、惡、分別等諸般習氣；擺脫各種情況的束縛，融入意識空性中。

意識空性：梵語 *chid-ákas*，由 *cid+ákása* 兩字組成。*cid* 意思是意識、明覺、清淨覺，*ákása* 是虛空、乙太、空元素的意思；此時瑜伽行人因身心清淨故，見本然意識如虛空般不受諸相影響，而入定境。

一大秘密

30. There is no posture like that of *Siddhásana,* no power like that of *kumbha*, no *mudrá* like the *Khechari*, and no absorption like that of náda (the mystic sound).

無有坐式如完美坐，無有力量如瓶息法，無有身印如明空身印，無有甚深禪定之法如秘音。

31. Now I shall describe to thee, O dear, the foretaste of salvation, knowing which even the sinful aspirant may obtain salvation.

親愛的弟子們，現在我要向你們述說「自在解脫之先修法門」；達悟此法之志道者，即使罪業在身亦能得到自在解脫。

自在解脫：人心融入天心，個體意識融入俱屬性本體，得大自在之謂；而究竟解脫的梵文是 *mokśa*，個體意識融入無屬性本體，與永恆真性融而為一。

32. Having adored the Lord God properly, and having completely performed the best of the *Yogas*, and being in a calm and steady state and posture, let the wise *Yogí* initiate himself into this *Yoga* by pleasing his *Guru*.

虔心禮敬上主，傾全力修習上品瑜伽之法，修習時保持寧靜與姿勢的安穩；透過取悅其上師，智瑜伽行人正其心意進入此瑜伽。

33. Having given all his cattle and property to the *Guru* who knows *Yoga*, and having satisfied him with great care, let the wise man receive this initiation.

將自己所有的畜養和財產供施通曉瑜伽的明師，悉心令師滿意，智者當如是接受明師的啟蒙。

明師：上師、導師之謂；字義是驅逐黑暗者，能引導弟子達悟目標者，亦是密乘瑜伽的必要條件。

譯按：捨卻帶不走的有限的個人所有，求得永恆宇宙無限本體的門鑰。古印度傳統將人生分為學習、家居、林棲、行腳四期，通常這是林棲期以後的作為，當然也有可能提早（詳《希瓦本集》第二章 51 節經句及註文）。

34. Having pleased the *Brahmans*(and priest), by giving them all kind of good things. Let the wise man receive this auspicious *Yoga* in my house(i.e., the temple of *Śiva*) with purity of heart.

供養婆羅門或出家僧所有好的東西，使其歡喜；願明智之行人秉持清淨心，在吾道院受學此吉祥瑜伽。

婆羅門：古印度四姓階級之首，此字之梵文本義是指以服侍上主或無上本體為生命職志或依歸之人；後來亦指乞法於天，乞食於人的出家僧。此一階級在古代印度有承啟天意的地位。

35. Having renounced by the above methods all his previous bodies (the results of his past karma), and being in his spiritual (or luminous) body, let the *Yogí* receive this highest *Yoga*.

如是透過前述方式散盡所有，所有習者宿世業身（累世業力的結果）化入其靈性光身，故瑜伽行人當接受此最上品瑜伽。

36. Sitting in the *padmásana* posture, renouncing the society of men, let the *Yogí* press the two *vijñána nádis* (vessels of consciousness, perhaps coronal arteries) with his two fingers.

於僻靜處取蓮花坐姿安坐，出世行人以其兩指按壓兩側唯識脈。

唯識脈：此處或是指頸動脈竇處。根據近代瑜伽大師艾揚格表示唯識脈是將生命能量傳輸至潛意識中心（例如丘腦）的脈道。然按壓此處有潛在的危險性，力度須非常小心，也禁止同時按壓兩側，故醫事上頸動脈竇按摩一般都是在指導之下進行。對頸動脈狹窄者、中風患者及頸動脈內有粥樣斑塊者忌按壓。從生理觀點看，頸動脈竇按壓可刺激副交感神經和抑制交感神經，緩解心跳過速情形。

37. By obtaining success in this, he becomes all happiness and unstained; therefore, let him endeavor with all his might, in order to ensure success.

依此法獲得成就者，內心清淨無染且充溢喜悅；因此，為確保成功，當全力以赴。

38. He who practices this always, obtains success within a short time; he gets also *váyu-siddhi* in course of time.

常行此法者，得於短期內獲得成功；假以時日，習者也能獲得御風成就。

39. The *Yogí*, who does it even once, verily destroys all sins; and undoubtedly in him the *váyus* enter the middle channel.

此法即便只有一次成功，也能滅一切罪；且其內氣亦必能行入中脈。

40. The *Yogí* who practices this with perseverance is worshipped even by the gods; he receives the psychic powers of *ańimá, laghimá*, etc., and can go everywhere, throughout the three worlds, at pleasure.

堅持不懈習練此法之行人，甚至受到眾神的景仰；他得到「能小」、「能輕」等等超然力，隨意能到三界內一切處。

譯按：「能小」、「能輕」等超然力為瑜伽八種神通或妙自在成就，詳見《哈達瑜伽明燈》第三章 8 節譯註。

41. According to the strength of one's practice in commanding the *váyu*, he gets command over his body; the wise, remaining in the spirit, enjoys the world in the present body.

根據行人修煉制氣而得之力量，他能夠控制己身；如是智者，安住於自性之中，以此身安享世樂。

42. This *Yoga* is a great secret, and not to be given to everybody; it might be revealed to him only, in whom all qualifications of a *Yogí* are perceived.

此瑜伽乃一大奧秘，非可輕意傳人；往昔只可能傳給身具瑜伽行者所有條件之人。

不同的執持法門

43. Let the *Yogí* seat himself in the *padmásana,* and fix his attention on the cavity of the throat, let him place his tongue at the base of the palate; by this he will extinguish hunger and thirst.

取蓮花坐式安坐，意注喉穴，舌尖捲置上顎咽；藉此可消除飢渴。

44. Below the cavity of the throat, there is a beautiful *nádi* (vessel) called *kúrma*; when the *Yogí* fixes his attention on it, he acquires great concentration of the thinking principle (*chitta*).

在喉穴下方有一條名為龜脈的美麗經脈，當瑜伽行者專注於此時，能獲得心靈高度集中的能力。

龜脈：位於喉胸區域的竇狀小管神經，是與聲帶有關的能量管道，亦有說其位於鎖骨中央凹陷處下約一英吋及往內半英吋處。《瑜伽經》第三章 32 節述及「依合參法集中此脈能令身心堅穩」。

45. When the *Yogí* constantly thinks that he has got a third eye – the eye of *Śiva* – in the middle of his forehead, he then perceives a fire brilliant like lightening. By contemplating on this light, all sins are destroyed, and even the most wicked person obtains the highest end.

當瑜伽行者持續思惟彼之第三眼——希瓦之眼（位於前額中央處的第三眼），他將內見有如閃電般的光焰。冥思此光，眾罪即消，即使最邪惡之人也能獲得最高目標。

第三眼：意指魯德羅之眼；魯德羅是希瓦教化人的五種面容之一，字義是能令人嚎哭流淚者，故亦是希瓦的名號。魯德羅之眼是指希瓦的第三眼，位於前額中央，神秘學認為第三眼是通往內在與更高層意識的入口。科學家不認為人有第三眼，也有人認為松果體即是第三眼。

46. If the experienced *Yogí* thinks of this light day and night, he sees the (adepts), and can certainly converse with them.

有此經驗之行人若晝夜繫念此光，即能見諸成就者，甚且能與之交流。

成就者：悟道者，已成就道業之人；亦指能幫助瑜伽士在修行道上進步的天人。

47. He who contemplates on *śunya* (void or vacuum or space), while walking or standing, dreaming or waking, becomes altogether ethereal, and is absorbed in the *chid-ákas*.

靜慮空性之瑜伽行人，或行或立，或夢或醒，全體是空，並融於意識空性之中。

空性：又名實相，萬法真實不虛的本相；意指萬法之本源，因緣而生萬法，然本質性空，不受萬法侷限・

48. The *Yogí*, desirous of success, should always obtain this knowledge; by habitual exercise he becomes equal to me; through the force of this knowledge, he becomes the beloved of all.

渴望獲得成就的瑜伽行者，應常思惟此空性智，透過規律的練習即能如我一般；緣此智之力，行者為眾人所愛戴。

49. Having conquered all elements, and being void of all hopes and worldly connections, when the *Yogí* sitting in the *padmásana*, fixes his gaze on the tip of the nose, his mind becomes dead and he obtains the spiritual power called *Khechari*.

已然控制了所有元素，放下了一切希望與世緣；如是行者以蓮花坐姿正念安坐，繫意鼻端，心寂若亡，即可獲得名為明空的屬靈力量。

明空：意指明空身印「內悟空性」的成就。

50. The great *Yogí* beholds light, pure as holy mountain (*Kailás*), and through the force of his exercise in it, he becomes the lord and guardian of the light.

大瑜伽行人觀此淨光，潔若聖妙高峰，通過從修煉中所得之力，他成為此光的主人及護衛。

51. Stretching himself on the ground, let him contemplate on this light; by so doing all his weariness and fatigue are destroyed. By contemplating on the back part of his head, he becomes the conqueror of death. (We have described before the effect of fixing one's attention on the space between the two eyebrows, so it need not be enumerated here).

舒展全身仰躺於地，默照思惟此光，由此可消除全身之倦乏。行者若能思惟其腦後部分，則能成為死亡的征服者(前曾述及習者定意眉心的效果，故此處不再贅述)。

思惟腦後：思惟腦後時的生理反應可放鬆頸椎部位，鬆開頸側血脈使血氣充分供給腦部，有助意舒神凝。

52. Of the four kinds of food (i.e., that which is chewed, that which is sucked, that which is licked and that which is drunk), which a man takes, the chyle fluid is converted into three parts. The best part (or the finest extract of food) goes to nourish the *linga sharira* or subtle body (the seat of force). The second or middle part goes to nourish this gross body composed of seven *dhátus* (humours).

有四種食物為人所取，食物成乳糜狀後被消化成三部分；其中最好的部分轉為根舍利或精細身，次等的部分滋養由七種體組織組成的粗重身。

四種食物：指咀嚼的、吸吮的、舐食的和啜飲的四種飲食。

根舍利或精細身：由精細脈組成，可增加感官潛能的微妙身。

七種體組織組成的粗重身：舊譯身界，根據印度之生命科學，七種體組織分別是：血漿、血液、肌肉、脂肪、骨骼、骨髓神經及腎精。

53. The third or the most inferior part goes out of the body in the shape of excrement and urine. The first two essences of food are found in the *náis*, and being carried by them, they nourish the body from head to foot.

第三或最粗濁的部分以大、小二便之形式排出體外。在經脈之中可以發現前兩部分的食物精華，這些精華藉由經脈之輸送，從頭到腳滋養全身。

54. When the *vayu* moves through all the *nádis*, then, owing to this *váyu*, the fluids of the body get extraordinary force and energy.

當內氣藉由所有的經脈運行通暢後，由於這些內氣，身內的體液得到非凡的活力與能量。

內氣：吸入的空氣或吃下的食物經由臟腑轉化而成的較精細

的能量形式。

55. The most important of these *nádis* are fourteen, distributed in different parts of the body and performing various functions. They are either weak or strong, and the *prána* flows through them.

這些經脈中最重要的有十四條，分布在身體的不同部位並執行著各種功能；無論這些經脈是弱是強，生命能都需藉助它們流通。

六脈輪

一、根持輪

56. Two fingers above the rectum and two fingers below the *linga*, four fingers in width, is a space like a bulbous root.

後陰之上兩指，前陰之下兩指，邊寬四指，狀若球莖根之大小。

57. Between this space is the "*yoni*" having its face towards the back; that space is called the root; there dwells the goddess *Kundalini*. It surrounds all the "*nádis*", and has three coils and a half; and catching its tail in its own mouth, it rests in the hole of the *sushumná*.

於此空間內之區域即會陰，其面朝背；此空間名「根門」，軍荼利女神居於其中。她圈繞著所有經脈，總三圈有半；口銜其尾，沉睡在中脈入口。

根門：據本文所述位在前後陰之間；此位置和《哈達瑜伽明燈》所述有別，《哈達瑜伽明燈》第三章 113 節謂其在後陰之上一掌高，類若丹家所言之下丹田位置。

58. It sleeps there like a serpent, and it is luminous by its own light. Like a serpent it lives between the joints; it is the goddess of speech, and is called the seed (*bija*).

彼沉睡該處若冬眠之蛇，以自體光明閃爍發光；彼如蛇般蜷居此交會處，彼是妙音女神，亦被稱作「種子」。

妙音女神：微妙的語言能力在吠陀文化裡被人格化成為女神，為她所愛的人提供表達和能量，而能說出如詩一般或啟迪人心的話語。她也是吠陀之母，因為時人認為吠陀是天啟的知識；在往後的文化裡，她成為學習及智慧女神。

種子：比喻四種生命根本心緒傾向——物質渴望、心理渴望、法性渴望及靈性渴望，隨著這四種渴望不同比例的發展，衍生出生命不同的景象，有如樹木種子根據環境及灌溉的情形發芽、成長為不同的樹貌。

59. Full of energy, and like burning gold, know this *Kundalini* to be the power (*shakti*) of *Vishnu*; it is the mother of the three qualities – *sáttwa* (rhythm), *rájas* (energy) and *támas* (inertia).

能量滿實如冶煉黃金，知此靈能軍荼利即維世努之力；此力亦是悅性、變性和惰性等三德之母。

悅性：造化力的悅性作用，喚醒從束縛中解脫的欲望。

變性：造化力的變性作用，保持心思參與行動的作用力。

惰性：造化力的惰性作用，創造所有因循成習的作用力。

三德：上述造化勢能所包含的悅性等三種作用力。

60. There, beautiful like the *Bandhuk* flower, is placed the seed of love *lam*; it is brilliant like burnished gold, and is described in *Yoga* as eternal.

彼處美若午時花，置有愛的種子「ळं -*lam*」，明亮若拋光之金，在瑜伽中言彼為不朽。

61. The *sushumná* also embraces it, and the beautiful seed is there; there it rests shining brilliantly like the autumnal moon, with the luminosity of millions of suns, and the coolness of millions of moons. The goddess *Tripúra Bhairavi* has these three (fire, sun, and moon) taken together, and collectively she is called the *vija*. It is

also called the great energy.

彼亦含於中脈之內，美麗的種子即藏於彼處，彼所歇處明若秋月，有光輝燦如百萬太陽，皓似百萬夜月。三明女神拜拉維集日、月、火三明於一身，總言之彼即種子，亦稱之為大能。

三明女神拜拉維：又名杜爾加女神。代表著生、住、滅之能力及毀滅之後的變革，亦代表著靈能的非常力量。

三明：英文括弧內註為日、月、火三明，有說是日、閃電、火等三明。三明於身內是指左、右、中三脈，於身外指的是代表物質界、星界和因界的三種光明，亦可說是地界、天界和空界的三種光明。

62. It (*bija*) is endowed with powers of action (motion) and sensation, and circulates throughout the body. It is subtle, and has a flame of fire; sometimes it rises up, and at other times it falls down into the water. This is the great energy which rests in the perineum, and is called the *swayambhu-linga* (the self-born).

彼種子賦予行動與知覺之能力，循行周身；其質精微，且具火焰；有時火焰上炎，有時下沉落水。此為暫眠於會陰根門的巨大能量，被稱之為史瓦央布靈根。

史瓦央布靈根：靈能軍荼利具有逆向而上的特質，而此逆向運動的起點，即名史瓦央布靈根，位於根持輪。

63. All this is called the *ádhár-padma* (the support lotus), and the four petals of it are designated by the letters *(v), (ś), (ṣ), (s)*.

此根門球莖名為根持蓮花，彼有四花瓣，瓣面有四字母。

根門球莖：此處未取英譯用詞，而採用梵語原作；梵語原是 *yoni kanda*，直譯即會陰球莖或根門球莖。

根持蓮花：即是有四蓮瓣之海底輪，為地大脈叢。

四字母：意指四花瓣每一花瓣有一字母；每一字母代表一種心緒傾向的音根，此四字及其對應羅馬拼音為 - ष（*ṣa*），

श（*śa*），व（*va*），स（*sa*）。見本章 58 節註 2。

64. Near this *Swayambhu-linga* is a golden region called *kula* (family); its presiding adept is called *Dviranda,* and its presiding goddess called *Dákini*. In the centre of that lotus is the *Yoni* where resides the *Kundalini*; the circulating bright energy above that, is called *káma-bija* (the seed of love). The wise man who always contemplates on this *Muládhar* obtains *Dárduri-siddhi* (the frog-jumping power); and by degrees he can altogether leave the ground (i.e., rise in the air).

在史瓦央布靈根附近是名為庫拉的金色區域，主理庫拉的男神名毗蘭達，女神名達吉妮。蓮花中心是胎藏所在，靈能軍荼利於其中深眠；彼處上方是旋轉著的光輝能量，其名為愛種。常冥思此根持輪，聰敏行人可得達杜里成就 ，成就深厚者甚至能全然地騰離地面。

庫拉：字義為根基，也有家族血統之意；生理位置意指脊椎尾端，薦椎第五節的位置。

男神毗蘭達：代表根持輪看不見但可感覺到的生理作用。

女神達吉妮：代表來自根持輪生理作用所起的心理變化。

愛種：梵語 *káma bija*，愛欲的種子，對有限事物或世間事物的欲望，達吉妮亦見於藏密，譯作空行母。

達杜里成就：一種身形輕捷，躍遠如飛的輕身成就。

65. The brilliancy of the body is increased, the gastric fire becomes powerful, and freedom from disease, cleverness, and omniscience ensue.

身體因之增添光澤，胃火也更有力，疾病難侵，人也更為聰明，功深者甚至能知一切事。

66. He knows what has been, what is happening, and what is to be, together with their causes; he masters the unheard of sciences together with their mysteries.

彼能知過去已發生之事、當下正發生之事和未來將發生之事，並且知其事因；亦能掌握尚未聽聞的科學及其相關奧秘。

67. On his tongue always dances the goddess of learning, he obtains *mantra-siddhi* (success in mantras), through constant repetition only.

妙音女神常於彼舌之上舞蹈，唯有通過精勤不懈的修習，行者才能獲得持咒成就。

持咒成就：通過持咒，喚醒靈能上升，克服或超越脈輪之心緒傾向之影響。

68. This is the dictum of the *Guru*: "It destroys old age, death, and troubles innumerable." The practitioner of *pránáyáma* ought always to meditate upon it; by its very contemplation, the great *Yogí* is freed from all sins.

明師有言：「成就彼法能滅老死，解諸煩惱。」調息練氣之士當常修此法；藉此非常之觀想思惟，大瑜伽行者得免於一切罪染。

69. When the *Yogí* contemplates this *Muládhár* lotus – the *Swayambhu-linga* – then, undoubtedly, at that very moment, all his sins are destroyed.

當行者觀想此根持蓮花史瓦央布靈根時，那麼毋庸置疑，於其時，所有彼之罪染已然消除。

70. Whatever the mind desires, he gets; by habitual exercise he sees Him, who gives salvation, who is the best both in and out, and who is to be worshipped with great care. Better than Him, I know none.

無論心中欲想為何，行者都能如願；透過經常性的修習，行人得見度脫者，彼是內外在最好的，最值得虔心頂禮；吾未見有能出其右者。

度脫者：給予、賦予或賜予解脫者。

71. He who leaving the *Śiva* who is inside, worships that which is outside (viz., worships external forms), is like one who throws away the sweetmeat in his hand, and wanders away in search of food.

內心疏遠希瓦，只敬拜其外在形像之人，猶如扔棄手中蜜果，然後外出漂蕩覓食。

希瓦：至上意識、無限意識的同義詞；或謂內在的自性或內在的至上意識。

72. Let one thus meditate daily, without negligence, on his own *Swayambhu-linga*; and have no doubts that from this will come all powers.

是故行人當日日思惟身內之史瓦央布靈根，不得輕忽；循此用功，毋庸置疑，所有的力量都將隨之而來。

73. By habitual exercise, he gets success in six months; and undoubtedly his *váyu* enters the middle channel (the *sushumná*).

透過日常規律的修持，行者可於六個月內獲得成就；且其內氣亦必能進入中脈。

74. He conquers the mind, and can restrain his breath and his semen; then he gets success in this as well as the other world, without doubt.

如是征服心靈，且能夠調御出入息及煉化其精之行人，可從此生以及他世中獲得成就，真實不虛。

二、生殖輪或自我輪

75. The second *Chakra* is situated at the base of the penis. It has six petals designated by the letters *b, bh, m, y, r, l*. Its stalk is called *Swádhisthán*, the color of the lotus is blood-red, its presiding adept is called *Bálá,* and its goddess, *Rákini*.

第二個脈輪位於前陰根部，彼有六片花瓣，瓣面閃亮著六字母；其莖稱自我座處，蓮花顏色為血紅色，此輪之主理男神名巴拉，主理女神為娜吉妮。

六字母：意指每一花瓣有一字母，每一字母代表一種心緒傾向的音根。此六字及其對應羅馬拼音為：ब（*ba*），भ（*bha*），म（*ma*），य（*ya*），र（*ra*），ल（*la*）。

自我座處：此處屬生殖輪（腹輪、自我輪）管轄。為水大脈叢，包含冷漠、恍惚、縱溺、缺乏自信、絕望、冷酷等六種心緒傾向，種子音根 *vam*。

男神巴拉：代表生殖輪看不見但可感覺到的生理作用，如性腺之作用。

女神娜吉妮：代表來自生殖輪作用所起的心理變化。

76. He who daily contemplates on this *Swádhisthan* lotus, becomes an object of love and adoration to all beautiful goddesses.

每日觀修此自我蓮花輪之行人，將成為受人愛慕的對象且易受到所有美麗天女的愛慕。

77. He fearlessly recites the various *Śástras* and sciences unknown to him before; becomes free from all diseases, and moves throughout the universe fearlessly.

行者能無畏地吟誦或講述經論以及前所未曾涉獵的學問，成百病不侵之身，無所畏懼地周行於世間。

經論：意指典籍、聖教、正論、諸論等；意指透過書中所述之微言大意能在解脫道上引領奉行者之典籍或經文，如吠陀、奧義書、往世書等等。

78. Death is eaten by him, he is eaten by none; he obtains the highest psychic powers like *animá, laghimá*, etc. The *váyu* moves equably throughout his body; the humours of his body are also increased; the ambrosia exuding from the ethereal lotus also increases in him.

死亡為彼所噬，彼為空性所吞，可得如若能小、能輕等最高的超然力量。內氣在彼周身均勻流佈，彼身荷爾蒙亦持續增加；從彼身內微妙蓮花所散發出的靈氣也因而漸增。

三、臍輪

79. The third *Chakra*, called *Manipur*, is situated near the navel; it is of golden colour, having ten petals designated by the letters *d, dh, n, t, th, d, dh, n, p, ph*.

第三個脈輪名臍輪，位近肚臍，其色金，有花瓣十片，瓣面各有一燦麗字母。

臍輪：此處為充滿秘寶之處，通名臍輪。為火大脈叢，包含害羞、酷虐、羨慕、遲鈍、憂鬱、暴躁、貪求、癡迷、嫌惡、恐懼等十種心緒傾向，種子音根 *ram*。

瓣面各有一燦麗字母：意指每一花瓣有一特定字母，各代表一種心緒傾向的音根。此十梵文字母及其對應羅馬拼音為 - ड（*ḍa*），ढ（*ḍha*），ण（*ṇa*），त（*ta*），थ（*tha*），द（*da*），ध（*dha*），न（*na*），प（*pa*），फ（*pha*）。

80. Its presiding adept is called *Rudra* – the giver of all auspicious things, and the presiding goddess of this place is called the most sacred *Lákini*.

臍輪的主理男神為魯德羅，是一切吉事的賦予者，主理女神是最神聖的蘿吉妮。

男神魯德羅：代表臍輪看不見但可感覺到的生理作用，如腎上腺等之作用。

女神蘿吉妮：代表來自臍輪作用所起的心理變化。

81. When the *Yogí* contemplates on the *Manipur* lotus, he gets the power called the *pátál-siddhi* – the giver of constant happiness, He becomes lord of desires, destroys sorrows and diseases, cheats death, and can enter the body of another.

當瑜伽行者觀修臍蓮花輪，彼可得博多成就：綿綿喜悅的給予者；行者成為欲望的主人，除憂祛病，欺瞞死神，且能進入他人之身。

博多成就：一種有能力控制欲望、消除悲傷和療癒疾病的成就。

82. He can make gold, etc., see the adepts (clairvoyantly), discover medicines for diseases, and see hidden treasures.

他具有點金等能力，還有超然的遙視能力，能應病予藥，且得見隱匿的寶藏。

四、心輪

83. In the heart, is the fourth *Chakra*, the *Anáhat*. It has twelve petals designated by the letters *k, kh, g, gh, n, ch, chh, j, jh, n, t, th*. Its colour is deep blood-red; it has the seed of *váyu- yam*, and is a very pleasant spot.

第四脈輪位於心口，名心輪。具十二片花瓣，其色血紅，瓣面各有特定之字母；中有風大種子音根 *yam*，是處非常悅人之所。

心輪：為風大脈叢，包含希望、憂慮、喚醒潛能之力、愛執、虛榮、良知、神經崩潰、我執、貪婪、虛偽、浮誇易怒、懊悔等十二種心緒傾向。

瓣面各有特定字母：意指每一花瓣各有一特定字母，各代表一種心緒傾向的音根。此十二梵文字母及其對應羅馬拼音為：क(*ka*)，ख(*kha*)，ग(*ga*)，घ(*gha*)，ङ(*ṅa*)，च(*ca*)，छ(*cha*)，ज(*ja*)，झ(*jha*)，ञ(*ña*)，ट(*ṭa*)，ठ(*ṭha*)。

風大種子音根：其音根的梵文是यं。

84. In this lotus is a flame called *vánalinga*; by contemplating on this, one gets objects of the seen and the unseen universe.

於此蓮花中有光焰名梵靈根，觀想此光焰，行人能取得可見與不可見世界之物。

梵靈根：梵語 *vánalinga*，原為象徵希瓦的特別石雕，此處代表相應希瓦的某種感應。

85. Its presiding adept is *Pináki,* and the *Kákini* is its goddess. He who always contemplates on this lotus of the heart is eagerly desired by celestial maidens.

心輪的主理男神是賓納吉，女神是卡吉妮；常觀想此心輪蓮花者，受諸天女所傾慕。

男神賓納吉：代表心輪看不見但可感覺到的生理作用，如胰腺等腺體之作用。

女神卡吉妮：代表來自心輪作用所起的心理變化。

86. He gets immeasurable knowledge, knows the past, present and future time; has clairaudience, clairvoyance and can walk in the air, whenever he likes.

彼可獲得無盡的知識，能知過去、現在和未來；隨其心意，即具有耳通、眼通之力，並能行於空中。

87. He sees the adepts, and the goddess known as *Yoginis*; obtains the power known as *Khechari,* and conquers all who move in the air.

心輪成就者能見諸神及人稱瑜伽母之諸女神，獲得明空之力，收服一切行於空中之存在。

瑜伽母：又名空行母；一般指女性瑜伽行者，本節或指有修持有成的女性修行人。

明空之力：能行於空中之成就。

88. He who contemplates daily the hidden *Vánalinga*, undoubtedly obtains the psychic powers called *Khechar*i (moving in the air) and *Bhuchari* (going at will all over the world).

每日觀想此隱秘之梵靈根，當可獲得稱作明空和地行之超然能力無疑。

地行：能遍行於世間及降伏野獸之能力。

89. I cannot fully describe the importance of the meditation of this lotus; even the Gods *Brahmá*, etc., keep the method of its contemplation secret.

我不能逐一盡述冥思此蓮花的重要性，甚至於梵天諸神亦不能，保守此觀想法之秘奧吧。

五、喉輪

90. This *Chakra* situated in the throat, is the fifth, and is called the *Vishuddha* lotus. Its colour is like brilliant gold, and it is adorned with sixteen petals and is the seat of the vowel sounds (i.e., its sixteen petals are designated by the sixteen vowels – *a, a, i, i, u, u, ri, ri, lri, lri, e, ai, o, au, am, ah*.). Its presiding adept is called *Chagalánda*, and its presiding goddess is called *Śákini*.

第五脈輪位於喉嚨，名為喉蓮花輪；其色猶若明亮之黃金，蓮瓣十六片，各配有一母音字母。主理男神名為恰嘎蘭達，主理女神是夏吉妮。

喉蓮花輪：為空大脈叢，包含孔雀、牛、山羊、鹿、布穀鳥、驢、象、唵、吽、將理想付出實現、世俗知識的表達、精細層面的福祉、從事高尚的行為、臣服於至上、令人厭惡的表達、甜美的表達等十六種心緒傾向。前七種只有聲音，如音樂的基本七音階。種子音根 *ham*。

十六母音字母：意指每一花瓣各有一特定字母，各代表一種心緒傾向的音根。此十六梵文字母及其對應羅馬拼音為－अ (a)，आ (*á*)，इ (*i*)，ई (*í*)，उ (*u*)，ऊ (*ú*)，ऋ (*ṛ*)，ऋ (*ṝ*)，ऌ (*ḷ*)，ॡ (*lrr*)，ए (*e*)，ऐ (*ai*)，ओ (*o*)，औ (*au*)，अं (*aṁ*)，अः (*aḥ*)。

男神恰嘎蘭達：代表喉輪看不見但可感覺到的生理作用，如甲狀腺、副甲狀腺等腺體之作用。

女神夏吉妮：代表來自喉輪作用所起的心理變化。

91. He who always contemplates it, is truly the lord of the *Yogís*, and deserves to be called wise; by the meditation of this *Vishuddha*

lotus, the *Yogí* at once understands the four *Vedas* with their mysteries.

常觀修喉輪者實為諸瑜伽士之先導，堪稱是睿智之士；藉靜慮此輪蓮花，行者可立即領會四吠陀之奧義。

四吠陀：吠陀原意為正確或真正的知識，又稱作明論或智論，印度古老的靈性文化遺產，最早是由阿利安人帶入印度。梨俱吠陀成書於五千至一萬五千年前，夜柔吠陀成書於五千至一萬年前，阿闥婆吠陀成書於三千年前，娑摩吠陀則是結集前三部吠陀中有關詠唱、音樂的部分成為第四吠陀。

92. When the *Yogí*, fixing his mind on this secret spot, feels angry, then undoubtedly all three worlds begin to tremble.

若瑜伽行者一心專注於此秘密點時感到憤怒，那麼所有三界肯定也會開始顫慄。

93. Even, if by chance, the mind of the *Yogí* is absorbed in this place, then he becomes unconscious of the external world, and enjoys certainly the inner world.

即使瑜伽行者心識是隨機融入此處，亦可息諸外緣，細啜內觸妙樂。

94. His body never grows weak, and he retains his full strength for a thousand years, it becomes harder than adamant.

彼之身體永不孱弱，且可保千年之充沛體力，其力更比石堅。

95. When the *Yogí* leaves off this contemplation, then to him in this world, thousands of years, appear as so many moments.

當行者從禪境中出定，於彼而言，雖所處世界已歷千年，顯現猶如剎那頃。

猶如剎那頃：梵文 ***manyato tat Ksanam Krtiı***。直譯「感覺上就像一剎那」。玄奘法師取經西域途中，曾遇過幾位這種入定僧。

六、眉心輪

96. The two-petalled *Chakra*, called the *Ajna*, is situated between the two eye-brows, and has the letters h and *ksh;* its presiding adept is called *Shuklá Mahakála* (the White Great Time); its presiding goddess is called *Hakini*.

眉心輪有兩片蓮瓣，位於兩眉之間，蓮瓣字母為 *ha* 與 *ksa*；主理男神名蘇卡拉摩訶噶拉，女神名哈吉尼。

眉心輪：屬月亮脈叢結，亦稱月亮曼陀羅。眉心輪包含世俗知識及靈性知識兩種心緒習性，唯後者與自性真常相連結。

ha 與 *ksa*：蓮瓣上對應的梵文字母是ह與क्ष。

男神蘇卡拉摩訶噶拉：神話上是大護法神，代表眉心輪看不見但可感覺到的生理作用，如腦垂體之作用。

女神哈吉妮：代表來自眉心輪作用所起的心理變化。

97. Within that petal, there is the eternal *bija* (the syllable *tham*), brilliant as the autumnal moon. The wise anchorite, by knowing this, is never pulled down.

蓮瓣中央有種子音根，明亮如秋月；慧智修士達悟之後，即永不退轉。

種子音根：眉心輪的種子音根是ठं（*tham*）。

98. This is the great light held secret in all the *Tantras*; by contemplating on this, one obtains the highest success, there is no doubt of it.

此廣大光明的奧秘保存在一切密續經典中；觀想此蓮輪能得最上勝成就，毋庸置疑。

99. I am the giver of salvation, I am the third *linga* in the *turiya* (the state of ecstasy, also the name of the thousand-petalled lotus). By contemplating on this, the *Yogí* becomes certainly like me.

我是解脫的賜予者，我是處於意識最高狀態的無限本質；冥思此蓮輪，行者自然能夠如我一般。

意識最高狀態：瑜伽哲學將意識分為四種狀態，分別是醒、夢、眠和此處所講的第四種狀態，亦即意識的最高狀態，又稱千瓣蓮境界。

無限本質：此處翻譯是採意譯，直譯的意思是第三靈根。此處靈根係指希瓦靈根，是一種石製的圖騰；圖騰呈陽物狀，分成三部分；底部三分之一表梵天，即宇宙的創造部分；中段三分之一表遍在天，表貫穿於一切受造物中的存在；頂端三分之一表希瓦神，即自性無限的本質。

100. The two vessels called the *idá* and the *pingalá* are the real *Varana* and *Asi*. The space between them is called *Váranasi* (*Benares*, the holy city of *Śiva*). There it is said that the *Vishwanátha* (the Lord of the universe) dwells.

此輪的左脈和右脈即是真瓦魯納與鄂西二河，兩河間之地名為瓦拉納西；有言此城市是宇宙之主維盧瓦納塔的住處。

瓦魯納與鄂西二河：瓦魯納河在瓦拉納西城之北，鄂西河在瓦拉納西城之南，兩河北自南流入恆河。本節言地理上的瓦魯納河與鄂西二河如同左右脈。

瓦拉納西：又譯貝拿勒斯；印度人認為此地是通往神的入口，又名光明之城、聖希瓦城。本節瓦拉納西喻眉心輪。

維盧瓦納塔：宇宙的治理者，主希瓦的別名。

101. The greatness of this holy place has been declared in manifold scriptures by the truth-perceiving sages. Its great secret has been very eloquently dwelt upon by them.

這處聖地的偉大已由領悟真理的先哲在多部經典中描述過，他們也非常詳細地辯論過其中的奧秘。

102. The *sushumná* goes along the spinal cord up to where the *Brahmarandhra* (the hole of *Brahma*) is situated. Thence by a certain flexure, it goes to the right side of the *Ájná* lotus, whence it proceeds to the left nostril, and is called the Ganges.

中脈沿著脊柱向上直達梵穴所在，從彼處透過一定的撓曲，達到眉心蓮花的右側，然後轉入左鼻孔，此路徑稱之為恆河。

恆河：印度的母親河，本節以恆河喻左脈。

譯按：左脈與心理導向靈性的活動相關，右脈和肢體活動相關，兩脈相繞中脈而上，終於左、右鼻孔。

103. The lotus which is situated in the *Brahmarandhra* is called *Sahasrára* (the thousand-petalled). In the space in its centre, dwells the moon. From the triangular place, elixir is continually exuding. This moon-fluid of immortality unceasingly flows through the *idá*. The elixir flows in a stream – a continuous stream. Going to the left nostril, it receives from the *Yogís* the name of the "Ganges."

座落在梵穴中的蓮花稱作千瓣蓮，彼中心處有明月安住。從月中三角處，涓涓不斷地有靈藥滲出，這股不朽的月露不絕地流經左脈；此靈藥形成一股綿延細流，流向左鼻孔，瑜伽行者名之為「恆河」。

104. From the right-side portion of the *Ájná* lotus and going to the left nostril flows the *idá*. *Varana* (the northward-flowing Ganges). It is here called

從眉心蓮花右側部分流向左鼻孔的左脈，此處名之為瓦魯納河（恆河的北向支流）。

左脈：也稱月脈，色淡藍；載送精細情緒能量的脈道，在心靈從事心理—精神活動時變得活躍。

105. Let the *Yogí* contemplate on the space between the two (i*da* and *pingala*) as *Varanasi*. The *pingalá* also comes in the same way from the left side portion of the *Ájná* lotus, and goes to the right nostril, and has been called by us the *Asi*.

行者冥思兩河之間的聖地瓦拉納西。右脈以同樣的方式從眉心蓮花的左側走向右鼻孔，我們稱之為鄂西河。

右脈：也稱日脈，色泥黃；載送世俗情緒能量的脈道，心從事肢體活動時變得活躍。

106. The lotus which is situated in the *Muúládhár* has four petals. In the space between them, dwells the sun.

位於海底根持輪的蓮花有四片花瓣，於其間空處，有日脈居於其中。

107. From that sphere of the sun, poison exudes continuously. That excessively heating venom flows through the *pingalá*.

從日脈轄域裡，接連地滲出毒液，此種過熱之毒流向右脈。

108. The venom (sun-fluid of mortality) which flows there continuously in a stream goes to the right nostril, as the moon-fluid of immortality goes to the left.

於脈河中接連沁出的毒液流向右鼻孔，猶如不朽的月露流向左鼻孔。

109. Rising from the left-side of the *Ájná* lotus and going to the right nostril, this northward flowing *pingalá* has been called of old the *Asi*.

從眉心蓮花左側升起走向右鼻孔，這條向北流的右脈被稱作老鄂西河。

110. The two-petalled *Ájná* lotus has been thus described where dwells the God *Maheshwara*. The *Yogís* described three more sacred stages above this. They are called *vindu*, nada and *śakti*, and are situated in the lotus of the forehead.

此具有兩片花瓣的眉心蓮花裡居住著大自在天。瑜伽師們還提及此處另外三種神聖的階段，它們是觀明點、聞密音和喚醒造化力，其位置是在前額的蓮花中。

大自在天：音譯摩醯首羅，意思是所有控制者的控制者，控制著宇宙的思想波，是有屬性本體的控制者，不受任何一切束縛的存在。

111. He who always contemplates on the hidden *Ájná* lotus, at once destroys all the karmas of his past life, without any opposition.

常於此神秘眉心蓮花輪靜慮之人，往世宿業當即消融，無有乖違。

靜慮：梵文音譯禪那，常見譯名有禪定、坐禪、禪思、思惟、靜慮、冥思等，瑜伽八支中的第七支。

112. Remaining in this place, when the *Yogí* meditates constantly, then to him all forms, worships and prayers appear as worthless.

安住此處，行人持恆地思惟，如是將視一切形色、禮拜和祈禱如草芥。

113. The *Yakshas, Rákshashas, Gandharvas, Apsarás,* and *Kinnaras*, all serve at his feet. They become obedient to his command.

藥叉、羅剎、香音天、飛天及緊那羅等，都隨侍在彼足前，聽候差遣。

藥叉：字義迅捷，護法天人之一；種類不一，能助有緣人，天人之一，又名嗜財天；生前正派心善，靈性修為亦深厚，常勸募為善，因常掛心為善所需，費心張羅，反離道旨漸遠，辭世後成為此類天人。

羅剎：字義可畏，護法天人之一，亦名護法神。

香音天：音譯乾闥縛，天人之一；生前受音樂藝術吸引，熱心鑽研音樂，能作美樂，臨終猶記掛於所好，辭世後成為此類天人。

飛天：天人舞者，有男有女，可飛天起舞。

緊那羅：天人之一，又稱慕美天；生前執著於身貌之魅力，熱衷打扮、穿著及裝飾，甚至祈求諸天護佑增益魅力，臨終猶記掛於所好，辭世後成為此類天人。

114. By reversing the tongue and placing it in the long hollow of the palate, let the *Yogí* enter into contemplation, that destroys all fears. All his sins, whose mind remains steady here even for a second, are

at once destroyed.

捲舌輕抵上顎內凹處，行者凝神靜慮，可祛除一切恐懼；即便內心只有瞬間安止此處，所有身負罪業亦得迅即滅除。

115. All the fruits which have been described above as resulting from the contemplation of the other five lotuses, are obtained through the knowledge of this one *Ájná* lotus alone.

靜慮前述其他五處蓮輪的所有結果，僅從這一處眉心蓮花的領悟，便能獲得。

116. The wise one, who continually practices contemplation of this *Ájná* lotus, becomes free from the mighty chain of desires, and enjoys happiness.

慧智者即是常於此眉心輪蓮花靜慮之人，得擺脫巨大的欲望鎖鏈而安享大樂。

117. When at the time of death, the *Yogí* contemplates on this lotus, leaving this life, that holy one is absorbed in the *Paramátmá*.

彌留之際，行者於靜慮此蓮花中辭世，彼虔誠行者即融入最高自性。

最高自性：原梵文譯名甚多，有無上大我、至上真我、至上靈魂、宇宙心靈運作的見證者等等。

118. He who contemplates on this, standing or walking, sleeping or waking, is not touched by sins, even if it were possible for him to do sinful works.

或立或行，或眠或醒，皆能靜慮此輪不輟之人，即使犯錯亦不受罪染。

119. The *Yogí* becomes free from the chain by his own exertion. The importance of the contemplation of the two-petalled lotus cannot be fully described. Even the gods like *Brahmá*, etc., have learnt only a portion of its grandeur from me.

行者需憑藉一己之努力來擺脫鏈鎖，故靜慮此兩瓣蓮的重要性言之不盡；即便梵天諸神，也只從我處學習到一部分它的榮光。

七、千瓣蓮花輪、頂輪

120. Above this, at the base of the palate, is the thousand-petalled lotus, in that part where the hole of that *sushumná* is.

在顎根之上，是千瓣蓮花，彼處有中脈之口。

121. From the base or root of the palate, the *sushumná* extends downwards, till it reaches the *Muládhár* and the perineum: all vessels surround it, or are supported by it. These *nádis* are the seeds of mystery, or the sources of all principles which constitute a man, and show the road to *Brahma* (i.e. give salvation).

自顎根部，中脈向下延伸，直至根持輪與會陰，所有的經脈圍繞著它或說由它支持著。這些經脈是神秘種子，或說是構成吾人一切要素的源頭，並且顯示出通往至上本體之路徑。

至上本體：包含了時間、空間，一切有無存在總稱；今名本體、法界本體，亦名宇宙本體。

122. The lotus which is at the root of the palate is called the *Sahaśrar* (the thousand-petalled); in its centre, there is a *yoni* (seat or force-centre) which has its face downwards.

顎根上的蓮花輪稱作千瓣蓮花，中有蓮座其面朝下。

千瓣蓮花：心理－靈性的神經叢，身上最高的脈輪，故又稱頂輪，相對應的生理組織為松果體。

蓮座：意指球形胎藏（能量中心），形似蓮蓬或花托；靈能軍荼利未達此處之前，蓮瓣是向下的。

123. In that is the root of the *sushumná*, together with its hole; this is called the *Brahmarandhra* (the hole of *Brahma*), extending up to the *Múládhár padma*.

彼處係中脈根，連同其口，喚作梵穴，向下延伸至根持蓮花。

124. In that hole of the *sushumná* there dwells as its inner force the *Kundalini*. In the *sushumná* there is also a constant current of force called *chitrá*, its actions or modifications should be called, in my opinion as *Brahmarandhra*, etc.

於中脈穴內有其內在靈能軍荼利居於彼處。又中脈之內尚有一恆定之力名妙色脈，我認為其作用或變化有如梵穴。

妙色脈：中脈中間稱梵脈，圍繞住梵脈的就是妙色脈，其外有金剛脈包覆。餘可參考《希瓦本集》第二章 18 節註釋。

125. By simply remembering this, one obtains the knowledge of *Brahman*, all sins are destroyed, and one is never born again as man.

單憶及此，人即能獲得本體之智，滅一切罪，不受後有。

126. Let him thrust the moving thumb into its mouth: by this the air, which flows through the body, is stopped.

行者可迅以拇指推入其口，如是循行身內之氣得以暫歇。

譯按：此節敘述甚簡，根據前文推斷，或是以拇指輕巧迅速地伸入口中（指腹朝上），封住喉咽之謂。此法未見於他處，練習需先洗淨指掌，以保衛生。亦有可能本節關鍵字誤植，拇指其實是指舌頭，伸入其口意指以舌頭封住喉咽孔穴，如明空身印之做法。還有一種可能，就是明空身印對常人而言頗為困難，故取此方便法。

127. Owing to this (*váyu*) man wanders in the circle of the universe; the *Yogís*, therefore, do not desire to keep up this circulation; all the *nádis* are bound by eight knots; only this *Kundalini* can pierce these knots and pass out of the *Brahmarandhra*, and show the way to salvation.

世人因此風息滯世遊蕩輪迴，瑜伽行者無意再陷此輪迴；

所有的經脈皆受八結所縛，唯有靈能軍荼利能穿透這些結使並通達梵穴，從而顯示出解脫之道。

風息：此處意指內息及身風，內息是由鼻吸入經肺轉化後供給身體的動能；一種是搧動心靈情緒，令心不安。通常前者曰氣，後者曰風，皆是生命能之作用。林語堂考證宋代文人蘇東坡曾習練瑜伽，留有「八風吹不動，端坐紫金蓮」之名句。

八結：本書全文未解釋此節所謂之八種結縛為何，然人生反應出來的障礙多以心結或情緒傾向為主，而這些心結或情緒傾向幾都是脈叢不平衡的反映，故推測八結或是指五個脈叢結（脈輪）及維世努結、魯德羅結、梵結等三結。

128. When the air is confined full in all the vessels, then the *Kundalini* leaves these knots and forces its way out of the *Brahmarandhra*.

當風息盡被封於所有脈道之內時，靈能軍荼利便能脫離這些結縛並迫使風息離開梵穴。

梵穴：至上意識與人身的接觸點，亦表示千瓣蓮花輪。

129. Then the vital air continually flows in the *sushumna*. On the right and the left side of the *Múládhár*, are situated the *idá* and the *pingalá*. The *Sushumná* passes through the middle of it.

然後生命氣繼續地流入中脈 。位於根持蓮花的左、右兩側是左脈和右脈，中脈則從左右兩脈中間穿過。

130. The hollow of the *sushumná* in the sphere of the *ádhár* is called the *Brahmarandhra*. The wise one who knows this is emancipated from the chain of *karma*.

位於中脈入口處之穴名梵穴，知悉此秘之智者即不為業識鎖鏈所拘束。

中脈入口處：原文梵語 *susumnádhárá*，*ádhár* 有口唇之意，故譯為中脈入口處。

業識：字義行為，又名業行或業力；集積過去無明煩惱招感或反作用力影響所產生的行為，此行為復形成未來的果報力量。

131. All these three vessels meet certainly at the mouth of the *Brahmarandhra*; by bathing at this place one certainly obtains salvation.

所有三脈交匯於梵穴之口，浸浴於此者必得解脫。

神聖的三河

132. Between the *Ganges* and the *Jamuna*, flows this *saraswati*: by bathing at their junction, the fortunate one obtains salvation.

在恆河與賈穆納河之間流著薩拉斯瓦蒂河，浸浴於此三河交匯處，即是得獲解脫之幸運者。

恆河：印度北部的聖河，也是印度的母親河，全長兩千五百餘公里。

賈穆納河：恆河支流，源於印度西北，和恆河在印北的阿拉巴哈德匯合。

薩拉斯瓦蒂河：傳說中位於前述兩河之間的神秘河流，已乾涸了四、五千年，今印度政府有計劃嘗試恢復。

133. We have said before that the *idá* is the Ganges and the *pingalá* is the daughter of the sun (the *Jamuna*), in the middle the *sushumná* is the *saraswati;* the place where all three join is a most inaccessible one.

前曾述及左脈即恆河，右脈是太陽神之女賈穆納河，其間之中脈則為薩拉斯瓦蒂河；當此三脈交匯處是最難契入之地。

134. He who performs mental bathing at the junction of the White *(idá)* and the Black *(pingalá)* becomes free from all sins, and reaches the eternal *Brahma*.

能將心意浸浴於此白、黑之交匯處者，即不受一切罪染，通達至永恆的至上本體。

白、黑交匯處：白喻水色清之恆河，供給精神性活動的能量；黑喻水色深之賈穆納河，供給物質身活動的能量。

135. He who performs the funeral rites of his ancestors at the junction of these three rivers (*Triveni*) procures salvation for his ancestors and himself reaches the highest end.

於此三河交匯之處舉行先人葬儀者，可超度先人，己身亦能達到最高的目的。

三河交匯處：此三河地理上的交匯處即本章 132 節註二所言之阿拉巴哈德。

136. He who daily performs the threefold duties (i.e., the regular, occasional and optional ones) by mentally meditating on this place, receives the unfading reward.

於此交匯處靜慮內觀，履行日常行、依例行和揀擇行等三方面職責之人，得不朽之勝果。

交匯處：此處交匯處指的是生理上三脈的交匯處——梵穴。

日常行、依例行和揀擇行：請參考《希瓦本集》第一章 23 節註釋。

137. He who once bathes at this sacred place enjoys heavenly felicity, his manifold sins are burned, he becomes a pure-minded *Yogí*.

曾於此聖地沐浴之人得享天界之樂，燒去眾多罪業，而成為內心清淨的瑜伽行者。

138. Whether pure or impure, in whatever state one might be, by performing ablution at this mystic place, he becomes undoubtedly holy.

無論垢淨，無論身處何種狀況，能於此神秘聖地淨身沐浴者，即可成聖。

譯按：正統瑜伽行人則常浸浴於此身內的聖河。

139. At the time of death let him bathe himself in the water of this *Triveni* (the Trinity of rivers): he who dies thinking on this, reaches salvation then and there.

臨終之時浸浴於此三河交匯處且命終仍繫念於此之人，即得解脫。

140. There is no greater secret than this throughout the three worlds. This should be kept secret with great care. It ought never to be revealed.

三界之內無有秘密大過於此，當慎守此秘，永不揭露。

141. If the mind becomes steadily fixed even for half a second at the *Brahmarandhra*, one becomes free from sins and reaches the highest end.

若能全心繫念此梵穴，即便須臾，行者亦不受罪縛且能到達最高悟處。

142. The holy *Yogí* whose mind is absorbed in this, is absorbed in Me after having enjoyed the powers called *animá*, *laghimá*, etc.

如是心靈融入其中之虔誠瑜伽士，在體驗能小、能輕等神通之後復融入於「**我**」。

143. The man knowing this *Brahmarandhra*, becomes my beloved in this world; conquering sins, he becomes entitled to salvation; by spreading knowledge, he saves thousands of people.

明此梵穴之人，成為世間吾之摯愛；彼能克服諸罪，成為授記解脫者；而透過知識的傳播，彼可以解救成千上萬之人。

144. The Four-faced and gods can hardly obtain this knowledge, it is the most invaluable treasure of the *Yogís*; this mystery of the *Brahmarandhra* should be kept a great secret.

四面梵王及眾神很難獲得此知識，它是瑜伽士們最無價的珍寶，是故當嚴守此梵穴之秘奧。

四面梵王：梵語 *catur mukhadi*，*catur* 字義四，一般認為四面梵王擁有慈、悲、喜、捨等四面特質；然 *mukhadi* 兼有面、口等義，所以此處也有可能是以四口宣說四吠陀的梵王。兩者分別象徵著功德和學問。

神秘的月亮

145. I have said before that there is a force-centre (*yoni*) in the middle of the *Sahasrára*; below that is the moon; let the wise contemplate this.

前曾言及在千瓣蓮中心有能量中心，於其下方即清涼月，明智行人當思惟此月。

能量中心：梵語 *yoni* 一字象徵意義很強，衍生出產門、根門、源頭、會陰、胎藏等義，視上下文用法而異。此處與前面 122 節一樣是指靈性能量的中心。

清涼月：就脈輪學而言，指的可能是月叢或眉心輪。

思惟：禪那之別譯，一般譯作禪定，通用譯名有靜慮、思惟修，皆有如法觀照，心一境性之義。

146. By contemplating on this the *Yogí* becomes adorable in this world, and is respected by gods and adepts.

緣思惟此月，行者漸得世人愛戴，且得到諸神與成就者之推崇。

147. In the sinus of the forehead let him contemplate on the ocean of milk; from that place let him meditate on the moon, which is in the *Sahasrára*.

行者當於額竇處觀想乳海，自彼處思惟千瓣蓮內之明月。

於額竇處觀想乳海：大海之意，喻由眉心處靜慮觀想而顯現的浩瀚境界。

148. In the sinus of the forehead there is the nectar-containing moon, having sixteen digits (*kalás*, i.e, full). Let him contemplate on this

stainless one. By constant practice, he sees it in three days. By merely seeing it, the practitioner burns all his sins.

額竇中有月，滿貯甘露，具十六光瓣，行者當思惟此無瑕明光。透過持續的修持，行者可於三日內見此光明；而僅是見此光明，行人即能燒去己身所有罪業。

具十六光瓣：直譯是具有兩對八瓣光芒，喻圓滿無瑕之光。

149. The future reveals itself to him, his mind becomes pure; and though he might have committed the five great sins, by a moment's contemplation of this he destroys them.

未來景象揭露於彼前，行者內心轉為純淨；即或犯下五欲大罪，若得片刻入定彼光，亦得消弭。

五欲大罪：意指因貪著色、聲、香、味、觸而執著於世間之財、色、名、食、睡；若是沉溺過深，即易涉險犯罪，甚至犯下瀰天大罪。

150. All the heavenly bodies (planets, etc.,) become auspicious, all dangers are destroyed, all accidents are warded off, success is obtained in war; the *Khechari* and the *Bhuchari* powers are acquired by the seeing of the moon which is in the head. By mere contemplation on it all these results ensue, there is no doubt of it. By constant practice of *Yoga* one verily becomes an adept. Verily, verily, again most verily, he becomes certainly my equal. The continual study of the science of *Yoga*, gives success to the *Yogís*.

所有天象轉為吉祥，所有危險都被清除，所有意外均得避開，戰場上亦常獲勝出，明空和地行二力因見此額竇中清涼月而成就。緣能融入所觀，所有這些成果隨之而來，真實不虛。透過不斷的瑜伽修持，習者逾趨嫻熟；此言實在，無有虛假，行人必當等同如我；如是不斷地參究瑜伽之學，必為行人帶來成就。

神秘的須彌山

151. Above this (i.e., the lunar sphere) is the brilliant thousand-petalled lotus. It is outside this microcosm of the body, it is the giver of salvation.

於此清涼月之上是為光耀無比之千瓣蓮花，位置在人身小宇宙之外，乃解脫之賜予者。

152. Its name is verily the *Kailás* mount, where dwells the great Lord (*Śiva*), who is called *Nakúla* and is without destruction, and without increase or decrease.

此處定名須彌峰，偉大的上主希瓦居於彼處，人稱不增、不減、不壞的納固羅。

須彌峰：又名妙高山，印度境內之最高峰；本節表人身頂輪之所在。

納庫羅：字義無盡的、無邊際的，希瓦的名號之一。

153. Men, as soon as they discover this most secret place, become free from re-births in this universe. By the practice of this *Yoga* he gets the power of creating or destroying the creation, this aggregate of elements.

行人一旦親見此最秘之境，在宇宙間即不受後有；通過如是瑜伽修習，行者可得此能生滅造化、能聚散五大元素之大能。

154. When the mind is steadily fixed at this place, which is the residence of the Great Swan and is called *Kailás*, then that *Yogí*, devoid of disease and subduing all accidents, lives for a great age, free from death.

當內心定持於此，安住於名為須彌峰之天鴻居處時；彼時之行人，無有疾病，免遭橫逆，長生不死。

天鴻：梵語 *Paramahansa*，象徵瑜伽最高成就、心中視眾生平等一如者之尊稱。

155. When the mind of the *Yogí* is absorbed in the Great God called the *Kulá*, then the fullness of the *samádhi* is attained, then the *Yogí* gets steadfastness.

當行者之心念融入於人稱庫拉的上主，即達圓滿三摩地，行者入於不動之境。

庫拉：字有多義，一般表示根基、族群、家世、家園等。在密續用詞裡，此字又指絕待圓融的陰性造化原力（*shakti*），偶爾此字會用來描述宇宙意識與宇宙原力合一的神妙經驗。

不動之境：內見自性不動之境。

156. By constant meditation one forgets the world, then in sooth the *Yogí* obtains wonderful power.

透過持續地觀照思惟，行者忘卻身外世界，得真實微妙能力。

157. Let the *Yogí* continually drink the nectar which flows out of it; by this he gives law to death, and conquers the *kulá*. Here the *kulá kundalini* force is absorbed, after this the quadruple creation is absorbed in the *Paramatman*.

行者連續地啜飲從彼處流出之甘露，如是行者生死由己，不再受造化力之影響。原蜷曲於此之靈能軍荼利已融入〔千瓣蓮花〕，四種根本心緒亦隨之消融於至上絕待之境。

四種根本心緒：梵語 *catur vidhá*，直譯為四種造作，即物質渴望、心理渴望、法性渴望及靈性渴望等四種心緒傾向。

融於至上絕待之境：形容此絕對待、絕能所、絕名相之實相境地。

勝王瑜伽

158. By this knowledge, the modifications of the mind are suspended, however active they may be; therefore, let the *Yogí* untiringly and unselfishly try to obtain this knowledge.

通過如是學問，無論心思如何活躍，其變化均得降伏，故而行者們當精進且不懈地悟得此門知識。

159. When the modifications of the thinking principle are suspended, then one certainly becomes a *Yogí*; then is known the Indivisible, holy, pure Gnosis.

當善變的心念消停，其人自然成為一位瑜伽行者，明了一切是不可分割的、神聖的、純淨慧智的。

心念：意表內心所起之種種念想、思緒。

160. Let him contemplate on his own reflection in the sky as beyond the Cosmic Egg: in the manner previously described. Through that let him think on the Great Void unceasingly.

行者於超越宇宙胎藏之虛空中靜觀所映，依前述方法，持續思惟無盡之空性。

宇宙胎藏：被創化出來的橢圓形宇宙，因形似卵且生生不息而有此名。

161. The Great Void, whose beginning is void, whose middle is void, whose end is void, has the brilliancy of tens of millions of suns, and the coolness of tens of millions of moons. By contemplating continually on this, one obtains success.

此過去、現在、未來皆無變異之無上空性，其光耀若千萬顆太陽，其涼淨又若千萬輪明月；不斷地思惟入於其中，行者即能獲得成功。

162. Let him practice with energy daily this *dhyána*, within a year he will obtain all success undoubtedly.

日日篤行，用心禪定於此者，一年之內必能得到所有成就。

163. He whose mind is absorbed in that place even for a second, is certainly a *Yogí*, and a good devotee, and is reverenced in all worlds.

心思若得消融於彼處，即便剎那，如是行人及虔誠者，能於諸世間受人尊敬。

164. All his stores of sins are at once verily destroyed.

一切過往諸罪亦必立等滅除。

165. By seeing it one never returns to the path of this mortal universe; let the *Yogí*, therefore, practice this with great care by the path of the *Svádhiśthán*.

若得親見空性即不再重返此生死世界，因此瑜伽行人當著意依此自我之道修習。

自我之道：梵文字面義為自我之居所，引伸為自我開展之道路。

166. I cannot describe the grandeur of this contemplation. He who practices, knows. He becomes respected by me.

此門禪法之殊勝難以言喻，有從實修達悟者，吾亦敬之。

167. By meditation one at once knows the wonderful effects of this *Yoga* (i.e., of the contemplation of the void); undoubtedly he attains the psychic powers, called *animá* and *laghimá*, etc.

依此禪法，行者迅即領悟此門〔空觀〕瑜伽之微妙旨趣；且必能獲得能小、能輕等超然之力。

168. Thus have I described the *Rája Yoga*, it is kept secret in all the *Tantras*; now I shall describe to you briefly the *Rájadhirája Yoga*.

此為我所講述之勝王瑜伽，其秘藏於一切密續之內；現在我將略說王中之王瑜伽要旨。

勝王瑜伽：一門控制己身內在能量，將之從身體導向心理，從心理導向俱屬性靈性本體的瑜伽修持。

王中之王瑜伽：一門控制己身內在能量，將之從身體導向心理，從心理導向俱屬性靈性本體，再從俱屬性靈性導入無屬性靈性本體的瑜伽修持。

王中之王瑜伽

169. Sitting in the *Svastikásana*, in a beautiful monastery, free from all men and animals, having paid respects to his *Guru*, let the *Yogí* practice this contemplation.

遠離人群和動物，覓一幽靜之修院，頂禮上師後，瑜伽行人以吉祥坐式安坐，開始修習此禪法。

吉祥坐式：詳第三章 95 節。

170. Knowing through the arguments of the Vedanta that the *Jiva* is independent and self-supported, let him make his mind also self-supported; and let him not contemplate anything else.

從吠檀多之論點得知，個體靈魂是無所緣止的，且令其心亦無所緣止，則思惟自淨。

無所緣止：意指獨立不倚，自在無著之安止心境。心無所緣止即無掛礙，然此境微奧，非是思量可得。

171. Undoubtedly, by this contemplation the highest success(*maha-siddhi*) is obtained, by making the mind functionless; he himself becomes perfectly Full.

透過如是禪法，行者必得甚深成就；一旦心妄湛寂，行人即得大圓滿。

心妄湛寂：內心染塵盡淨，湛然清寂之意。

172. He who practices this always, is the real passionless *Yogí,* he never uses the word "I", but always finds himself full of *Átman*.

如是修習不輟者，是謂真離欲之瑜伽行人；彼從不言「我」，然總能見及自性之圓滿。

是謂真離欲：意指如是行人，無有執著、疑惑，故為真離欲者。

173. What is bondage, what is emancipation? To him ever all is one; undoubtedly, he who practices this always, is the really emancipated.

何為束縛？何為解脫？於彼已無差別；如是不斷修習之人，無疑是真解脫者。

174. He is the *Yogí*, he is the true devotee, he is worshipped in all worlds, who contemplates the *Jivátmá* and the *Paramátmá* as related to each other as "I" and "Am", who renounces "I" and "Thou" and contemplates the indivisible; the *Yogí* free from all attachment takes shelter of that contemplation in which, through the knowledge of super-imposition and negation, all is dissolved.

彼為瑜伽行者，彼為真虔誠者，彼受到諸世界的崇敬；彼視個體意識和至上意識猶如「我」和「是」之間的關係；他已離捨人我二見，觀人我眾生無有二致。如是瑜伽行者出離一切，以所觀為安歇處；透過破除一切疊加假象的世智，一切歸真。

破除一切疊加假象：梵語 *adhyaropapavadabhyam yatra sarvam viliyate*。古吠陀觀念：心本清淨，因無明影響而生諸妄，諸妄即疊加於清淨上之念想，去此疊加之念想，即顯本來清淨。

175. Leaving that *Brahma*, who is manifest, who is knowledge, who is bliss, and who is absolute consciousness, the deluded wander about, vainly discussing the manifested and the unmanifested.

離開那顯現出的、知識上的、喜樂的、絕對意識的，以及那徘徊在迷惑中的、妄談其顯化與否的梵。

譯按：本節義涵是指離開那些無有實義，只存在於想像、言說和爭辯中的梵或本體。

176. He who meditates on this movable and immovable universe, that is really unmanifest, but abandons the supreme *Brahma* – directly

manifest – is verily absorbed in this universe.

於思惟中照見此動靜宇宙之真性本空，且不執著於此有相宇宙者，方是得大定之人。

177. The *Yogí*, free from all attachment, consistently exerts himself in keeping up this practice that leads to Gnosis, so that there may not be again the upheaval of Ignorance.

如是行人，離一切執著，持續傾全力依此通向直覺智之法修持，即可避免再次受到無明襲捲。

178. The wise one, by restraining all his senses from their objects, and being free from all company, remains in the midst of these objects, as if in deep sleep, i.e., does not perceive them.

明智者收攝所有外馳之官能，令心無掛礙，即使身處器世間，如處深眠境，常住無所緣。

179. Thus constantly practicing the Self-luminous becomes manifest: here end all the teachings of the *Guru*, (they can help the student no further). Henceforth he must help himself, they can no more increase his reason or power, henceforth by the mere force of his own practice he must gain the Gnosis.

如是持續修習，自性光明現前，即進入離師自修階段。此後行人不再有外力加持，唯有自助，亦即必得以自修之力來獲得直覺智。

180. That Gnosis from which the speech and mind turn back baffled, is only to be obtained through practice; for then this pure Gnosis bursts forth of itself.

從言說和心念而來的是困惑，直覺智只能從修持而得；待時機成熟，直覺淨智自會迸發。

181. The *Haṭha Yoga* cannot be obtained without the *rájayoga,* nor can the *rájayoga* be obtained without the *Haṭha Yoga*. Therefore, let

the *Yogí* first learn the *ha hayoga* from the instructions of the wise *Guru*.

沒有勝王瑜伽，哈達瑜伽無法有成；少了哈達瑜伽，勝王瑜伽也難以奏功；是故，行人宜先從明師指示修習哈達瑜伽。

182. He who while living in this physical body, does not practice *Yoga*, is merely living for the sake of sensual enjoyments.

寄居人身而不修瑜伽，是只為感官欲樂而活。

183. From the time he begins till the time he gains perfect mastery, let the *Yogí* eat moderately and abstemiously, otherwise, however clever, he cannot gain success.

從開始修行到能圓滿自主之時，瑜伽行人飲食應節度知量，否則即使再聰穎，也無法成就。

184. The wise *Yogí* in an assembly should utter words of highest good, but should not talk much; he eats a little to keep up his physical frame; let him renounce the company of men, let him renounce the company of women, verily, let him renounce all company, otherwise he cannot attain *mukti* (salvation); verily, I tell you the truth.

明智行人於聚會中應說上善之語，不宜多言；飲食知量以維繫身命；需避男女之嫌，如實離群索居，否則無由達到解脫；此實真理之言。

185. Let him practice this in secrecy, free from the company of men, in a retired place. For the sake of appearance, he should remain in society, but should not have his heart in it. He should not renounce the duties of his profession, caste or rank; but let him perform these merely, as an instrument of the Lord, without any thought of the event. By thus doing there is no sin.

避開群眾，於安靜處，隱密地修習此法。為觀感形象，行者應心無所住地留居社會。不應放棄己身之職責、階級與身份，且需履行本分所當為，視己有如上主之工具，於諸人事不起分別之想。如是行之即無罪疚。

186. Even the house-holder (*grihastha*), by wisely following this method, may obtain success, there is no doubt of it.

即便在家居士，若能明智地依循此法，亦得成就，毋庸置疑。

在家居士：居家、白衣、世俗之人。

187. Remaining in the midst of the family, always doing the duties of the house-holder, he who is free from merits and demerits, and has restrained his senses, attains salvation. The householder practicing *Yoga* is not touched by sins, if to protect mankind he does any sin, he is not polluted by it.

居於家中，克盡家主之責，不著意於功過是非，密護根門，可得解脫。在家居士修習瑜伽應離諸邪行，若為護持人道而犯諸罪，亦得不受其行染污。

一些梵咒

188. Now I shall tell you the best of practices, the *japa* of mantra: from this, one gains happiness in this as well in the world beyond this.

現在我將語汝最佳修行之法 - 持咒法；循此法，行者可得超越世間之喜樂。

189. By knowing this highest of the *mantras*, the *Yogí* certainly attains success (*siddhi*): this gives all power and pleasure to the one-pointed *Yogí*.

明此最勝持咒之法，行人必得成就；是法能予制心一處之瑜伽士所有能力及喜樂。

190. In the four-petalled *Muladhar* lotus is the *bija* of speech, brilliant as

lightening (i.e., the syllable aim).

於四瓣根持蓮花中有言語種子音 ऐं(*aim*)，其光耀如閃電。

191. In the heart is the *bija* of love, beautiful as the *bandhuk* flower (*klim*). In the space between the two eyebrows (i.e., in the *Ájná* lotus), is the *bija* of *Śakti* (*strim*), brilliant as tens of millions of moons. These three seeds should be kept secret – they give enjoyment and emancipation. Let the *Yogí* repeat these three mantras (i.e., *Om*, *aim*, *klim*, and *strim*) and try to attain success.

其中心是愛的種子 क्लीं（*klim*），美若午時花；在兩眉之間有造化力種子 स्त्रीं（*strim*），光輝若千萬輪明月。此三種子應當保密，它們能夠帶來安樂與解脫。瑜伽行人應常持誦此三種子咒，努力獲得成就。

應常持誦此三種子咒：即 *Oṁ*——*aim*、*klim* 和 *strim*，*Oṁ* 為咒語之前的起始音，表都攝一切，亦包含贊嘆的意味。

譯按：這些種子心咒的音形並未錄於梵文本文字，依傳統規矩，需由明師口傳心授。

192. Let him learn this mantra from his *Guru*, let him repeat it neither too fast nor too slowly, keeping the mind free from all doubts, and understanding the mystic relation between the letters of the mantra.

學人應從其師處學習這些種子咒，持咒時不應太快也不應過慢，保持內心不起疑念，並了然梵咒文字間的神秘關聯。

193. The wise *Yogí*, intently fixing his attention on this mantra, performing all the duties peculiar to his caste, should perform one hundred thousand *homs* (fire sacrifices), and then repeat this mantra three hundred thousand times in the presence of the Goddess *Tripúra*.

明智之行人一心專注在此梵咒上，從事己身責份時，應進行十萬次的火供，進而在三明女神前重覆此梵咒三十萬次。

火供：又稱火祭，佛教中稱護摩，早在吠陀時期已有相關記載。上古時期發現火之大用後，將火視為諸神之口，復循一定儀軌將酥油等投入火壇中，供作神食，神依之得力以降伏諸魔。而宗教之火供或護摩，其作用則更形複雜。

三明女神：管理日、月、火三明的女神拜拉薇，詳本章 61 節註解。

194. At the end of this sacred repetition (*japa*), let the wise *Yogí* again perform homa, in a triangular hollow, with sugar, milk, butter and the flower of *karari*.

於此神聖的持誦結束時，明智行人再次於三角形火壇中，以糖、牛奶、醍醐和羊躑躅進行火供。

羊躑躅：植物名，音譯名迦羅毘囉，本草綱見稱鬧羊花。陀羅尼集經八曰：「迦囉毘囉樹脂，唐云羊躑躅也，若採其葉即脂汁出。」

195. By this performance of *Homa-Japa-Homa*, the Goddess *Tripúra Bhairavi,* who has been propitiated by the above mantra, becomes pleased, and grants all the desires of the *Yogí*.

透過這種火供及梵咒之吟頌，以取悅三明女神拜拉薇，祈請應允行人所有的想望。

196. Having satisfied the *Guru* and having received this highest of mantras, in the proper way, and performing its repetition in the way laid down, with mind concentrated, even the most heavy-burdened with past *Karmas* attains success.

以得宜之方式，博取上師滿意，領受此上善咒語；繼而集中精神，如法反覆持誦，則即便身負深重之宿業，亦能成就。

197. The *Yogí*, who having controlled his senses, repeats this mantra one hundred thousand times, gains the power of attracting others.

感官諸根已得控制之瑜伽行人，持誦此咒十萬遍，即具吸引他人之能力。

198. By repeating it two lacs of times he can control all persons – they come to him as freely as women go to a pilgrimage. They give him all that they possess, and remain always under his control.

持誦二十萬遍之行者，能服眾人，他們自發地前來如同婦女之進香朝聖；並供施所有，任由其支配。

199. By repeating this mantra three lacs of times, all the deities presiding over the spheres as well as the spheres, are brought under his dominion.

持誦此咒三十萬遍，所有域內域外諸神，均由其統理。

200. By repeating this six lacs of times, he becomes the vehicle of power – yea, the protector of the world – surrounded by servants.

持誦此咒六十萬遍，彼行人身負大能，且成為世界之守護者，受信眾之擁戴。

201. By repeating this twelve lacs of times, the lords of *Yakshas, Rákshas* and *Nága*s come under his control; all obey his command constantly.

持誦此咒一百二十萬遍，能主使藥叉、羅叉和龍王諸天，彼諸天人皆從其指揮。

龍王：司興雲降雨，護法世間。觀世音菩薩兩側侍立的童男童女中，童女即海龍王之女。

202. By repeating this fifteen lacs of times, the *Siddhas,* the *Viddyadharas,* the *Gandharvas*, the *Apsaras* come under the control of the *Yogí*. There is no doubt of it. He attains immediately the knowledge of all audition and thus all-knowinghood. Become ominiscient.

持誦此咒一百五十萬遍，行者能主使諸成就天、持智天、香音天和阿修羅，無有虛假。彼立即獲得一切音聲的知識及所有相關的知識。

成就天：天人中之最勝者；生前精進修持，得神通法力，依然未得解脫者，辭世後成為此類天人。這類天人會以指導者的角色，用各種方式協助靈修行人；

持智天：天人之一；生前受知見吸引，一心鑽研學識，臨終若猶記掛於所好，辭世後成為此類天人。

203. By repeating this eighteen lacs of times, he, in his body, can rise from the ground: he attains verily the luminous body; he goes all over the universe, wherever he likes; he sees the pores of the earth, i.e., he sees the interspaces and the molecules of this solid earth.

持誦此咒一百八十萬遍，行者之身能從大地騰空，身出光明；可隨心意遍行宇內，亦能透見大地世間。

透見大地：大地亦有世間之意；觀本節句意，或為能見大地孔竅或分子結構，或為能透見世間，故中譯為「亦能透見大地世間」。

204. By repeating this 28 lacs of times, he becomes the lord of the *Viddyadharas,* the wise *Yogí* becomes *kamarup*i (i.e., can assume what-ever form he desires). By repeating these thirty lacs of times he becomes equal to *Brahmá* and *Vishnu*. He becomes a *Rudra*, by sixty lac repetitions, by eighty lac repetitions he becomes all-enjoyer, by repeating one tens of millions of times, the great *Yogí* is absorbed in the *Pram Brahman*. Such a practitioner is hardly to be found throughout the three worlds.

持誦此咒兩百八十萬遍，行者成為持智天之首，聰穎者可成就隨心變化之能。若持誦此咒三百萬遍，行者成就等同梵天與妙毗天。若持誦此咒六百萬遍，成為魯陀羅天；若持誦此咒八百萬遍，行者成為一切之享受者；若持誦此咒一千萬遍，大行者融入至上大梵，如是行者甚難從此三界覓得。

梵天：至上意識即無限的意識，結合造化力即具創造一切萬有的能力，故又稱至上本體；這種創造力的神格展現，即是梵天神。

遍在天：即維世努或妙毗天，至上意識具有無所不在，遍及一切的特性，此特性的神格化即是遍在天。

魯陀羅天：梵語 ***Rudra***，又譯為樓陀羅，印度神話中司風暴、打獵、死亡和自然界之神；亦被視為破壞神希瓦的早期型態，名字含義為「在宇宙崩潰之時令全世界哭泣的人」或「帶走悲傷者」。他也被稱為治療者。

一切之享受者：英譯作 all-enjoyer，原梵語作 *amara*，字義有不死、無死、天人、不朽等義。較接近的譯文應是「無死仙人」。

至上大梵：英譯作 *Parama Brahma*，原梵語作 *Parama Pade*，義為至上之果位；此處至上之果位即至上本體，至上大梵。

205. O Goddess! *Śiva*, the destroyer of *Tripúra*, is the One first and highest cause. The wise attains Him, who is unchanging, undeceiving, all peace, immeasurable and free from all ills – the Highest Goal.

噢，女神吶！希瓦是三界的毀滅者，是第一因亦是究竟因；唯上根者能親證於祂，祂是不變的、不可言喻的、全然和平的、無可量度的以及遠離一切病的究竟最高目標。

三界：此字與前述三明女神的三明相同；三明除為日、月、火三明，也代表地界、天界和空界的三種光明，故此譯詞處用「三界」。

206. O Great Goddess! this science of *Śiva* is a great science (*mahavidyá*), it had always been kept secret. Therefore, this science revealed by me, the wise should keep secret.

噢，超凡之女神！此希瓦之學乃是大明之學，當永保其秘；我今傳承此學，明智者亦應保守其秘。

大明之學：梵語 *mahavidyá*，*vidya* 字義是直覺智、屬靈的知識，驅暗趨明的知識；*maha* 音譯摩訶，意思是大；故中譯為「大明之學」。

207. The *Yogí*, desirous of success, should keep the *Haṭha Yoga* as a great secret. It becomes fruitful while kept secret, revealed it loses power.

冀望成就之瑜伽行人，應如大秘密般守護哈達瑜伽；保守其秘者受益豐碩，披露者喪失其力。

208. The wise one, who reads it daily from beginning to end, undoubtedly, gradually obtains success in *Yoga*. He attains emancipation who honors it daily.

每日持恆勤習之明智者，必能漸次階及瑜伽成就；彼得解脫者，當屬日日虔修之人。

209. Let this science be recited to all holy men, who desire emancipation. By practice success is obtained, without it how can success follow?

願此實學能向一切冀望解脫之至誠者宣說。成就須通過修習獲得，不如此何能成就？

210. Therefore, the *Yogí* should perform *Yoga* according to the rules of practice. He who is contented with what he gets, who restrains his senses, being a householder, who is not absorbed in the household duties, certainly attains emancipation by the practice of *Yoga*.

是故，行人應根據修法來鍛煉。能知足所獲之人，能調御感官之人，在家卻未陷溺於家務之人，必能透過瑜伽修持而得解脫。

211. Even the lordly house-holders obtain success by *japa,* if they perform the duties of *Yoga* properly. Let, therefore, a householder also exert in *Yoga* (his wealth and condition of life are no obstacles in this).

若能妥善履行瑜伽修行日課，發心之在家居士透過持咒亦得成就；因此，在家人習練瑜伽也能有所發揮（不致因經濟和生活條件而形成障礙）。

212. Living in the house amidst wife and children, but being free from attachments to them, practicing *Yoga* in secrecy, a householder even finds marks of success (slowly crowning his efforts), and thus following this teaching of mine, he ever lives in blissful happiness.

雖居家生活於妻兒之間，於內心無有執著，且密行瑜伽不輟之在家居士，甚至可為成就之典範；如是信受奉行吾之教導者，得永住於無上喜悅之境。

〈結語〉
成就瑜伽的關鍵是對目標發展出全然的愛

時光如逝水，生命漂沉其中，隨波擺盪在希望和失望之間。佛門晚課有首普賢菩薩的偈子——「是日已過，命亦隨減，如少水魚，斯有何樂？當勤精進，如救頭燃，但念無常，慎勿放逸」。透過瑜伽打破時間幻象而融入至上意識，是瑜伽人的終極理想。 印度傳統上視瑜伽行者為修道者，亦即靈修之人，而其道旨及修持心態則視修行者之識見而有差別。如前述偈子，若為瑜伽行人或是「但念真常，慎勿放逸」。

古今行者在修習瑜伽的過程中，興起過許多有關生命的實際問題，也或漸或頓地逐一解開了生命的問題；其中洞悉人生本質與離幻證真的佼佼者，亦是完成生命大戲的成就者。從譯書的過程中，筆者一方面窺見了早期瑜伽行人的鍛煉經歷，對哈達瑜伽也更加認識。哈達瑜伽、勝王瑜伽都是橋接無上瑜伽的鍛煉，其中關鍵就是在修習過程中的心態。在《葛蘭達本集》、《希瓦本集》和《哈達瑜伽明燈》中都發現了這種以虔誠為本的心態，這是圓滿成就的關鍵。

在瑜伽歷史的長河裡，代代有人徜徉其中吸收生命養分，然而瑜伽精神亦代代難為時人真正理解，故每個時代都有人解釋瑜伽，以呈現一己之領悟。《瑜伽秘要》之出版亦是希望透過書面詞句內涵，讓喜好瑜伽的學人有機會窺見自古以來瑜伽的一貫要旨。只是瑜伽真境，非關文字，如欲透悟，尚須秉持淨念相續之心訣修行，不離不棄，生死相依，否則仍只是知解功夫，瑜伽行人不可不察。

傳統上凡是以瑜伽為目的修練者，即可名為瑜伽行人。瑜伽史上練習瑜伽的人口從來沒有像今日這麼蓬勃，那麼瑜伽真正的內涵是什麼？為什麼值得作為目的？我們再從瑜伽經典中的敘述來回顧瑜伽古來一貫的核心本義。如書中所記，瑜伽的本義為相應、聯結、合一或融合。這裡有兩個問題，一是和誰和什麼相應？ 二是依循什麼方法來相應？ 前者涉及習者個人的認知與了解，後者涉及習者個人的機緣與揀擇。在《瑜伽經》中帕檀迦利盡其所能地提出了他所知的瑜伽見解，即便不是最圓滿直捷的途徑，但絕對值得後世有心深入瑜伽的人琢磨。

《瑜伽經》開篇所說的「瑜伽之道在使妄心湛寂。」不是帕檀迦利的原創觀點。薄伽梵歌第六章二十六節經句：「搖蕩不定之心，總是紛飛外馳；宜當攝心息念，歸寂清淨自性。」即有類似的意涵，可知息妄歸真一直是印度傳統修行的重點。帕檀迦利也認為這一點非常重要，故一開始就舉出揭明。初唐牛頭智威禪師有首偈子「余本性虛無，緣妄生人我；如何息妄，還歸空處坐」，亦點出禪宗和瑜伽之間有著精神上的呼應。故對於瑜伽所追求的終極目標，究其實可說是人性的共同追求。

清初學通儒、道、釋、回等四教的經師真回老人王岱輿曾言：「無物之初，唯一真宰之本然，至清至靜，無方所，無形似，不牽於陰陽，不屬於造化。實天地人物之本原也。」這段憾動人心的領悟，明指出人性共同覓求的目標，即此無物之初的真宰本然；此真宰本然亦是瑜伽中所稱的真我、真常、真常自性、至上意識、至上本體等等。雖然這些名詞在嚴格的哲學析理上或有著細微差異，但在理念上其實是一致的。

真常自性如果是可以達到的目標，那麼達到目標的關鍵為何？通過書中所敘，讀者或已看出關鍵不在體位法或呼吸法，帕檀迦利認為主要還是在起心動念。六祖惠能大悟金剛經密旨後回秉五祖黃梅的第一句話是：「何其自性，本自清淨。」意思是說心性本淨，只要受到熏染的心能夠復歸清淨，即得契入瑜伽定境。《瑜伽經》第四章 31 節「彼時一切塵垢業障泯除，無量真知現前。」講的是相同道理。帕檀迦利在一開始就點出瑜伽之道在使妄心湛寂的重點，六祖惠能無相頌亦有言「起心即是妄」，故歸寂妄心雖不等於瑜伽，然而卻是達成瑜伽成就的重要條件。在密乘瑜伽中還有一項成就瑜伽目標的緊要關鍵，就是對於此一目標需發展出全然的愛。這一關鍵在《瑜伽經》裡未明述，但在《希瓦本集》中可體會一些。如果真體會到了這種愛，就會對泰戈爾寫在《漂鳥集》中詩句「我的存在，對我是一個永久的神奇，這就是生活。」產生會心的微笑。

後文筆者摘譯了一段瑜伽行人實修的記述，讀者可藉之了解一些哈達瑜伽較深入的內涵。這是聖施化難陀（*SwamiSivananda*、1887-1963）的弟子維世努德瓦難陀（*SwamiVishnudevananda*、1927-1993）講述自己在喜馬拉雅山苦修時的經歷：

「我在苦修時所從事的鍛煉幾乎與《哈達瑜伽明燈》中所述相同。承上師的恩典和上主的福佑，我前往烏塔喀西修行。從清晨、中午到傍晚和午夜，我規律的練習生命能控制法、體位法、身印和鎖印以及三到四個小時的梵唱靜心；每晚難得有兩三個小時的睡眠，但是不會覺得睡眠不足。身體並不需要太多的睡眠，因為強大的能量在身內流轉，我親身經驗到這股能量。」

「承上主和上師的恩典，我們能夠從事強而有力的修持來淨我的物質身、星光身和致因身。前面我說過，先一一修習體位法、生命能控制法、各種身印和鎖印，然後結束於本然持氣法（將生命能從左右脈行入中脈之法），入定於無有二元對待的心寂定境」。

「要達到心寂定境需要多世的修持。別因路遙而中止現在的練習，為己建立一個穩健、虔誠的生活。不要有一步到位的念頭，欲速則不達，也不要走太慢，以免因喪氣而中斷修持。心與業的作用常使靈性的道路充滿著障礙，要避免焦慮不安；縱使心境起起伏伏，也要常繫念於自己的靈性進展。保持勇氣往上攀爬！登頂之前，必須步步為營，用無畏和虔誠的愛心粉碎挫折、沮喪，勝利才會屬於你！」

「善用此生，高山頂立，深海徐行，當我們力氣放盡時，莫忘祈禱、臣服。我們的願望需要上主的恩典和福佑，因為我們的願望只是小小水滴，上主的恩典則如大海汪洋！讓祂牽著我們的手前行吧。」

「縱使道途險阻，但決不可忘懷自己的目標。始終心繫目標，每次前進一點，直到生命最後一口氣息。不要中止自己的靈修和進化，前進、前進、再前進！始終仰望著至上主，向祂祈禱：幫助我，不要讓我陷於一蹶不振！放下、臣服於祂！單憑自我的努力是不足恃的，我們很難看到隱藏的陷阱，但是由於臣服以及誠心一意地奉行內、外在規範，就一定會達到目標。也衷心祝願每一位瑜伽學子都能達到自在的成就和解脫。」

從這位瑜伽師的故事裡，可以看見行動瑜伽、知識瑜伽和虔誠瑜伽的整體修持，不以自我的意志為意志，時時保持虔誠自省之心，如是在身心的交互影響下，啄啐同時，當有明悟之時。筆者再略舉一些生理上身心相互影響的例子，現代認知心理學和大腦神經科學的研究成果，顯示出身心彼此影響的深度超乎我們的想像。例如肌肉緊繃、脂肪堆積或腫瘤可能和心中綁住自己卻又放不掉的死板想法有關！ 層層難消的脂肪可能是我們用來隱藏或保護記憶的設防，若減重成功可能表示我們敞開心扉褪下了自我保護的外殼等等，不勝枚舉。而在練習瑜伽的過程中即使習者不知道自己的問題，但會發現自己心情逐漸比較舒暢了，與此同時似乎覺得健康也有所改善。如果在自己的練習中添入從書中所領會到的精神，則必將感受到生命中真正永不乾涸的生機。更願世人都能觸及這一股源源不絕的生機，獲得精神上的富足。

《瑜伽秘要》內容豐碩，書中所敘述的各種瑜伽修法，展現出瑜伽多元的面向，指出生命的神聖本質，而神聖亦是生命的基礎。事實上一切宇宙創造都是建基在此神聖的基礎上，此一基礎或本源的神格就是上主、大梵、清淨本然或至上本體。而每一個人乃至芸芸眾生、宇宙萬象，都與此神聖有著超乎想像的緊密聯結，親近此一聯結，抓住此一聯結，從此聯結融入其中，即是瑜伽的終極成就。

王家衛執導的「一代宗師」膾炙人口，劇中有兩句對練武人的建言，對瑜伽學人同樣適用。這兩句話，一是「見自己，見天地，見眾生」，此語儼然是瑜伽修持不同階段的境界；第二句話是「念念不忘，必有回響」，秉此態度，精勤修習，則日久功深，亦必獲得回響，何愁不得成就？

「合一至上本體，安住本然自性；如是其心既不憂愁，亦無欲求。」

——薄伽梵歌 18：54-1

書末以一首當代靈性導師雪莉 普羅巴・阮將・沙卡先生（*Srii Prabhát Ranjan Sarkar*）作詞作曲的曙光之歌，作為本書的結尾。沙卡先生於一九八二年九月開始，八年間利用餘暇創作了五千零一十八首，全面的表達出志道者在尋道、修道、見道、合道等不同階段裡的心境。以下列引用的這首為例，在如詩的歌詞裡，充分顯現一位虔誠的瑜伽行人並不把至上意識視作抽象的空性，他視至上意識為生命中至親的人，是可以相互溝通的摯愛。這是虔誠瑜伽行者心中甜美的秘密。

曙光之歌 第 158 首 *

你您在眾生心中	*Tumi sabár mane ácho*
眾生也在您心中	*Sabái tomár mane áche*
在痛苦與快樂裡，不知不覺	*Duhkhe sukhe ná jene tái*
眾生都祈望您的恩典	*Sabái tava krpá jáce*
靠近我，請再靠近一點	*Eso káche eso áro káche*
眾生都祈望您的恩典	*Sabái tava krpá jáce*
您悲憫一切眾生	*Tumi sabár vyathár vyathii*
您是永恆的伴侶	*Nityakáler tumi sáthii*
您優美的笛聲和甜美的笑容	*(Tava) Mohan bán̂shii ár madhur hási*
使我滿懷歡愉	*Bán̂dhbháun̂gá sukh dey upce*
您是黑暗大海上的光明	*Án̂dhár ságarpáre tumii álo*
您的愛勝於一切	*Sabár ceye báso beshi bhálo*
宛如在夢中，不經意地	*Svapanghore ánmane tái*
眾生隨著您的旋律舞動	*Tomár chande sabe náce*

ॐ

* 本曲徵得阿南達瑪迦香港區總秘書阿闍黎舒巴尼亞薩南達（A'c *Shubhaniryasananda*）同意轉載，謹此致謝。

譯者簡介

楊台基，修習瑜伽數十年，喜探索各宗教擱置名相之後的哲學旨趣，受所習之阿南達瑪迦瑜伽哲理啟發頗多。曾任阿南達瑪迦瑜伽靜坐協會創會理事長、阿南達瑪迦基金會董事長、阿南達瑪迦出版部負責人、十年社大瑜伽教師；現任阿南達瑪迦瑜伽老師、私人瑜伽課程教師。參與之翻譯有《大師在喜馬拉雅山》、《瑜伽自然療法》、《細說摩訶婆羅多》等書。電郵信箱：yogascriptures@gmail.com

國家圖書館出版品預行編目資料

瑜伽秘要：瑜伽經、哈達瑜伽明燈、葛蘭達本集、希瓦本集合集 / 帕檀迦利 (*Maharsi Pantanjali*), 史瓦特瑪拉 (*Swatmarama*) , 葛蘭達 (*Gheraṇḍa*)著 ; 楊台基譯著. -- 二版. -- 臺北市 : 啟示出版 : 家庭傳媒城邦分公司發行, 2022.04
面； 公分. -- (SKY系列 ; 7)

ISBN 978-626-95477-9-1 (精裝)

1.CST：瑜伽

137.84　　111001734

啟示出版線上回函卡

SKY系列 ; 7

瑜伽秘要：瑜伽經、哈達瑜伽明燈、葛蘭達本集、希瓦本集合集

作　　者／帕檀迦利（*Maharsi Pantanjali*）、史瓦特瑪拉（*Swatmarama*）、葛蘭達（*Gheraṇḍa*）
譯 著 者／楊台基
企畫選書人／彭之琬
責任編輯／彭之琬
版　　權／黃淑敏、江欣瑜
行　　銷／周佑潔、周佳葳
業　　務／黃崇華、賴正祐
總 經 理／彭之琬
事業群總經理／黃淑貞
發 行 人／何飛鵬
法律顧問／元禾法律事務所 王子文律師
出　　版／啟示出版
臺北市104民生東路二段141號9樓
電話：(02) 25007008　傳真：(02)25007759
E-mail:bwp.service@cite.com.tw
發　　行／英屬蓋曼群島商家庭傳媒股份有限公司城邦分公司
台北市中山區民生東路二段141號2樓
書虫客服服務專線：02-25007718；25007719
服務時間：週一至週五上午09:30-12:00；下午13:30-17:00
24小時傳真專線：02-25001990；25001991
劃撥帳號：19863813；戶名：書虫股份有限公司
讀者服務信箱：service@readingclub.com.tw
城邦讀書花園：www.cite.com.tw
香港發行所／城邦（香港）出版集團
香港灣仔駱克道193號東超商業中心1F　E-mail: hkcite@biznetvigator.com
電話：(852) 25086231　傳真：(852) 25789337
馬新發行所／城邦（馬新）出版集團【Cite (M) Sdn Bhd】
41, Jalan Radin Anum, Bandar Baru Sri Petaling, 57000 Kuala Lumpur, Malaysia.
電話：(603) 90578822　傳真：(603) 90576622
Email: cite@cite.com.my

封面設計／李東記
排　　版／邵麗如
印　　刷／韋懋印刷事業有限公司

■ 2020 年 1 月　7 日初版
■ 2022 年 4 月 12 日二版
定價 880 元

Printed in Taiwan

城邦讀書花園
www.cite.com.tw

 ISBN 978-626-95477-9-1